ISBN 978-1-331-21006-1
PIBN 10158766

1 MONTH OF
FREE
READING

at

www.ForgottenBooks.com

By purchasing this book you are eligible for one month membership to ForgottenBooks.com, giving you unlimited access to our entire collection of over 1,000,000 titles via our web site and mobile apps.

To claim your free month visit: www.forgottenbooks.com/free158766

English
Français
Deutsche
Italiano
Español
Português

www.forgottenbooks.com

Mythology Photography **Fiction**
Fishing Christianity **Art** Cooking
Essays Buddhism Freemasonry
Medicine **Biology** Music **Ancient
Egypt** Evolution Carpentry Physics
Dance Geology **Mathematics** Fitness
Shakespeare **Folklore** Yoga Marketing
Confidence Immortality Biographies
Poetry **Psychology** Witchcraft
Electronics Chemistry History **Law**
Accounting **Philosophy** Anthropology
Alchemy Drama Quantum Mechanics
Atheism Sexual Health **Ancient History**
Entrepreneurship Languages Sport
Paleontology Needlework Islam
Metaphysics Investment Archaeology
Parenting Statistics Criminology
Motivational

HEALTH SECURITY ACT OF 1993

HEARINGS

BEFORE THE

COMMITTEE ON
LABOR AND HUMAN RESOURCES
UNITED STATES SENATE

ONE HUNDRED THIRD CONGRESS

FIRST SESSION

ON

EXAMINING THE ADMINISTRATION'S PROPOSED HEALTH SECURITY ACT, TO ESTABLISH COMPREHENSIVE HEALTH CARE FOR EVERY AMERICAN

NOVEMBER 17, 18 AND DECEMBER 8, 1993

PART 3

Printed for the use of the Committee on Labor and Human Resources

S. Hrg. 103–216, Pt. 3

HEALTH SECURITY ACT OF 1993

HEARINGS

BEFORE THE

COMMITTEE ON
LABOR AND HUMAN RESOURCES
UNITED STATES SENATE

ONE HUNDRED THIRD CONGRESS

FIRST SESSION

ON

EXAMINING THE ADMINISTRATION'S PROPOSED HEALTH SECURITY ACT, TO ESTABLISH COMPREHENSIVE HEALTH CARE FOR EVERY AMERICAN

NOVEMBER 17, 18 AND DECEMBER 8, 1993

PART 3

Printed for the use of the Committee on Labor and Human Resources

U.S. GOVERNMENT PRINTING OFFICE

77–135 CC   WASHINGTON : 1994

COMMITTEE ON LABOR AND HUMAN RESOURCES

EDWARD M. KENNEDY, Massachusetts, *Chairman*

CLAIBORNE PELL, Rhode Island
HOWARD M. METZENBAUM, Ohio
CHRISTOPHER J. DODD, Connecticut
PAUL SIMON, Illinois
TOM HARKIN, Iowa .
BARBARA A. MIKULSKI, Maryland
JEFF BINGAMAN, New Mexico
PAUL D. WELLSTONE, Minnesota
HARRIS WOFFORD, Pennsylvania

NANCY LANDON KASSEBAUM, Kansas
JAMES M. JEFFORDS, Vermont
DAN COATS, Indiana
JUDD GREGG, New Hampshire
STROM THURMOND, South Carolina
ORRIN G. HATCH, Utah
DAVE DURENBERGER, Minnesota

NICK LITTLEFIELD, *Staff Director and Chief Counsel*
SUSAN K. HATTAN, *Minority Staff Director*

(II)

CONTENTS

STATEMENTS

WEDNESDAY, NOVEMBER 17, 1993

STATEMENTS

THURSDAY, NOVEMBER 18, 1993

STATEMENTS

THURSDAY, NOVEMBER 18, 1993

ADDITIONAL MATERIAL

STATEMENTS

WEDNESDAY, DECEMBER 8, 1993

THE HEALTH SECURITY ACT OF 1993 PUBLIC HEALTH AND HEALTH CARE REFORM

WEDNESDAY, NOVEMBER 17, 1993

U.S. SENATE,
COMMITTEE ON LABOR AND HUMAN RESOURCES,
Washington, DC.

The committee met, pursuant to notice, at 11:30 a.m., in room SD–430, Dirksen Senate Office Building, Senator Edward M. Kennedy (chairman of the committee) presiding.

Present: Senators Kennedy, Simon, Wellstone, and Durenberger.

OPENING STATEMENT OF SENATOR KENNEDY

The CHAIRMAN. The committee will come to order.

We first want to express our apologies to our witnesses today for inconveniencing them and delaying the start of the hearing. It was due to circumstances beyond our control, with the Senate trying to conclude a very lengthy and extensive debate on crime, necessitating our voting earlier in the course of the morning on that issue. So at the outset of the hearing, I want to apologize to all of our witnesses. We had intended to perhaps reschedule it, but because of the various schedules of a number of our witnesses, we decided to move ahead and do the best we can this morning. So I appreciate their patience.

Today's hearing deals with the important issue of the relationship between health care reform and the role of public health. Health care reform can make our health care system strong only if it encompasses strengthening our public health infrastructure.

America's public health system has an enormous burden today and is in serious disarray. The missions of our public health agencies are crumbling under the pressure of heavy fiscal burdens, epidemics like AIDS and TB, and the large number of uninsured who must depend on State and local agencies to obtain medical care.

Currently, our public health system performs not only its traditional function, but has become the provider of last resort—the "safety net" that delivers essential health services for those most in need—low-income women, infants and children, the elderly and minorities. It provides prenatal care, and it treats a range of infectious diseases. It also deals with childhood lead poisoning and many other health-related problems.

The public health system protects the public through disease surveillance and epidemic control. Intervention by the public health department in identifying the Hanti virus in the western United

(1)

States in the "Four Corners" area demonstrates the necessity of this vital work. State and local public health agencies must be given the resources to provide these vital functions.

My hope is that as part of comprehensive health reform, we can assure that adequate and appropriate resources are available to public health agencies to address State and local concerns. The President's plan is a step in the right direction, and I hope that Congress will strengthen its promises.

Chronic disease is responsible for three-quarters of the deaths and disability in our society. Heart disease and cancer are the two top killers in our population. We must emphasize health promotion and disease prevention. We must strengthen programs delivering broad, community-based health education. Public health must promote healthy living as well as deliver medical care. Above all, we need a stronger partnership between State and local public health agencies and the Federal Government.

Our witnesses today will consider many important aspects of this approach to public health. First, we will hear from Dr. Phil Lee, Assistant Secretary of Health, who will discuss the administration's proposals for public health initiatives.

We will hear from Ms. Anthony, director of the Michigan State Health Department, representing the viewpoint of a rural region.

Dr. Maurice Mullet, the county health officer of Knox and Holmes County in Ohio, will discuss public health programs from a county perspective.

Dr. Fernando Guerra, director of the San Antonio Metropolitan Health Department, will describe a city outlook on this important issue.

And finally, Dr. Helen Halpin Schauffler will discuss ways to improve the delivery of public health services under health care reform.

I welcome all our witnesses, and I look forward to their testimony.

Dr. Lee will arrive momentarily, but I think we will move ahead with our other witnesses, and then when he arrives, we will hear his testimony and then come back and conclude the panel.

So I would ask Dr. Mullet, Vernice Anthony, Dr. Guerra, and Dr. Schauffler to please come forward.

We welcome all of you and express our appreciation. I am strongly committed in this area. Even if we get a little card that says "Health America", it will not remove the nonfinancial barriers to health care unless we have a system that can deliver public health services, we are going to fail in a very important way. And there are a lot of concerns out there, particularly at the community level, about the role of public health.

Let me just mention one. We visited a TB center in Massachusetts, where they treat TB for about $600 or $700 per patient. In Harlem, it is $22,000 to $25,000 per patient. Massachusetts' TB control program has been successful in treating TB and preventing the case of multidrug resistant TB found in New York City. This difference also underscores the importance of having an effective public health system in place. We are fortunate in my State to have maintained a skeleton structure during a long period of very serious cutbacks, but the public health service that generally was in position in the country 30, 40, 50 years ago has been decimated in many important respects. We are very, very strongly committed to doing what we can to strengthen that and help it.

And as one who has a son who is working on the issue of lead paint poisoning up in New Haven, I hear weekly from him about some of the successes and failures and gaps in terms of public health policy; and I know Dr. Lee is strongly committed to strengthening the public health system..

I will recognize Senator Simon just before we begin.

OPENING STATEMENT OF SENATOR SIMON

Senator SIMON. Thank you, Mr. Chairman.

I think there is no question that public health will be restructured somewhat as we move into a national health program, but it will give our public health programs a chance to really focus on some things that, frankly, have been spread so thin that we really have not had a chance to focus on.

So I look forward to having a national health care program and having public health do an even more significant job in the future.

Thank you, Mr. Chairman.

The CHAIRMAN. Thank you.

Before we begin I have a statement from Senator Mikulski.

[The prepared statement of Senator Mikulski follows:]

PREPARED STATEMENT OF SENATOR MIKULSKI

Good morning Mr. Chairman. I want to thank you for agreeing to hold this hearing today. As you know, this issue is one I feel very strongly about. In fact, I proudly characterize myself as an outspoken advocate for public health.

And I am very pleased that you too saw the importance of the public health issues which need to be addressed as we proceed with health care reform in America.

It is no secret that I was working on a degree in public health when my plans were interrupted by my first community-centered political fight. While I never returned to my intended career, I never lost my commitment to programs that promote good health and prevent disease on a community-wide basis.

There is a lot in the President's health care reform proposal that I like. I agree with the objectives of universal access, affordability, portable and comprehensive benefits, cutting costs without cutting quality, eliminating hassles, and preserving doctor-patient relationships.

But I believe that the President's plan can be improved.

Reducing red-tape, reforming malpractice, eliminating pre-existing conditions clauses, establishing managed competition, and all the rest will go a long way in making health care more accessible, and this is great, but it won't keep people from getting sick and it won't make them healthier.

As the New York Times pointed out last week, "many people who disregard advice to have children vaccinated or to have a pap smear or to exercise or eat less fat or drink less alcohol will not change their ways because they have health insurance."

To change their ways we need to look at public health in a comprehensive way and address everything from alcohol and drug abuse to violence, to infections like tuberculosis, to sanitation, to hazards in the workplace, to diet and nutrition, to a smoke-free environment.

And if our objective is to improve the health of the American people, it is not enough to offer a list of covered services in a benefits package. We also need to make sure people get services—such as screening and preventive tests—at the right time.

The public health community has had considerable experience with the delivery of services to the poor and near poor who are most underserved and most difficult to reach because they are often poorly educated. And they have learned some hard lessons on that score that we should hear.

As Robert Blendon, from the Harvard School of Public Health said in that same New York Times article, "if you remove the financial barrier, some will come in, but not all. Another group comes in after an educational effort. As for the third group, you literally have to send the vans out to get them."

The President's proposal will address the financial barrier by providing coverage for basic services but it is not clear that enough is being done to deal with education or service delivery.

We have had some success stories in reaching women with information and with women reaching the public health clinics for breast and cervical cancer screenings.

Those successes have been dependant on an infrastructure supported by a public-private partnership such as the YWCA "encore" program in Baltimore.

The "encore" program provides transportation, information, peer support, and what is called "navigator" services—guiding women through the fears as well as the physical maze which must be negotiated in order to receive these tests.

That kind of infrastructure is hard to build and needs to be nurtured. But it is essential.

I am concerned that the need for this kind of infrastructure to really improve the health of Americans is not understood, appreciated or adequately addressed in the reform proposal.

For example, existing community-based providers, a fragile group which we have been building and nurturing for many years, will be phased-out after 5 years unless no other provider can be found.

This provision fails to recognize that the issue here is not just the need for someone to provide a given test, but the more sophisticated need to reach the people who need the test.

And the public-private partnership I mentioned has traditionally provided matching federal funds to help support this more sophisticated need. It is not clear if that will continue.

So it is many things—from alcohol to smoking to diet and preventive medicine—along with being the health care provider of last resort—that represent the challenge of our community-based public health system.

That is why it is important to listen carefully to what these witnesses have to say to us today. What we are about cannot be accomplished without effectively responding to the fundamental issues these people bring to the table.

We should not let this opportunity pass.

So I want to thank these witnesses for appearing here today and I look forward to their testimony.

Thank you Mr. Chairman.

The CHAIRMAN. Dr. Mullet.

STATEMENTS OF DR. MAURICE MULLET, HEALTH COMMISSIONER, HOLMES AND KNOX COUNTIES, OH, REPRESENTING THE NATIONAL ASSOCIATION OF COUNTY HEALTH OFFICIALS; VERNICE DAVIS ANTHONY, DIRECTOR, MICHIGAN DEPARTMENT OF PUBLIC HEALTH, ANN ARBOR, MI; DR. FERNANDO A. GUERRA, DIRECTOR OF HEALTH, SAN ANTONIO METROPOLITAN HEALTH DISTRICT, SAN ANTONIO, TX; AND HELEN HALPIN SCHAUFFLER, UNIVERSITY OF CALIFORNIA, SCHOOL OF PUBLIC HEALTH, BERKELEY, CA

Dr. MULLET. Thank you, Mr. Chairman, Senator Simon.

I am Maurice Mullet, the family physician and health officer for Holmes and Knox Counties, OH. Those are two small rural counties in north central Ohio. I am here today as the president of the National Association of County Health Officials, also known as NACHO. NACHO represents the 3,000-plus local health departments across the country and is the national voice of those local health officers.

I am also vice chair of the National Association of Counties subcommittee on public and environmental health, and my testimony today is endorsed by the National Association of Counties, and I have included several of those concerns in my prepared testimony.

On behalf of the public health officers represented by NACHO, it is a pleasure to have this opportunity to discuss core public health functions and practices with you; the role of local public health in delivering those core functions; and the effect of the President's health care legislation on the ability of the public health system to protect the public's health.

Public health leaders at national, State and local levels are working together to achieve a shared vision of healthy people in healthy communities. This can be done by fulfilling the public health mission of assuring the conditions in which people can be healthy. And I hope that as you consider and debate health care reform legislation that you keep focused on the belief that the primary objective of your effort should be the improved health status of Americans, not just the creation of a more efficient or less costly illness care system.

As you know, local health departments are responsible for assuring that all citizens within their jurisdiction are served by the following set of core public health functions that has been identified by Dr. McGinness and others in the Office of Disease Prevention and Health Promotion of the Public Health Service. These include: health-related data collection, surveillance and outcomes monitoring, protection of environment, housing, food and water, investigation and control of diseases and injuries, public information and education, accountability and quality assurance, laboratory services, training and education, leadership, policy development and administration.

We are pleased that the Health Security Act proposed by President Clinton incorporates the above core functions as a public health initiative. This is important because I very firmly believe that improving the health status of Americans depends on more than just providing a health security card, making sure that everybody has access to care, paying for clinical preventive services. If we do not strengthen and reinvent the public health system, I think we will not achieve what we are really setting out to do.

An important part of that is that the public health system needs to be adequately funded. It has been estimated that 0.9 percent of total national health care expenditures now are devoted to the support of core public health functions. We believe that this amount really ought to be somewhere in the range of 3 to 5 percent if core public health functions are really going to be available to all citizens.

When the public health system works, it is really largely invisible; because people stay health, they become ill less frequently. So when the system erodes a result of lack of or absent political support and inadequate financial resources, public health crises frequently result. Examples include the measles epidemic that results from a failure to adequately immunize kids; a resurgence of multiple drug-resistant tuberculosis resulting from inability to apply known control measures; and foodborne disease outbreaks due to E. coli, resulting from a breakdown in proper food-handling techniques.

I would like to cite another example from one of my jurisdictions in Holmes County. We are a small rural county with the largest Amish population in the world. You know the importance of horses for both work and travel to this religious group. We also have a very large marsh and wetlands that was established by the Ohio Department of Natural Resources. This is a huge breeding ground for mosquitoes. And we were constantly reminded of that by the numerous nuisance complaints that we received. However, we did not and still do not have the adequate resources to do the kind of a surveillance program that is needed. In the summer of 1990, we had an outbreak of Eastern equine encephalitis that killed 19 horses. Now, that is horses, not people, but it very easily could have been kids or adults.

With the assistance of the State department of health and the Centers for Disease Control and Prevention, we were able to identify the vector mosquito in the marsh; however, there were no funds available for any control activities. In the last two summers, we have conducted very limited surveillance of the marsh. We know the vector mosquito is still there, but there are inadequate financial resources to do the kind of surveillance that is needed, let alone any kind of control activity. Fortunately, there has been no recurrence of the encephalitis, and we continue to keep our fingers crossed.

Another example of the value of core public health functions, I believe, is illustrated by a community health assessment that was done in our county in the mid-1980's. A community leadership group reviewed the mortality data, did a risk behavior survey, and identified injuries resulting from motor vehicle accidents as the leading cause of years of productive life lost. As a result of that, a Community Highway Safety Task Force has been organized. The task force developed a video, which is shown at tourist locations, and we are either the first or the third leading tourist location in the State now because of the Amish community. This video emphasizes the need for tourists, who are not used to driving around on small country roads, to drive carefully where an Amish buggy or a kid on a bicycle might be around the next curve or over the crest of the next hill.

We have taken the Safety Town program and customized it to our county and have incorporated it into our elementary school curricula. A public education campaign has resulted in increased use of seatbelts and child safety seats. While it is too early to document results, I believe efforts such as this will eventually lead to fewer injuries and deaths due to motor vehicle accidents.

Examples such as this could be replicated from each of the 3,000 health departments across the country. What is even more important, however, is to understand the importance and value of community- or population-based services in the health system. The public health system must have the capacity of responding effectively to emerging and newly-recognized public health problems, examples of which include HIV infection, injury prevention and violence, both intentional and unintentional. I would suggest that violence is perhaps the major public health problem in our country today.

You are all familiar, I am sure, with the usual list of leading causes of death in the United States. Mr. Chairman, you referred to that in your opening remarks. I think it is imperative that we begin focusing on the actual causes of death, not those usually listed, if we hope to constrain the increase in health care costs. In a study published in the Journal of the American Medical Association by Dr. McGinness and Dr. Faige, they really identified the actual causes of death from 1990 data; 400,000 of them are the result of the use of tobacco. The next largest group is the result of diet and activity patterns. I would cite that article for your reading; it makes the case much more eloquently than anything I could say.

Section 3312 of the Health Security Act addresses the core public health functions. The following provisions would, in our opinion, greatly enhance the ability of the public health system to protect the public's health. The Act authorizes up to $12 million for fiscal year 1995, to reach $750 million by the year 2000. We do not believe this is adequate to do the job you expect, and as stated previously, we believe this amount should be in the range of 3 to 5 percent of total national health care expenditures.

Although the Health Security Act provides for an authorization, there is no guarantee that an adequate amount of funding will be appropriated. The public health system needs a dedicated source of funding, such as a Public Health and Prevention Trust Fund, to assure that core public health functions are always adequately supported.

The public health system must also be held accountable for providing the core functions and practices to all people in this country, whether they live in rural areas such as mine, inner cities, or the suburbs.

Effectively addressing local health problems requires an understanding of the needs and resources of individual communities. Local officials are best-positioned to ensure that health problems are identified and appropriate programs are developed and implemented at the local level. The Health Security Act, however, gives sole responsibility to the States for planning, prioritizing and allocating resources. The expertise of local public health officials is lost, and we think there needs to be a strong partnership between Federal health officials, State health officials and local health officials to assure that local needs are targeted and met.

By definition, core public health functions are essential services and must be available to all citizens. I would respectfully suggest that funding the core public health functions through any kind of competitive grant system makes no sense. NACHO supports a formula grant for supporting core public health functions and practices.

Mr. Chairman, thank you for the opportunity to share our views. I would be happy to respond to any questions.

The CHAIRMAN. Thank you very much.

[The prepared statement of Dr. Mullet follows:]

PREPARED STATEMENT OF DR. MAURICE MULLET

Good morning Mr. Chairman, and distinguished members of the Senate Committee on Labor and Human Resources. I am Dr. Maurice Mullet, health commissioner for both Holmes and Box Counties, which are rural jurisdictions in central Ohio. As a family physician, I provide personal health care services in addition to overseeing the population-based services provided by the health departments in both counties.

I am also the president of the National Association of County Health Officials, also known as NACHO. NACHO is the voice for local health officials nationwide, representing more than 3,000 local governmental agencies. In addition, I am the vice chair of the National Association of Counties' Public and Environmental Health Subcommittee. The National Association of Counties endorses this testimony, and they have incorporated some positions in my prepared testimony.

On behalf of NACHO, I am pleased to have this opportunity to discuss core public health functions, the role of local health departments in providing core public health functions, and the effect of the President's health care legislation on the ability of local health departments to protect the public's health.

Public health leaders at the federal, state and local levels are working together to achieve a common mission: to assure conditions in which people can be healthy. In order to fulfill this mission, we embrace the following core public health functions:

> Health-related data collection, surveillance and outcomes monitoring.
> Protection of environment, housing, food and water.
> Investigation and control of diseases and injuries.
> Public information and education.
> Accountability and quality assurance.
> Laboratory services.
> Training and education.
> Leadership, policy development, and administration.

Health departments are responsible for providing core public health functions, and NACHO is pleased to see that President Clinton's Health Security Act incorporates the eight core functions of public health. Improving the health status of this country's population will only be achieved by going beyond health payment reform and personal health services reform, and by assuring adequate resources for our public health system as well although not well known, core functions are responsible for many advances that have been made in health and longevity.

When public health "works," it is largely invisible. People stay healthy, and do not become ill. However, when services have eroded and a public health crisis emerges, for example, measles epidemic, food-borne outbreak, or resurgence of tuberculosis, the need for public health services is apparent.

I would like to give you an example of how a coordinated approach using the core public health functions works at the local level.

The jurisdiction of a colleague suffered a hepatitis A outbreak approximately one year ago. The local health department identified the outbreak and its cause, and instituted measures to prevent further spread of the illness and future outbreaks. Through the core function of data collection and surveillance, the health department became aware that an unusually high number of hepatitis A cases were developing. Through another core function, investigating and controlling diseases, the health department traced the source of the disease to food improperly handled by a local caterer, and contacted additional individuals at risk of contracting the illness. Laboratory services, another core function provided by the health department, identified people needing treatment. The health department followed up with all cases to assure that appropriate treatments had been received. To prevent recurrences, additional education regarding proper handling and storage techniques was provided to food handlers.

This is just one example that illustrates the multitude of ways in which core public health functions keep people healthy.

While section 3312 of the Health Security Act addresses the eight core functions of public health, additional provisions would greatly enhance our national ability to protect the public's health, as follows:

The Health Security Act authorizes up to $12 million for fiscal year 1995, to reach $750 million by fiscal year 2000.

Public health leaders agree that no less than three percent of current total national health care expenditures, or $27 billion, is needed to support the core functions.

Although the Health Security Act provides for an authorization, there is no guarantee that an adequate amount of funding would be appropriated. We need a dedicated source of funding to assure that core functions will always be adequately supported.

By definition, "core," functions are essential. We are concerned that competitive grants will not fund all essential services. Therefore, NACHO supports noncompetitive funding for core functions.

Effectively addressing local health problems requires an understanding of the needs and resources of individual communities. Local health officials are best positioned to ensure that health problems are identified and appropriate programs are developed and implemented at the local level. The Health Security Act, however, gives sole responsibility to states for planning, prioritizing, and allocating resources. The knowledge and expertise of local officials is lost. Mandated participation of local health departments in planning, prioritizing and allocating resources would ensure that local needs are targeted and met.

Under the proposal, states will bid competitively on one or a number of grants for core functions. In order to receive funds, states are required to identify the amount of current local funding spent towards a specific core function, and assure that those funds will be maintained. If states use local money in their grant application, the counties must have significant input into the process.

There is also no recognition that states creating new health systems overall must consult with their political subdivisions, primarily counties, which actually deliver or administer health care currently to uninsured populations. County governments must be involved in the creation of the new state systems. If there are system failures, we will ultimately pick up the pieces. We are under no illusion that any state will repeal their provisions making counties the providers of last resort. Meaningful consultation must occur between county and state officials in designing new state systems.

We are pleased that the concept of essential community provider is included in the President's legislation but are troubled by the lack of specificity for county facility eligibility. Automatic designation is given to certain recipients of federal discretionary health funds. Since most local public health departments receive maternal and child health or Ryan White aids funds, we assume that many of them will receive automatic federal designation. Left unclear is whether that specific program would be designated or the entire facility.

Some may argue that this is a county "turf" issue. It is not. A truly reformed system should not re-create a two-tier delivery system. Under a capitated payment, health plans have little incentive to reimburse providers that they have no contractual obligation with. Access to universal coverage must be accomplished and a short-term, special status will help accomplish that principle. We support the essential community provider status through the transition to universal coverage.

Thank you for the opportunity to appear before you today. I would be happy to answer any questions.

The CHAIRMAN. Dr. Lee has arrived, and if our panel would be good enough to be seated in the first row, then we will hear from him and resume with the testimony of the panel. I thank you very much, and I appreciate your indulgence.

Dr. Lee, we have, as you know, had a series of votes on the Senate floor.

It is a pleasure to have you back. Dr. Lee is an outstanding educator, physician, researcher and administrator. He has had a lifetime of commitment to health issues and good health policy for the country. We are delighted to have you with us, and we look forward to your testimony.

STATEMENT OF DR. PHILIP R. LEE, ASSISTANT SECRETARY OF HEALTH, DEPARTMENT OF HEALTH AND HUMAN SERVICES, WASHINGTON, DC

Dr. LEE. Senator Kennedy and Senator Simon, thank you very much for this opportunity to discuss the public health initiatives in the Health Security Act.

I will submit my full statement for the record, and I would like to review a few of the issues, particularly the rationale for the public health initiatives within health care reform, and then obviously would be pleased to respond to any questions that you might have.

I think it is important that we focus this morning on the public health aspects of the reform. There has been so much attention devoted to personal health care piece of it. With that, and with the link of the public health initiative and the personal health care reforms, we believe that it will be possible to achieve two of the fundamental objectives outlined in Healthy People 2000—first of all, to improve the health of all Americans; and second, to reduce the disparities in health status among Americans.

We have made good progress in recent years on the first; we have not made any progress in reducing disparities in the second.

We will achieve the third objective, which is providing clinical preventive services. That is a core benefit. So that third objective in Healthy People 2000 will in fact be achieved.

The President's plan is really health-oriented; it emphasizes accountability, prevention, and a close working relationship between personal health care and public health. Central to this approach is restructuring the personal health care system, enabling it for the first time to focus on keeping people healthy as opposed to simply treating the sick.

An old friend of mine, Dr. Jacques May from France, used to describe our system as "a one ill, one pill, one bill" system. This will really transform that to a system that really focuses, through the alliances and the plans, on populations and a population perspective, as well as treating appropriately the individuals in the plans.

One of the unique features of the reform is that the payment system rewards plans for keeping people healthy. When you have a capitated system of payment rather than simply an open-ended, fee-for-service system, you change the incentives dramatically.

Health plans will receive a fixed annual premium to cover total patient care. To the extent that the enrollees are kept healthy, the plans will benefit. This is one of the crucial factors in enhancing the public health infrastructure as well as providing access to care for everyone. By improving public health, we will diminish the demands for medical care on the personal health care system. It is a crucial interrelationship and linkage between those two systems, and it is a linkage that is not there today.

The changes in personal health care will permit us to strengthen the public health system, making it more effective in protecting and promoting the health of our individuals in communities and, in fact, the health of communities.

In recent years, as health insurance has had diminishing capacity to meet the needs of the population, more and more uninsured were dependent on the public sector or things like community health centers, federally-funded, to assure their access to care, so local tax funds, which could have been used to provide public health services, have been forced to be used to provide acute care in emergency rooms and outpatient hospitals for the uninsured. Medicare did a good job for the elderly; Medicaid covered those who were on cash assistance. But for the growing number of working families who are uninsured, it did not provide any real protection.

We know that we live in an environment of limited resources and that this shifting of the State and local funds toward personal expenses has had a devastating effect on public health. The Institute of Medicine report in 1989 declared public health in disarray, and I quote, "a threat to the health of the public." The American Public Health Association in its recent report, "Public Health in a Reformed Health Care System: A Vision for the Future," reiterated these problems. And over the last 9 months, working with State and local governments, we have really identified the same problems identified by the IOM report, and we document and list those in the testimony, so I do not need to discuss those.

I believe that we have an historic opportunity to improve the health of the American people with the President's health care reform act. If we reform the personal health care system as the President has proposed, the public health system will no longer need to provide coverage services to indigent populations. Instead, it can turn its resources and expertise to its original role, removing barriers to medical care or personal health care and protecting the health of communities. By working closely with alliances and health plans under the new system, public health agencies can be far more effective than they are now in achieving community-wide improvements in health.

Reforming the public health system is not supplemental to, but is core, to health care reform. The programs contained in Title III of the Health Security Act are the means by which the President proposes to strengthen and restructure the public health system. The success of these programs will ultimately determine how well health security is provided for all Americans and how well the health disparities are reduced between lower-income populations and the rest of the population. They will also play a vital role in determining the extent to which we will be able to contain the costs of health care; the extent to which we strengthen public health, we enhance our opportunities for controlling the cost of health care.

Three approaches are included in the public health initiatives. One, to build the capacity and capability of communities to protect the health of their populations and address high-priority local health problems. Second, to assure access to necessary health services for all Americans, particularly low-income, isolated, hard-to-reach populations. And third, to provide the knowledge base and information systems necessary to prevent disease more effectively and provide medical care more appropriately and more efficiently.

The core public health and prevention initiatives are at the heart of the reform, and these are detailed in my testimony. We have our core public health programs, which are competitive grants to provide funds to State health agencies to strengthen a series of essential functions which are described in the testimony.

The question was raised why should these be project grants instead of formula grants. We believe grants will be given to every State, but we believe there are some areas where there are priority needs, and with limited resources, initially at least, we need to move to meet those needs are the outset. Downstream, we think every State will be funded, and all States will have to account for and determine what the local needs were, and in the proposals will have to define how much funding will go to the local level.

We believe that is the best way to begin this approach, as opposed to beginning with a formula grant. It will help to correct the inequities across the States as well.

The second area is the preventable priority health problems which will be dealt with through a grant program that will let the communities decide which needs have a priority. It will help to integrate the multiple categorical grants that we are currently funding and we would propose to continue.

The initial priorities we think might be targeted on such things as prevention of smoking by children and adolescents, violence prevention, and reductions in behavioral risks that contribute to the incidence of chronic disease, including heart disease, cancer, stroke, or adult-onset diabetes.

The second set of initiatives are the access initiatives. There, we would continue our current safety net programs; we would increase practitioner supply in underserved areas—among the approaches would be expanding the National Health Service Corps, ultimately about a 5-fold expansion. There would be a capacity expansion initiative both for urban inner city areas and for rural areas that would include loans, loan guarantees, and grant programs. There would also be an expansion of outreach and enabling services—such things as transportation, translation, child care, outreach—to help the underserved populations access to care, whether it is a homeless group in Long Beach, CA, whether it is a nonEnglish-speaking group in inner city New York, whether it is a low-income group in Chicago. Different populations have different needs, and these enabling grants would help us do that.

Also, a school-aged initiative—and this builds, Senator Kennedy, on your initiatives for a school-based adolescent initiative. We would have two elements to this—a comprehensive school health education initiative, K through 12; and school-related health services that would be primary care and psychosocial support services, providing youth with skills to help them cope with the multiple stresses and problems that they face.

The final element is the mental health and substance abuse initiatives, which we would expand significantly, particularly with enabling services, to expand outreach to hard-to-reach, chronically mentally ill or substance abusers who need more than just a card to have access to care.

And finally, the prevention and health services research initiatives, expansion of NIH prevention research, significant expansion of health services outcomes, medical effectiveness research, dissemination of information to practitioners, practice guideline development.

Let me just say in closing, Mr. Chairman, that the public health initiative is not separate from health care reform. It is essential to the success of reform. Together, the components of the public health initiative provide the building blocks vital to our reform efforts. They shift financial incentives away from paying for disease and their complications toward paying providers and plans to keep people healthy. They assure integration of private and public health care providers and mainstreaming of vulnerable populations too long neglected. They build on the new responsibilities of health plans and alliances for entire populations, while providing funds to States and local health agencies to work in partnership with the personal health care system. The promote the goal of quality health care at affordable cost by relying more on primary care providers, proven clinical interventions, and a strong information base and performance monitoring to support quality assurance efforts.

In summary, the President Health Security Act is designed to provide all Americans, including those currently underserved, with real health security at an affordable price.

Mr. Chairman and members, we appreciate this opportunity to appear before the committee, and we look forward to the opportunity of working with all of you to take full advantage of this really unique opportunity to improve the health of all Americans.

Thank you very much.

[The prepared statement of Dr. Lee follows:]

THE PREPARED STATEMENT OF DR. PHILIP R. LEE

Mr. Chairman, Senator Kassebaum and members of the Committee, I welcome this opportunity to discuss the public health initiatives in the President's Health Security Act.

This morning, I urge the Committee to shift its attention to an important, but not well appreciated, purpose of the President's plan—the reform of our public health system. Under the Health Security Act, we will do far more than just treat people when they are sick. We will achieve the two fundamental goals set out in Healthy People 2000, our nation's health promotion and disease prevention agenda:

improve the health of all Americans; and
reduce health disparities among Americans.

THE NEW HEALTH-ORIENTED FRAMEWORK OF REFORM

The President's plan has a new health-oriented approach that emphasizes accountability, prevention, ad a close working relationship between the personal care and public health systems.

Central to this approach is a restructuring of the personal health care system, enabling it—for the first time—to focus its energies on keeping people healthy. Under reform, all Americans will have comprehensive benefits including preventive services without deductibles or copayments. Regional alliances ad health plans will be responsible for making sure that their populations have access to these covered services. And report cards will focus the attention of health plans on achieving healthy outcomes for their enrollees and will monitor how well they accomplish these goals.

Another unique feature of the President's reform is that the financing and payment system will reward alliances and health plans for keeping their populations well. Health plans will receive a feed annual premium to cover total patient care. To the extent their enrollees are kept healthy, plan health care costs will be lower and premiums paid by individuals and employers will be lower. This will provide a strong incentive for health plans to make sure that their enrollees are aware of and get the preventive services they need and for both alliances and health plans to work closely with public health agencies.

These changes in the personal care system will make it possible to strengthen and restructure the public health system, making it far more effective in protecting ad promoting the health of our communities. In recent years, as the health insurance system failed more and more working Americans, public health agencies were required to meet a growing need for medical care and mental health services. National, State, and local health agencies became increasingly involved in providing basic medical services to those shut out of the private health insurance system. While Medicare solved many problems for the elderly, Medicaid did not solve the problem for the growing number of working people and their families who were uninsured.

In an environment of limited resources, this shift of public spending at the State and local level toward personal medical care has been at the expense of its essential role in keeping communities healthy. This steady erosion of public health led the Institute of Medicine in 1989 to declare public health "in disarray" and a "threat to the health of the public". The American Public Health Association, in its recent report "Public Health in a Reformed Health Care System: A Vision for the Future" reiterated these problems. We have confirmed them in our own analyses during the past nine months.

When public health fails, people and communities suffer and personal health care costs increase. Let me give you a few examples.

Every year, an estimated 900,000 people fall ill—and 900 die—from contaminated drinking water. In Wisconsin alone, a failure to protect the quality of drinking water, and to detect and control Cryptosporidium, caused over 370,000 people to fall ill—4,000 of whom required hospitalization—and led to over $15 million in medical care costs.

State public health staff report that they have had to severely curtail or even close down restaurant inspection efforts due to lack of funds, despite the fact that in 1991 and 1992, 212 cases of Hepatitis A in Missouri, Wisconsin, and Alaska were traced to infected restaurant workers. In 1987, Hepatitis A outbreaks infected 75,000 Americans, at a cost of $766 million.

An outbreak of E. coli linked to a restaurant chain recently resulted in 500 laboratory-verified cases of bloody diarrhea in Washington State, Idaho, California, and Nevada. The costs of treatment were $ 100-$200 for every case not requiring hospitalization and much more for those young children and frail elderly who had to be hospitalized.

Hepatitis B infects up to 300,000 people each year in the United States, at a cost of $750 million per year, despite the fact that a vaccine to prevent the disease has been available for the past decade. Yet only one percent of the estimated 28 million young adults at risk for hepatitis B have received it.

Substance abuse is not only an epidemic in and of itself; it is also at the root of other public health problems. Substance abusers are the fastest growing segment of the HIV/AIDS population, and substance abusers with AIDS are a major factor in the spread of multi-drug resistant tuberculosis. Fifteen percent of women delivering babies in Harlem hospital use cocaine. According to the Center on Addiction and Substance Abuse at Columbia University, substance abuse is currently estimated to add $140 billion to our country's direct and indirect health care costs every year, including $500 million to treat cocaine-affected infants during their first month of life.

I can't emphasize enough that we now have an historic opportunity to improve the health of the American people. If we reform the personal care system as the President has proposed, the public health system will no longer need to provide covered services to indigent populations. Instead it can turn its resources and expertise back to its original role: removing barriers to medical care and protecting the health of communities.

By working closely with alliances and health plans under the new system, public health agencies can be far more effective than they are now in achieving community-wide improvements in health. For example, they can work alliances and health plans to inform and educate individual patients and providers. And they can reinforce the efforts of alliances and health plans by protecting communities against environmental hazards, identifying and controlling community outbreaks of infectious diseases, and instituting community-wide education programs.

As you can see, reforming the public health system is not supplemental to health care reform but instead is an integral part of achieving the goals of reform. The programs contained in Title III of the Health Security Act are the means by which the President proposes to strengthen and restructure the public health system. The success of these programs will ultimately determine how well health security is provided for all Americans and how well health disparities among Americans are reduced or eliminated. They will also play a vital role in determining the extent to which we will be able to contain accelerating health care costs.

SPECIFIC PUBLIC HEALTH INITIATIVES IN THE HEALTH SECURITY ACT

The programs in the Public Health Initiative do not scrap the old model of public health. Instead they create a new health-oriented partnership between government, alliances, health plans, and communities that will:

Build up the capability of communities to protect the health of their populations and address high-priority local health problems;

Assure access to necessary health services for all Americans, particularly low-income, isolated, hard-to-reach populations; and

Provide the knowledge base and information systems necessary to prevent disease more effectively and to provide medical care more appropriately and efficiently.

Core Public Health and Prevention Initiatives

Health care reform simply cannot meet its cost-containment targets or address pressing health problems—such as teenage pregnancy, lead poisoning, diabetes, tobacco and drug abuse, and violence—successfully without strengthening our capacity to provide population-based public health activities. We must define the population groups for whom particular problems are most common. We must identify effective interventions by learning why some communities are hard-hit by a problem while others somehow seem to escape. We must target public education and prevention interventions to populations at highest risk and populations with different cultural backgrounds. And we must create alliances between public health agencies, health plans, and providers as well as sectors outside health, such as public schools, law enforcement agencies, and social service agencies. The close interrelationship between health problems such as HIV/AIDS, tuberculosis, substance abuse, infant mortality, and violence highlights the importance of pursuing integrated approaches that cut across individual problems and that unite the personal care and public health systems.

Two programs included in Title III take advantage of universal coverage under reform to shift the focus of public health agencies from providing personal care services toward identifying, preventing, and controlling high-priority local health problems.

Core Public Health Program. This competitive grant program will provide funds to State health agencies to strengthen the following essential public health functions at state and local levels:

(1) surveillance of communicable and chronic diseases—essential to define the magnitude, source, and trends of health problems so that limited resources can be directed to populations at greatest risk.

(2) control of communicable diseases and injuries—essential to ensure that new problems are identified early, that contact tracing and partner notification occur effectively, and that sources of infectious exposures are removed.

(3) environmental protection—essential to safeguard the physical and social environment (e.g., water, food, workplace, housing) against causes of disease.

(4) public education and community mobilization—essential to prevent major causes of premature death and disability that are behavioral and societal in nature.

(5) accountability and quality assurance—essential to protect consumers from medical and health services that do more harm to health than good.

(6) public laboratory services—essential in the diagnosis of major infectious and environmental threats to health.

(7) training and education of public health professionals—essential to ensure a workforce capable of carrying out public health functions.

The program fosters greater accountability to the federal government than has been realized previously for the definition and reporting of progress in achieving public health objectives.

Preventable Priority Health Problems. A second competitive grant program will provide funds to public and private not-for-profit agencies to address health issues that affect local communities or specific populations within communities. Many of these problems do not affect the country uniformly and call for tailored, community-based interventions. For example, in some inner-city communities, diabetes or heart disease is a major problem; in others, priority may be accorded to programs that deal with cigarette smoking; while in still other areas, teen pregnancy is an issue of great concern. In cases where multiple factors contribute to a health problem, as with violence, grants will support approaches that cut across individual problems.

Among the initial set of priorities, the program will target prevention of smoking by children and adolescents; violence prevention; and reductions in behavioral risks that contribute to the incidence of chronic diseases, including heart disease, cancer, stroke, and adult-onset diabetes.

Access Initiatives

Congress—particularly members of this Committee—has demonstrated great concern about the ability of underserved populations to obtain access to personal health care services. You have also expressed concern about the ability of health care providers currently serving underserved populations to become effective participants in the reformed system. The President recognizes, as you do, that a Health Security Card will not, in and of itself, guarantee that all Americans receive necessary health care services. To achieve this goal, universal health insurance must be backed up by an adequate system of practitioners, facilities, education, outreach, and information.

Special initiatives contained in Title III will assure that all Americans—no matter who they are or where they live—have access to the full range of services included in the comprehensive benefit package under health care reform. Currently 72 million Americans live in inner-city and rural areas where there are neither sufficient numbers of providers nor adequate facilities. And many isolated, culturally diverse, and hard-to-reach populations confront other barriers that reduce their access to care. The Health Security Act uses five interrelated approaches to remove these barriers to care and to facilitate transition to a single-tier system in which all Americans have an adequate choice of culturally-sensitive providers and health plans.

Current Safety-Net Programs. Current safety-net programs such as community and migrant health centers, programs for the homeless, family planning, Ryan White, and maternal and child health will be maintained. To assure access and continuity of care during the early years of reform, providers funded under these programs will receive automatic designation as essential community providers, guaranteeing them payment for covered services from all health plans.

Practitioner Supply. The supply of practitioners in underserved areas will be increased. This will be accomplished by expanding the National Health Service Corps approximately five-fold from its current field strength of 1,600; by redirecting residency training to substantially increase the ratio of primary care physicians to specialist physicians; and by supporting the training of primary care physicians, physician assistants, and advanced practice nurses. Special programs to increase the representation of minorities and disadvantaged persons among health professionals will overcome access barriers that stem from cultural gaps.

Capacity Expansion. Capacity expansion in inner-city and rural areas will be supported. This will be accomplished both by expanding the successful community and migrant health center program and through a new program supporting the development of community practice networks and health plans.

The new program will integrate federally funded providers with other providers in underserved areas, equipping them with skills to coordinate care, negotiate effectively with health plans, and form their own health plans. It will increase the level of service available in underserved areas by supporting the creation of new practice sites and by renovating and converting existing practice sites, including public and rural hospitals. In addition, it will improve access to specialty care in urban and rural underserved areas—and improve coordination of care—by linking members of the practice networks with each other and with regional and academic medical centers through information systems and telecommunications.

Outreach/Enabling Services. The Access Initiative also incorporates a new competitive grant program that will expand federal support for enabling services—such as transportation, translation, child-care, and outreach. These grants will assure that isolated, culturally-diverse, hard-to reach persons not served by other programs get the supplemental services they need to obtain access to medical care and to use the health care system effectively. Awards will be made to community practice networks, community health plans, and other public and private not-for-profit organizations with experience and expertise in providing enabling services for underserved populations, complementing existing Public Health Service programs.

For many years, groups that have been denied access to the traditional medical care system have come to rely on emergency room care, often waiting until their problems are far more difficult and costly to treat. These individuals must be assisted in shifting their care patterns and learning to use the health system more effectively by receiving earlier and more appropriate primary care services. Enabling funds in the new program will not only improve access to care for these vulnerable populations, but will also reduce the excessive costs associated with avoidable emergency and tertiary care services.

School-Age Youth. The final component of the Access Initiative will address the problems of one of our Nation's most vulnerable groups: adolescents and young adults. The current health care system has failed to provide our youth with the information and services they need to avoid risky behaviors and make healthy decisions. Adolescents are also often reluctant to seek help, ignorant about what help is needed or where to get it, and concerned about confidentiality. These barriers contribute to the substantial problems with substance abuse, unwanted pregnancy, and HIV/AIDS among this age group.

The Health Security Act will reach out to school-age youth and adolescents in two ways. The Comprehensive School Health Education initiative will establish a national framework within which States can create school health education programs that improve the health and well being of students, grades K through 12, by addressing locally relevant priorities and reducing behavior patterns associated with preventable morbidity ad mortality. This program will be targeted to areas with high needs, including poverty, births to adolescents, and sexually-transmitted diseases among school-aged youth.

The School-Related Services program will support the provision of health services—including psychosocial services and counseling in disease prevention, health promotion, and individualized risk behavior—in schoolbased or school-linked sites. Grants will be made to states for the development and implementation of state-wide projects targeted at high-risk youth ages 10-19. In states that do not take this initiative, grants will be available to local community partnerships including public schools, experienced providers, and community organizations.

Mental Health and Substance Abuse Initiatives

New funds authorized in Title III will assure that low-income, hard-to-reach individuals in inner cities and other neighborhoods know about and take advantage of the expanded mental health and substance abuse treatment benefits included in the comprehensive benefits package. Working through the existing Community Mental Health Services and the Substance Abuse Prevention and Treatment formula grants, these funds will support enabling services—community and patient outreach, transportation, translation, education—for low-income individuals and other vulnerable groups (such as the homeless, dually-diagnosed, or severely mentally ill). In addition, they will build up the currently inadequate infrastructure for delivering mental health and substance abuse services in communities and facilitate integrating these services within the broader health care system.

Prevention and Health Services Research

The final components of the Public Health Initiative will support a prevention research initiative in the National Institutes of Health and a health services research initiative in the Public Health Service. These efforts will provide a knowledge base to prevent disease and promote health more effectively, and to elucidate the factors that affect health care costs, quality, and access.

Prevention research is the foundation for both clinical preventive services and the public health interventions included in the Health Security Act. Expanded prevention research will ensure the availability of effective preventive measures against existing diseases as well as new and emerging health threats. Progress in preventing disease will help to offset escalating acute health care costs and the disproportionate impact of disease and disability among women, minorities, and the elderly.

Health services research will elucidate what works best in medical care and how to organize providers and institutions most effectively in the new health care system. This investment will build on the considerable expertise of the Agency for Health Care Policy and Research in investigating outcomes and quality research, identifying practice variations with unnecessarily high costs, and developing practice guidelines to improve the appropriateness and effectiveness of the treatment decisions made by health professionals. Further development of these methods will provide more accurate measures to evaluate the performance of alliances and health plans and to assess the extent to which reform is making health care available to all Americans.

The Health Security Act also includes provisions to develop health information systems that improve the quality of health data and simplify the collection and analysis of health related data. These data will be essential to monitoring the quality and performance of health plans and providers, and monitoring the effectiveness and costs of specific clinical or administrative functions within organized delivery systems.

CONCLUSION

In closing let me emphasize that the Public Health Initiative is not separate from health care reform. It is essential to the success of reform. Together, the components of the Public Health Initiative provide the building blocks vital to our reform efforts. They shift financial incentives away from paying for diseases and their complications toward paying providers and plans for keeping people healthy. They assure integration of private and public health care providers and mainstreaming of vulnerable populations too long neglected. They build on the new responsibility of health plans and alliances for entire populations by providing funds to state and local health agencies to work in partnership with the personal health care system. They promote the goal of quality health care at an affordable cost by relying more on primary care providers, proven clinical interventions, and on a strong information base and performance monitoring to support quality assurance efforts.

In summary, the President's Health Security Act is designed to provide all Americans—including those currently underserved—with real health security at an affordable price. Mr. Chairman, I appreciate this opportunity to appear before this Committee and look forward to the opportunity to work with you to take full advantage of this unique opportunity to improve the health of all of our people.

The CHAIRMAN. Thank you very much, Dr. Lee.

We will have 6-minute rounds for questioning, and I will ask staff to keep track of the time, and if there are further questions, we will come back to them.

One of the observations that have been made by some of the people up in my home State is whether we are really in the shape for being able to move toward transition, and whether there is appropriate time available given the magnitude of the issue.

What is your own sense with regard to the public health aspects of this program; do you feel that we can move ahead—we have the expansion in the national health service, we have school-based clinics, and a lot of other features that you have mentioned as well in terms of other kinds of support systems. What can you tell us in terms of the time or the movement in reaching the goals that have been established by the President's program, and also the resources that will be needed?

Dr. LEE. I think in terms of the public health initiatives, particularly, that we do have the capacity. At the Centers for Disease Control, Health Resources and Services Administration, the Agency for Health Care Policy and Research, substance abuse and mental health at NIH, we have a very strong professional capability, and I think we are able and would be able to move forward in these areas.

I think the transition, however, as we are going through a great deal of change in personal health care out in the country right now, with very dramatic shifts, I think this transition is a very difficult one. Until the Congress is able to act on the reforms, and there is a very clear signal to everyone where we are going to go, I think there is going to be a lot of uncertainty. And my concern is during this transition, there will be more people uninsured, there will be more demands on local governments to provide for the uninsured during this transition period before enactment. Then, once it is enacted, I think the clear signals to the States and to the providers will help us deal with that transition far more effectively than we can right now, which is a period of uncertainty. But I think on the public health side, we are ready to move promptly; I think we do have the capacity. We do need to rebuild that infrastructure, particularly at the local level and the State level in terms of public health, but I think we have the capacity to do that.

The CHAIRMAN. Of course, there are many features of public health that are not included in terms of the coverage—cleaning up of the lead paint poisoning sites for example—and the President has talked, certainly, about the importance of preventing violence. So I see it as sort of a continuing process, besides just the legislation; if we are really serious about these issues, we have to deal with the parts which are outlined in the administration's bill and also try to begin to develop a focus on some of these other aspects.

In terms of the funding and the financial support, it is always challenging. I read a very interesting article the other day, which gave some hope, described that in Hawaii—which for some of us, in terms of the employer mandate, has some appeal—they are 35 percent higher in cost of living, they are 40 percent lower in terms of the costs of health care, they have twice as many people who visit doctors in terms of utilization of preventive services, and they have half the number of hospitalizations. So that is what we are all looking for.

Dr. LEE. That is exactly right.

The CHAIRMAN. When you come back to that, in terms of some of those who are sharp-shooting this program—and that is without the business subsidies, which we can talk about another day—but it is the delivery services and the preventive aspects and early intervention that are such important aspects. And you are not going to be able to do that unless you have a strong public health component, I do not think.

In the time remaining, I would say that we are going to hear from Joycelyn Elders next week, but in terms of the school-based clinics, I am a very, very strong supporter. We have one in Cambridge in the Latin School, and how they were able to get it in there over a long period of time is an enormously interesting subject for another day. But there is not a parent in that school who would support taking it out at this time, and I think that will be the case generally.

We have not talked much about the importance of providing that range of services particularly in the inner city—and I am sure it is true in rural America as well—but particularly in the inner cities. And I am not just talking about sexually-transmitted diseases and health education, but the other great pressures that are on children in this climate and atmosphere. I am just wondering if you could expand on your own understanding of the needs for the development of school-based systems and how you see those developing.

Dr. LEE. Yes. My experience goes back to San Francisco, Senator Kennedy, when we worked to develop a school-based clinic at Balboa High School. That is now being expanded to a second high school in San Francisco. Our initial objective was to provide family planning services. But when we surveyed the kids in the schools, that was not their priority. Their priority was for psychosocial support services to help them cope with family problems, social problems, peer pressures. What we developed, then, was a primary care, nurse practitioner-led service, but the major component was the psychosocial support.

Now, some of those services will be included in the health benefit. And of course, the plans will have to pay the schools who develop these services for all the services included in the benefit package. We believe that would best be done on a capitation basis, rather than on a fee-for-service basis, simply for recordkeeping purposes and other reasons.

Some of those services are not included. They would be included in the package in our core benefit. One of the issues—and we want to work with you on this—is how do you reach the kids who drop out of school. And we believe with the access initiative and with the enabling services that are possible, that we can at least begin to meet that need—but that is as important a need as for the kids who are in school. And as you know, we are proposing to limit this program at the outset to kids from low-income school districts where half or more of the kids come from families with incomes of less than 100 percent of poverty, so we reach the highest-risk kids in the beginning.

We also know that adolescents, even when they have health insurance, do not go to their primary providers. There are a lot of reasons for that, but they are one of the most underserved groups in the population. And you identified several of the problems—HIV/AIDS, problems associated with violence and the stresses, substance abuse, sexually-transmitted diseases, teenage pregnancies. Those are all interrelated problems related to empowering the individual, giving these young people coping skills. We would hope to make that an integral part of these school-based programs and the programs that would be developed with the access initiative as well.

The CHAIRMAN. My time is up, but I think we have about 350,000 kids a year dropping out.

Dr. LEE. Yes, it is at least that many.

The CHAIRMAN. Yes, I think it might be even higher than that. And we are attempting through this program, as well as well as the school-to-work program and the national service program, to reach this group of young people who are just being left out. I am sure we are not doing it as well, obviously, as we can or should, but hopefully, we are trying to establish some links with these young people to try to bring them into the whole process, whether it is in a continuing education program or capturing them through programs like City Year and national service and others.

We all understand there is no single silver bullet that is going to do everything that's needed, but I think we must recognize the importance of access to health service for adolescents and children.

Dr. LEE. The core public health funding, providing data for surveillance and monitoring at a local level, will help communities identify those high-risk groups within the community, even neighborhoods, or within census tracts or within ZIP codes—where are the neighborhoods where the problems are the greatest, and where can they concentrate their resources to make the most effective use of those. And that is why the core public health element is really integral to meeting these other objectives.

The CHAIRMAN. And I think parts of Goals 2000, in terms of the education and the mentoring systems, are beginning to identify those young people who are falling through the process as well.

Senator Durenberger.

Senator DURENBERGER. Thank you, Mr. Chairman.

Phil, I am sorry I was not here for all of your presentation, and just so everybody knows, I have known Phil for a dozen years or so now, and I care a lot about you, and I respect you a great deal.

I have read your statement, and I must say that, sitting on this committee and on the Finance Committee, I care a lot more about the kinds of things we do here, than the things we do over there. Over there, we are funding Medicare and wasting a lot of money the way we do it; and we are funding Medicaid and putting people in nursing homes and not getting the right care to the right people; and we cannot come to grips with a tax policy that rewards people for buying huge policies they do not need, yet penalizes other folks.

But here, this is a place where over 30 years now, people have cared a lot about community failures in one way or another and have come to Washington, DC, to find solutions. They have found them, and have developed over 500 different approaches, most of which have been developed in communities like Boston, MA, Minneapolis, MN, and Chicago, IL, and so forth; they come out here, and they become a categorical program. Now, they are back in 39,000 communities in America, and the situation seems to be getting a lot worse than it ever was before.

I do not think that situation started in 1981. I think that has been developing over a long period of time. The kinds of things that the President talked about in Memphis did not start with Ronald Reagan; they started in our communities a long time ago and for a wide variety of reasons. This is supposed to be a solution place, but I cannot find the solutions in Federal answers, Federal categorical programs, Federal mandates, and so on. I see public health as a community problem, and as a series of relationship problems. I see failures in our face.

Paul Wellstone and his wife have been committed, a long time before they ever got here, to talking about violence in a wide variety of ways, but you cannot put $10 million or $20 million in a Federal program here and solve that problem in America. The best he can do is call attention to it and say that somebody in Washington hears you, and somebody in Washington cares, and somebody in Washington, including the President, says that as a nation we need to do something about it.

I would just like to know where in that basic benefit package in the Health Security Act, and where in the dollars that the administration recommends we spend through the Public Health Services, we are going to take on the challenges that the President talked about in Memphis, we are going to take on the challenges of the behavior deterioration in this country, we are going to take on all of those kinds of challenges. The chairman talked to you about the interrelationships between education, social services, health, and so forth. We are dying in the State of Minnesota to co-locate these services, but you cannot break down the barriers in the system. There are smart people all over this country who we are choking on the smokestacks of Federal categorical programs—but do not say we are going to substitute for that a 58-page series of health benefits, because that is not going to do it.

You can say preventive this and preventive that, but you do not have it in there, and it is not in there because you cannot afford to put it in there. So we are struggling between resource availability and a national solution to problems that really start in our local communities.

So I just need you to help me understand how it is that the administration's Health Security Act and related proposals are going to accomplish this job of improving the health of all Americans and reducing health disparities among Americans, and over what period of time.

Dr. LEE. I think the first thing, and it is fundamental—and of course, you have really been a leader in this area for many years—is the development of capitated plans. The alliances are regional, and therefore a population-based approach to personal medical care, personal health care.

In the plans, capitation payments, so that population is in a plan, so that we can begin to focus and to achieve public health objectives through the plans. We need to strengthen the core public health—and that is this whole public health initiative—so that as you take a problem, whether it is, let us say, tuberculosis in New York—the patient can go from New York to Minneapolis. We cannot afford to have a good prevention program in New York but not a good one in Minneapolis.

Violence issues. The kind of core infrastructure that we are proposing will help the community identify the problems, decide—in Minneapolis, maybe it is one type of problem, in Chicago, it is somewhat different. That core funding is going to be critically important.

Senator DURENBERGER. Maybe we could just concentrate on the District of Columbia. We all live around here, we are working here. We are sitting in the middle of it right now.

How is the postal workers' health plan, if it becomes an accountable health plan in the District of Columbia health alliance going to solve the problems that we read about in our newspapers in this community every, single day?

Dr. LEE. Well, there some problems we read about; there are a lot of problems that we do not read about, like sexually-transmitted disease, teenage pregnancy. We read about the violence end of it, and that is one piece, actually, for some populations. For African American males, I think between the ages of 20 and 40, AIDS produces a higher mortality than violence. We hear about the violence. We do not hear as much about the prevention of HIV. This would permit, with the preventive components of the plan, combined with the public health initiatives, as well as continuing our major CDC HIV prevention program with States and local communities, and bringing into that in a new approach which is being proposed by CDC to work with nonprofit organizations and community-based organizations.

I think we will see a much more effective approach. Now, we do not have a solution to all the problems——

Senator DURENBERGER. My time has run out, but maybe you could respond to this in writing. Let us just take the District of Columbia as an example, if you would, Dr. Lee, and tell me how long it is going to take, how much it is going to cost, and how the money is going to get into the system. I care about this community, but I read in the newspaper this morning about a wonderful little Russian girl who, if she were on Medicaid in this country, would get $80,000 or $100,000 to get a bone marrow transplant, but we cannot find $100,000 to do prenatal care the way it ought to be done in this community. And I can go on and on and on and on and on. But I need to know how you are proposing the accountable health plan is going to change that situation. Maybe you could just take the District of Columbia.

Dr. LEE. We can describe that and how the plans as well as the core public health, combined with the existing efforts—it is a Federal-State-local partnership, and it is a public-private partnership if we are going to make this happen successfully.

Senator DURENBERGER. Thank you.

Dr. LEE. Thank you.

The CHAIRMAN. Senator Simon.

Senator SIMON. Thank you, Mr. Chairman.

As I mentioned to you on the telephone the other day, Dr. Lee, I saw a picture of a young Philip Lee with Lyndon Johnson in some newspaper or magazine article recently. And I note that sitting in back of you is the sister of Hubert Humphrey, and of course, we have the brother of Jack Kennedy presiding here. So we bring together the spirit of a lot of people who have been wanting to see this day come.

Dr. LEE. I could not be more honored than to have you associate me with those two individuals.

The CHAIRMAN. We are all honored.

Senator SIMON. I think they feel honored, too, I am sure.

Last Saturday, we held a hearing in Springfield, IL, and Dr. Lasker of your staff was there and did a superb job, and I think you ought to know that.

The CHAIRMAN. I would second that as well. Dr. Lasker has done an outstanding job.

Dr. LEE. We have a good team.

The CHAIRMAN. Good.

Senator SIMON. You do have a good team.

As I read Title III, we have the Public Health Service initiatives fund, $400 million for fiscal year 1995. That is new money entirely?

Dr. LEE. Correct.

Senator SIMON. OK. Then, as I go through, and you talk about competitive grants, here is my problem and my question. Madison County, IL, the fourth-largest county in the State, has a lot of problems. It has no county health department. Now, how does Madison County, IL benefit, and how do we make sure that some of the areas of great need, where we may not have the agencies that are going to apply for competitive grants, how do we make sure they benefit from this?

Dr. LEE. The State has basic responsibility for public health, the State public health agency, for the health of the public in the entire State. Some States have county health departments, others have city health departments, and others have city-county. In this case, the State of Illinois would apply, would identify the needs, and if they felt that the priority need was in Madison County, and they needed to deploy State employees into that county or develop the infrastructure in the county by funding through the county the development of these core purposes, like sexually-transmitted disease control or communicable disease control, that would be through that grant to the State.

In California, for example, almost half of the counties do not have a local health department; the State actually runs the local health departments, because they are very, very small counties, very rural. So it differs in different States, but that would be absolutely possible, if that is a priority in Illinois, for that county to get the support through this grant that would be necessary.

Senator SIMON. Will the States be the only entities that can apply for that?

Dr. LEE. The States would be the grantees for that core public health function, because basically they have that responsibility. They would identify in their grant request both how much money and what particular functions would be performed at the local level. That would have to be part of the original grant, so the grant would be made, although to the State agency, it would then be passed on to the local Government if that were a priority as determined in the State.

Senator SIMON. Well, my concern is—and I think maybe we can work out some language to deal with this—that if the State makes these judgments in terms of the competitive grants, the people who are going to apply to the State are going to be people who have been leading, understandably. And I commend the counties that have the programs. Obviously, in Cook County, IL, you have huge needs, but you also have—and I am not saying there are not needs in Du Page County, IL, which has a county health department, and many others—but we have some areas of huge need that do not have county health departments—and maybe Illinois is the only State like this; I have no idea——

Dr. LEE. No, it is not.

Senator SIMON [continuing]. My concern is that those who follow this and who are going to be on top of this are going to have some proposals, then, to the public health department in the State of Illinois, and the grant money will be heading in the direction of those who have departments and missing areas where we do not have anyone.

Dr. LEE. Well, we will need to make sure. One, we will need to provide technical assistance. We will need also to be making a determination in a given State if they are not meeting the areas of greatest need. And as we go forward and get better information, we will be able to identify those areas, and we would be able to ask, why is it that you are not dealing with these areas of greatest need, let us say, in Illinois.

I think we have to find some way, and I do not think we have it spelled out clearly enough in the plan just how we would do that, because I think it is a central question for us to be able to answer, and it is a central need, because we want to meet those needs where the priorities are greatest, I mean, the areas of greatest need. That is what the Federal Government should be doing is helping reduce those disparities.

Senator SIMON. Right. And it seems to me that maybe we ought to work out some kind of an amendment that requires the States to look at those areas that may not be covered by county health departments or whatever you call it in a particular State.

Dr. LEE. That is true. In many rural areas, they do not have an adequate public health infrastructure. And as they are underserved in terms of personal medical care, many of them are also underserved in terms of public health infrastructure protecting water supplies, a number of other fundamental public health protections.

Senator SIMON. Thank you very much.

Dr. LEE. We would be very glad to work with the committee on that, Mr. Chairman.

Senator SIMON. We would like to work with you in drafting some kind of an amendment to make sure this is covered.

Thank you, Mr. Chairman.

The CHAIRMAN. Senator Wellstone.

Senator WELLSTONE. Thank you, Mr. Chairman.

First of all, Dr. Lee, I agree with what Senator Simon said. When I look at the chairman, and I know of his leadership in health care over the years, and I look at Frances Humphrey and Senator Simon and others, I feel really honored to be a part of this—and Senator Durenberger. He and I do not always agree, but I know what his commitment is to health care reform.

Since I only have a short time, let me first of all express my frustration, which am I sure everybody has. I have been looking forward to this hearing, and because things got rearranged, I have a commitment in about 6 or 7 minutes that I cannot get out of—it was set up months ago. And I want to talk about the importance of public health, and maybe put all three of my questions to you, and then you can answer, because I fear that if I do one, then we will have gone over our limit.

As you know, the American Public Health Association is a strong supporter of single-payer, and that is always my framework as I evaluate legislation and think about where we are going. And I think this focus on public health and this focus on community outreach and empowerment—I heard you use that word—is critically important, and I would say to you that it has to be there, because I do see schematically and conceptually a huge gap where you have these accountable health networks, run by whom, question mark, competing on the basis of cost. And I am not at all sure, when I travel around the country, people who are in public health and people who work with community health care clinics and people who work with the most vulnerable low-income citizens, worry about where they fit into that. So you really are focusing on an incredibly important piece, that is, what is going to be the commitment to this infrastructure of delivery of care, which I think all of us believe in.

So here are my questions. First of all, could we not look to a more stable source of funding? I have been on this committee, and I know we authorize great things, and then I know we do not get the appropriation. I am very worried—it seems to me we ought to have a more stable funding mechanism for this if we are going to say it is absolutely of priority importance.

The second question. When it comes to those who apply for this, one of the concerns I have heard from some of the 330 community health care clinic people is that they do not really see a priority in terms of where they fit in. And they have been doing this; I mean, they have got a proven record. In fact, Mr. Chairman, I think that is one of the great success stories is the community health care clinics, which goes back well over two decades now. And I am wondering why there is not a priority for people who have been doing this in terms of applying for the funding.

Then, finally, a cautionary note. We had just a great hearing last week in this committee on mental health. We had some people who came in with some very important, I would say, actuarial numbers that work with Fortune 500 companies that I think are going to be helpful to the President and Mrs. Clinton and the task force. But one concern—I heard you mention mental health—is if in fact—I do not know that you want to respond, but I just want to sound this as a warning—if we further contract the benefits in terms of inpatient, outpatient, copays and all the rest, then all those folks get thrown into the public sector. And we have people from some of the large cities really worried about whether there is going to be adequate funding and support for them.

So that is the stream of my three questions, if you could take them one by one—did I thank you for being here? Thank you very much for being here.

Dr. LEE. Thank you, Senator. On the funding stream, the administration feels very strongly that we need to develop a secure funding stream for the public health initiatives, and we definitely want to work with this committee and work with the Congress to identify that and determine how that can best be accomplished.

We know that in the bill that was proposed, we did include authorization; we did not identify that secure funding, but we hope that working with you, we can identify that and find the answer to that. But it is a key question.

On the 330 clinics, many others, of course, have been at the front lines—rural family practitioners in private practice, public hospitals—many other providers in addition to the 330 clinics.

Senator WELLSTONE. Right. I used that as an example.

Dr. LEE. Of course, the 330 clinics have been central, as a Federal initiative, to meet a need that was identified in the 1960's. It has been a very successful program, and there is both an expansion of support for that, but more particularly in the access initiative, the capacity expansion part of the access initiative and enabling services. They would be not only eligible for but would be one of the groups that we believe would be in the leadership by taking advantage of those new authorities.

On the mental health side, one of the key problems is with the chronically mentally ill and long-term. And the benefit that has been developed thus far is principally more of an acute care benefit. It does not deal with the homeless mentally ill. That is why we are proposing expansion of our public sector funding in mental health and substance abuse to help deal with some of those problems in the transition and to make sure that we have a safety net that is there.

We will find for many chronically mentally ill individuals, people with depression, for example, that they can be treated through mainstream providers with no limit on those benefits. Those are standard. That is not part of the mental health benefit. That really comes under the treatment of those individuals where there is a medical treatment available, an effective treatment—like depression, some people with chronic anxiety and some other disorders. Those can be treated without these other limitations that have been necessary because of the difficulties in really calculating the cost side of it. As we go forward, we think those figures will be more clear-cut, and we think that by the year 2000 or a little bit after, those benefits can come fully onstream.

Senator WELLSTONE. Yes. Please convey to HHS and to the administration that we are very anxious to work with them on the numbers, because I really think the data so far is a bit outdated, and I think we have more recent numbers from those who have really managed some of these Fortune 500 companies, and I think we can do the comprehensive and flexible benefits.

Dr. LEE. We have seen some of that same data from New York State, and it is very, very important.

Senator WELLSTONE. Then, finally, on the language, I will want to get back to you. I appreciate your response on the 330 clinics. I am not clear that the actual language that we see gives priority to those. In fact, I think it may give priority to anyone not currently providing health——

Dr. LEE. No. We want to make sure about the language.

Senator WELLSTONE [continuing]. OK, let us be clear about that language if we can.

Dr. LEE. Absolutely.

Senator WELLSTONE. Thank you very much.

Dr. LEE. Let me just say a single word about single-payer. Of course, that is in the plan, it is an option. The President, of course, has gone for the employer mandate because that is the way most people experience access to health insurance now, and that seemed to us to be the most feasible way to cover everybody. But covering everybody is bottom line, with a comprehensive benefit package.

Senator WELLSTONE. Thank you.

Thank you, Mr. Chairman.

The CHAIRMAN. Thank you very much.

Dr. LEE. Thank you, Mr. Chairman.

The CHAIRMAN. We appreciate very much your presence here.

We will return now to our panel and hear now from Ms. Anthony.

Ms. ANTHONY. Thank you, Senator Kennedy.

It certainly is to my advantage to be following Dr. Mullet and Dr. Lee because they have done a good job describing things like the core functions, and I will not have to repeat that.

But I am very pleased to be here before this committee, and I do want to commend the committee for your strong support and interest in health care reform and recognizing the crucial role that public health has to play.

I come here representing the State of Michigan as well as the Association of State and Territorial Health Officers. The public health community is very excited about the potential for health care reform, the potential for universal access, and certainly, if public health is strengthened, we will have the opportunity to actually improve the health status of our population. And we would certainly fall short as a nation if we had universal access and discovered that we had not actually improved the health status of citizens of this country. So public health is very anxious to offer this opportunity to our country.

Out of necessity, as has been mentioned, public health has served a role in providing clinical services to vulnerable populations. It was a necessary safety net, if you will. And, while that has been very important, it has diverted us away from our primary mission for public health and the core services that are so important.

In order for public health to provide these core services, as was described by Dr. Lee and Dr. Mullet—assessment, prevention, health promotion and protection, as well as access to needed care—we must address the twin issues of resources and flexibility—resource level, adequacy of funding, and greater State flexibility, to use these funds more effectively and efficiently through block grants and other methods of funding.

States are in the best position to develop a consensus and provide the appropriate forum for determining statewide needs using local planning processes. A cookie-cutter, categorical-type approach dictated federally will not work in Michigan. While we run the gamut of very rural, such as in the upper peninsula of our State, to very urban, such as in the city of Detroit with its intense urban concerns, our needs are ever changing, and we do need that flexibility at the State level.

I think some of the questions that have been asked earlier in terms of how do you meet the local needs were very good questions. With the State providing the forum to bring together local planning processes, that is how you do that. And if the funding is based on health data, health statistics, demographics and causes of death, you can assure a statewide approach that does indeed target all areas of the State.

First, to the issue of the level of resources. Currently, less than one percent of aggregate national health expenditure support population-based public health services. How much is enough to adequate fund population-based services is difficult to say, but a recent draft paper from the U.S. Department of Health and Human Services estimated that a reasonable level of per capita support for population-based public health services at the current rate of spending would be $61 per capita, or 1.7 percent of total national health expenditures. If the population-based services were brought to a level of full effectiveness, it is estimated that $100 per capita would be needed, or 2.7 percent of total national health expenditures.

Given the State maintenance of effort clause in the Clinton plan, one way to address this could be a redirection of direct clinical services spending that is currently being spent by public health back into population-based core public health functions.

As an example, in the State of Michigan, we estimate that we currently receive over $90 million from Federal grants and Medicaid for clinical services. If this funding were redirected to population-based public health services, it would go a long way toward an effective level of funding.

I would like to compliment the administration for including tobacco tax as a source of revenue for health care, because as a public health community, we know that the use of tobacco is the single most significant modifiable risk behavior we can change if we want to make a difference in health status, and an increase in cost would reduce consumption.

While the total amount of dollars available for public health population-based service is of paramount concern, the issue of flexibility in the allocation and use of these funds also is critical. State flexibility must be an integral characteristic to address a number of concerns which include the minimum capacity to carry out core public health functions, the ability of State and local public health agencies to identify needs and priorities and target resources, and the recognition that a single funding method such as per capita allocations will not be able to respond adequately to the needs of rural areas or of special vulnerable population groups.

For example, when we look at the State of Michigan, a larger portion of our population may reside in urban areas or metropolitan standard areas, but a very large number of our residents are in rural areas, and a straight per capita type of funding would short-change those areas, and there are many unique needs, especially in terms of access, in rural areas that cannot be addressed with a simple per capita allocation.

While each type of grant has its advantages and disadvantages, our experience tells us that categorical grants lack the broad flexibility for States and communities to target resources based on greatest need. Because each categorical program comes with its own requirements related to reporting, data collection, and other administrative functions, States end up spending huge amounts of resources on these types of activities rather than the actual provision of services.

To make matters worse, definitions used by one categorical program may be contrary to those used by another program. For example, the definition of a child can cover the whole range from birth through age 21. My favorite definition conflict is whether the unborn child of a pregnant woman is counted when you are determining the size of a family for poverty status. One Federal program counts the fetus in calculating eligibility for family size, while another program does not, so a woman may come for services and be eligible in the same building for one Federal program and not for another one, and that really creates all kinds of problems for the families and for those who are delivering services.

Restrictive Federal categorical language can and often does create unexpected problems for the implementation of good public health at the State and local level.

Another example is the breast and cervical cancer prevention program at CDC. While this program was meant to help women have access to quality and low-cost mammograms, Federal legislation actually prohibits this from occurring in some rural areas. Legislation stated that health departments could only contract with not-for-profit organizations in the provision of these services. However, in many rural areas, there are limited services, and oftentimes there may be only for-profit organizations to contract with. With the reauthorization of the program this year, this problem was corrected, but it is a good indication of what can happen when there is not flexibility for States to best determine how to get services to their local communities.

There is, however, some merit to the use of competitive grants to fund demonstration projects and projects which go beyond the core public health function to test new, creative approaches. The Association of State and Territorial health officials, of which I am a member of the executive committee, strongly advocates for formula grant programs such as the preventive health and health services block grant, which provides States with general Federal guidelines but still provides them with the much-needed State flexibility.

To ensure that these grants meet the needs of rural as well as more populated States, we advocate for a base funding level for each State based on population, with the remainder of the grant distributed based on appropriate indicators, such as poverty, number of elderly or children, etc.

We are fortunate in the State of Michigan to have a Governor, John Engler, who has given prevention a high priority. Recognizing the impact of smoking on cardiovascular disease and cancer, the Governor has been a strong advocate in changing policies to protect the public's health. For example, he has signed recent bills to ban smoking in schools and day care centers, increase nonsmoking seating in restaurants, and prohibit minors from purchasing cigarettes in vending machines.

Also, we are very fortunate in our State to have a very strong local public health network. We have 50 local health jurisdictions covering all 83 countries, and we are governed by a relatively new public health law which directs State and local governments to safeguard the public's health. And our public health activities in Michigan are, by statute, partnership between local and State government. In Michigan, we recognize local public health as the key front line for public health service delivery.

Recently within our State, we have undertaken a State and local public health consensus process to develop a paper on the future of public health under health care reform, called "Promoting Healthy Michigan Communities: The Role of Public Health and Health Care Reform." I would be glad to make that document available to this committee when it is completed.

In addition to this, we have also in the process of competing a State strategic planning process identified four priority areas for the State: influencing health risk behaviors, focusing on crime, disease, and prevention; reducing the minority health status gap; survival of the African American male, and the reduction of adverse environmental and occupational health effects, and the evolution of the public health system.

I share these experiences with you as an example of the capabilities of State and local governments to demonstrate that they have a solid foundation to build upon.

In closing, I would like to reiterate that we in the public health community believe that health care reform represents both new opportunities and challenges. The medical system can and should become more accountable for a full range of health services in ways that meet the needs of vulnerable populations as well, so that the mainstream public health agencies can again make population-based services their primary priority.

Each community will respond in its own unique way, but Government, through local and State public health, must retain responsibility for assessment, prevention, health promotion and protection, and access to needed health services. These population-based services, or core public health functions, must be supported adequately at all levels of Government, starting at the Federal level, and the support must be in a form which allows State flexibility to meet the unique and ever-changing needs of our States.

A strengthened public health system for the future, coupled with a reformed medical care system, can produce a more efficient and more equitable health system that actually improves the health and quality of life of all of our citizens.

On behalf of the State of Michigan and the Association of State and Territorial Health Officers, I would like to thank you for this opportunity to speak before you today.

Thank you.

The CHAIRMAN. Thank you very much.

[The prepared statement of Ms. Anthony follows:]

PREPARED STATEMENT OF VERNICE DAVIS ANTHONY

My name is Vernice Davis Anthony, and I am the Director of the Michigan Department of Public Health. I am honored to be able to come before you at this hearing, representing the public health interests of my state, as well as the Association of State and Territorial Health Officials. I commend Senator Kennedy, and members of the Senate Labor Committee for your current and future efforts to reform our nation's health system and your recognition of the importance of public health in this effort.

The past, present and future discussions on health care reform have this country's public health agencies very excited because it offers the potential of significantly altering what we think is wrong and improve upon what is right. It offers us an opportunity to fix a broken medical care system, assure universal health coverage, and if public health is strengthened, to actually improve the health status of our citizens. Assuring access to medical care will only impact 10% of the causes of premature death. Seventy percent of these deaths can be linked to health behaviors and environmental causes, both of which can best be addressed by public health strategies. (The other 20% of premature deaths are caused by inherited or genetic factors.)

We readily acknowledge that none of this will be easy. Health reform will require some very tough negotiations and consensus building. One key element of reform is changing how health care is financed so that the incentives work for prevention and this will require investment in areas that have not always received the highest priority in the past.

My testimony will focus on getting back to basics in public health, getting truly excited about prevention and the core functions of public health. In order to accomplish this, the public health system will require increased investment in funding, and maximum flexibility for states and local areas to set priorities and target funding to areas in greatest need. States are in the best position to develop a consensus (forum) for determining needs of its citizens with local input. Because of this, it is important that the federal government establish general guidelines for the use of resources, but provide the states with the flexibility to determine specific programs to be implemented to meet local needs on a statewide basis.

I would like to take a few minutes now to talk about the public health vision in health reform, how we get there, and what we are doing in my state of Michigan to position ourselves for what needs o occur.

Whether we look at a recent report on "Public Health and Health Reform" from the U.S. Department of Health and Human Services, or the 1988 report on The Future of Public Health from the Institute of Medicine, or each state's own assessment of needs and resources, the same conclusion can be reached: *while public health has a vital role to play in maintaining and improving the population's health, it lacks the resources to carry out this role.* Public health has, out of necessity, served an important role in filling the gap in providing both clinical prevention and primary care to vulnerable and underserved populations, often being supported by Medicaid and state and local tax dollars. This has taken us away from our primary mission of assessing the health of the population and delivering services that prevent disease, promote and protect health, and increase access to care. Our current health system has perverse financial incentives. The system lavishes money on the most costly specialized medical services but underfunds prevention and public health population based services. While health is the most rapidly growing component of both state and federal budgets, the growth is occurring in entitlement programs that pay for medical care. Grant-supported public health programs have lost financial ground despite their potential to help deter the steep rise in medical care spending. Public health has paid the price for this diversion. While year-to-year budgeting pressures make it difficult to remedy this imbalance, we have an opportunity in reforming our entire health system that we must not lose.

The Institute of Medicine's report on The Future of Public Health opens its discussion with the observation that the existing public health system is in disarray at a time when the health of the public is under severe attack. Not only does society face the immediate crisis of the AIDS epidemic, violence, and other major health problems, but there are also the enduring problems, such as injuries and chronic illness; growing challenges such as the aging of our population, and the toxic by products of a modern economy, transmitted through air, water, soil or food. The issue of how to support and strengthen the public health system, while recognizing the fundamental responsibility of government in protecting the health of the public is one of the challenges we now face.

The United States health system can be viewed as the union of two components--the medical care system and the public health system. These two components are not independent. Rather they must, and do, complement and support each other. While the medical care system's primary focus is on the treatment of medical problems, the public health system's primary emphasis is on disease prevention, health promotion, and environmental and personal health protection. While the medical care system provides medical services to individuals seeking care, the public health system activities extend beyond the boundaries of individual providers and facilities to encompass the entire population. We refer to these public health activities as *population-based services*. You might also hear them referred to as "core public health functions", as the Clinton health care reform proposal does.

Population-based services have a long history. The recognition that diseases were transmissible from one person to another led to development and application of population-based infectious disease control services by state and local public health authorities. Early in this century, epidemics of cholera, yellow fever, diphtheria, polio, typhoid and many other diseases were virtually eliminated and millions of lives were saved. Other population-based health measures were directed at protecting the public's health through things like milk sanitation, and adding iodine to salt to prevent goiter and other thyroid disease. Population-based public health efforts directed at preventing present day health problems are expected to yield similar results. The importance of population-based efforts to the personal and environmental health of the nation cannot be underestimated

Let me give you a few examples of what I am referring to as population-based services, so you can appreciate what I am talking about

This first example relates to public health's responsibilities in health protection. You probably know about the major outbreak of the E-Coli bacteria infection that occurred in this country a short time ago. The foodborne infection started with heavily contaminated meat which was passed on to others, mainly children, when the meat was undercooked by fast food restaurants. While private sector medical practitioners provided emergency room services and quickly hospitalized stricken individuals for medical care and follow-up, the public health system immediately interviewed families to determine where they had been, what they had eaten and what else they had been in contact with. They discovered that fast food restaurants were undercooking infected meat, the result of packing house practices. Public health providers also noticed many of the cases were children of day care age and promptly contacted day care centers, reinforcing instructions on sanitation with toddlers, and thus preventing hundreds more cases of secondary infections.

A second example relates to public health's responsibilities to assess the population's health. Adults in Michigan households are interviewed by telephone to determine their knowledge, attitudes and behaviors that contribute to chronic disease, injury and other health problems. Information is collected on such things as smoking, drinking, cholesterol, hypertension, exercise, diet, seat belt use, smoke detectors, and preventive health practices. The data have shown that the high rate of chronic disease deaths in Michigan can be accounted for, at least in part, by Michigan being the state with the highest proportion of its adult population who are overweight and the third highest proportion of smokers. In contrast, this survey data demonstrated that legislation requiring car seat belt use resulted in a higher proportion of the population who "buckle up". These data are an invaluable resource to use in identifying risk behaviors, planning programs and evaluating their effectiveness.

A third example relates to public health's responsibilities in promoting the health of the population. A community coalition of health-related organizations, coordinated by one of Michigan's local health departments, worked to change many factors in its community that support the continuation of smoking. The group successfully petitioned the county commission for an ordinance that restricted smoking in all workplaces. With the coalition's encouragement, local television and radio stations agreed to play public service announcements which stressed the health effects of secondhand smoke, especially on children. All advertisements included a toll-free number to call for help with quitting smoking. Letters to the editor encouraged restaurant patrons to avoid eating establishments that didn't adequately keep tobacco smoke away from non-smoking diners. As a result of these combined efforts, many community residents decided to quit smoking and some contacted their private medical practitioners for smoking cessation counseling and nicotine patches.

A fourth example relates to public health's responsibilities to prevent disease and death in the population. Every newborn in Michigan is screened, through a simple heel-stick blood test, for a number of devastating genetic diseases. One of these diseases is galactosemia, a rare inherited medical disorder that has a rapid onset in the first few weeks of life. The earliest symptoms are Jaundice and poor feeding which rapidly progresses to severe liver damage and death. Five days after birth, an infant was found to have a positive test for galactosemia by our Newborn Screening Laboratory. By this time, the baby had become ill and jaundiced and the physician had readmitted the baby to the hospital. The physician was notified of the screening result the same day as it was discovered. The physician had been trying unsuccessfully to treat Jaundice and the infant's condition had deteriorated. His response was "I never considered galactosemia." The infant was immediately switched to a soy based infant formula and all symptoms of the disorder were resolved in a few days. The physician was convinced that the baby would have died if he had not been notified of the newborn screening test result.

A fifth and final example relates to public health's responsibilities to assure access to needed health care and support services. A 14 year-old Detroit girl with a third grade education became pregnant and delivered a daughter. She was unmarried and lived with her mother in a home without heat or a stove. The baby died of malnutrition when she was seven months old. She was brought to the hospital with her fingernails polished but weighing only a few ounces more than her healthy birth weight, and died within a few hours. She had not seen a doctor since she was discharged from the hospital following

her birth. She had been fed mashed potatoes, iced tea and cold whole milk. This baby did not die because her family had no medical insurance. She was covered by Medicaid. She did not die because good medical care was not available. Some of the finest medical care in the nation is located within blocks of where she lived. She died because health is a more complex issue than medical care alone. In this case, we failed to give her family the kind of non-medical help they needed to keep her healthy. Shortly after this tragedy, Michigan's state health department, working closely with the state's Medicaid agency and child protection personnel, designed a program and a system which would assure that such a tragedy would not be repeated. The program is called Infant Support Services and is designed for high-risk families such as the one I just described. Services include intensive home visiting by a nurse, nutritionist, social worker, and infant mental health specialist, where available, administered by community providers. It is paid for by Medicaid funds, one of the first in the country to be approved by HCFA to provide enriched services to pregnant women and their children.

Providing a health insurance card alone will not solve our nation's health problems. We know this in Michigan because we have a very fine Medicaid program. Despite this, the Medicaid population is the most unhealthy. Lifestyle, poverty and other non-medical factors contribute to the health problems and must be addressed by public health and others if we are going to make this country healthier.

These examples are the best ways I know to describe to you what we mean by population-based services, or core public health functions, and why they are so important to the overall health and well-being of our population. These population-based services may vary from community to comm nity, depending on needs and resources. Regardless of what we do to i i prove our medic il care system and expand the availability of health coverage for all individuals, governmment at the federal, state and local levels must retain responsibility for:

- assessment
- prevention
- pro i otion
- protection
- access to needed health services

These are the population based services.

To be i ore specific, we must provide leadership in developing and imple i enting strategies to address non financial barriers to health services, which the tragic death of our i edically insured infant in Detroit so vividly illustrates. We also need to invest in a co i prehensive public health surveillance system and information network that is able to detect health problems, monitor trends, evaluate effectiveness, assess changes in the delivery of health services, and link the public and private health sectors. We need to hold health systems accountable for providing services which i i prove the health status of the population. We need to increase the provision of personal health and environmental population-based services by public health. And we need to develop a strengthened partnership between public health and the private sector to avoid duplication of personal health services and assure access for all populations, including low-income, hard to reach and other vulnerable populations. Again, this can be accomplished through increased resources and greater flexibility.

Currently, less than 1% of aggregate national health expenditures support population-based public health services. In Michigan, over $700 i illion of federal, state and local i oney has been allocated to public health, with over $500 i illion, or 73%, going to support population-based services. How much is enough to adequately fund necessary population based services? It's di fficult to say exactly, but a recent draft paper from the U.S. Department of Health and

Human Services estimated that a reasonable level of per capita support for population-based public health services at the current rate of spending would be $61 per capita, or 1.7% of total national health expenditures. If the population based services were brought to a level of full effectiveness, it is estimated that $100 per capita would be needed, or 2.7% of total national health expenditures. Given the state maintenance of effort clause in the Clinton plan, one way to address this is a redirection of direct clinical service spending by public health agencies to population based core public health functions. As an example, in Michigan, we estimate that we currently receive over $90 million from federal grants and Medicaid for clinical services. If this funding were redirected to population-based public health services, it would go a long way toward an effective level of funding.

In looking at the financing for health reform, I need to compliment the Clinton Administration for recommending a tobacco tax as a source of revenue for health care. We know the ill health effects of tobacco use. We need to do whatever we can to reduce the number of people who use tobacco products and to prevent people from starting to use this products. An increase in the tax on tobacco will serve as an incentive to get people to quit, and as a disincentive for people to start. Research shows that an increase in tobacco prices is particularly effective in lowering the use of tobacco by youth.

While the total amount of dollars available for public health population-based services is of paramount concern, the issue of flexibility in the allocation and use of these funds also is critical. An effective public health system requires the capacity to identify and respond to needs at the state and community level.

The way in which population based services are funded is very important to their effectiveness. Flexibility must be an integral characteristic to address a number of concerns which include the minimum capacity to carry out core public health functions, the ability of state and local public health agencies to identify needs and priorities and target resources, and the recognition that a single funding method, such as per capita allocations, will not be able to respond adequately to the needs of rural areas or of special vulnerable population groups. Public health has a long history of experience with various funding approaches from competitive grants, to categorical grants, to block grants. Using Michigan as an example, we receive 10 major categorical grants totalling over $125 million, with WIC comprising $90 million of this total. We also receive 3 block grants, totalling $70 million. The largest of these block grants is substance abuse, totalling over $40 million.

While each type of grant has its advantages and disadvantages, our experience tells us that we need to stay away from categorical grants because they lack the broad flexibility for states and communities to target resources based on greatest needs. Because each categorical program comes with its own requirements related to reporting, data collection and other administrative functions, states end up spending huge amounts of resources on these type of activities rather than the actual provision of services. To make matters worse, definitions used by one categorical program may be contrary to that used by another program. For example, the definition of a child can cover the whole range from birth through age 21. My favorite definition conflict is whether the unborn child of a pregnant woman is counted. The Medicaid program in HCFA counts the fetus in calculating eligibility of family size versus income, while the WIC program in USDA does not. The two federal agencies have been working for years to reconcile this difference but, to the best of my knowledge, they have not yet done so.

Restrictive federal categorical language can and often does create unexpected problems for the implementation of good public health at the state and local levels. A good example is the breast and cervical cancer prevention program at CDC. While this program was meant to help women have access to quality and low-cost mammograms, federal legislation actually prohibited this from occurring in some rural areas. Legislation stated that health departments could only contract with not-for-profit organizations in the provisions of these services. However, in many rural areas, there are limited services and often times these are for-profit organizations. With the reauthorization of this program this year, the problem was corrected, but it is a good indication of what happens when there is not flexibility for states to best determine how to get services to their local communities. There is, however, some merit to the use of competitive grants to fund demonstration projects and projects which go beyond the core public health functions to test creative new approaches. The Association of State and Territorial Health Officials, of which I am a member of their Executive Committee, strongly advocates for formula grant programs such as the Preventive Health and Health Services Block Grant which provides states with general federal guidelines but still provides them with much needed state flexibility. To ensure that these grants meet the needs of rural as well as more populated states, we advocate for a base funding level for each state based on population, with the remainder of the grant distributed based on appropriate indicators such as poverty, number of elderly, children, etc.

We are fortunate in Michigan to have a governor, John Engler, who from the outset gives prevention a high priorities. Recognizing the impact of smoking on cardiovascular disease and cancer, Governor Engler has been a strong advocate in changing policies to protect the public's health. The Governor has signed into law several bills to ban smoking in schools and day care centers, increase non-smoking seating in restaurants, and prohibit minors from purchasing cigarettes from vending machines. He also has been a strong supporter of breast and cervical cancer screening programs, and expanding support services for pregnant women and infants. Michigan also is blessed with a strong local public health system. We have 50 local health jurisdictions covering all 83 counties in the state. We are governed by a relatively new public health law which directs state and local governments to safeguard the public's health. Public health activities in Michigan are, by statute, a partnership between local and state government. While health reform may require us to update our public health laws, we believe we already have a substantial foundation upon which we can build.

Recently, we have undertaken a state and local public health consensus process to develop a written articulation of what we envision the future role of public health to be. The document is just being completed and is called: "Promoting Healthy Michigan Communities: The Role of Public Health in Health Reform". I can provide copies to you as soon as we have it printed. We are also moving ahead to take on the next steps--operationalizing public health's future role. In addition to these state/local efforts, we will be guided by another recently completed document, a state health department strategic plan which provides us with directions to use in targeting our resources and programs for the future. After assessing demographic, economic and health trends, we have focused our future efforts on four priority areas: influencing health risk behaviors, survival of the African American male, influencing the reduction of adverse environmental and occupational health effects, and public health system evolution.

I share our experience with you as an example of the capabilities of state and local public health agencies to carry out the responsibilities which are so critical to the health of our population.

In closing, I would like to reiterate that we in the public health community believe that health reform presents both new opportunities and challenges. The medical system can and should become more accountable for a full range of health services in ways that meet the needs of vulnerable populations as well as the mainstream and public health can again make population-based services its primary priority. Each community will respond in its own unique way, but government, through local and state public health, must retain responsibility for assessment, prevention, promotion, protection and access to needed health services. These population-based services, or core public health functions, must be supported adequately at all levels of government, starting at the federal level. And the support must be in a form which allows flexibility in the way that funds get allocated to best meet needs. The past history of public health has demonstrated effectiveness in preventing disease and disability and improving the health of the population. A strengthened public health system for the future, coupled with a reformed medical care system, can produce a more efficient, more equitable health system that actually improves the health and quality of life of all our citizens. On behalf of the state and local public health community, we stand ready to make our contribution of this vision for the future. I thank you, on behalf of the Association of State and Territorial Health Officials and the State of Michigan for the opportunity to speak before you today on such an important concern in our overall efforts to reform the health system.

The CHAIRMAN. Dr. Guerra.

Dr. GUERRA. Senator Kennedy and members of the staff of the Committee on Labor and Human Resources, for me it is a privilege to offer testimony pertaining to local public health roles, responsibilities and services in the context of giving, perhaps, the local public health scenario as it relates to my community, which is the community of San Antonio, TX, with a population base of 1.1, a community very much in transition, a community that presently has a majority of Mexican Americans. It is a community that is, as you know, close to the U.S.-Mexico border, a community very much in transition.

My department of public health has an annual budget of $23 million, of which $11.1 million is provided by the city general fund, and $12 million by the State, Federal, as well as some foundation support and some corporate sector support to provide the basic level of public health services for an urban community.

To give you a glimpse through the window of local public health to bring to this discussion perhaps a more practical consideration in stating the importance of public health at the local level, where it provides a consistent level of quality, basic services to assure the health, the quality of life, and respond to the basic public health needs of the community, I will simply State initially some experiences from a recent day in my department of health that relate to some of the discussion that has been presented this morning.

In the time of the daily operation of a public health department as prenatal clinics, family planning, well-child clinics, Head Start examinations, the processing of vital records for births and deaths in the community, the provision of which services, the operation of the sexually-transmitted disease clinics, the community outreach for populations at risk for the spread of tuberculosis, HIV and STDs, the cancer screening programs, the multitude of restaurant inspections, the inspections of child care centers, the inspection of food service areas in the schools, the capturing of stray animals, the assurance of trying to keep in place a tracking program for immunization records, a variety of case management services for at-risk populations, the assessments of public inebriants that are brought in by the police officers for having created a public nuisance of one sort or another—all of those are amongst a list of many different services that go on in a local health department.

In the office of the director of a local health department, as those services are going on around one, yesterday I had a meeting with the city manager pertaining to a concern about an increasing number of young children with elevated lead levels from lead in their living and play environments. There was the concern also about the revision of our animal control ordinances. We continue to address what is a major public and social problem in the community, that every year, we pick up upwards of 50,000 strays and also the changing population demographics, with a growing number of animals, including a variety of exotics, that put people at risk, let alone the need for preventing the spread of rabies.

During the same time, I sent a letter to primary care physicians in our community, recruiting their support for participating in a field trial of immune acellular pertussis for young infants, a public-private linkage that is so essential in a community. I also reviewed the protocols for the community-based coalition of case management services and the service providers for the high-risk populations in our community.

We conducted a meeting in our department for the HIV and AIDS community-based service providers who provide the full array, from case management to early intervention, diagnosis treatment, counseling for testing, as well as the array of clinical services.

We reviewed with our staff also the need for submitting a proposal for a therapeutic community for substance-abusing mothers who are pregnant.

We were also preparing to staff an emergency response training exercise for our community to maintain a State of preparedness in the event of some unanticipated catastrophic event that puts a community at risk.

We also participated in the review and comments of a video promoting breast feeding to a community, especially to a community of minority women.

We also discussed computerized restaurant inspections with some of our fellow health officers around the State to see if in fact we can maintain some consistency in the quality of restaurant inspections which, as you know, with the thousands of people who in one way interact with the food service industry, there are tremendous risks for the spread of a variety of diseases related to some contamination of food products.

There was also the additional responsibility for addressing the relocation of a tuberculosis community-based clinic because of having outgrown the space in our present facility, and then having to prepare for a meeting with community groups that are very much opposed to having a TB clinic within their community, even though they have in those sectors a very high incident rate of TB with the numbers continuing to increase.

Perhaps that glimpse through the window of public health services to emphatically State the case for why it is so important to assure the presence and the adequate support of public health in every community, be it urban or rural, throughout this country.

In this long tradition, public health has never been a static or a set set of services and programs in communities. It has been involved since the pioneering efforts of the 18th and 19th centuries, when controlling epidemics of contagious diseases and the early initiatives in public sanitation, to find the original limits of our field.

This willingness to seek out and embrace change will be an extremely important hallmark of public health as we prepare for the next century.

With or without comprehensive health care reform, this is a reality that we cannot afford to ignore. With the transformation of the American society from rural to urban and the emergence of large concentrations of poor, unskilled, uneducated in our cities, public health became de facto the primary health care resource for those disenfranchised from the traditional and mainstream models of service delivery. The attachment of public health and its legacy continues to serve public health, especially in large, very complex urban communities, extremely well.

Today in our urban communities, this situation persists and is even more complicated. It is at the center of the current public debates about access to, availability of affordable and appropriate health care for the most needy in our urban communities. Mine certainly is no exception.

It goes to the heart of the issue of whether we can continue in good conscience and in keeping with the noble ideals of the healing arts to perpetuate a two-class system of care. This is clearly the case in many parts of our Nation.

How this public policy debate is ultimately resolved will define in a very real way how public health will be reconfigured in the remaining years of this century and the early years of the next. It will be a test of political resolve coupled with the vision and commitment of this country's medical and health care institutions and the providers within those systems of care to insist on some basic assurances for every resident—and I emphasize "resident"—in this country.

The mission of public health has been defined as fulfilling society's interest in assuring those basic conditions in which people can be healthy. This was clearly stated in "The Future of Public Health," a report from the Institute of Medicine. This is achieved by mobilizing and organizing the community behind public health issues and by bringing to bear the latest knowledge and technology to prevent disease and prevent good health and healthy lifestyles. Perhaps this is easier said than done.

We must design programs and implement strategies for a society that is undergoing rapid and profound change. As you well know, interpersonal violence is the leading cause of injury across the country for women, for children, and for minority groups. The population of young Mexican American males in my community and the incident rate of assault and homicide and the mortality associated with that is the leading cause of death. If this is not a public health issue, then perhaps we have some of our priorities confused.

The 80-and-over age cohort in our country is amongst the fastest-growing segment of our population. Do we have a public health strategy to address some of these sociodemographic phenomena? Nationally, one in five children live in poverty today, and this number has increased by one-third since 1970. In my own community, the rate is one in four, as it is in other communities around the country.

Within the same time frame, the number of attempted and successful teenage suicides has doubled, and the reported incident rate of child abuse has quadrupled. What is the rate of depression? Do we know that in our communities? Do we know what the rate of unwanted childbearing is, or poorly-timed childbearing, that have very significant health outcomes and consequences in communities. How do we use these indicators of the social and personal health of our Nation in assessing the basic and important core functions of public health, and the presence of public health in a reconfigured health care system?

This is the real world in which public health must function and survive. These are not independent variables to be noted and recorded as we go about our principal tasks. They are clearly linked to root causes and, as impediments, must be recognized, addressed and overcome if the mission of public health as described earlier is to be achieved. In public health, we sometimes think that getting lead out of our soil and fluoride into our drinking water are uphill battles. They certainly are, but there are a lot of other uphill battles, many that continue to challenge and perplex us, and for which we do not always have the resources or, unfortunately, the science and the scientific base, to give us the kind of compelling information that we need to more clearly State some of those efforts and important interventions.

Looking at my own community, I can point with pride to the success of many of our own public health initiatives. We have experienced an enviable record in the past two decades in San Antonio County in terms of improving infant and maternal health, life-expectancy and infant mortality rates. We are recording levels of infant mortality that are below the national and State figures and are coming close to satisfying the objectives of the Healthy People 2000 initiative.

I call attention to an important pioneer effort in our community of the immunization tracking system that allows us to use the birth records for tracking populations of young children to assure compliance at an appropriate time for maintaining immunization levels. That has served our community very well in the prevention of outbreaks of vaccine-preventable diseases.

There are many other important public health conditions that require the basic public health services and programs in the area of prevention and the delivery of services, especially for populations that presently cannot be served within the ongoing private system of medical care, pertaining to sexually-transmitted diseases, to the homeless populations, the incarcerated, those who are at risk because of immunodeficiency states.

Through all of these experiences, we have learned that carefully crafted, well-targeted, and vigorously implemented public health interventions are successful. Programs related to first-time parents for adolescents, where we can prevent the continued rise in second and third pregnancies, are programs that are worth the continued support and investigation in terms of evaluation and assessment for continued provision of those kinds of services.

Every physician and health care worker has both a role and a vital stake in this effort that we call public health. This includes all of our professional societies and the academic medical centers that train our future practitioners as well and give some basic assurances to the competencies that they must maintain. I feel strongly that the public must also be more visible and informed about public health.

Second, in speaking to the central issue of how to finance and support this new and expanded public health agenda, I am sensitive to the competing and sometimes conflicting forces that must be reconciled. I would not be true to this vision of public health for urban communities if I did not encourage you to be steadfast in your support in identifying and releasing new resources for this most critical priority. Current levels of categorical funding available to address public health must be stabilized and expanded. There must be consensus reached on how to creatively leverage State and local resources as well.

Public policy at all levels of Government as well as in the private sector must be tightly focused on recognizing the need to maintain a pool of resources that are clearly and exclusively earmarked for pursuing the public health agenda, the public health set-aside fund at a level of 3 to 5 percent to assure the provision of those basic core functions of public health.

And finally, I want to thank you for the opportunity to present to your committee. We must continue to articulate the strong and compelling case for public health within the reformed health care system.

Thank you very much.

The CHAIRMAN. Thank you very much.

[The prepared statement of Dr. Guerra follows:]

Prepared Statement of Dr. Fernando A. Guerra

The brief comments and observations I bring to you today are drawn
from my experiences as the Director of a public health department
serving a large urban metropolitan population. The variety of
services and programs which constitute the public health presence in
my community is mirrored in many communities both large and small
throughout our country. More often than not the physicians, nurses,
nutritionists, sanitarians and laboratory technicians perform their
daily tasks in relative obscurity. Public health historically has not
been a high profile component of this nation's health care delivery
system. The remarkable advances in recent years in clinical medicine
have understandably captured the public's eye and very often the
lion's share of the public resources directed into health care.
Public health has come to realize that it must address this imbalance
if it is to survive and remain a viable force in this period of health
care reform and reorganization. Our legacy and tradition is rich,
deep and rooted in the development of this country from the earliest
colonial times. Public health has been the voice and the conscience
behind basic and fundamental changes in our communal life that have
laid the groundwork and made possible today's remarkable progress in
hospitals and research laboratories across the land. In the late 19th
and early 20th Century, public health created the essential
infrastructure that allowed for modern urban society to develop and
flourish. The provision of basic sanitation services, the protection
of our water and food supply, the pioneer immunization campaigns
against contagious diseases, the transformation of our hospitals from
human warehouses to healthy, curing and caring environments are all
part of this legacy. Without those fundamental safety nets in place
modern urban society as we know it would not have developed as rapidly
as it has. It is a fact, however, that this very urban environment
which we have helped to foster has in turn spawned new threats and
challenges which must be addressed if public health and safety are to
be protected. Societal changes in the last two to three decades have
unleashed forces that none of us anticipated. Risk-taking behaviors,
substance abuse, interpersonal violence, teen pregnancy, depression,
injury and AIDS have replaced cholera, polio and diphtheria and
occupational injuries as major threats to the public's health. Add to
this, environmental abuse and impact from over use and poorly
regulated industries, we face with a cumulative challenge for public
health. In many of our largest urban centers they have reached
epidemic proportions and have frustrated our best efforts to control
and contain the damage.

Increasingly, public health does recognize that this is the new arena in which it will have to adapt if it is to survive. This is the new agenda it will have to address. Public health's traditional strength has been its ability to assess and track the health status of the communities it serves. Out of these assessments it formulates recommendations which in turn develop into regulations, policies and laws for the common good. Clinical medicine and practice or hospital based models of care are ill equipped and poorly prepared to address societal problems on this scale which are increasingly behavior driven. New models and strategies need to be developed that recognize the need to address community based problems with community based solutions. Given adequate funding and support, public health will be uniquely positioned to do this! It has the history, legacy and important presence in urban communities. We cannot run the risk of retreating from these challenges. To do so would compromise both the progress we have made already (a tragic case in point being the totally avoidable increase in tuberculosis cases and vaccine preventable diseases we are now experiencing) and threaten a delay in developing an effective response to the equally tragic phenomenon of children killing children in the streets of our cities.

The CHAIRMAN. Ms. Schauffler.

Ms. SCHAUFFLER. Thank you. Good afternoon, Senator Kennedy. My name is Helen Halpin Schauffler. I am an assistant professor of health policy, and the King Sweesy and Robert Womack Chair in Medical Research and Public Health at the University of California at Berkeley School of Public Health.

Prior to coming to California, I was a Pew Health Policy Fellow at Brandeis University, and I worked in Massachusetts for over 15 years, both in the department of public health, directing the State's community-based prevention programs, as well as chairing the Boston Regional Health Promotion Council. And I was also a lecturer in public health policy at the Harvard School of Public Health.

I recently served as the principal investigator and the primary author of a report that was released this morning and that has been made available to you and the other members of the committee prior to this hearing. It makes specific legislative recommendations on how to incorporate public health and health promotion in health care reform. It was developed by consensus by a very distinguished group of leading health care and public health practitioners and scholars in California. The list of all the advisory group members is in the report and also in my written testimony.

I just want to make three main points this afternoon about the report that address several issues that I think the Clinton health care plan does not adequately address. I have looked at the Clinton health care plan, and I am pleased to say that in fact it addresses most of our recommendations. But there are three critical issues that I think require strengthening if we are really serious about improving the public's health.

The first is that we need to make improved health status an explicit goal of health care reform. I do not think it is right now. I think it is implicit, but it is not explicit. And we need to hold every part of the health care system accountable for improving health status. That includes not only health plans, but also health departments and community-based organizations.

We recommend in our report that all States be mandated to collect data on population-based health outcomes using uniform measures established at the Federal level. We recommend that every State by provided with the resources necessary to support the development and operation of comprehensive and fully integrated automated data systems for the collection, analysis and reporting of health outcomes data.

We recommend that all States' and local health departments' health plans, and community organizations, be required to establish measurable goals for improving health status, using the uniform measures and that they be held accountable for making progress toward those goals.

Second is comprehensive public policy. I think we need to give health departments a central role in developing and implementing comprehensive public policy for public health.

The CHAIRMAN. In Goals 2000, we are doing something similar to that in education, and just listening to you, I am wondering why we should not be doing it. You might take a look at that—I will ask the staff to give you a rundown—to see if there are parallels.

Perhaps there are, and if we are doing it there, why shouldn't we do on this.

Ms. SCHAUFFLER. Exactly. I think we need to integrate the goals of Healthy People 2000 into the health care reform bill. I think we need to hold all parts of health care reform accountable for achieving those Healthy People 2000 objectives.

The CHAIRMAN. Good.

Ms. SCHAUFFLER. But I think we have a long way to go, even within Healthy People 2000, in defining what those uniform measures might be.

The second point is comprehensive public policy. We recommend that every State and local health department in the country be required and funded adequately to develop and implement what we call comprehensive public policy. As we have heard this afternoon, increasing access to individual clinical preventive services, while important, will have relatively little impact on the health of the population compared to broader public policy approaches. State and local health departments need to be supported in using their authority and expertise to use all of the policy tools available to them, including public education, public participation, incentives, taxation, and regulation, to address all of the health priority areas identified in Healthy People 2000.

As an example, comprehensive public policy for tobacco—which I know you are very familiar with—illustrates the point. We know that if all physicians routinely counseled their smoking patients to quite smoking that approximately an additional 5 percent of patients might quit. But if we are really serious about reducing the overall use of tobacco products in our society and the rates of tobacco use, we will be much more effective if we complement that strategy with taxing cigarettes and other tobacco products, restricting smoking in all public places, restricting tobacco advertising, countering the advertising of the tobacco industry, and involving communities, meaningfully, in activities like removing billboards, removing vending machines, enforcing sales to minor laws, and educating young people about the dangers of tobacco.

In our report, in appendix A, we have developed on pages 42 to 49 comprehensive public policy that can be used to address every, single one of the target areas in Healthy People 2000, and hopefully, this is a major contribution that will help not only the Federal Government but State and local governments to begin to approach each of those areas from a comprehensive perspective.

The third is integration and coordination. We need to make the most efficient and effective use of the limited resources available for public health by requiring an integrated and coordinated approach to public health at the State and local levels. As we have heard, the public health system is in need of reform, and I think health care reform presents us with an opportunity to achieve some of the goals.

We need to reduce the tremendous fragmentation and duplication in the way we currently fund and organize our public health system. We recommend that in every State as appropriate at the local level, an integrating structure be identified and funded to take responsibility for coordinating the prevention activities of not only public health departments and local community-based organizations, but also other governmental agencies that have a role in health and health plans.

Right now, in the current administration bill, there is no mechanism for coordinating the prevention activities of health plans, health departments, and community-based organizations, and yet it is only when they work in partnership that I think we will have the best chance of really influencing the public's health.

At the State level, we imagine the responsibility could be given to the State health department or to a new umbrella organization. We would leave the selection of the integrating structure up to each individual State and community to decide what is best for them. At the local level, it could be given to the local health department or a single community prevention council. In our report on pages 12 through 16, we outline the specific functions that this integrating structure would be required to perform.

Finally, as we have heard, increased and stable Federal funding is needed to support population-based public health. We recommend in our report that the sources of revenue for public health be a combination obtained from health care premiums, increased Federal taxes on tobacco, alcohol, firearms, ammunition, and other products harmful to the public health, and pooling of existing Federal categorical disease program funds.

We recommend that the States have flexibility in using categorical funds in a way that best meets their needs. Our report concludes that if we do not strengthen the role of public health in health care reform with respect to accountability, comprehensive public policy and an integrated, coordinated approach, we will fall far short of our goal of health security for all Americans.

I would be happy to elaborate on these or any of our other recommendations.

Thank you.

[The prepared statement of Ms. Schauffler follows:]

PREPARED STATEMENT OF HELEN HALPIN SCHAUFFLER

Good morning Chairman Kennedy, Senator Wellstone and other distinguished members of the committee. My name is Helen Halpin Schauffler. I am an Assistant Professor of Health Policy and the King Sweesy and Robert Womack Chair in Medical Research and Public Health at the University of California at Berkeley, School of Public Health.

Prior to coming to the University of California, I worked in the Massachusetts Department of Public Health, directing the state's high blood pressure education program and community-based multiple risk factor intervention program, and I chaired the Boston Regional Health Promotion Council. For four years I was a lecturer in public health policy at the Harvard School of Public Health, and for ten years I was a health care consultant to state and federal governmental health agencies.

I have recently served as the Principal Investigator and primary author of a report that was released this morning that makes specific legislative recommendations for health promotion and public health in health care reform. The project was funded by The California Wellness Foundation.

The recommendations were developed by consensus by the Prevention in Health Care Reform Advisory Group, created by the California Wellness Foundation to guide my work. The recommendations reflect our collective wisdom and experience. Just to give you an idea of the breadth and depth of experience of the group, it was chaired by Dr. Joyce Lashof, Dean Emeritus of the UC Berkeley School of Public Health, past president of the American Public Health Association (APHA), and former associate director of the Office of Technology Assessment (OTA), and some of its members include Clark Kerr from Bank of America, Dr. David Lawrence, CEO of Kaiser Permanente, Dr. Caswell Evans, president-elect of APHA and a county health officer, Dr. Kenneth Kizer, former Director of Health Services for the state of California, Robert Gomez, the past president of the National Association of Community Health Centers and Executive Director of the El Rio Health Center, Dr. Sheldon Margen, Editor of the UC Berkeley Wellness Letter, and several leading scholars in public health.

It was a privilege to work with this distinguished group and I am pleased to share with you the results of our thinking on how best to address public health in health care reform and its relation to health promotion.

I have reviewed the President's plan as it was released last Wednesday and have compared it against our recommendations. While I am pleased to see that the President's plan addresses many of our recommendations, and includes some additional funding for public health and community based programs, there are three critical issues which I believe it does not adequately address.

1. Accountability: We need to make health status an explicit goal of health care reform and hold every part of the health care system—health plans, public health departments and community-based organizations—accountable for improving the health status of the population.

We recommend that all states be mandated to collect data on three population-based health outcomes, using uniform measures established at the federal level (incidence of preventable health outcomes, prevalence of risk factors, and rates of preventive services utilization). We recommend that every state be provided with the resources necessary to support the development and operation of comprehensive and fully integrated automated data systems for the collection and analysis of uniform health outcomes data, that can be integrated with data from health plans, employers and population surveys. We recommend that all states and local health department, health plans and community based organizations be required to establish measurable goals for improving health status using the uniform measures and be held accountable for making progress towards these goals.

The President's Plan holds health plans accountable for access and qualit (Section 5005). It requires the development of uniform measures for health promotion and prevention of disease and the criteria for selection of uniform measures "may incorporate . . . standards for meeting public heath objectives" (Section 5003), but it does not go the next important step to use these prevention and public health data as the basis for holding all state health departments, health plans and community based organizations accountable for improving the public's health, nor does it identify which of the public entities will be responsible for holding health plans accountable.

2. Comprehensive Public Policy: We need to give health departments a central role in developing and implementing comprehensive public policy for prevention using every weapon in our arsenal of public policy tools to combat the leading causes of death—not just health insurance policy to cover the costs of medical care.

The health of the population is largely determined by their social, economic and physical environment, as well as health behaviors. Individual preventive services have an important role to play in preventing disease, but their impact is limited compared to population-based and public health approaches to prevention, combined with comprehensive public policy.

Our efforts to reduce smoking illustrate this point. We know physician counseling is cost-effective in smoking cessation, that only about half of all physicians advise their patients to quit, and that, if all physicians routinely counseled their smoking patients to quit, an additional 5% of smokers would quit. However, individual approaches to smoking cessation, while important, have relatively limited impact on total smoking rates compared to broader based public policy approaches to prevent tobacco use among our young people. Reducing the use of tobacco in our population will be most effective if we also tax cigarettes and other tobacco products, restrict smoking in public places, restrict tobacco advertising, counter the advertising of the tobacco industry, and involve communities in efforts to remove billboards and vending machines, enforce sales to minor laws, and find alternative sources of funding for community projects than that offered by the tobacco industry.

The President's plan recognizes that one of the core public health functions is health policy (Section 3312). We recommend that every state and local health department in the country be required and funded to develop and implement comprehensive public policy for public health. They need to be supported to use all of the policy tools available to them, including public education, public participation, incentives, taxation and regulation.

In our report, we have prepared a table in Appendix A (p. 36-44) that provides examples of comprehensive public policy for all of the major health problems identified in Healthy People 2000.

3. Integration and Coordination: We need to make the most efficient and effective use of the limited resources available for public health by requiring an integrated

and coordinated approach to public health at the state and local levels. The public health system is in need of reform. We need to reduce the tremendous fragmentation and duplication inherent in the way we currently fund and organize our public health system.

We recommend that in every state, and as appropriate at the local level, that an integrating structure be identified and funded to take responsibility for coordinating the health promotion and disease prevention activities of public health departments, other governmental agencies, health plans, and community-based organizations in order to reduce the fragmentation and duplication in the present system. At the state level this responsibility could be given to the State Health Department or a new umbrella organization to coordinate the many state agencies with a role in public health (for example health, welfare, employment, housing, environment, criminal justice). At the local level this responsibility could be given to the local health department or a single prevention council with representation of health plans, health departments, community organizations, and the many coalitions addressing single issues (e.g. AIDS, tobacco, etc.).

In our report (p. 12-16) we outline the specific functions that the integrating structure would be required to perform. We also recommend that states be given the option of consolidating federal categorical grant funds to address the state's health priorities (p. 17).

There is little question that present funding levels are inadequate to support either the core functions of public health at the state and local levels, or community-based health promotion and disease prevention programs. There is a need to both consolidate and increase the federal funding available to support population-based public health functions. We estimate, based on calculations performed by the Department of Health and Human Services, that between $15 and $25 billion per year (of which $11 to 21 billion are federal funds) are presently required to adequately support the core public health functions and community-based organizations. We recommend that the sources of revenue from which to develop stable financing be a combination obtained from health care premiums, increased federal taxes on tobacco, alcohol, firearms, ammunition and other products harmful to the public health, and pooling of existing categorical program funds.

If we continue down our current path and support fragmented approaches, do not hold public health departments, community-based organizations, and health plans accountable for improving the public's health, and focus primarily on the individual as the target of prevention interventions, we risk increasing, rather than decreasing, the enormous health status gaps between the most advantaged and disadvantaged members of our society.

Our report concludes that if we do not strengthen the role of public health in health care reform with respect to accountability, comprehensive public policy and an integrated, coordinated model, and provide adequate and stable funding for population-based approaches, we will fall far short of our goal of health security for all Americans. Thank you.

[Additional material is retained in committee files.]

The CHAIRMAN. In the coordination of the policy, isn't that what the States are supposed to be doing? Do you have suggestions about that?

Ms. SCHAUFFLER. They are, but there are tremendous differences across States in terms of the approaches that they are using. I think States are not learning from each other. We are not systematically looking at what approaches States are pursuing, what is effective, sharing the results of that.

I think we need to encourage States and hold them accountable for pursuing and making use of all of those policy tools in effecting improved health status. I think that is not happening now. I think it varies tremendously from State to State, and I think in Federal legislation, we can set the expectation that all States should be doing that.

The CHAIRMAN. Perhaps we will submit some additional questions about how that can be done. We could get caught up in establishing more bureaucracy.

Ms. Schauffler. We are not arguing for establishing another bureaucracy, Senator.

The Chairman. I know you are not, and that is why I am interested in how you think we can do it, and the different ways of trying to do it.

In our education programs, we are trying to establish competitive programs that will respond to some of the local challenges—it may be dropout rates, it may be improvement in mathematics, or other areas—and then the community gets the grant, and then they have to meet those goals. And we give them a period of time like 3 years, 4 years, to be able to do that.

So I think the concept of accountability is generally supported, but as to how we do that, I think we would be interested in hearing more from you on that.

Ms. Schauffler. My experience in terms of accountability with many public health programs is that frequently they are health accountable for what we would call process evaluation measures—how many people were served, how many people participated, how many brochures were distributed—but not how much disease was prevented or how much risk status was reduced, or how many preventable health outcomes were avoided.

I think we need to start using those kinds of measures as the basis for holding plans and programs accountable, and we are simply not doing that right now.

The Chairman. I will submit questions for all of you. Your testimony has been very helpful and useful, and we obviously invite your continuing observations as the legislation moves along. There have been a lot of excellent comments.

Ms. Schauffler. Thank you, Senator.

The Chairman. Senator Durenberger.

Senator Durenberger [presiding]. Mr. Chairman, thank you.

I do not intend to keep you long. I know you came a long way to be here, and you would probably stay all afternoon—and I would love to stay all afternoon with you and deal with this subject because I love it.

I have mentioned many times before, and I suppose I reflected it in my questions of Phil Lee, the notion that I use in my speeches, and that is that if we try to commit all of our financial resources to universal access, to universal coverage or whatever it is, and buy insurance plans for everybody in America, and do not deal with the problems that you are telling us to deal with in this wide variety of ways in different parts of the country that we have to deal with, I do not think we have licked the health care problem in this country.

I wish, and I pray every day, that the President and Mrs. Clinton would talk to us about the health of America in the context that you are speaking of it and then say one of the ways we need to deal with that, of course, is to guarantee equal access to every American to high-quality care through a system of universal coverage. I really believe that unless we make the same commitment to public health that we make to public education, i.e., in our communities, we are not going to lick this problem. We are not going to lick it here, at that table, or at this side of the table; it is not going to get resolved. It is too big, too interconnected. There are environmental issues involved, there is poverty. There is such a wide variety of issues.

We have our role to play. Certainly, when you talk about poverty, you talk about economics, you are talking about the folks around here who make NAFTA decisions and tax decisions and big-time stuff like that. But when you are talking about its impact on individual people and on communities, whether they are relationships in a family or a would-be family, or relationships in neighborhood or workplace or whatever, it just strikes me that we are not going to get a handle on this problem until we take back responsibility in our communities.

Now, having said that, the answer is that we cannot take back responsibility in our communities because we do not have the resources. My community in Minneapolis says we are resource-rich—mainly in people. We have people now that we did not have 30 years ago, and some of you 30 years ago might not have contemplated careers in the field you are in. But because of the encouragement of people like Senator Kennedy and a lot of the activities here in this committee, y u are encouraged to go into a wide variety of public health, social œervice, and education related areas, as well as to practice medicine in ways that are more socially responsible than some people accuse people in medicine of practicing.

So I would argue that, whether it is in our churches, our non-profits, in our caregivers, or whatever, the resources are there. The problem and challenge is matching up needs and resources.

So I am in the process of proposing officially, as I have unofficially a number of times, including to the Public Health Association and others, that we get about the job of federalizing the access to doctors and hospitals and acute care services through the Health Security Act and that the national Government take responsibility, through vouchers to health plans or whatever it is, for making sure that, whether it is the 58-page benefit or the 3-page benefit like we have, everybody has the security of that health security card. But when it comes to community health and public health and all the rest of these problems that all of you articulate so well part of the bargain is that State governments and local communities take back responsibility for community health and for a lot of the things that you have talked to us about here after States save about $60 billion a year by having us federalize access for low-income people and rearrange the long-term care program so we do that one better.

That is the essence of the proposal, and there is a little bit more to it so that nobody gets cheated, and we do not worry about Mississippi, which has half the capacity that Texas has to meet people's needs, coming up short. You have to deal with the issues of fiscal disparity, because from a governmental standpoint or a tax standpoint, not all States are situated the same. Not all cities are the same. We know that in the 1950's, people took their money and their cars and everything and made suburbs; they kept their jobs downtown, but they left the problems downtown, and they let the inner cities decay while they took their paychecks to the suburbs, and we decided here that we had to tax those paychecks and send them programs instead.

There is more to it than that, but as I was reading your presentations, I read into all of your statements some argument that we consider giving people the opportunity to take back some of this responsibility, that we rearrange the way we look at accountability, that we do try to look at outcomes, and we help in the outcomes measurement, and that we find ways to break down some of these categorical barriers.

So I would appreciate if any of you would comment on that. I think the chairman said he is going to submit questions for the record, and I will submit questions for the record, and there may be others who will want to do the same thing, because you are a very, very talented panel and have had a lot to contribute.

Ms. ANTHONY. I would just like to support what Ms. Schauffler mentioned in terms of accountability and outcomes and stress that she focused on all providers being accountable for health outcomes. We think that certainly public health needs to be accountable, and we are willing to do that. But all providers who provide health care need to also be accountable for some health status and outcomes.

Your comment on the involvement of the community, I think you are absolutely right. If we do not have a process whereby the community assumes some ownership not only of the process but also of the outcome, then we can never have a solution that can be federally-driven, State-driven, or Government-driven. And most communities are willing to do that. Part of our core functions in terms of public health strategy allows for supporting things like community coalitions and direct involvement of the people who are most affected by the health situations within their communities. They must be involved, and they must have ownership, but they must also feel some responsibility for the outcome, and they will, and public health can provide the forum for those things to happen.

Senator DURENBERGER. Dr. Mullet.

Dr. MULLET. I agree with you, Senator Durenberger. I believe that every person in America should have a right to access to appropriate health care, and I think we are in the process of developing that right through legislation.

I think, though, that if we lose sight of what ought to be the real objective, which is improving the health status of Americans, not just access, I think we will have missed the boat, and we will not have solved the problem, and a few years from now, we are going to have a lot of disappointed if not angry people.

I think at the same time that we provide access, and we pay for clinical preventive services which are extremely important, it is also essential that we provide and supportive the community preventive services. Like politics, all health is local, I believe, and I think that is where the rubber meets the road, and that is where the health status of Americans will really improve.

I would just echo Ms. Anthony's comments about the testimony on accountability; I agree with that whole-heartedly.

Senator DURENBERGER. Dr. Guerra.

Dr. GUERRA. Senator Durenberger, I would certainly echo also the matter of accountability and assessing outcomes in a way that allows us to more clearly understand what it is that we have been able to accomplish in assuring the health and well-being of communities.

At the same time, however, we have to understand that sometimes what we do in public health has a very weak science associated with it that is very difficult. It is a soft science; it is one that we cannot always get a good handle on, unless you are looking at large numbers and population sort of outcomes and trends over time.

But in the process, it seems to me that as we are trying to maybe find a better fit for public health in a reconfigured medical and health care system, we also have to at the same time redefine the society that these systems are going to be changed and working in, because society for quite a few years has become tremendously complex, and a lot of the things that have always been so much at the heart of what we have done in public health are not going to work because of the complexities of society. But we do not have a science or a scientific base that allows us to sometimes take those leaps into those areas where we have to learn. And so many of those relate to social and behavioral issues and conditions, the risk-taking behaviors. A lot of it relates to the changing family structure. A lot of it relates to a community that we really do not know how to define. Communities are very different.

Senator DURENBERGER. We do not have to wait for the American Psychiatric Association to tell us what to do, though, do we?

Dr. GUERRA. I am not sure that they can. I think they have struggled with that.

We do not know, as I stated in my testimony, what the incident rate of depression is in a community. If we could get a handle on that, I feel quite strongly that we could do a lot about preventing and also improving outcomes in many, many instances. I have looked at it from an immunization standpoint, for example. Missed opportunities will account for some of the low compliance rates at age-appropriate levels, but the missed appointment side of it, that relates to so many things going on in the lives of the people, when that is coupled with depression because of stress or domestic violence or loss of job or whatever, mothers are not going to keep appointments to an immunization clinic or WIC or whatever.

Senator DURENBERGER. I understand.

Dr. Schauffler.

Ms. SCHAUFFLER. I just wanted to comment a little further on your question about the fragmentation in the categorical funding. This is, as I am sure you are aware, an extremely difficult question, one that the advisory group I worked with spend a great deal of time on, considering whether or not one could merge Federal categorical disease grant programs at the Federal level or whether those would have to remain intact and just to give more flexibility to the States.

We came down in favor of, rather than trying to tackle that bear within the context of health care reform, which I think might be very difficult and potentially sink the health care reform bill if we alienate all of those public health interest groups, that it might be much better to give that flexibility to the States and let them take the responsibility to use those funds in the way they best see fit.

Right now, I think form is following funding, and the kinds of problems that Ms. Anthony was talking about, I think, are rampant in every community. In San Francisco alone, we have a proliferation of these coalitions, each of which addresses a different disease, and even for one disease, we have several coalitions, be-

I think you made the observation and sin taxes and whatever else it is.

Ms. SCHAUFFLER. Yes.

Senator DURENBERGER. I appreciated hearing that, because I think I am the only one here who does not mind if we have to raise sin taxes. I used to think that is something State and local government ought to do, for precisely the reason that you stated, but I now acknowledge the fact that unless we raise them out here, they will not get raised. But the idea of putting them into the Health Security Act in order to access more people to insurance plans, when you know that the more you raise the tax, the more over time your revenue is going to go down, never made much sense to me. But it does make some sense to me to use that source, send it back to the States and local communities, to deal with precisely the kinds of problems we are talking about here.

Ms. SCHAUFFLER. Hopefully, we can put ourselves out of business.

Senator DURENBERGER. OK. Thank you all very much for being here.

The hearing is adjourned.

[Whereupon, at 1:22 p.m., the committee was adjourned.]

THE HEALTH SECURITY ACT AND THE NEEDS OF RURAL AMERICA

THURSDAY, NOVEMBER 18, 1993

U.S. SENATE,
COMMITTEE ON LABOR AND HUMAN RESOURCES,
Washington, DC.

The committee met, pursuant to notice, at 10 a.m., in room SD–430, Dirksen Senate Office Building, Senator Harkin presiding.

Present: Senators Harkin, Pell, Wellstone, Wofford, Jeffords, and Gregg.

OPENING STATEMENT OF SENATOR HARKIN

Senator HARKIN [presiding]. Good morning and welcome to today's Labor and Human Resources Committee hearing. This hearing will focus on rural health care issues and the extent to which the Health Security Act meets the needs of rural Americans.

I personally have held a series of town meetings in Iowa, in many small communities, and it is clear to me that people in rural areas want health care reform as much as people in cities, but they are very apprehensive about it.

Health care reform must work for rural and small-town America. People in those areas, I think, have the same right to access to high-quality care as those who live in Beverly Hills or West Palm Beach or Washington, DC. I as well as others on this committee have continued to express this point to the administration.

My own background is one of coming from a small town and rural area. No one in my family was born in a hospital. I was born in a house. No doctor attended my birth. The neighbor woman came across the road and helped my mother deliver babies. That is the way things were done in those days. I cannot remember the first time I ever saw a doctor—probably when I was in school, grade school or high school, I cannot remember which. So I have a full background and knowledge of what lack of health care means in rural America.

Well, we have come a long way since those times, but in many parts of rural Iowa and other parts of America, we have a dire need for health care professionals. Universal coverage to people in rural areas is not going to mean much unless we have health care providers there to provide the health care services.

We all use the term "rural" rather generically, but we have to acknowledge at the outset that rural America is a place of great variation; there are a lot of differences between rural Iowa and

(61)

rural Georgia, rural New Mexico and rural Pennsylvania. Any health care reform plan must recognize these differences.

The Health Security Act does have a number of very positive features targeted at rural areas—it seeks to increase the number of providers by expanding the National Health Service Corps; providing incentives such as tax credits and loan forgiveness for providers willing to serve in rural areas, and so on.

I do have some very serious concerns. I am concerned about the impact of the proposed Medicare cuts. When you have a State like my own, which ranks third nationally in the percentage of citizens over age 65; first in the Nation in the percentage of our citizens over age 85; and over 60 percent of all patient days in rural hospitals attributed to people over age 65; Medicare cuts hit hard.

So when I am told that these Medicare cuts can be achieved because the average is such-and-such, I say that may be the average, but we are not average. And when those deep Medicare cuts come, it is going to hurt States like Iowa and other rural areas where you have a high proportion not only of elderly, but elderly poor. So I believe something has to be done in that area.

The purpose of this hearing is to examine these and other issues further. Dr. Phil Lee will testify on behalf of the administration, and then we will hear from rural health care providers and experts who have struggled to meet the health care needs in our rural communities. They will tell us about the innovative programs and networks that they have developed. We will hear their reactions to the President's plan and how that plan addresses the needs of rural areas and how they believe it could be improved.

Before we begin I have statements from Senators Dodd and Hatch.

[The prepared statements of Senators Dodd and Hatch follow:]

STATEMENT OF SENATOR DODD

I thank the Chair for holding this morning's hearing. I feel that it's essential to examine the views of those in rural America because these communities pose special challenges in the health care system, both for those who need services and those who provide them.

Earlier this week, at a hearing I co-chaired on maternal and child health, I heard about the challenges of serving pregnant women and children in rural areas from a family physician in Kansas. He told the committee that 2,000 square miles in his area have no readily available Ob care. He said that "it will be only a matter of time before the distance that expectant mothers have to travel to receive obstetrical care results in injury to an infant or mother. "I do not come from a rural state, but I maintain that this situation cannot continue. The needs of rural America must be addressed in the health care reform debate.

CURRENT SITUATION IN RURAL COMMUNITIES

A total of 34 million people—half of them with incomes under 200 percent of poverty—live in rural areas with inadequate health care. The fragile economies in many of these areas often mean that many residents have little or no insurance, making it difficult for rural communities to attract and keep doctors and maintain local hospitals.

Twenty-one million rural residents have no access to consistent primary care providers, and the population of younger rural physicians has not expanded to replace those who retire. Rural communities worry that the current shortage of physicians will continue and limit their access to care even further.

Since rural areas have a disproportionate number of uninsured, underinsured and Medicaid recipients, providing universal coverage will help channel significant new resources into rural health care systems. Americans in these areas also have a harder time getting to the services they need. More than half of the rural poor do not own a car, and nearly 60 percent of the rural elderly are not licensed to drive.

Under the President's plan, new workforce initiatives, including tax incentives, increased reimbursement, retraining, scholarships, and loan forgiveness programs, will encourage health care providers to practice in rural underserved areas. The proposal also calls for an expansion of the National Health Service Corps, placing at least 3,000 primary care practitioners in rural areas by the year 2000. This would help us reach many more individuals in isolated areas.

Other elements that will improve the situation in rural communities include: health networks that link rural communities to larger referral centers and academic health centers; a greater investment in community and migrant health centers; and the provision of technology and services that is available in urban areas to these communities.

I look forward to the testimony of representatives from rural communities and learning about their ideas and concerns. I thank them for addressing the committee this morning.

PREPARED STATEMENT OF SENATOR HATCH

Mr. Chairman: I appreciate the work you have done to hold this hearing on the "Health Security Act and the Needs of Rural America." Health care for rural areas is not just another academic topic in Utah. There are almost 224 thousand residents in my state who live in rural areas. My state understands first hand some of the challenges involved in providing medical treatment and facilities for individuals scattered over large geographical areas.

Utah, like many western and midwestern states, prides itself on the independence and self-reliance of its rural citizens. These families and individuals should not be penalized for living outside of traditional urban areas. Yet they have historically been denied access to the same level of health care and medical facilities more populated areas enjoy.

I commend President Clinton for addressing this issue within the broader context of overall health care reform. However, I question whether the specific proposals contained within the "Health Security Act" will adequately change the status quo and yield better health care for rural America.

I am very interested in hearing the views of our panel members, and I hope they will address not only the needs of our rural areas, but also the Administration proposals and the impact they will have on meeting those needs.

I particularly want to welcome our Assistant Secretary of Health, Phil Lee, to this hearing. Mr. Lee's leadership and expertise is already proving to be an important asset to HHS. It has been my privilege to work with Mr. Lee on other issues, and I am looking forward to having his input on this critical health care issue.

Mr. Chairman, America is the land of opportunity and that should include the opportunity for all citizens of this great country, both urban and rural, to have access to affordable, comprehensive, and quality health care. This hearing is an opportunity to discuss how we can best obtain that goal. The independent, hard-working Americans in less developed areas of this great country deserve no less.

Thank you, Mr. Chairman.

Senator HARKIN. Our first witness is Phil Lee. He is assistant secretary of health for the Department of Health and Human Services, and he is well-known to our committee; he was just here yesterday. And I have the feeling you are going to be here a lot in the next few months, Phil. But Dr. Lee is perhaps one of the most knowledgeable and committed individuals in our country toward true health care reform and making universal coverage available to all Americans.

Dr. Phil Lee, it is good to have you here again. Your statement will be made a part of the record in its entirety. Just proceed as you so desire.

STATEMENT OF DR. PHILIP R. LEE, ASSISTANT SECRETARY OF HEALTH, DEPARTMENT OF HEALTH AND HUMAN SERVICES, WASHINGTON, DC, ACCOMPANIED BY DR. HELEN SMITS, DEPUTY ADMINISTRATOR, HEALTH CARE FINANCING ADMINISTRATION

Dr. LEE. Mr. Chairman, thank you very much.

I am accompanied by Dr. Helen Smits, who is the deputy administrator of the Health Care Financing Administration, and will respond to questions that you may have with respect to Medicare.

Let me first say that we certainly agree with your opening statement and the fact that people in rural areas deserve the same kind of high-quality health care that is available in the rest of the country. That is a principal objective.

I would just like to say a personal word about the process, having been involved in this since January. One of the things that impressed me from the beginning was the President and the First Lady's commitment to the issues in rural areas and meeting the needs. And the First Lady particularly has, as she has gone around the country, listened and listened and listened. And as we then review various options that are being developed and the various ideas that have come forth, she judges it against how it affects individual patients. Some would say that is an anecdotal approach to policy, but she asks what is going to happen to the housewife in Des Moines with breast cancer; what is going to happen to the small business in a rural area; what is going to happen to a family with a child with a severe congenital defect in New London, CT?

So as we go through the plan, she is constantly judging it on that basis, and her contribution has been, I think, of enormous importance as we have developed both the personal health care piece of the plan and the public health initiatives which are an integral part of the plan.

The first thing that was recognized was that there were unique problems in rural areas—and you are very familiar with these, and I will just recite a few of them—but in terms of health problems like injuries, for example. There are other problems in the delivery of personal care. There are other problems in terms of poverty or high percentage of elderly. So that the rural areas have unique needs, and there are unique public health problems in rural areas, prevention of injury being one of those.

So that those problems, as we went through and developed the plan, were under consideration constantly. We know, first of all— and this is one of the things that the plan is really designed to correct—that residents in rural areas are more likely not to have health insurance or, if they do have it, to pay more than people in nonrural areas. More than 8 million rural Americans have no health insurance—no health insurance. That is 18 percent of all farm families. And, according to a recent New York Times series over this last weekend, the agricultural sector, the farm sector, is now the highest rate of uninsured in the country. So that is a fundamental problem that is dealt with.

The rural resident lacks the purchasing capacity that somebody in an urban area does who works for a large employer. Either they are self-employed, or they may work for a small employer. And with the current insurance system, they lack the purchasing capacity. If they get health insurance, as much as 40 percent of the premium may go for administrative costs—for marketing and other things—so that only 60 percent ends up as a benefit. And they pay more; they not only get less, but they pay more even for the same benefit.

They lack the choice that people have in urban areas in terms of health plans.

In comparison with other parts of the country, a higher percentage of people in rural areas are elderly, and they have higher rates of chronic illness or other serious illnesses. Now, it is interesting— Iowa is obviously one of the healthiest States in the country, because if you look at the percentage of those over 65 and those over 80, it suggests that you are doing something right in Iowa. One of the goals of the health plan would be to bring the health of people in the rest of the country up to that level of health. There are obviously things that affect the health status that go far beyond the health care system, and many of those are apparently present in Iowa.

Rural areas experience many other challenges in access to care— fewer physicians, fewer other providers—and there have been few incentives for physicians or others, nurse practitioners or physician assistants, to settle in rural areas.

As a result, over 400,000 rural Americans live in counties without a single doctor; 34 million people live in areas with too few physicians to care for them, what we call "medically underserved areas."

The undersupply and maldistribution of physicians and other providers in rural areas exacerbates geographic barriers. I mean, some areas are called "frontier areas." It is not just rural; there are long distances that people must travel to get access to care.

Well, what are we proposing in the plan? And I could go on and on, and you, Senator Harkin, could detail this in much more detail, and I am sure your hearings have been very helpful in identifying the problems we have to address in the plan.

First of all, everybody will be covered; universal coverage with a comprehensive benefit package that, with the insurance reforms, with the alliances, these benefits cannot be taken away—whether somebody moves, whether they lose their job, whatever happens, they will be insured—which would have an enormous benefit because of the large number of uninsured in the rural areas.

One of the key problems, however, relates to choice. We know that in a number of rural areas, the only plan currently available is a fee-for-service plan. Even in States like Minnesota, where they have extensive development of preferred provider organizations and health maintenance organizations, in many of those areas, still the only plan available is a fee-for-service plan.

So one of the things we have to do in developing the alliance structure is to assure choice of plan for people living in rural areas. The creation of the alliance, of course, will be a State responsibility. It is our view that the States can make a better judgment about the breadth of those alliances. There will be certain Federal requirements, but they are in a better position to judge how to include people in rural areas in the same alliance area that are in urban areas, so they will have a choice of plans.

They need to have an active role in assuring at least a fee-for-service and a preferred provider option in rural areas. Now, one of the things we are doing in the public health initiative part of the plan, in the access initiative, we have a capacity expansion program, significant because it will provide funds for physicians in rural areas, or physicians in rural hospitals, nurse practitioners, other providers, to work together to develop practice networks with other physicians in those areas and then linking them with, say, group practices in smaller towns or larger communities, so they would be part of a practice network. They would then be in a better position in negotiating with plans to assure one choice of plan for people living in the rural areas and improving the capacity of rural areas to meet the needs.

In other words, our intention is to expand capacity. There are a number of incentives in the Medicare program to improve payment to physicians in rural areas, and Dr. Smits can discuss those in somewhat more detail, but there would be increased bonus payments for primary care physicians, there would be modifications of the practice expense payments that would improve payments for office-based physicians. These should help improve the Medicare payments. In terms of others, when they are insured with comprehensive benefits, there would be assured payments for the other services, and many of those, of course, are uncompensated currently.

So that capacity expansion is going to be important. Another would be an expansion of the National Health Service Corps. Currently, about 55 percent of the physicians in the National Health

Service Corps work in rural areas. We are going to have a 5-fold expansion of the National Health Service Corps, which should significantly increase the availability of not only physicians, but nurse practitioners and physician assistants, in rural areas.

Also as part of our public health initiative, there will be a significant expansion. The current proposal would be that we would ask for about $400 million additional funds for expansion of training programs for physicians and nurse practitioners, and half of that money would be to expand nurse training programs at various levels, again to improve the availability of personnel to serve in underserved areas.

One other element would be the designation of the so-called safety net providers. Those will be continued. Like migrant health centers, they would also be called essential providers, and plans would have to contract with them, so that if there is a rural area where there is a migrant health center, there would be a requirement that the plan contract with those providers. And of course, physicians in rural areas could also be designed as essential providers because they would be serving in areas that would otherwise have needs unmet. They do not have to be a federally-qualified health center. They do not have to be a migrant health center. The Secretary could determine that a network of general practitioners in a rural area could be designated as essential providers.

You have already mentioned the tax credits. That would also improve the situation. One other thing we want to do is improve the practice environment. The access initiative will help to do that, but our goal would be to make the physicians, and the nurse practitioners and the physician assistants in rural areas, who have been isolated, much more part of network, much more part of a collegial group of providers, and link those through telecommunications. We have had some experiences in this area, Public Health Service and HCFA. We are going to be carefully evaluating those—there has been great interest in that area—to improve access of those rural physicians to immediate consultation with respect to a patient when there may be a problem and they need that consultation.

We believe that these activities will enhance that practice environment. We also want to enhance the ability of individuals in rural areas to access services. We are expanding what we call enabling services, again with this capacity expansion, increased funds to provide outreach to people in their homes; in some cases, transportation; in other areas, if there is a large number of non-English-speaking rural workers, translation services to help them access the services.

So those would be the activities that we would be developing around the practices in rural areas. We will also be expanding school-based health services, particularly in low-income areas. Many rural areas are poverty areas, and the school-based initiative would provide adolescents access to care through the schools, because many of them, even now when they are part of a health maintenance organization or part of a health plan, do not have access, do not take advantage, do not go to doctors. There would be both primary care, mainly nurse practitioners, and also psychosocial support services available through the schools. The plans would be required to contract with them as essential providers. So the adolescents would have some of their most difficult psychosocial problems and emotional problems dealt with.

Finally, in the core public health initiatives, we will be strengthening the core public health functions and strengthening and providing funds for communities to develop public health programs to meet their own particular needs. We will continue the categorical prevention programs, but core public health has got to be strengthened. We have seen a significant deterioration of the public health infrastructure in this country over the last 15 years, as more and more dollars, local tax dollars, State dollars, have had to go to pay for acute care for the uninsured. That meant those funds were not available to protect all of us from issues around contaminated water supplies, patients with drug-resistant tuberculosis, other communicable diseases, other chronic disease problems which have emerged, like diabetes, in some communities. We have not been able to respond to those needs, and that is particularly the reason.

For example, we have seen in the Midwest with the floods, which you are very familiar with, Senator Harkin, the response that was necessary to protect communities because of contaminated water supplies. That was a Federal-State-local response, and fortunately, we were able to prevent any serious outbreaks of waterborne disease.

In Iowa, the surveillance has revealed the very high prevalence of farm-related injuries. CDC reported in one 3-year period 7,797 injuries, 263 deaths, 1,263 hospitalizations, making farm-related injury the leading cause of traumatic occupational injury in Iowa. That has been a problem that has not been adequately dealt with, and it is one that with this public health infrastructure, with the reforms we are proposing, we could begin to deal with that in a preventive way.

Let me close, Mr. Chairman, by saying that we believe these initiatives will go a long way toward correcting some of the gross inequities with respect to access to care and quality of care and public health protections in rural areas. We believe the Health Security Act has taken into account the special problems in rural areas and targeted provisions to deal with them. We recognize the very special interest of this committee in rural health and health care in rural areas and look forward to working with you and the members of the committee as we go forward with carefully reviewing the plan and perfecting it and making it really work in ways that we all want it to work for people in rural areas.

Thank you very much.

[The prepared statement of Dr. Lee follows:]

PREPARED STATEMENT OF DR. PHILIP R. LEE

Mr. Chairman and Members of the Committee:

I am pleased to have the opportunity to discuss the Health
Security Act and how the plan can not only help improve access to
affordable health care for people living in rural areas, but also
improve the health status of people in rural communities.

Health Care in Rural Areas -- Special Problems

Rural America faces special health care problems. In terms of
individual care, primarily these are problems in obtaining
affordable health insurance and barriers in accessing the health
care system. There are also special public health problems in
rural areas, which will be discussed separately in a moment.

Residents in rural areas are more likely not to have health
insurance or, if they do have insurance, to pay more for it than
people in non-rural areas. More than 8 million rural Americans
have no health insurance, including 18 percent of all farm
families. Residents of rural areas generally lack the benefit of
being a part of a large business or purchasing group. Rural
Americans who have health coverage may obtain it through
employment at a small business or through a rural cooperative,
but many rural families have no choice but to purchase separate
coverage at high market rates.

In comparison with other parts of the country, a higher
percentage of people in rural areas are elderly, with higher
rates of chronic or serious illness. Rural areas also have much
higher rates of serious accidents due to the risks inherent in
farming, mining, and other rural occupations. Rural Americans,
perhaps more than any other segment of the population, live in

fear that their insurance will be canceled if they get sick or have an accident. They live with the fear that a "pre-existing condition" will force them to go without health insurance, and that medical bills will have to be paid out-of-pocket, depleting family assets.

The Administration understands that having a Health Security Card in your pocket may guarantee coverage, but it doesn't guarantee that you'll get to see a doctor when you need one. This is one reason why the programs in the Public Health Initiative are so integral to meeting the goals of health care reform.

Rural areas experience many challenges in the area of access. Physicians and other providers currently find few incentives to practice in rural areas. Fewer and fewer new medical school graduates choose the career of family practitioner needed in rural areas. Over time, the average age of rural doctors is increasing while rural areas compete for a decreasing pool of new graduates in family medicine and primary care. Long hours, professional isolation, and outmoded facilities and equipment

People in rural areas have limited access to health plans, especially ones that are built upon the providers in their community. For example, a PPO may be offered in a rural area and it may be a lower cost option than a fee-for-service plan. However if, for example, you have to travel over 60 miles one-way to see most of its member physicians, it is not really a "lower cost option."

These problems have put the rural health care system on the critical list and nothing short of complete health care reform will bring it back to health.

contribute to high turnover among health providers in rural areas
and difficulties of rural communities in attracting new health
care providers. As a result, over 400,000 rural Americans live
in counties without a single doctor and 34 million people live in
rural areas with too few physicians to care for them.

The undersupply and maldistribution of providers in rural areas
exacerbate the geographic barriers faced by patients. Rural
Americans may have a long distance to travel and have a harder
time getting to the services that are available. Public
transportation systems are seldom available in rural areas. More
than half of the rural poor do not own a car, and nearly 60
percent of rural elderly are not licensed to drive.

Basic System Changes and the Benefits for Rural Health

The basic tenet of the Health Security Plan, universal coverage
with a comprehensive benefit package that can never be taken
away, will go a long way toward alleviating the health issues and
problems in rural areas. Because of the alliance structure,
rural Americans will have the purchasing power necessary to
bargain for lower rates. Self-employed people, including farm
families throughout the nation, will be able to deduct 100
percent of the cost of their health insurance premiums instead of
the current 25 percent.

Rural areas will benefit from the small business and low income
premium discounts -- further stretching their health care
dollars. Rural families will finally have the security they need
and will no longer be concerned about pre-existing conditions and
situations in which their insurance could be taken away.

With the proposed plan, shopping for and selecting a health plan
will become easier for rural Americans. The alliances will

develop and distribute literature clearly showing the differences
in price and quality and in consumer satisfaction among the area .
health plans. Alliances will also monitor health plan
performance and publish a report card showing the how well the
plans perform in outcome terms that consumers will be able to
understand.

Because of the incentives of managed competition, health plans
will be motivated as never before to control costs and provide
the preventive services people need, providing total patient care
instead of care only when a person is sick or injured.

Choice of Health Care in Rural Areas

I want to now turn to the issue of whether rural American will
really have a choice of health plans. All rural Americans will
have access to a fee-for-service plan as one option. Rural
Electric Cooperatives and Rural Telephone Cooperatives that
currently offer group plans will have the option to function as
corporate alliances for their members.

However, rural residents want more choices, preferably lower cost
options that are community-based. One goal of health care reform
is to provide new incentives for expansion and creation of new
networks in rural areas modeled on HMOs and PPOs.

To accomplish this expansion, alliances will be able to offer
financial incentives for health plans based in urban areas to
establish satellite operations or subsidiaries in rural areas.
In addition, through the Public Health Service, community
capacity expansion grants will be available to cover start-up
costs and encourage new health plans to develop in rural areas.
Specifically, a rural coalition including some combination of
rural hospitals, clinics, physician groups and other providers

could use these grants to develop their own network and serve as
a health plan to their community.

We cannot expect to provide rural consumers with the same range
of choice in health plans offered elsewhere; but, with these
incentives to expand and create new low cost networks in rural
communities, choices will improve. Rural Americans will have
more choice after health care reform than they have today.

Access to Health Care in Rural Areas

In addition to supporting the development of community practice
networks, current safety-net programs funded through the Public
Health Service, such as community and migrant health centers,
programs for the homeless, family planning, Ryan White, and,
maternal and child health will be maintained. Some of these
programs will be expanded. Community and migrant health centers
will undergo significant expansion that will create new centers
in many rural areas.

During the transition under health care reform, many rural
providers, including the categories of grantees just cited, will
be eligible to apply for status as essential community providers.
This will ensure that these providers receive payment for covered
services from all health plans.

In order to succeed in rural America, health care reform must
address the shortage of health care providers. National goals
involve incentives in medical schools to get more students to
choose a career in primary care. Over the next ten years the
goal is to have 55 percent of the incoming medical school class
select primary care. Funding will be increased for nurse
practitioners, midwifery, and physician assistant training, and
changes will be made to expand the delivery of services by
persons in these fields.

The National Health Service Corps, which places about 55 percent of its providers in rural areas, will undergo approximately a five-fold expansion from its current strength of about 1,600.

A number of other provisions in the plan are specifically targeted to help attract more primary care physicians to rural areas:

o   Tax credits will be offered for primary care providers serving in underserved areas. Up to $1,000 per month will be available for primary care physicians and $500 for non-physician providers for up to 5 years of service. The tax credit may be recaptured on a sliding percentage scale for service less than 5 years in a designated area.

o   Allowable depreciation expense for medical equipment will be increased by $10,000 for primary care physicians practicing full time in designated underserved areas.

o   The Medicare bonus payment for primary care physicians practicing in underserved areas will be increased from 10 to 20 percent, while other specialists will continue to receive a 10 percent bonus.

One disadvantage of practicing medicine in a rural area is the professional isolation. Several components of health care reform will make significant changes in the practice environment which is so important to attracting and retaining providers and to the overall quality of care.

Major improvements in the practice environment will result from the community practice network and health plan program mentioned above that will stimulate formation of new community-based networks of providers in rural areas.

New communication technologies linking academic health centers
and rural providers will assure access to specialty diagnostic
and treatment services. The PHS community practice network and
health plan program will provide grants to bring the latest
medical technology to rural areas and expand the professional
interaction needed by rural physicians. A beneficial by-product
of the expanded communication linkages will be to enrich the
referral patterns for specialty services needed by rural
patients.

The community practice network and health plan program will also
include loans and loan guarantees to provide capital needed for
renovation, modernization, and conversion of health care
facilities in rural areas. Like all facilities, rural hospitals
will benefit because, after reform, uncompensated care will no
longer be the financing problem it is under the current system.
Also, rural facilities stand to gain from inclusion of a
geographic factor in the risk adjustment premium.

Another key aspect of the access issue in rural America is the
need for outreach or enabling services, especially
transportation, support and other services needed by those who
are elderly and geographically isolated. Increased grant funds
during the transition will be available to public and private
non-profit entities to provide these supplemental services people
need to gain access and effectively use the medical system.

Rural residents will also benefit greatly from reforms in the
area of long term care. Chief among these is the new home and
community-based services program tailored to the unique needs of
people with severe disabilities. Because people of all ages are
equally eligible, this program will be well-positioned to serve
farm families experiencing tragic accidents with disability-

related consequences. This program is a federal /state
partnership, like Medicaid, but with a federal share up to 95
percent of the program cost. The rural elderly will likewise
benefit from long term care insurance market reforms and from the
following changes in Medicaid long term care requirements: (1)
the increase in the Medicaid asset exemption in the long term
care eligibility calculation and (2) the increase in the amount
of income residents may keep for their personal needs.

The final change to discuss in the area of access is the school
health initiative. Our health system has failed to provide our
youth with the information and services they need to avoid risky
behaviors. Adolescents are also reluctant to seek help, ignorant
about what help is needed or where to get it. Rural youth face
many of the same health risks as urban teens -- drug and alcohol
abuse, unwanted pregnancy, tobacco use, poor nutrition, and,
increasingly, HIV infection.

In order to address these problems, states will have access to
resources to create school health education programs for grades k
through 12, to address locally relevant priorities. Funds can
also be used to provide some health services including counseling
in disease prevention and risk behavior -- in school-based or
school-linked sites. In states that do not take advantage of the
initiative, these grants will be available to local community
networks.

Core Public Health and Prevention Initiative

Just as the personal health care system administers to the health
of the individual, the public health system cares for the health
of the community. When the public health system is not
maintained and falls into disrepair, the health of the community
suffers and, inevitably, the health risks, volume of care, and
cost of care to the individual increases as well.

I cannot overemphasize the importance of this connection between the public health and personal health care systems.

As mentioned earlier, rural areas have a much higher rate of serious accidents due to the risk of farm, mining and other occupations. Just as in urban areas, rural areas must cope with public health problems like drug and alcohol abuse, food-borne illness, teen pregnancy and AIDS. Rural areas can experience mysterious infections as we witnessed in the Four Corners region last year and they experience natural disasters including flood, fire, hurricanes, tornados, and earthquakes.

Let me give several examples of how essential public health resources are in rural areas:

o   The recent midwest floods required an immediate response to protect whole communities against infectious disease. Specifically, health departments of Missouri and Iowa, with federal support, directly intervened to ensure that families protected themselves against polluted well and municipal water supplies. In Missouri, immune globulin was administered to stem a resulting outbreak of hepatitis A.

o   Public health surveillance has focused attention on agricultural injury in Iowa. Over a three year period a system supported by grant funds from CDC's National Center for Injury Control reported 7,797 injuries, 236 deaths, and 1,263 hospitalizations, making farm-related injury the leading cause of traumatic occupational injury in the State. The data system is able to define the types of injury and causes linked with age groups and type of farm activity. Such data is invaluable in mounting injury control and prevention efforts to help reduce this toll.

The promise of universal health coverage, cost containment, and
quality will not be complete in rural America unless it is
supported by a public health structure with solid programs in the
key areas of infectious diseases, teen pregnancy, lead poisoning,
drug and tobacco abuse, injury and violence control, and others.
As is evident in the above examples, rural areas will benefit
substantially from the competitive grant programs in Title III
that will strengthen the core public health functions at state
and local levels. These include:

o   surveillance of communicable and chronic diseases;

o   control of communicable diseases and injuries;

o   environmental protection;

o   public education and community assurance;

o.   accountability and quality assurance;

o   public laboratory services; and,

o   training and education of public health professionals.

Another grant program will provide competitive grants to public
and private community-based organizations to address special high
priority issues of the community. For example, this could be a
prevention program targeted at farm injuries, drunk driving, teen
smoking, violence, proper nutrition, or any number of other
prevention agendas.

Conclusion

In many ways the Health Security Act has taken into account the
special problems of rural health care and targeted provisions to
deal with them. We recognize the special interests of this
Committee in rural health, and look forward to working with you
as Congress considers the issue of health care reform.

This concludes my statement today. I would be pleased to answer
any questions you may have.

Senator HARKIN. Phil, thank you very much for your statement, and you are right, we will be working together to improve the Health Security Act and to make sure that we meet the objectives and the goals that you have just outlined.

A couple of things. Let me put on my appropriations cap now. This is the authorization committee, and I am on the authorizing committee, and authorizations are nice. But authorizations do not do anything about funding of programs, which we have to do in appropriations. And I am concerned about how we are going to finance the public health initiatives that you have outlined, those targeted at rural areas. We do need them.

As you know, we are under a discretionary spending freeze for the next 5 years. In your statement, you say that "Funding will be increased for nurse practitioners, midwifery, and physicians assistant training. Changes will be made to expand the delivery of services by persons in these fields." I think you mentioned a figure of $400 million. I do not know if that was related to that.

Dr. LEE. It was related to that.

Senator HARKIN. I just do not know how we are going to fund it. Authorizations are nice, but in many ways, I have got all the authorization I need; I just do not have the dollars.

Dr. LEE. We recognize that as we put the proposal forward, it is for an authorization. And the administration is committed to working with the Congress to identify an assured source of funding for these programs and to develop that in the course of these discussions. In the process of developing the plan, it was not possible to do that, and we felt it was really better to work with Congress to do that than it was to come up with some idea that might not really be acceptable.

Senator HARKIN. So you are saying that we are going to be discussing this.

Dr. LEE. We are going to be working with you all to do that, and our goal is to develop an assured source of funding, because it is just as critical—as a matter of fact, in some ways more critical—to have the public health infrastructure put in place than it is some of the other elements of the plan.

Senator HARKIN. Precisely. I agree with you on that.

Second, in terms of nurse practitioners and physician assistants, is there anything in the plan that speaks about reimbursements for them? In other words, will they be part of a provider network that will be reimbursed for their services?

Dr. LEE. Well, our goal in this, of course, is to have the plans capitated, working with networks of hospitals and physicians, and the compensation of those individuals. In some, they would be part of a fee-for-service plan, and in others, they would be part of a group practice, capitated and on salary. For example, the Permanente Medical Group, they have nurse practitioners. There are other groups that use nurse practitioners and physician assistants. They are on salary, because those groups are capitated. Where there is a fee-for-service arrangement, the physicians and nurse practitioners and physician assistants in the group would determine what the fee schedule would be. In the plan, those fee schedules will be negotiated at the alliance level. So those determinations would be made at the alliance level—what would be the level of compensation, say, for a PA or a nurse practitioner or a physician for a particular service.

Senator HARKIN. But the national board, or we here, as we develop this legislation, will sort of set the parameters for what these alliances will do. And what I am concerned about is expanding the provider network out there to think beyond what we thought in the past. I mentioned physician assistants, nurse practitioners, and you just mentioned midwifery—but how about just nurses, period, not nurse practitioners, but just nurses themselves, many of whom live in rural areas and who are out there, who could provide many preventive services such as health education? As a matter of fact, I think that is in one of the covered parts of the plan.

Dr. LEE. It is absolutely part of the plan.

Senator HARKIN. Well, it would seem to me that that should be looked upon as something that ought to be reimbursed.

Dr. LEE. Yes, it will be. The clinical preventive services—and health education is part of that—would be reimbursed without copayments or deductibles. But again, the level of payment would depend in each alliance area on the level of premiums, and then whether it is fee-for-service or it is not fee-for-service.

It is interesting, Senator Harkin, in a recent study that NIH did, called the Diabetes Complications and Control Trial, where they showed dramatic improvements in outcomes for Type I diabetics when they had very strict control of their blood sugar, I asked the professor at Vanderbilt who directed this program who was the most important person on the team. He said the nurse educator; the nurse who educated the patient on how to manage his diabetes.

It is a very important element. Nurses can play a critically important role in prevention and certainly in working as a team. We see this much more as a team operation. Medical care or health care has become much more—it is no longer possible to just do it as a solo practice doctor in a rural area. There has to be a team approach. And that physician has to not only have a team in that area, but has to be linked up with specialists or subspecialists in regional or academic medical centers. And I think you will be hearing a little bit later from the Geisinger Clinic in Pennsylvania, which is one of the models showing how this can be accomplished.

Senator HARKIN. Just a couple of last things before I recognize Senator Jeffords who has joined us. You said the National Health Service Corps will undergo approximately a 5-fold expansion. By when? Is there a target date on that?

Dr. LEE. That would be by about 2004. There will be a 3-fold expansion by the end of the century. We will do that in two ways—one, by expanding the loan forgiveness programs, so you will get people who are ready to go into practice immediately; but also to get the pipeline going and get enough people available to make sure that they are going to be there, about half of those funds will go for scholarships, and that takes longer, of course.

Senator HARKIN. OK, and who will be eligible for these?

Dr. LEE. Well, those who wish to go into the National Health Service Corps. The scholarships will be available to those who want to get into the National Health Service Corps, who are willing to serve in rural areas or urban inner city areas.

Senator HARKIN. Physicians?

Dr. LEE. Physicians, nurses, nurse midwives, physician assistants.

Senator HARKIN. That is the point I wanted to get across. You are thinking of expanding the concept of the National Health Service Corps.

Dr. LEE. Absolutely right.

Senator HARKIN. I appreciate that.

One last thing. A September outline of the plan indicated that alliances would have the capacity to require urban plans to serve rural areas in the alliance. The draft legislation presented, however, indicates that alliances may use financial incentives to get urban plans to serve rural areas, but does not indicate that alliances can require that they serve rural areas.

Is this correct, and is this a weakening of the initial position—because obviously, this is a big concern in rural areas where an urban plan can set up in an urban area and then not extend to cover a rural area.

Dr. LEE. The risk adjustment which would be made for rural areas is one of the incentives. As the discussions have gone on, there has been a desire to not have regulation to the extent that that was possible, to not have Federal regulation—to minimize that regulatory role. But in a particular State, let us say Iowa, there could be one or two alliances. The determination will be made at the State level as to what areas they have to cover. In certain areas where it is a standard statistical metropolitan area, like New York City, Putnam County, Westchester County, and the New York counties will all be in a single alliance area. Putnam is partly rural, at least.

When a standard statistical metropolitan area includes rural areas—and I would say in a number of rural States, it may well do that, but I am not sure because I have not looked at that—that would include the rural areas that are adjacent to those urban areas. It would not include the more remote rural areas under ordinary circumstances. If that is not a satisfactory approach, clearly, we have to find a way to provide choice for people in rural areas, and that would be one area which would certainly in my view be open for further careful examination by the Congress.

Senator HARKIN. But could the States require that an alliance serve a rural area?

Dr. LEE. Let us take Montana. They could have a single alliance for the whole State. So in a State that chooses to have one alliance for a State, that would automatically include it.

In those States where the alliance would be in an urban area, the current plan does not require that alliance to go beyond its geographic area.

Senator HARKIN. But under your provision, could the State require the alliance to serve a rural area?

Dr. LEE. Well, I am not a lawyer, but I would say that I would hope so. I mean, it is not required. The point is that the Federal Government is not requiring the alliance to do that. It does not prevent a State from doing it; it does not say a State cannot do it.

Senator HARKIN. I see. Thank you very much. I appreciate it.

I will turn to Senator Jeffords.

Senator JEFFORDS. Thank you, Mr. Chairman.

Dr. Lee, that was very excellent testimony, and I appreciate it very much. I want to pursue the question of the expansion of the health service corps from this perspective. One of the problems that we have had with the present system is that you cannot keep the doc out on the farm. So if you are trying to service the rural areas, and every time you put someone out there, and the time for their commitment expires, and they leave, the ability to expand and cover the areas is going to be greatly increased in the sense of time if we cannot find out how to keep them out there, so that every new crop does not just replace an old crop of doctors.

What is your solution for that? One, certainly you have already talked about, and that is reducing the stress factor by having nurses or others who are qualified to relieve the doctor at times; but how are you going to keep the doc on the farm?

Dr. LEE. Well, in the past, because of the shortage, because of the limited numbers—I was visiting recently with a former University of California San Francisco graduate. I was on the faculty at UCSF. She had gone with her husband to rural Tennessee as a National Health Service Corps physician. She wanted to continue to practice in rural Tennessee, and the National Health Service Corps said, well, we have a shortage in Alaska, so you have to go to Alaska. She resigned from the National Health Service Corps and is still practicing, fortunately, in rural Tennessee.

We have to not have that kind of, in a sense, arbitrary movement of people in the corps. We need to have them settle in communities, be part of the community. And we need to provide, through the access initiative and through these other initiatives, a much more friendly practice environment, a much more supportive practice environment, a much more linked—we must link those physicians so they are not isolated. That has been one of the problems, is isolation in the rural areas. We intend, through these other mechanisms, to reduce that.

We also want to provide a better selection process—in other words, match the physician or the nurse practitioner much more carefully. They are already beginning to do that. And as we look to provide the scholarships for students in medical schools, we will then be looking to match those, picking, for example, kids from rural areas. We know they are much more likely to go back to a rural area. We have seen that. Some of the medical schools—for example, the University of Minnesota, which has "rural" explicitly as one of the their criteria for admission, and University of Washington, which has had the WAMMI program, giving residents and medical students opportunities to train with doctors in rural areas—have a much higher percentage of their graduates who end up in those environments.

So we would encourage medical schools also to be more involved both in the training, preparing physicians to work in those areas, having training experiences in the rural areas, and then supporting the doctors. For example, when a doctor is in rural practice 7 days a week, 365 days a year, some of the medical schools are giving doctors time off—in other words, a weekend—and they will have one of their residents or one of the faculty go out and work in that rural practice. And they will do that repeatedly so that they know the practice. So there are a number of other things that we can do to support that National Health Service Corps doctor or the other doctors in rural practice to make it a livable, professional experience.

One of the things we cannot change is when those doctors and the doctors' wives, when their kids reach the point of going to high school, for example, they often then say they have to move into the city to give their kids an adequate educational opportunity to really be competitive. Those are things that, obviously, with health care reform, we cannot change, but we will do a great deal to try to enhance that practice environment both through the National Health Service Corps, through the recruitment, selection and placement, as well as through providing a more supportive environment.

Senator JEFFORDS. I had an interesting discussion with one very large provider that will be competing for business, and they indicated that they are willing to help subsidize the doctors out in the rural areas for their own self-interest, because they want to ensure that they capture the volume that they need in order to keep their medical center viable. I had never thought of that.

Dr. LEE. One of the things they are doing already is they are paying off the loans of physicians when they recruit primary care physicians. A number of major plans are already doing that. In other words, a resident—particularly in family practice, or general medicine, or one of the general specialties—will have the loan paid off by his plan in order to induce him to join the plan. That is not uncommon. It is not too common yet, but I think it will be increasingly common as they strive to recruit physicians for rural areas and also for the generalists' roles in health plans.

Senator JEFFORDS. I had not thought of that, but it makes sense that they are going to want to make sure they get as many people as they can through their system. And the way you do that is by hiring the gatekeeper, so to speak.

Dr. LEE. My notion of a gatekeeper is someone who facilitates the patients getting access to the most appropriate care and not blocking them from necessary specialty or subspecialty care. The gatekeeper has got to be someone who opens the gate, not someone who closes the gate.

Senator JEFFORDS. I understand. That is probably not the appropriate term to use——

Dr. LEE. Well, no, but it is very, very widely used, and as you talk to other witnesses, ask them about the gatekeeper role.

Senator JEFFORDS. Thank you very much.

Thank you, Mr. Chairman.

Senator HARKIN. Senator Wellstone?

Senator WELLSTONE. Can I ask one question?

Senator HARKIN. You sure can. You can ask more than that.

Senator WELLSTONE. I apologize for being late, Dr. Lee.

Senator Jeffords has left, but I was going to say that part of the problem with the use of the language of "gatekeeper" is, at least with some of our experience, to lay it on the table, with managed care and HMOs, it does not have a very positive connotation, because some of the gatekeeping has been underutilized.

Dr. LEE. I agree with that, yes. That is a very serious problem.

Senator WELLSTONE. That is correct.

I think the one question that I would have is a broad schematic question. With the President's proposal, you have in each State some regional alliances, or maybe some States will decide to just have one alliance or one single-payer. I think the language has changed dramatically for the better, and that could be a real option.

Dr. LEE. It could be, right.

Senator WELLSTONE. And then you have these accountable health care plans or networks that compete against one another on the basis of cost and, of course, we hope also on the basis of quality of care.

My concern—and maybe you went through this, and I apologize to Senator Harkin if you have—I think one of the things that has people in rural America sort of scratching their heads is that all too often, not only can people not afford a doctor, but they cannot even find a doctor. So now they are hearing about this sort of framework of managed competition and these networks competing against one another. They read in the papers and hear about how Humana cannot wait to come in and take over these networks. They are reading about all the plans of the big insurance companies, like CIGNA, Aetna, Travelers, Prudential. And I think people are really wondering where they fit into this.

I mean, this could really be the future of health care, and it looks like it could very well go into a kind of—and I asked you this yesterday, Dr. Lee, but in a different way—bureaucratized, corporatized medicine, oligopoly. In Minnesota, we have very good things. But the fact of the matter is we only have three hospital chains now. We are really moving toward consolidation here.

I think rural America has always had a healthy distrust of concentration of economic power, and I just want to know where you see rural people fitting into this. And if I could make one final point, I think it could be argued that given the number of older people that we have in rural areas, and Mr. Chairman, given the fact that even though people think of poverty in the cities actually disproportionately, we have poverty in rural America—it is more hidden, but it is no less real—it is not at all clear to me that some of these outfits that I think are going to move in, or that is what they say they are going to do, why would they even want to be setting up programs to serve such people? I mean, if you want to compete to keep costs down, you really would not locate out in rural America, and you really would not try to serve rural people.

This is what I see as the flaw to this. Now, reassure me.

Dr. LEE. Well, first, that everybody is insured and with a good benefit package makes the rural person more attractive in terms of physicians moving there to practice, or nurse practitioners or physician assistants. In other words, people will be able to pay for their care, and they will be able to pay for a good benefit, and the doctor or the other provider will be able to provide the necessary care, which is really lacking today because of the high percentage of uninsured in rural areas. So that is number one.

Second, I think the example of Minnesota begins to tell us what it is going to look like in the future. And one of the things that has been evident in Minnesota—and I do not know if you are going to be hearing more about this later—but as you know, the managed care plans did not move into rural areas. The only plans available were fee-for-service. So people living in rural areas paid a higher premium and higher out-of-pocket costs. This would be, for example, State employees living in rural areas, and they have a good benefit, but they did not have the choice.

So what is the State now doing? It is moving to work with plans like Blue Cross to develop a preferred provider option to give people choice who are insured in the rural areas.

As everybody gets insured, I think the States, through the alliances, or through some other mechanism if they choose it, will have to do that to make sure that people have choice in the rural areas. And that is going to vary. Minnesota is unique because of the development of group practice, and one other development that is, I think, very important and is part of the access initiative, the capacity expansion initiative. My view is that the physicians and other providers have to be working together; otherwise they will be picked off by the plans.

In other words, there is strength in numbers. There is strength in developing—I am a great believer in group practice. And of course, Minnesota has one of the best in the world certainly in terms of the Mayo Clinic. And they are now moving to develop networked or affiliated relationships.

So I think we see Minnesota as an example of where we would be going with this approach. We look at Hawaii as another example. The thing that has happened there, with an employer mandate, as you know, since the early 1970's, is there has been a very big increase in ambulatory care with a big decrease in inpatient care, and very good health status in Hawaii—I am not sure if it is as good as Iowa, but it comes pretty close. And I think Minnesota is actually number one in terms of health status in the country. But what they have done is shift the locus of care.

Now, where they could not meet the needs, the States have provided district health centers or local health centers to meet needs in underserved areas that were not otherwise met. And I think we may have to do that through migrant health centers or other plans that we currently have to extend those as essential providers to meet needs for particular populations.

And of course, in Minnesota, we also have the Indian Health Service, which is designed for a particular population in areas that are very underserved otherwise.

So I think that there are approaches that can help to meet these needs.

Senator WELLSTONE. Just one final question, and this ties into yesterday's discussion, on the public health/community health care clinic infrastructure of delivery. We have to have a good, stable funding source for it because I think it is going to be critical not just in the inner city, but in rural America as well.

The only thing I would like to mention from the Minnesota experience, and I do no damage to the truth, is that it is interesting to me—as you know, I am a strong single-payer supporter—that among the rural family doctors, 60 percent in a Minnesota Medical Association Survey said they preferred single-payer. And we also had a situation about a month ago where the AMA State chapter came very close to recommending that the State study single-payer.

And the experience has not been uniformly good from the point of view of caregivers vis-a-vis some of these large HMOs; not at all in terms of the micro-management and the gatekeeping in the negative sense.

So I would still sound a cautionary note with the administration—when we say there is going to be choice, but when the fee-for-service option is going to be more expensive for people, and some of those very people live in rural America, and that is really what they want to have, I think a lot of people are going to say, "You say it is choice, and then you tell me it costs more. And we do not view that as choice."

And finally, even though the package of benefits will be the same—and I think you are right, that will be very helpful, and I am so appreciative of the focus on universal coverage and comprehensive package of benefits—as you well know, I worry about this average price plan, when there is also a low-cost plan, and then many people bidding up to a higher-cost plan. And my prediction, Mr. Chairman, is that what is going to happen is that because of the cost of the plan—you can have the same package of benefits for everyone, but in terms of where the really good doctors and nurses and caregivers are, who answers your phone call, who provides the best services, who reads the Pap smear tests the most accurately, my fear is we are going to have a stratification, and a whole lot of people in this country who can afford to are going to buy up to a higher-cost plan. There should be a band. We should not be able to go above the average price plan more than 10 or 20 percent. But we do not have that, and as a result, I think we are going to have tremendous hierarchy, and I think rural people are going to find themselves either in the average or low-cost plan, and many other people in our States are going to be in the higher-cost plan, and you are going to have the very stratification we are trying to avoid. And that is why, again, I think we ought to pass an amendment in the Senate that says all Senators and Representatives should be at a minimum in the average price plan so we can see whether it is working for the majority of our constituents.

u I think rural people are going to get the short end of the stiBk.t

Dr. LEE. As you know, a State could choose single-payer in the President's plan, and it has improved the way to do that. But currently in the United States, we are different from other countries that have used single-payer. We have a far higher percentage of specialists. We have a large oversupply of both hospital beds and technology, particularly in the suburbs. We do not have it in the rural areas, we do not have it in the inner cities.

We also have incentives. If we use single-payer now, we will fix the fee-for-service system, I think, and what we will do is we will increase physician supply, which it is going to do; as more technology comes on line, we are going to have more and more Government regulation of fees and payments to hospitals, and a more contentious system. And the decisionmaking moves away from the doctors deciding how resources should be allocated for appropriate care to a level of regulation. And that is one of my major concerns about single-payer, and that is why I am very enthusiastic about the approach the President has proposed that gives this option for organized systems. And it is not just big insurance plans. It is——

Senator WELLSTONE. I am not arguing single-payer. I am just telling you that you have an 80-20 contribution to the average price plan. I am delighted it is set at average and not low, but I am telling you that most rural citizens are not going to be able to vote with their dollars and opt into higher-cost plans, because that is about all most people are going to be able to afford in rural America, and I can see real possibilities of stratification.

That is my only point.

And finally, yesterday, since you were here, I have to express my disappointment, not in a sense of pretention. We talked about the mental health/substance abuse benefit. I said that people all around the country are telling us that if you cut it back even further, there is going to be a tremendous strain on the public institutions. And today, I read in the paper that in fact we are cutting it back even further. You are making a huge mistake—or someone is, not you—a huge mistake, and there is going to be a big battle over that.

Dr. LEE. I think there is very broad concern about those benefits, and the problem obviously has to do with how much can you afford at the beginning and how soon can you phase them in.

Senator WELLSTONE. The people in HCFA who have been doing the numbers, their numbers are outdated; there are a lot of people who manage Fortune 500 plans who can give them more up-to-date data. I just think it is crazy that we are going in this direction right now.

I have said enough.

Thank you, Mr. Chairman.

Senator HARKIN. I just want to thank you, Senator Wellstone, for your insight. I think you understand what is happening to people in rural areas better than anyone else on this committee, and we are going to look to you for your leadership in this. We have got to make sure that this thing does work for people in rural areas and that they are not stratified. And of course, as Senator Wellstone points out, if there is a stratification, I know where rural residents are going to wind up—not on the top layer; maybe down on the bottom layer.

I just want to perhaps correct one thing. I am appreciative of your comment that Iowa must be doing something right, and that we must be one of the healthiest States in the Nation because we have such a large proportion of elderly who are living over 85. I daresay I think that has more to do with the out-migration of young people during the 1980's than anything else. We were second only to West Virginia in the number of people who left our State during the 1980's. We had a terrible time because of the loss of our farm population, and the loss of jobs, and that is why we have so many people over 85. Now, obviously, I think we are fairly healthy, too, but that is the reason why we have such a high proportion of elderly.

Dr. LEE. I will also report back to you, Senator Harkin, on the comparisons by State and see where Iowa stands. I just have the impression it is a pretty healthy place to live.

Senator WELLSTONE. Are you going to disagree with that, Senator Harkin?

Senator HARKIN. How can I disagree with that? [Laughter.] Obviously, it is very healthy.

Finally, I just want to clear up this issue of nurse practitioners and nonphysician providers. How do we ensure that the plans include others, like chiropractors, for example? Should we have a nondiscrimination clause?

Dr. LEE. Well, there is an "any willing provider" provision, so that at least one plan will have to include any willing provider.

Senator HARKIN. That means anyone licensed by the State.

Dr. LEE. Yes, right. Not an unlicensed practitioner, I would hope; they might be willing providers, but they need to be licensed.

And those determinations as to who gets a license and what they are licensed to do, States have always been the primary determinants of that.

Senator HARKIN. So what you are saying is that at least one plan must have a nondiscrimination clause.

Dr. LEE. That would have the "any willing provider" provision; that is right. And other plans—I mean, if you look at some of the larger capitated group practice pre-payment plans, they employ nurse practitioners and physician assistants because it is more efficient, and they employ nurse midwives because it is better quality care than a pure physician system. That team approach is clearly the way we are going to go. But at the moment, there is not a requirement that each plan do that.

Senator HARKIN. Well, I think that is something we ought to fix, because I really believe that if you do not have it for every plan—if you only require one—then fee-for-service will have the other practitioners, the willing providers, and the other plans will not. And that means that people who want to go into a lower-cost plan will not have the option of having other types of services. I really think that is something we are going to have to fix here. We are going to have to have a nondiscrimination clause that any willing provider, anyone licensed by the State to provide services that are covered under this plan ought to be included in any plan.

Dr. LEE. Well, let us say you have a group practice like the Mayo Clinic that is part of a plan. Would you say to the Mayo Clinic that they have to hire any willing provider?

Senator HARKIN. Yes. They would have to provide to anyone who participates in their plan. If I want to see a chiropractor, or a naturopathic, or someone who is licensed by the State, they have to cover it, absolutely.

Dr. LEE. Because that is very different than what is in the plan as it is currently proposed.

Senator HARKIN. Well, I know, but my goal is to expand the concept of who provides health care. Well, I do not want to get into the whole philosophy of this, but I think we need to move ahead or we are going to continue to pay for a sick care system. What I want to do is to rearrange it so we start focusing on a health care system.

Dr. LEE. I totally agree with that.

Senator HARKIN. I know you do.

Dr. LEE. Absolutely, that is right.

Senator HARKIN. Keeping people healthy in the first place. That is why I am saying we need a better mix, an appropriate mix, of different providers, not of services to get you well when you are sick, but to keep you healthy in the first place. And that is why I think some of these alternate providers—maybe that is the wrong choice of words—but other types of providers of health care services ought to be included in these plans. If they are not, let us face it, I know what power structures are like and how they operate, and they will squeeze those people out, and we will have a set of providers much like what we have today. So we will rearrange how we pay them, but we will not rearrange how we provide health services.

So that is something I think we are going to have to fix.

Finally, on Medicare, I mentioned in my statement, and I know Senator Wellstone feels this way, that you have all these big cuts in Medicare. Mrs. Clinton has been wonderful on this, but she talks about averages, and how the average is going up, and so on. But when you have a State like Iowa that has a high proportion of elderly, those Medicare cuts are going to kill us. So we have got to figure out some other way of doing this, and I just do not know how we are going to live with those kinds of Medicare cuts proposed in the plan.

Has the administration looked at how this is going to impact the rural areas?

Dr. LEE. I can ask Helen to respond to that. Let me just say a word based on my 6 years as chair of the Physician Payment Review Commission. The cuts are not really cuts, of course; it is a slower rate of increase. Instead of going up at 10 percent per year, it will go up at, I think, about 6 percent per year. Now, some particular institutions will be more affected by those reductions than will others. Physicians, particularly those in general practice or family practice or general medicine, because of the bonus in rural areas, because of the change in payments in Medicare, will tend to benefit even though the rate of increase is slower than it would have been had these others not been in effect.

Rural hospitals are a different situation, and I would like to ask Dr. Smits if she would comment on that, because I know that is an area of particular concern for both of you.

Senator HARKIN. Yes, please.

Dr. SMITS. In terms of the Medicare reductions in rates of increase, there are really four elements. First is the indirect medical expense, which really does not affect rural hospitals. In fact, some of the changes in education, we would hope, would begin to put more training out in the rural areas. But at the present time, that has very little effect.

The second big one is decrease in what are called disproportionate share payments that are related to hospitals that care for very large numbers of the uninsured. Rural hospitals get a very small percentage of that money now and will continue to get, as it is reduced, in the ball park of the same percentage. Remember how many uninsured people there are in rural areas, so that we think that rural hospitals will in fact in that area come out considerably better.

The other two big cuts are, first of all, a reduction in capital payments, the rate of increase of capital payments. That basically takes the base years and changes them somewhat and then trends forward with a 5 or 6 percent increase. Roughly the same happens with the overall market basket adjustment for Medicare case payments, and that base is reduced, the rate of increase is reduced, but it still continues to increase.

The important thing to remember is that the administration would not support these cuts without reform and universal coverage. Hospitals of all types, especially rural hospitals, could not handle this change without reform.

The other thing, as you have said before, is that we have to face the spending caps, and this is one way to help Medicare face those spending caps. Continued growth, faster growth, in fact, than the rest of the health care system, because Medicare has been held down more recently, but still continued growth.

Finally, let me say for smaller rural hospitals—and you know more about them in many ways than I do—simple manipulation of the case-based payment really is not enough. A little rural hospital of 25 beds or less is a very unusual organization. I trained entirely on the East Coast, and I had the privilege of visiting those hospitals when I was on a Johnson Foundation Committee that gave them grants. They do different things. They have a very important relationship in the community.

Working with Congress over the last 10 years or so, HCFA has done a number of things to recognize that unique function—the creation of swing bed payments to allow them to do long-term care; the creation of rural transition grant payments that go to rural hospitals that want to change what they do, and most recently, very importantly, the creation of a program known colloquially as EACHs/PCHs, the essential access community hospital arrangement, that is designed to try to set up networks of very small rural hospitals that are essentially primary care hospitals, linked to larger hospitals. That involves both grants, to help hospitals work toward that, and modifications in payment systems so that those hospitals will function better.

One of the most important things is that that contains a provision that allows the smallest hospital to leave the DRG system, a system based on averages, and to go back to actual cost, which I think makes a great deal of sense.

Finally, the President's proposal would allow States to set up a statewide system that could be single-payer, but as long as it meets the plan's standards, could be something a little different from single-payer, but that could fold in Medicare provided beneficiaries are protected in their out-of-pocket costs and their benefits. I think that makes a lot of sense for rural States. I think part of why you hear the concern of both physicians and hospitals about single-payer is that for a hospital to have 40 percent the new plan and 60 percent Medicare, no matter what we do with Medicare, is still difficult. So I think it is very important to keep those options in the plan.

Senator HARKIN. Very good.

Thank you both very much.

Dr. LEE. Thank you. Could I just close with a little story, Mr. Chairman, that the Secretary related after a visit to Detroit? It is apropos of who should be a provider.

She was in Detroit, gave a talk to the AFL-CIO, and then went to an Arab-American health center, where she saw her elderly Mennonite priest from Cleveland was there. He came up to her afterward, gave her a big hug, and whispered in her ear in Arabic: "Don't forget the chiropractors." [Laughter.]

Senator HARKIN. Thank you very much, Dr. Lee.

Thank you, Dr. Smits.

Our second panel includes Craig Thompson, a family practitioner at Strawberry Point Medical Center in Strawberry Point, IA. Dr. Thompson testified at the health care forum that Mrs. Clinton held in Iowa this past March. Also, candidate Clinton and Senator Gore visited the clinic in Strawberry Point during their bus tour through Iowa.

Frank Trembulak is the executive vice president of operations for Geisinger Health System in Danville, PA. I understand that Mr. Trembulak's HMO has been held out as a model and praised for its integration and delivery of services in rural areas.

Charlene Hanson is an advanced nurse practitioner in Georgia, and an instructor at Southern Georgia University's Nurse Practitioner Program in Statesboro, GA. Ms. Hanson also practices in a rural health department clinic.

Frances Hoffman is chief executive officer for Franklin General Hospital in Hampton, IA. I am looking forward to hearing your testimony about the relationship you have with Mercy Hospital in Mason City.

Ron Nelson is a physician assistant and director of the Cedar Springs Clinic in Cedar Springs, MI. Last summer, I visited a physician assistant-operated rural health clinic in Redfield, IA, so I am interested in hearing your thoughts on how nonphysician health care providers can play an expanded role in our health care system.

I thank you all for being here. All of your prepared statements will be made a part of the record in their entirety. I would like to ask each of you if you could limit your testimony to 4 to 5 minutes. I always ask witnesses what is the most important thing you want to leave in our minds when we leave here today, and focus on that; what is it you want to have us think about when we finish this session today?

So again I welcome you all here. We will start in the order in which I read off the names. First, Dr. Thompson. It is good to see you again, and we appreciate your coming to testify.

Please proceed as you so desire.

STATEMENTS OF DR. CRAIG B. THOMPSON, STAFF PHYSICIAN, STRAWBERRY POINT MEDICAL CENTER, STRAWBERRY POINT, IA; FRANK J. TREMBULAK, EXECUTIVE VICE PRESIDENT OF OPERATIONS, GEISINGER HEALTH SYSTEM, DANVILLE, PA; CHARLENE M. HANSON, RURAL FAMILY NURSE PRACTITIONER PROGRAM, GEORGIA SOUTHERN UNIVERSITY, STATESBORO, GA; FRANCES HOFFMAN, CHIEF EXECUTIVE OFFICER, FRANKLIN GENERAL HOSPITAL, HAMPTON, IA; RON NELSON, PHYSICIAN ASSISTANT, CEDAR SPRINGS CLINIC, CEDAR SPRINGS, MI

Dr. THOMPSON. Thank you, Mr. Chairman. It will take me 6 minutes.

Senator HARKIN. All right.

Dr. THOMPSON. I am a family physician from northeast Iowa. I am in my 15th year of practice in the small town of Strawberry Point, with a population of 1,500.

Strawberry Point is a community with no hospital. The nearest hospitals are approximately 20 miles away. I serve 5,000 patients in a solo practice. There are a few of us, contrary to Dr. Lee's comments earlier.

I have been asked to give you an overview of our practice model that we have developed and offer some comments on the administration's health care plan.

As you have already heard, agriculture is the deadliest occupation in the Nation and the dominant in the area I serve. About a decade ago, I realized that we needed advanced life support capabilities within our community. We started out using only private funds to build a system that would allow the day-to-day doctor's office care you would expect from a family physician, including preventive care, as well as emergency services that you would expect delivered by small community hospitals, specifically, stabilization and treatment of motor vehicle accidents, farm injuries, heart attacks and so on. This included emergency room special equipment, x-ray, building and strengthening the community's ambulance service, as well as a helipad in the community to allow air ambulance safe and rapid transit.

We strive to be innovative in a number of ways. We were in an original study, sponsored by the University of Iowa, that looked at the use of automatic defibrilators. After study, these were found to be safe and effective and are not used widely throughout the State of Iowa and other States in the Union.

Teleradiology, interestingly, has been something that we have applied for in rural health outreach grants the last 3 y r, and I was interested to hear Dr. Lee mention that as part of thesupcoming program.

Strawberry Point Medical Center was also the first nonhospital facility in the Midwest to use thrombolytics on an acute heart attack patients. As you are aware, this is lifesaving medicine that dissolves blood clots in the artery of the heart when one is having a heart attack. Strawberry Point has since been recognized by Iowa Blue Cross and Blue Shield plans as a unique provider situation, allowing an increase in emergency care remuneration.

We have seen a change in the State rules, allowing our hybrid model to evolve. We are not a doctor's office or a hospital, but we find many times, somewhat frustratingly, we fall somewhere between. We have been held up nationally as a potential model for alternative rural health care delivery. However, this threatens to die on the vine because of the continued decrease in reimbursement for Medicare and Medicaid patients, and the ratcheting down of private patient fees as well.

It is a known fact, as we have heard, that rural areas are paid less than urban areas to provide the same level and quality of care, based on the false belief it is cheaper.

Senator HARKIN. What is your percent right now for reimbursement?

Dr. THOMPSON. As far as——

Senator HARKIN. Medicare reimbursement.

Dr. THOMPSON. Presently, the hospital is about one-half to two-thirds.

Senator HARKIN. So, 66 percent.

Dr. THOMPSON. Yes, and roughly the same in office fees. this is based on real estate values, primarily, and some misunderstanding, because staff wages must be comparable to metro areas, or our staff will simply compute. And comparable equipment costs the same or more because we cannot buy in big networks. It is illegal in many places, because we are a private, for-profit, quote, entity.

For these reasons, you probably will not see models like ours springing up all over the countryside, because presently, start-up simply costs too much the way the plan is currently paying in rural areas. I would point out, however, that our turnkey cost was less than most small community hospitals are spending on renovation right now. This is not to replace hospitals. This is meant to be in an area where services are needed, where there has never been one, or a hospital is no longer viable. Unfortunately, we have seen that in Iowa.

I have been asked to comment specifically on some segments of the administration's health security plan. We are all happy to see universal coverage for all. Anyone who is close to the people they serve feels that way.

Pharmacy coverage for Medicare is a strong plus as well. But I am concerned that these changes, as you have voiced, will cost more than expected. Looking at pharmacy charges alone, I would expect to see a 10- to 20-fold increase, potentially, in outpatient costs for Medicare just because of this alone. I can expound on that later, if you wish. I am just afraid that this will be carried on the back of further pay cuts to providers, which will make it that much more difficult to have providers in rural areas.

Specifically in regard to rural health, as Dr. Lee has mentioned, there are some innovative features—the tax credit, the loan repayment. Those are all good things for rural areas, but primarily for those in the first 5 years of practice. It is still important that at the end of that phase-in period, the busy practice is also a financially viable practice. If it is not, the patients will be ultimately poorly discussed when, as has been discussed earlier, the practitioner simply gets up and moves.

I am a little concerned when I hear about choice of plans in rural areas, and I hope that we address this very carefully so we do not end up with two provider organizations in an area that can scarcely support one and ultimately will be underserved by both.

There are other issues that we could address, but I am limited on time, and I am sure other speakers will bring them out—transport in rural areas, which the plan does discuss and which is important; modifying the safe harbor rules to allow for progress in rural areas. It is unclear if the plan will do that, at my reading, other than changes that allow the plan to take effect. Also important is emphasizing family practice in graduate medical education, which the plan addresses; expand nurse practitioner training—we have long been a proponent to see this happen in the communities where these people work. They have families. They cannot necessarily take a year and leave. Sometimes, their income is the income that is keeping their husband on the farm. And also, I have concerns about corporate medicine and their concern for patients in general in rural areas.

We all hear about inefficiency and waste in systems. I would like to point out that I think rural providers are very cost-effective. As you have said, Iowa ranks third in the Nation in rural population, and we have a very elderly population, and yet we rank near the bottom of Medicare reimbursement in the country.

Also, we hear that physicians' fees are 15 to 20 percent of the health care dollar in various estimates. I have looked at what my personal percentage of health care expenditure was on the patients I serve, and I can explain my methodology, but it basically amounts to slightly over one percent. So as a family physician able to take care of 80 percent or more of my patients' needs, I am providing that at slightly over one percent of the per capita health care cost. Other family physicians are similarly cost-effective.

My intent is not to be self-serving, but truly, in my patient's future, I can leave, but most of my patients cannot. My perspective is not that of a fiscal expert, but as a family physician who cares about the people he serves. Where I live and work, this debate gets down to basics—human life, life and death. There is no average. It seems it is a matter of fairness. If we determine that basic health care is a right, then a rural basic health care system that includes good emergency care, equal to that in urban areas, surely is a right as well.

Thank you.

Senator HARKIN. Thank you very much, Dr. Thompson. Excellent testimony.

[The prepared statement of Dr. Thompson follows:]

PREPARED STATEMENT OF CRAIG B. THOMPSON

I am Dr. Craig B. Thompson. I am a family physician from Northeast Iowa. I am in my fifteenth year of practice in a small town named Strawberry Point with a population of 1500. Strawberry Point is a community with no hospital. The nearest hospitals are approximately twenty miles away. I serve 5000 patients in a solo practice. I am presently in solo practice. I have been asked to give you an overview of the practice model that we have developed and offer some comments on the Administration's health care plan.

About a decade ago, I realized that we needed advanced life support capabilities within the community. We started out using only private funds to build a system that would allow the day-today doctor's office care you would expect from a family physician, as well as emergency services that are delivered by a small community hospital (specifically stabilization and treatment of motor vehicle accidents, farm injuries, heart attacks, etc.). This included building and strengthening the community's ambulance service as well as building a helipad in the community to allow an air ambulance safe and rapid transit.

In 1988, in conjunction with STL, which is a subsidiary of St. Luke's Hospital in Cedar Rapids, we built a 6,000 square foot facility that not only offered the usual doctor's office care in a very pleasant setting, but also provided two emergency rooms and expanded radiography capability to allow us to effectively treat and stabilize emergency patients with the goal of rapid transit to the most appropriate distant hospitals.

We have strived to be innovative in a number of ways. Perhaps you are familiar with defibrillators, the machines that shock a heart that is in an abnormal beating pattern, to restore life. Strawberry Point was one of twenty Iowa communities in an original study sponsored by the University of Iowa which studied the use of automatic defibrillators. These were found to be safe and have now been used very successfully not only throughout the state of Iowa, but in growing numbers of states across the country.

The Strawberry Point Medical Center was the first nonhospital facility in the Midwest to use thrombolytics on an acute heart attack patient. As you are probably aware, this is a lifesaving medicine that dissolves blood clots in the arteries of the heart when one is having a heart attack. Strawberry Point has since been recognized by Iowa Blue Cross and Blue Shield plans as a unique provider situation allowing an increase in emergency care renumeration. We have seen a change in state rules allowing our hybrid model to evolve. You see, we are not a doctor's office or a hospital, but fall somewhere in between. We have been held up nationally as a unique model for rural health care delivery. However, it threatens to die on the vine because of the continued decrease in reimbursement from Medicare and Medicaid patients and the ratcheting down of private pay patients as well. It's a well-known fact that rural areas historically have been reimbursed less than urban areas to provide the same level of care. This has been based on a false belief that it is cheaper to operate in a rural area, based primarily on real estate values. This is a serious misunderstanding. While the real estate may be less costly, nursing wages are comparable to the metropolitan hospitals around us as it is not uncommon for nurses and lab technicians to commute an hour or more for the pay they wish. Hence, we must be competitive as this delivery model requires highly trained, hospital-experienced nursing staff. In addition, the defibrillator I was telling you about costs the same or more in a rural area because I am not part of a large buying network and under some federal rules can't be. That defibrillator protects a smaller number of people so its per capita cost is higher still. That is one reason why you don't see models like the Strawberry Point Medical Center springing up all over the countryside. It simply costs more than the system is now paying.

How did I make this concept of a free-standing clinic a reality? It was done by a team of people—myself, my nursing staff, and my business staff, all of whom recognized the need and believed in the dream of providing state-of-the art family medical and emergency care in even a tiny rural area.

Because of difficulty in recruitment and because of the low Medicare and Medicaid reimbursement, it may be very unlikely I'll ever recruit another physician to this area. In fact, it is difficult to recruit another physician assistant because of the hours involved for the pay. I am sure my story is not unique. It seems that this model and others are threatened with extinction unless there is an appropriate change in Medicare reimbursement.

It is felt that the National Public Health Service will take up the slack—that it will be expanded and that it will meet all these needs. It should be noted that because of funding and the way the criteria is organized, it is largely a crisis-based response in a crisis-based system. In other words, when there is a high neonatal death rate, when there is a high cardiac death rate, those areas are preferentially selected for loan repayment and placement of physicians. However, the system lacks, in my opinion, the ability to meet criteria for the maintenance of functioning systems that are starting to be spread very thin, and where the loss of one health care provider would result in a catastrophic change in the availability of health care. Once a crisis situation is reached, the System would then kick in gear, but at a much higher cost ultimately to the government and the system itself. We need to look at a way to make the public health service system more applicable to sustenance and maintenance of intact functioning viable systems that are being spread very thin and need more support.

I have been asked to comment specifically on some segments of the Administration Health Security Plan. I think universal coverage is certainly a strong point and pharmacy coverage for Medicare recipients would be a strong plus as well. However, I have some real concerns as a practitioner in a rural area. I understand that we will be cutting back on Medicare at the very time when we are expanding other benefits. For example, let's examine the drug coverage. When I see a patient during a maintenance exam for hypertension or diabetes or usually three to four different problems, my fee may be $18-$20 depending on the complexity of the visit. I may then send that patient home with prescriptions costing $100 a month. What the System is paying for is a $20 professional office call, and will now see over a four month span of time, perhaps a $400 pharmacy bill. Hence, that benefit alone may result in a twenty-fold increase in the cost to the System, even if one figures that with competitive bidding, careful formulary use and so on, that this can be reduced by a third or so. I fear that that is going to be carried on the back of further pay cuts to all providers which will, as it has historically, be passed down to the lowest paid providers, which are those in rural and underserved areas.

Specifically in regards to rural health, the plan has some innovative features. The tax credit for practitioners in underserved areas is attractive, but it will only benefit those who are in practice five years or less. Similarly, loan repayments are not going to be helpful once physicians are in an area and are established in practice. It is forgotten that those physicians need to recruit other health professionals and need to have the funds to do so. This grows increasingly difficult. Our biggest problem is not the uninsured patients. Our biggest problem is the underinsured government patients:the Medicare and Medicaid patients whose fees in what we are paid does not reflect what it costs to take care of them. Private insurances, not surprisingly, are growing tired of the cost-shifting and are not allowing that to happen. Hence, we get caught in a bind trying to provide quality service and to recruit quality personnel to an area that pays less than the metropolitan areas because of the historic fee schedule problem.

A year or so ago a physician left my practice after working with me for four years. He left because he couldn't make the income that he felt he needed to make in that rural setting. He left and joined a metropolitan hospital network at a satellite location at about a fifty per cent increase over what I make after fifteen years of practice. This sort of inequity will continue unless payment in rural areas reaches a reasonable level. It is interesting to note that nationally Iowa ranks second in rural population and first in people over age eighty-five. It is also known that the average elderly person has at least four different health problems or diagnoses, and that you consume fifty per cent or more of your health care expenditures in the last six months of your life. Additionally, Iowa ranks second or third from the bottom for Medicare reimbursement in the nation, so what you are seeing is a phenomena where we have the most expensive population to take care of and we are paid among the lowest in the nation. Is it any wonder that we are having difficulty in recruitment of health care providers?

The lack of meaningful malpractice reform is a disappointment as well. The new plan encompasses many requirements and restrictions of physicians, but I see virtually no similar expectations placed on the legal profession. Similarly, this has a real impact in rural areas as well, as many times we are called on to do high risk emergency medicine procedures because there they are life-saving and there is no one else to do it. It is easy to understand a rural physician's reluctance to get involved in that when it simply increases your risk of a malpractice suit, even in the absence of any negligence or wrongdoing.

Finally, I hear much about the inefficiency and the waste in the health care system. I know there is some waste in every system. Historically, there was more waste in the health care system and fee schedules than there is now. Even though the dollar figures are higher now, fees for the service that is rendered are not higher. When I assumed my predecessor's practice of thirty years, he was able to make three times as much as I make now and was seeing fewer patients than I do in the economic climate of that day.

Further, it is well known that supposedly physicians' fees comprise fifteen to twenty per cent of the health care dollar. I was curious as to what my personal percentage of that was. I compiled the number of active patients in my practice, multiplied the per capita health care expenditures published by HCFA last year, which was $3,170, and arrived at a figure that HCFA says was the total health care budget for every man, woman and child in my practice. I then looked at what my total billings were, mindful that I do radiographs or x-rays in the office because we have no hospital in town, and also do obstetrics. These are two services that all primary care doctor's offices might not provide, hence my percentage might be a bit higher. The results were enlightening to me. It is remembered that the family physician is deemed capable of meeting over eighty per cent of their patient's health care needs. So what was my per cent of that health care dollar? Was it twenty per cent? ten per cent? It was 1.14%. In other words, eighty per cent of the health care is being delivered for 1.14% of the health care dollar. Be careful when you take aim at the waste and the fraud and the abuse in the System that you don't deal a mortal blow to providers in underserved areas who are already operating as efficiently as they can.

I offered some heartfelt words to then Governor and Mrs. Clinton and Senator and Mrs. Gore when they visited the Strawberry Point Medical Center in August of 1992, and subsequently reiterated to Mrs. Clinton at the Conversations on Health Symposium in March at Ankeny, Iowa: that I say to you now that a rural life is worth no less than an urban life.

Senator HARKIN. Mr. Trembulak, executive vice president of operations for the Geisinger Foundation. Welcome.

Mr. TREMBULAK. Thank you, Mr. Chairman and members of the committee. I wish to thank you and especially recognize Senator Wofford for all your efforts and interest in rural health care and focusing on this health reform activity as proposed under the Health Security Act.

Geisinger is a rural integrated health system, assuming both the responsibility and financial risk of providing for total health care needs of an enrolled population in a rural area in Pennsylvania. Geisinger is comprised of a multispecialty group practice, now numbering 520 full-time salaried physicians, practicing in 48 practice sites in over 39 different countries; a rural regional tertiary referral center, one of only four nationally with more than 500 beds; a community hospital and chemical dependency treatment program; and the Nation's largest rural health maintenance organization and other related services.

We serve approximately 2.3 million people in a geographic service area encompassing 31 of 67 Pennsylvania counties, situated primarily in rural, central, and northeastern Pennsylvania.

We recognize the extreme variation in rural communities nationally; however, there is a commonality of rural health care delivery problems and issues which are skewed in severity by the degree of rural environment.

The successful formation of integrated health delivery systems in rural areas will be dependent on the number of hospitals, physicians, scope of other available resources, the practical expanse of geography to be covered and, naturally, time.

Integration is important for the delivery of rural health care in that rural health care has to be more than just a community hospital. Physicians need to be incorporated with broad networks and linkages to a spectrum of services, including perhaps even tertiary care as close as possible, and even medical education support, providing medical education in rural communities.

The opportunity to create multiple integrated competitive systems in rural areas will be limited if not impossible, as well as creating competitive health plans that would be positive for the communities. Rural hospitals must, however, be receptive to resizing, conversion to alternate delivery facilities, and move to create linkages for the services needed, as well as their economic survival.

Such restructurings and affiliations must be supported under the Health Security Act, with economic incentives, antitrust relief and, as already mentioned, safe harbor rules that are more clear.

With adequate financing, management of resources and delivery networks, health plans can be established in rural areas, but success may require the folding in of Medicare and other beneficiaries now excluded under the Health Security Act. This transition could be accomplished by enhancing and simplifying the Medicare risk contracting, AAPCC methodology, to ensure equitable rates for coverage provided.

The concept of financing the Health Security Act with significant Medicare funding cuts will not only not allow for such initiatives, but it will in fact jeopardize current service delivery and indiscriminately redistribute Medicare funds away from rural areas, such as the aging areas in central and northeastern Pennsylvania.

The health care reform proposal's complexity will overwhelm rural hospitals and physicians. The complexity in administration of such activities must be reduced along with costs. Regulation and bureaucracy must be minimized if rural hospitals and physicians are to survive and be able to network.

Primary care physicians will be in short supply, and the competition for their services will increase dramatically. And rural communities will be hard-pressed to meet the competitive price for primary care physicians. Therefore, it is imperative to continue to support other types of health care professionals, including physician assistants, nurse practitioners, midwives, and other allied health professionals. Support through economic and educational incentives allowing for a broader scope of practice are all appropriate initiatives.

The financing as noted for the Health Security Act will lead to significant economic pressure on rural hospitals, which will in turn respond with service and, naturally, manpower cuts, which cannot be afforded in an overall resizing and reshaping of work forces. Although other rural health professions will develop and grow, these professions and growth will not offset the overall decline in acute care hospital staffing.

Additionally, rural teaching hospitals—and there are some, such as the Geisinger Medical Center—which train rural providers will be negatively impacted by the loss of disproportionate share payments, a significant reduction in specialty graduate medical education payments, for which Geisinger Medical Center will be at risk for over $9 million on an annual basis.

Again, costs will be reduced through the downsizing and elimination of services, and manpower will be at risk, but we need to continue to grow alternative methods of delivery, particularly for rural areas.

I thank you for this opportunity and will be glad to answer any questions.

Senator HARKIN. Thank you very much, Mr. Trembulak. In your written testimony, which I went over last night, you have some good recommendations in there that I will want to go over with you.

[The prepared statement of Mr. Trembulak follows:]

PREPARED STATEMENT OF FRANK J. TREMBULAK

Geisinger's Principles for Health Care Reform –1993

In the spring of 1992, as the current national health care debate was being joined, Geisinger adopted a statement of reform principles (see Appendix B).

In brief, these principles encapsulate the thoughts of Geisinger's management concerning the accessibility, affordability, and accountability of health care, and the place of medical education, research, and public health in the reform debate from a rural health care system perspective.

During this year, Geisinger has been cited three times as a potential model for reformers to follow. (See Appendices C, D and E). That national attention has made us aware of two critical facets of the health care reform debate.

- *First*, a considerable amount of reform is occurring, without government intervention. And Geisinger is among the leaders in that reform movement.

- Second, there are specific areas in which federal action can empower and amplify those private efforts.

ACCESSIBILITY

The Geisinger experience shows how a private institution can effectively improve the *accessibility* of health care in a large rural region. Over the past 12 years, Geisinger has established 26 rural medical practices and expanded a number of additional existing practices. That has resulted in the addition of many physicians to our service area — the majority of them specializing in primary care. Geisinger physicians now represent 9.4 percent of primary care physicians in the 31-county area we serve.

Because of Geisinger's charitable charter, Geisinger physicians provide service without regard to ability to pay, which improves accessibility to medical care for all the residents of the area we serve. The declining economic state of rural providers, exacerbated by health reform initiatives, has led to many collaborative discussions on how best to restructure the combined resources of providers to meet the health care needs of the population. Those discussions focus on such issues as : The continuing need for certain rural providers entirely or as as "full-service" hospitals; the ability of private, primary-care practitioners to continue in solo practice; and the conversion or establishment of urgent-care centers and other alternative-delivery facilities, including the restructuring of home health services. Home health services represent a delivery alternative that is growing in importance in our rural setting.

But Geisinger currently has 66 vacancies for primary-care physicians. Recruitment in primary care has become increasingly difficult in recent years. Recognizing that we will be unable to recruit, nor possibly afford, all the primary-care physicians we need, Geisinger is emphasizing the necessity of expanding alternative-care providers in support of our clinical programs and is actively considering the development of training programs for such professionals.

Additionally, we will no longer be able to afford or recruit the high level of specialization that has been traditional throughout our workforce. We are studying ways to shift to a broader-based workforce and to alter the work we do in order to downsize and reduce our overall operating costs.

In order to continue, and perhaps to enhance, access to our services, Geisinger has established a technololgy strategy to link together our provider network for accessing and sharing medical information. Although an appropriate goal, it will be very difficult to accomplish in an environment of declining reimbursement and increased cost-containment.

RECOMMENDED FEDERAL ACTIONS:

Improve the quality of care and the quality of rural practice as a career choice by:

- *Using incentives to increase the number of physicians entering the primary care specialties.*
- *Using incentives to increase the number of primary care physicians who choose rural practice.*
- *Providing assistance to private institutions to develop rural practices.*
- *Supporting public transportation in rural areas, with a focus on increasing access to medical practices.*
- *Supporting research and development of communication and information technology to link rural generalists with specialty centers.*
- *Provide demonstration-project funding for hospital facility conversions to alternative-care facilities associated with health care networks.*
- *Use incentives to enhance the alternative-care professions and increase the number of such practitioners, especially those willing to locate in rural areas.*

AFFORDABILITY

Geisinger is demonstrating the effectiveness of an integrated health system in improving the *affordability* of health care. Geisinger's health maintenance organization, Geisinger Health Plan, has the lowest premiums of any HMO in Pennsylvania. It has the lowest premium of any HMO option being offered to federal employees in 1993. Yet the Geisinger Health Plan is able to provide high-quality care within a fixed budget and still contribute to the support of Geisinger's charitable, educational and research activities. Geisinger Health Plan now covers approximately 149,000 people and provides one-third of the total support of the Geisinger system.

In response to Geisinger Health Plan's success, we are seeing changes in the rest of the area's health care economy. Competition among providers (the typical medical arms race) is being replaced by competition among systems (in which the most efficient win). Meanwhile, competing health plans are moderating their premium increases and improving their managed care operations.

Employers in the area we serve are actively fostering competition by favoring the low-priced options in their employee health-benefit plans. They are already creating "managed *competition*" on their own.

Thus, directly and indirectly, Geisinger is having a positive impact on the affordability of care

RECOMMENDED FEDERAL ACTIONS:

- *Encourage the states to develop managed competition at the state and local level: allow waiver of the "ERISA preemption" of state laws pertaining to employee health benefits.*
- *Protect the access of non-profit institutions to low-cost capital by clarifying the criteria for charitable tax exemption (Section 501(c)(3)), to include health plans and other non-profit components of integrated systems engaged in the support and advancement of federal health policy.*
- *Encourage efficient integrated systems to enroll Medicare and Medicaid beneficiaries. That would include further improvement of the risk contract payment methodology (the AAPCC), and legislation to permit HMOs to function as medicare supplemental plans.*
- *Reduce the administrative costs associated with health care through an expanded use of communications technology such as Electronic Data Interchange (EDI).*

ACCOUNTABILITY

Geisinger has come to view *accountability* as more than periodic accreditation, even as accreditation and licensing requirements continue to be among our most important public accountabilities.

In the past year, one of our hospitals placed in the top ten percent of national reviews by the Joint Commission on the Accreditation of Healthcare Organizations (JCAHO). Geisinger Health Plan voluntarily went beyond the requirements of Pennsylvania law for external quality review, and applied for full accreditation by the National Committee on Quality Assurance (the HMO industry's accreditation body).

Beyond accreditation, we are working with a major corporate client to design a scorecard of quantitative and qualitative measures demonstrating quality and quality improvement to that employer.

Geisinger conducts formal, statistically significant patient surveys. We monitor the technical quality of care in a variety of ways; to do so, in fact, we conducted more than 400 studies last year. We track patient complaints and concerns, and we report them for management response. Results are considered major management accountabilities, and Geisinger's group practice structure makes our physicians continuously accountable to their peers in the group.

In general, however, the threat of litigation impedes public accountability for quality improvement in the health care industry, in the event that peer review data are made public.

RECOMMENDED FEDERAL ACTION:

- *Increase the willingness of health care institutions to publish comparative information about quality: enact a more equitable approach to identifying medical malpractice and compensating patients.*

EDUCATION

Geisinger's support for *education* dates from our earliest days. Since our founding, we have trained more than 2,400 interns, residents and fellows, graduated more than 3,200 registered nurses, and developed training programs in nine allied health professions. Total registration for the 1993 - 1994 school year was 181 resident physicians, 16 graduate fellows, 190 nursing students, and 72 students in allied technologies. Many of those students will remain in rural service when they complete their training.

Geisinger operates nine schools of allied health education:

- Cardiovascular Technology

- Dietetic Internship

- Histotechnology

- Medical Technology

- Nurse Anesthesia

- Nursing (diploma program)

- Radiation Therapy Technology

- Radiographic Technology

- Pastoral Care

Increased competition, however, will reduce the ability of medical institutions to subsidize the cost of education from patient revenues.

RECOMMENDED FEDERAL ACTION:

- *Provide direct support for educational programs, especially those that advance federal policy, such as primary care and rural practice.*

RESEARCH

Geisinger operates an $9 million basic science research program. Of that, nearly $4 million is supported by grant funding and endowment. Geisinger supports 11 full-time scientists and 408 separate research projects.

In addition, Geisinger has also begun research in health services and outcomes. The first project, measuring the short-term savings and health improvement from smoking cessation, has already produced encouraging data. We have seen a high cessation rate and nearly immediate savings from the reduced use of medical services among those who have successfully quit.

RECOMMENDED FEDERAL ACTION:

- *Increase support for outcomes research, especially in the setting of integrated health systems.*
- *Support methods to rapidly disseminate results of outcomes research.*

PUBLIC HEALTH

The medical community's interest in *public health* concerns has faded in prominence with the improvements in sanitation, immunization and treatment of disease that have characterized the second half of this century. Over the years,

Geisinger, like most institutions, had adopted a reactive posture in public health matters. We are a major source of care for accident and illness for much of our area. We are the place to go if a man, woman or child is sick, and especially if that man, woman, or child is sick *and* uninsured.

Geisinger employees, often acting on their own initiative, have continued a long tradition of voluntary public education about hygiene and safety in the communities we serve. Now, as an institution, we have come to recognize again the need to specifically incorporate a public health role in our business plans, and to support, encourage, and recognize the individual initiatives among our employees.

RECOMMENDED FEDERAL ACTIONS:

- *Provide support and recognition for health care institutions that adopt active public health agendas. Look to the nation's emerging integrated health systems as logical allies of federal and state agencies in identifying and ameliorating public health hazards.*

- *Support a public-private partnership to greatly improve the level of public knowledge about disease prevention, diet, exercise, safety, stress management, and the risks of chemical abuse.*

SUMMARY

In summary, the past few years have seen most of the components of proposed national health care reform develop in the private sector. Geisinger is a practical example. Managed care, managed competition, public accountability, access improvements: all can be found to some extent in various sections of the nation. The time is ripe for federal action to encourage the growth and spread of those developing systems.

While major reform is being debated, *we suggest a package of more modest reforms to continue that significant private sector activity.*

APPENDIX A

GEISINGER. HEALTH CARE SYSTEM
Corporate Structure

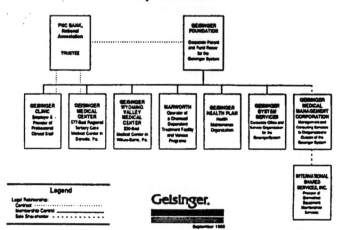

* – Geisinger is a registered service mark of Geisinger Foundation for operating medical, nursing and other health care educational programs through a multi institutional health care system. Throughout this document, the term Geisinger refers to the entire system of health care comprised of Geisinger Foundation and all corporate entities affiliated with or controlled by Geisinger Foundation.

Geisinger — A Regional System of Health Care
Hospitals and Group Practices

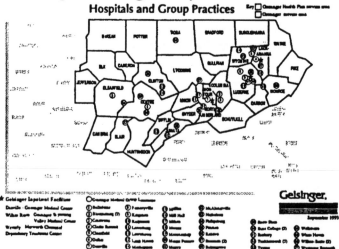

Mission Statement

The Geisinger health care system serves more than 2.3 million Pennsylvanians across 31 primarily rural counties, from the state's northeastern corner to its midpoint — and thousands of others through widely distributed outreach programs. That broad focus is consistent with the Geisinger mission:

To improve the health of the people of the Commonwealth through an integrated system of health services based on a balanced program of patient care, education and research.

Geisinger's primary values are enumerated as a commitment to constancy of purpose, continuous improvement, people caring, teamwork, tradition and financial stability. The New York *Times*, in a front-page article on March 18, 1993, applauded Geisinger's integration of its medical and administrative staffs in ways that contribute to cost-effective medical care.

The character of Geisinger health care management is recognized nationally. The National Committee for Quality Health Care last September offered the Geisinger approach as one of several national models for reforming American health care. The Geisinger management style integrates continuous formal planning and problem-solving methods with day-to-day control systems that assure efficient operating performance.

Geisinger's four driving corporate strategies are articulated succinctly this way:

• Geisinger functions as *one* organization.

• Clinical programs and clinical process improvements size and drive the Geisinger system.

• Managed care is Geisinger's primary business strategy.

• Geisinger seeks collaborative opportunities to increase access to cost-effective services.

Geisinger is focusing on its managed-care system, replacing fee-for-service business with capitated populations. That strategy will permit an even more effective management of limited resources, offer greater value to central and northeastern Pennsylvania consumers, and position Geisinger as the provider of choice in its region.

Crucial to the Geisinger concept of managed care is Geisinger Health Plan (GHP), which now has approximately 149,000 members. Founded in 1972 as one of the first rural health maintenance organizations in the United States, GHP is now the nation's largest rural HMO. The Geisinger Clinic's approximately 520 employed physicians offer GHP services at 45 primary care locations and 13 community hospitals in all or parts of 25 Pennsylvania counties. And, also through the Geisinger Clinic, GHP has agreements with 433 privately practicing physicians in central and northeastern Pennsylvania to deliver services complementing those that Geisinger specialists offer. GHP enrolled its 500th employer group during the past year.

Geisinger has introduced a variety of strategies to strengthen and improve its operational performance. Those strategies were aimed at sizing our system to respond to changes in the healthcare environment, and they included a system-wide workforce reduction.

A resiliently adaptive frame of mind is ingrained in the Geisinger approach to health care. Throughout its history, in fact, Geisinger has been a consistent example of the efficiency, effectiveness, and flexibility of medical group practice. The Geisinger group practice has changed in form and function over the years to respond to changing socioeconomic environments, but it has not deviated from the intent of its founder, Abigail A. Geisinger. Nearly 72 years after her passing, this organization retains Mrs. Geisinger's commitment of service to mankind.

History and Development

Founded in 1915 as the George F. Geisinger Memorial Hospital, Mrs. Geisinger's gift to her community in memory of her husband, the hospital was designed as a comprehensive regional health care institution that would offer specialized services to people in rural areas.

Harold Foss, M.D., was Geisinger's first chief of staff, and he served in that capacity from 1915 until 1958. Trained at the Mayo Clinic, Dr. Foss advocated the group practice of medicine and hired specialty-trained physicians who formed the full-time, salaried, closed staff of the hospital. The original hospital of 70 beds has grown to be one of the nation's four largest and most modern rural medical centers and now has 577 beds.

In 1961 the George F. Geisinger Memorial Hospital became Geisinger Medical Center. Twenty years later, in 1981, Geisinger Medical Center and its affiliates underwent a corporate reorganization and became a system of health care delivering medical and health-related services under the common control and direction of Geisinger Foundation.

A Geisinger Overview

- Approximately 520 physicians provide the excellence of Geisinger healthcare throughout central and northeastern Pennsylvania. Some of those physicians practice in small family health centers and some in large medical groups. Wherever they practice, they have access to hundreds of support services provided by the entire Geisinger system.

- Geisinger has two hospitals. Its 577-bed *Geisinger Medical Center* in Danville delivers specialized care—emergency medicine, cardiovascular surgery, newborn intensive care— actually 75 specialties and subspecialties in all. Geisinger Medical Center operates two medical helicopters, provides comprehensive trauma care 24 hours a day, and conducts outreach, educational and research programs in trauma care. The medical center is also home for the Janet Weis Children's Hospital, now under construction and scheduled for completion in 1994. Its other specialized care centers focus on kidney, neurosciences, trauma, heart, cancer, and infertility treatment. *Geisinger Wyoming Valley Medical Center* in Wilkes-Barre is a 230-bed secondary referral center serving as the eastern hub of the Geisinger system. Geisinger Wyoming Valley Medical Center cares for patients in the Greater Wyoming Valley and western Pocono region with comprehensive maternity programs and pediatric services, five medical/surgical units, the new Frank M. and Dorothea Henry Cancer Center, and a complete emergency department. Geisinger Wyoming Valley Medical Center also offers an extensive community-health education program.

- The Geisinger program for alcohol and chemical detoxification and rehabilitation is system wide. It includes the 77-bed Marworth inpatient treatment center in Waverly, Pennsylvania, which addresses the physical, social, psychological and family issues of dependency and recovery and coordinates outpatient chemical dependency services wherever Geisinger provides health care.

- Geisinger's health maintenance organization, GHP, offers members a variety of medical services for a flat fee. Medical expenses such as hospital and doctor bills are pre-paid under the plan, as are routine check-ups, immunizations, well-child care, and inoculations.

- ISS, a Geisinger affiliate in Plymouth Meeting, Pennsylvania, has responded to the requirements of the Joint Commission on the Accreditation of Health Care Organizations by offering hospitals clinical technology-management programs that can improve the quality of patient care while reducing hospital costs. ISS is one of the nation's largest independent clinical engineering firms. It has served hospitals and clinics throughout the mid-Atlantic region since 1972 and now has more than 160 corporate clients.

- Geisinger Foundation serves as the parent organization for the Geisinger system, which also includes Geisinger System Services and the Geisinger Medical Management Corporation. Geisinger Foundation coordinates fundraising, manages telethons, and facilitates community services.

1993 Fiscal Year

Admissions

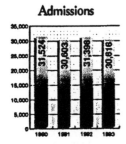

Clinic Visits

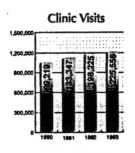

CME Programs

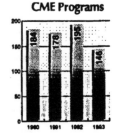

Number of Physicians

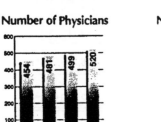

Number of Clinic Sites

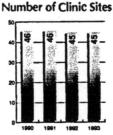

CME Attendance

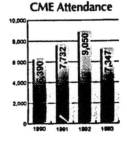

GHP Members

Active Research Projects

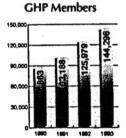
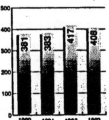

all figures as of June 30, 1993

GEISINGER STATISTICAL SUMMARY
(for fiscal year ending 6/30/93, except where noted)

Patients
GHP Enrollment *(as of 10/31/93)* 149,193
Outpatient Visits 1,225,556
Hospital Admissions *(including newborns)* 30,616
Life Flight Helicopter Retrievals 1,236

Employees
Physicians 520
Physicians in Training 207
Employees *(including physicians and physicians in training)* 7,301

Education
Residency Programs 15
Fellowship Programs 6
Medical Education Programs...146
Medical Education Participants...7,347

Research
Research Expenditures $9,215,000
Research Projects 408

Financial Indicators
Total Revenue...$786,564,000
(including operating and nonoperating revenues)

Allowances 278,245,000
(to insurers, government, third-parties,
charity care, and uncollectible accounts)

Total expenses 480,649,000

Funds Available for Reinvestment 27,670,000
Less Transitional Obligation...................................(14,683,000)
Less Loss on Defeasance ....(2,273,000)

Total Funds for Reinvestment...............................$ 10,714,000

Public Support ....$ 8,259,000*
(includes gifts and grants, plus revenue associated
with the Children's Miracle Network Telethon)

Charity Care, Policy Deductions, ...$ 12,040,000*
Uncompensated Care

* *included in the totals listed above*

APPENDIX B

Geisinger's Principles for Health Care Reform

Introduction

Government is a partner in the health care system.

Over time, the cost of this partnership has far exceeded original expectations.

As a result, and in the absence of a coherent federal health care policy, government's decisions about health care have been budget-driven, not program-driven.

This budget-driven approach has created conflicting incentives between patients and health care providers, and access issues for the uninsured and underinsured. Health care policy reform is key to the improvement of our nation's health care system.

Integrated regional systems of health care, like Geisinger, have a vital role to play in the delivery of health care and health care policy reform.

A national consensus on health care reform is yet to emerge. However, while no single proposal can claim majority support, we believe certain basic principles are already held in common. These principles, in turn, can serve as a framework to guide the design and construction of the actual components of reform.

Central to reform are the accessibility, affordability, and accountability of health care services. In addition, to be comprehensive, reform must also address medical education, research, and public health.

Health care must be accessible. Effective reform must remove barriers posed by cost and geography

• A basic set of essential services must be available to anyone, without regard to medical history, employment status, or ability to pay

• These basic services must be physically accessible in the urban core and the rural counties, as well as the populous suburbs.

Health care must be affordable. The cost of care, both to society and to the individual, must be within our means.

• Integrated regional systems which combine the financing and delivery of health care in a single economic unit offer the best mechanism to reward efficiency and penalize waste. Whether HMO's, PPO's or managed care networks, the formation and growth of such systems should be actively encouraged.

• In the long term, a competitive marketplace is the only effective means to control cost. Price controls and global budgets, unless created with perfect wisdom, produce perverse incentives and shortages This is demonstrably true in any industry, including health care.

• Competition must be among integrated systems, competing in the private sector on the basis of quality and cost. Competition on quality alone has produced excess capacity. Competition on cost alone has produced inadequate coverage and exclusion of individuals with pre-existing conditions among insurers. Lack of competition rewards unnecessary procedures and duplicative services

• There must be adequate financing, both public and private, to ensure that no one is excluded from the marketplace by personal financial circumstances The affordability of the basic set of services must be assured. In addition, individuals or groups wishing to purchase additional services or coverage should be free to do so

• The market price for the basic set of benefits must reflect true cost. Hidden subsidies, pricing by regulation, and cost shifting must be eliminated for the market to function. Tax subsidies should be limited to the cost of the set of uniform basic benefits. State mandated benefit levels above the basic set of benefits should be eliminated.

Health care must be accountable. To ensure a fair marketplace, the integrated regional systems providing patient care must be publicly accountable for the cost and quality of their services. The marketplace itself must be accountable for its structure and operation.

• Integrated regional health care systems should demonstrate the ability to measure and improve the quality of care, as a condition of participation in the competitive marketplace.

• Tort reform, to encourage rather than impede public accountability for quality, is a necessary corollary.

• To permit comparison among competing systems, all participants in the marketplace must offer, at a minimum, a uniform basic set of essential services.

• Establishment and modification of the basic set of essential services must, itself, be an accountable process. It must be directed to promote the general welfare, not secure private interests. Experimental procedures should be included only upon demonstrated efficacy.

Medical education must be supported and directed. Medical education should be financed and managed to produce an appropriate distribution of personnel among professions, specialties and localities, based upon anticipated public need.

Medical research must receive adequate support and direction. In addition to advancing the scientific frontier, medical research must focus on improving the quality and efficiency of current technology. Research should focus on practice guidelines to identify the best approach from among competing opinions and techniques. Research funding should be separate from patient care financing.

Public health must be reinvigorated. Improved control of preventable diseases and conditions could dramatically reduce the cost of patient care, while permitting the rededication of resources to improve both accessibility and quality

• Public education in health promotion and disease prevention should be greatly expanded. The message needs to be carried beyond our schools, into workplaces, shopping malls, and homes

• Public law and public funds must be dedicated to produce further reductions in environmental risks.

• Pressing public health needs must be given greater prominence in medical education and medical research.

• The health care system must educate patients to assume additional responsibility for their own health through healthier life-styles and participation in medical treatment decisions.

APPENDIX C

The New York Times

NEW YORK, THURSDAY, MARCH 18, 1993

Doctors Say They Can Save Lives and Still Save Money

By ERIK ECKHOLM
Special to The New York Times

DANVILLE, Pa. — Dr. James C. Blankenship, a cardiologist with a health-maintenance organization in central Pennsylvania, performs costly, risky procedures in which tubes are pushed to the heart to help find whether coronary vessels are clogged

In his catheterization laboratory, he studied X-rays revealing a partly blocked artery in a 55-year-old man "What are the chances this will shut off, causing a heart attack, versus the risks of surgery?" he asked "The studies differ."

"I'll advise him to watch and wait," said the doctor, whose salary would not be affected one way or the other. "I want to do everything that's necessary, but not too much "

As Americans consider a more frugal medical future, possibly dominated by competing H M O.'s or other forms of "managed care" that limit consumer choice, urgent questions are rising about the quality of care and how to protect it. Will people be pushed into health plans staffed by sullen, rushed doctors whose decisions are second-guessed and who are paid extra to scrimp on costly tests and operations?

Room for Judgment

Or will they find sensitive doctors who have no financial incentive to do too much or too little, have ready access to the best technologies and hold down costs by preventing illness and avoiding procedures with little benefit?

Medical experts are scrutinizing better health plans around the country to see how large savings might be gained through efficiency and prudence, not through shortchanging the sick. And the evidence suggests that institutions that foster physicians like Dr. Blankenship and allow them to exercise professional judgment may be in the best position to pursue that goal.

In the case of the 55-year-old man, some doctors would have recommended immediate surgery, but Dr. Blankenship felt sure, based on available science, that a trial period of drug therapy was in his patient's best interest.

At his organization, the Geisinger Foundation in Danville, the decision about how much is enough is left to the doctors. Their cautious style of medicine has held costs well below the national average. Increases here have still averaged 8 6 percent in recent years, though, raising questions about whether the country will be able to tame medical inflation without cutting into the quality of care.

The 530 salaried doctors who work here, and offer care through a prepaid insurance plan, do receive prodding from above But it involves not constant second-guessing or rewards for scrimping, but rather a steady flow of research news and tips that helps suffuse the institution with an ethic of conservative care

"Here, we don't police; we trust our doctors," said Dr. Howard G. Hughes, who directs the H.M.O., the Geisinger Health Plan.

In Danville, a town of 6,000 people, Geisinger runs an advanced 577-bed hospital as well as a network of clinics over a wide area of central and northeastern Pennsylvania Its growing H.M.O serves 142,000 members, while the same doctors and clinics also provide the same style of care to hundreds of thousands more people covered by government or other insurance.

The doctors insist that their brand of medicine improves on a system laden with incentives to overuse procedures.

And they are saving money The H.M.O. has the lowest rates in Pennsylvania, according to the state insurance department, with monthly premiums this year of $109.70 for individuals and $285 22 for families for a plan covering nearly everything but prescriptions

But the numbers suggest, too, just how severe the challenge is The health plan's charges have risen by an average of 8 6 percent a year since 1985, Dr Hughes said. That is a good record compared with that of most insurers' nationwide, H M O rates grew by an average of 11.7 percent per year from 1986 to 1992, and rates for traditional fee-for-service plans rose annually by 14.2 percent, according to A Foster Higgins & Company, a consulting firm

But it remains well above the national goal of steady real spending set by President Clinton Recent increases have mainly reflected the rising cost of nurses, technicians and other personnel, the soaring price of new drugs and other factors, officials said.

At What Point Will Savings Stop?

Geisinger doctors and administrators, most of them practicing physicians, insist that through steady refinement they can save much more without compromising care Just how much and how fast, though, no one is sure

"Price competition doesn't scare me," said Dr. Stuart Heydt, president of the Geisinger Foundation "If this model can't hold down prices enough, then I'm not sure it can be done in a way that fulfills the medical expectations of society "

While America's medical costs are increased by administrative waste, excess equipment, incentives to use procedures lavishly and outright fraud, in the end

spending mainly reflects the routine decisions of physicians. They decide when a patient needs a $70 electrocardiogram, when to order a $100 dollar antibiotic instead of a $10 one, and when $40,000 bypass surgery is truly likely to improve a patient's chances of survival or quality of life.

"The best way to control costs and preserve quality is to have the physicians do it," said Dr. Arnold S. Relman, the former editor of The New England Journal of Medicine. "The whole health-care system is built on the behavior of doctors, and that behavior is greatly influenced by the way health care is organized "

Dr Relman, who has been studying health plans around the country, praised Geisinger for high doctor morale and a system of mutual review that promotes excellent care

While no organizational structure guarantees quality care, Geisinger has several traits that promote it The bedrock, officials here say, is the careful selection of doctors who share the group philosophy and are happy to work for a salary Since they are not paid piecework, they make decisions with no direct financial interest at stake (Nationally, doctors are salaried in some but not all H M O 's or other forms of managed care)

The salaries here are enough to support an affluent life in this rural region, but for many doctors they are well below potential earnings in private practice. Primary-care doctors have starting salaries in the range of $75,000 to $90,000, while among the most experienced specialists who might earn several times as much elsewhere, "very few go beyond $300,000," said Dr. Laurence H. Beck, senior vice president charged with improving efficiency and quality.

Morale rests on the pleasures of patient care, collaboration, teaching and research, said Dr Francis J. Menapace, the director of cardiology "We look for a different type of physician, one who still looks at medicine as a profession, not a business."

Less Reliance On the Specialists

As in most H.M.O.'s, all patients must choose a primary-care physician in the plan Usually trained in family practice, internal medicine or pediatrics, these doctors provide most care and refer sicker patients to specialists only when necessary, holding down costs.

Now about 30 percent of the plan's doctors provide primary care, but studies suggest the proportion should rise to close to 50 percent, Dr. Beck said. This means cutting back on specialists, a painful and controversial topic among the medical staff.

Dr. Ernest W. Campbell, a primary-care physician and head of the Geisinger clinic in the nearby town of Bloomsburg, had been in independent practice for 18 years before he and his partner decided to join the salaried group in 1985.

"We looked at the H.M.O. and liked what they were saying," he said "It's more geared toward preventive medicine, keeping people healthy rather than just meeting the acute needs as they arise." He said the switch involved a significant loss in income, but offsetting this was a drop in work time to 60 to 70 hours a week so he could see his family more

Far from feeling pressure to avoid needed care, Dr. Campbell said, "I think the quality if anything has gone up." Since patients are in a prepaid plan, he said, "now we can tell them they have no excuse for not coming in when they are ill."

A large unified system like Geisinger's can also avoid duplication of costly equipment and readily monitor its use. For example, all cardiac catheterizations, which are Dr Blankenship's diagnostic specialty and require a million-dollar laboratory, are performed at the main hospital in Danville, as is open-heart surgery. This does mean, though, that some patients have to travel up to 100 miles for major procedures that in a less efficient system might be available at a community hospital.

With central control, too, can come imbalances in staffing, sometimes yielding long waits for non-urgent appointments. Currently, for example, because of a shortage of gynecologists in the group, an appointment for a routine pelvic checkup can take several months. Officials insist that is a temporary side effect of rapid growth and a national shortage, not a long-term shortchanging of patients.

But in surveys of H.M.O. patients that generally find high satisfaction with care and doctors, intermittent difficulty in getting quick appointments has been the most common complaint, said Dr. Duane Davis, medical director of the health plan.

When Supervision Is From Within

For all its emphasis on efficiency, Geisinger does little of the routine oversight that is now so prevalent in the health-insurance industry and so annoying to doctors. Instead, the doctors, with leadership from department heads, are expected to watch themselves for unjustified variations in individual practice and opportunities for improvement

"We have a high awareness of what our colleagues are doing in the next room," Dr Blankenship said "There's lots of intercommunication, lots of informal second opinions If someone is consistently doing something inappropriately, too much or too little, we'd notice "

Peer review is, however, increasingly backed up with research and suggestions from above. The H.M.O., for example, keeps track of prescribing patterns and sends out newsletters urging physicians to prescribe cheaper drugs or generic versions where they have been shown to be equally effective. One recent flyer warned that a drug company was "actively encouraging pharmacists to call physicians to switch patients" from current diabetes drugs to its new product, priced 40 percent higher even though it offers "no therapeutic advantage "

In another example, officials studied whether patients who were put on an expensive cholesterol-lowering drug were first asked to experiment with dietary change By sharing the results with other physicians and stressing the recommended course, doctors found that the proportion of patients trying diet changes had risen. Some will end up needing the drug anyway, but some will avoid indefinite use of a drug that can have dangerous side effects.

As the country seeks to flatten out its health costs, the question is how far even the best-organized providers can trim back without choking off tests and treatments of significant potential benefit.

Dr. Beck said he believes that Geisinger and other similar groups still have large opportunities to wring out expense. Increasingly important, he said, will be reliance on clinical guidelines that reflect research, done locally or nationally, on what sequences of tests and treatments yield the best results for particular conditions.

Still, Dr. Beck said, "At some point there will be tradeoffs between cost and quality." If price controls are too severe, he said, society will have to openly face the issue of rationing.

Modern Healthcare
September 7, 1992

Provider groups finding success with managed care, study says

Managed care, a key cost-containment and quality-improvement technique included in almost every local or national healthcare reform proposal, is being implemented by provider groups in communities across the country.

That's the finding of the National Committee for Quality Health Care, a Washington-based coalition of providers and suppliers, which has put together a report profiling 19 successful provider-based managed-care programs throughout the United States

The report, "Reinventing Health Care: The Revolution at Hand," will be released to the public late this week.

The study was prepared by New Directions for Policy, a fiscal policy consulting group based in Washington.

It's meant to be a companion study to last year's report by the NCQHC describing several successful managed-care projects initiated by healthcare buyers, said William Dwyer, director of corporate account development at Abbott Laboratories and chairman of NCQHC's managed-care subcommittee.

Many providers also have developed effective models of community-based managed-care programs, but policymakers and analysts have tended to overlook them because of all the publicity garnered by the corporate efforts, Mr Dwyer said.

The report shows that decision-makers can learn much from these lesser-known examples of how to construct successful quality-improvement programs and operate them within a coordinated healthcare system, he said.

The provider organizations profiled represent essentially two models for delivering services: those based on group practices, such as Lovelace Medical Center and Health Plan in New Mexico and Geisinger Medical Center and Health Plan in Pennsylvania, and hospital-based network systems, such as Sharp HealthCare in San Diego.

They represent a "small selection" of what provider-initiated programs can accomplish in reforming the healthcare system when they become leaders in promoting community health and wellness, he said.

—Paul J. Kenkel

Networking

by Frank Cerne

Sizing up Pennsylvania
Geisinger aims to reshape its delivery system

"If we as a nation are going to get a handle on the escalation of health care costs and if we are going to be able to provide better health care to more people for less cost sizing the delivery system is a fundamental part of making that happen." —Stuart Heydt M D , president and CEO of Geisinger Foundation, Danville, PA

At Geisinger health system, right-sizing has become a creed shared by executives and physicians alike that drives an organization singled out by some health care experts as one of several models for a nationwide reform

Geisinger's structure and operating strategies are built on the assumption that "we are going to have to provide better care to more people for less cost" says Heydt

Efficiency is the fundamental principle that allows Geisinger to accomplish that mission from the careful selection of primary care and specialty physicians—most of whom are salaried—to the placement of health care personnel and technology according to patient needs over a wide geographic area.

Integrating system components
Founded in 1915 as the George F Geisinger Memorial Hospital, a 70-bed facility with a multispecialty salaried group practice the hospital evolved into a series of separate corporate entities by the late 1980s under the control of the Geisinger Foundation

System components include the Geisinger Medical Center a 577-bed tertiary care teaching hospital in Danville with 75 specialties and subspecialties Geisinger Wyoming Valley Medical Center Wilkes-Barre PA a 230-bed secondary care referral center a 77-bed inpatient chemical de-

pendency treatment center, Waverly, PA, a 145,000-member HMO and the Geisinger Clinic, a 500-member multispecialty group practice

By 1990, Heydt says, it became apparent that Geisinger's management structure and corporate strategies had to change in response to foreseen changes in the health care environment, primarily the increasing emphasis on vertical integration of services and managed care

Geisinger executives then identified strategies that would be needed to carry the organization into the future
• Geisinger functions as *one* organization
• Clinical programs and clinical process improvements determine the size and direction of the Geisinger system
• Managed care is Geisinger's primary business strategy
• Geisinger seeks collaborative opportunities to increase access to cost-effective services

Although Geisinger still maintains separate corporate entities for legal purposes there are no independent boards or management structures that identify them as such. Geisinger has corporate and regional managers for the system's east west and central regions

The system spans 31 counties in north-central Pennsylvania a rural region with a population of 2 1 million Heydt says that Geisinger's approach

to "sizing" the system is to design the network in the most efficient and effective manner

To achieve that goal Geisinger has established a network of 45 primary care clinics staffed by salaried physicians employed by the Geisinger Clinic. The physicians offer services to Geisinger Health Plan (GHP) members as well as to other patients

GHP also contracts with other rural primary care clinics. 13 community hospitals and approximately 450 private-practice physicians in central and northeastern Pennsylvania

Heydt says that physicians and management determine how to best distribute resources throughout the system to build a vertically integrated network of primary, secondary and tertiary care that provides the appropriate level of care to communities

"We know that we have to size the system according to the needs of the population we serve." Heydt says "That way you not only provide greater access to high-quality services, but you also avoid duplicating services and adding expensive technology."

The right physician mix
"Sizing the system means placing physician specialists and referring primary care physicians in areas where

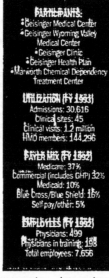

PARTICIPANTS:
• Geisinger Medical Center
• Geisinger Wyoming Valley Medical Center
• Geisinger Clinic
• Geisinger Health Plan
• Marworth Chemical Dependency Treatment Center

UTILIZATION (FY 1993)
Admissions: 30,616
Clinical sites: 45
Clinical visits: 1.2 million
HMO members: 144,296

PAYER MIX (FY 1992)
Medicare: 37%
Commercial (includes GHP) 32%
Medicaid: 10%
Blue Cross/Blue Shield: 16%
Self pay/other: 5%

EMPLOYEES (FY 1992)
Physicians: 499
Physicians in training: 198
Total employees: 7,656

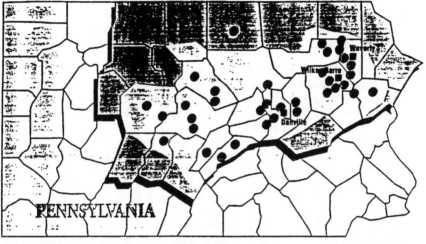

● Geisinger medical group locations ■ Geisinger inpatient facilities └ Geisinger health plan service area ⌐ Geisinger service area

they are most needed

"If you assume in a rural area that people will visit their family physician how many pediatricians and pediatric subspecialists do you need to have? Where would they be located in order to provide support for family practice physicians?" Heydt asks.

Geisinger plans to find the answer to those questions by analyzing the ratios of primary care physicians to specialists in populations served by other systems (such as Kaiser Foundation Hospitals), and by analyzing its own demographic and epidemiological data. an extremely difficult process, Heydt says

"We realize we can't simply build a system to suit our needs We have to make sure that our resources correspond to the actual needs of the populations we serve," he says

Geisinger has 500 salaried physicians. and 30 percent of the system's clinical practice comes from its HMO, so the alignment of physician incentives is a crucial part of Geisinger's strategy

Heydt says the system needs to be more creative with physician incen-

tives in the future with capitation expected to become the dominant payment method. Nearly 30 percent of Geisinger's gross patient service revenues come from GHP

"The concept of prospective payment for a defined population on a per-capita risk-adjusted basis with physicians managing that financial resource is something we need to learn to do." Heydt says "We need to be at risk in terms of utilizing resources to treat a defined population."

Heydt says quality assurance and utilization review activities are made easier by Geisinger's structure a salaried multispecialty group practice which allows physicians to police themselves

The Geisinger Health Plan contributes to this process by centrally collecting and disseminating information about all of Geisinger's quality improvement activities

"We are also trying to find ways of milking more information from our growing medical claims data base so that we can learn more about the practice of medicine as we conduct it," according to William MacBain, a senior

vice president and administrative director of GHP

Expansion through collaboration
GHP is licensed to offer coverage in 25 Pennsylvania counties and has contracts with 500 employers Managed care is the system's stated business strategy so Geisinger is looking for partners to integrate into its network.

Areas in which Geisinger will seek expansion will depend on the needs of the population, and on where resources need to be located to best serve that population

Heydt says Geisinger has approached providers in the region to determine how they can share their combined resources to better serve the needs of the populations they jointly serve

Such discussions have helped identify potential partners, but antitrust concerns have had a chilling effect "We think such discussions are appropriate, if they don't occur with the intent of violating some of the principles of antitrust, such as price fixing" Heydt says, "but we've had to tiptoe through this process" ■

Senator HARKIN. Charlene Hanson, please proceed.

Ms. HANSON. Thank you, Mr. Chairman. I am happy to be here this morning, and I commend you and your committee on your leadership in health care reform and your sensitivity to rural and nursing issues.

I have devoted most of my 30-year career in nursing as a nurse practitioner to meeting the needs of underserved individuals and families, and thus I feel very strongly about the need to reform our system. I would like to focus my remarks today mostly on access to health care for rural people.

I take your comment earlier about the need to be sensitive to all rural communities as very important. It is very different if you are from rural Montana than if you are from the poverty-ridden South or if you are from Iowa, so one fix is not going to work in a general way, and we will have to be sensitive to each area.

There is a need for flexibility. I think we need to really be able to match the public health system in rural areas, at least in my State, where we have 154 counties with health departments, with the private sector and be able to make linkages between different entities that are offering care. And communities will probably need some technical assistance to get that done.

Our public health initiatives can certainly help us in the area of school-based clinics. In Georgia, our infant mortality and our teenage pregnancy are off the paper; our elderly are growing, and mental health is a very serious concern. So we will need to think about public health and private ways to get that accomplished.

Our demand for nurse practitioners has risen sharply, and our demand is outstripping our ability to meet it. Right now, we think there are probably already four or five jobs to every nurse practitioner. If we consider migrant care and prison care and substance abuse and AIDS, it is even worse.

AIDS in rural Georgia right now—the highest rising statistic that I can give you is that in young black heterosexuals, we have almost a 300 percent increase, and we do not know how to take care of these AIDS patients. So we have to think about that spectrum of AIDS also.

There is serious concern on the part of many people that nurse practitioners are going to follow their physician colleagues into the larger communities where the supports are greater, so we do need to think about how we can shore up the rural areas with fiscal incentives and tax credits, which will require new appropriations, and we will need those.

I am concerned as you seem to be, Senator Harkin, about the ability of groups to be able to lock out nurse practitioners and others from being able to provide care through the purchasing groups. I think this is a very serious need in my State and worry that we could be shoring up all of these people for naught if we do not fix it so that they will be able to practice when we get finished.

I also feel that the system breaks down at the higher levels. At the grassroots level, in my 30 years' experience, physicians and nurses and PAs work beautifully together to get the job done, but then we cannot get the regulations in place to make it happen.

These barriers to nurse practitioners need to be lifted across all sites, not just in the rural areas. I think we are g ing to have urban underserved who are going to need this kind of care also.

An example that I can give you from Georgia about how the practice system may work is that by far, we have mostly sole providers in rural communities; single physicians who are practicing by themselves. The bad news is that most of these physicians are 65 years of age and are going to be retiring. And I do not think we have built into the system how we are going to make that transition, and I would see that as critical.

From an educator's standpoint, I do know that we must be able to educate rural nurses from their home bases—they have families, and they have children—and we need to be doing things like distance learning, telecommunications, to make it possible to bring educational programs to them in their home bases.

I know that the National Health Service Corps system is going to be expanded, but I am not sure that it really speaks to landlocked women and the need to be able to go back to their home base. I think Dr. Lee addressed that, and I would support it also.

There is a marked lack of access to both primary programs and continuing education. We need distance learning models, interdisciplinary approaches.

I am cautious about the GME dollars. Although I understand that they are in place, we need to be sure that they are going to rural community hospitals and agencies and that they are going to be used through nursing programs and others that can produce these people that we need. I am scared skinny about the ability of being able to retool faculty fast enough to get out the cadre of nurse practitioners that we need, and we will need to think about incentives to get faculty trained quickly and turned around.

We need to focus on minority and bilingual nurse practitioners, especially in the South, and we need to critically think about how we are going to get that done.

I just think that in the long run we need to be building a system that focuses on both the providers of care in rural areas and the consumers of care. We need to think very seriously about how we are going to build a collaborative network through teams of people to take care of the people in rural areas.

Thank you very much. I could say more, but I know we are in a time bind, and I will answer any questions.

Thank you.

Senator HARKIN. Charlene, thank you very much.

[The prepared statement of Ms. Hanson follows:]

PREPARED STATEMENT OF CHARLENE HANSON

Mr. Chairman and members of the committee, my name is Charlene Hanson, EdD, FNP-CS, FAAN. I developed, direct and teach in the rural family nurse practitioner program at Georgia Southern University in rural South Georgia. I have also been a practicing nurse and nurse practitioner working in rural areas in New York and Georgia for over 30 years. In addition to teaching, I currently maintain a clinical practice as a nurse practitioner within Georgia's Public Health System. Thank you for inviting me to testify before this committee on the American Health Security Act of 1993, specifically with regard to rural issues and nurse practitioner concerns.

Mr. Chairman, we, as nurse practitioners commend you and your colleagues on your leadership on health care reform and support the view of a bold new vision for providing care to the people of the United States. We thank you for your attention to nurse practitioner issues generally, and as they relate to special needs of rural areas for we feel that we can make a difference in searching for solutions to existing difficult rural health care problems.

I have devoted most of my career to providing health care to rural and under-served individuals and families both as an educator and a provider and thus I feel very strongly about the need for reform. The committee has heard and read testimony from other nursing groups about the concerns from nursing's point of view so I would like to focus my remarks today on specific rural issues dealing with the education, recruitment and retention of nurse practitioner providers, and access to health care for rural people.

Need for Flexibility to Implement Health Care Reform in Rural Communities

First and foremost, there is a need for sensitivity to the "uniqueness" of rural communities. They are all very different in terms of structure, leadership and capabilities to provide health care services, from the frontier west, to the big farms of the heartland, to the poverty the rural south.

There is a need for flexibility in the delivery of health services in rural communities. It must be possible for rural hospitals to build linkages with public health systems and other community based entities such as Home Health and Nursing Homes. In my home state of Georgia there are over 150 counties all with public health departments locally. In many of these rural communities the health department is the mainstay for health care. Flexibility for public health and other agencies as well as flexibility for rural hospitals to expand services to include primary and preventive health care and to be able to use swing beds as needed would be extremely important. Communities need technical assistance to assist in building the leadership and infrastructure necessary to carry out these associations between the public and private systems.

Prevention and Health Promotion

Nurse practitioners strongly support and advocate for a balance between illness care and a strong prevention and wellness focus to health care services. In fact, nurse practitioners are exceedingly well prepared to take the lead in this arena. Public health initiatives can certainly help us to build this better balance between illness and prevention. There is a need for school based clinics for children of all ages (K-12) in order to build an infrastructure for prevention and wellness lifestyles early on. In Georgia, we are confronting increasing levels of teen age pregnancy with high risk infants.

Supply and Demand for Nurse Practitioners in Rural Areas

The demand for nurse practitioners has risen sharply. There is short supply and a potential future shortage of health care providers ill rural America. The demand is outstripping our ability to meet it. A conservative estimate is that there are 4 to 5 jobs to every nurse practitioner. This supply problem is worse in rural areas and even more severe if we consider migrant care, prison care and the spiral of substance abuse, violence and AIDS in rural communities.

Rural areas in the south are riddled with poverty. Our rural areas in south Georgia are experiencing unprecedented increases in AIDS and sexually transmitted diseases secondary to crack cocaine abuse. In fact, AIDS in rural, young heterosexuals quoted at 300% increase, the fastest AIDS population growth in Georgia.

The demand for health services is steadily increasing. There is a need to create incentives, including financial incentives for health care providers who serve in rural areas at all levels. Physicians as well as non-physician providers need supporting personnel in order to practice. There is serious concern on the part of many people, and rightly so, that nurse practitioners will follow their physician colleagues into larger communities where the system is more stable and financial and supportive networks are in place. There needs to be incentives to rural based providers—tax incentives, and fiscal incentives such as those outlined by the Clinton plan. However, this will require new appropriations by Congress. We need to be sure that these funds are appropriated.

Key Barriers to Nurse Practitioner Practice in Health Care Reform

Nurse Practitioners advocate for universal access to health care for all and for the removal of barriers to consumer access to nurse practitioner care. We especially want to be viewed as legitimate providers of health care. Virtually every study of patient care by providers other than MDs has concluded that nurse practitioners can deliver services at the same quality as family physicians.

Economic competition and professional turf issues between NP's and other professional providers is evident and is cause for inequities for nurse practitioner practice. Over the years, it has become increasingly clear to me that grassroots providers at all levels in rural practice have a fine and productive professional relationship. The system breaks down at the higher levels of state and national association and in the policy arena. The most important issue to rural health care reform is the ability of mid-levels to practice their trade.

The barriers to nurse practitioner practice need to be lifted across all fronts. not just rural. In order to make the significant changes to our system needed for health care reform we will need a full compliment of nurse practitioners in all primary care settings, both urban and rural. Non-physician provider barriers are regulatory and supervisory and greatly hamper the nurse practitioners ability to diagnose and manage patients. Many states have softened regulations on NP prescriptive privilege, admitting, physician supervision, and reimbursement. But, there is a long way to go especially in the conservative rural south where restrictions are the most severe and the need for providers is the greatest.

Managed Competition

There is concern within the nurse practitioner community that nurse practitioners will be locked out as primary care providers within the new structure of purchasing networks. Congress needs to provide anti-competitive protection for nurse practitioners to ensure our inclusion. My understanding is that we were not listed in the current legislation. This is a major concern, from a rural standpoint, because we don't know how rural communities will fare as the plan is implemented from state to state. An example, from my own experience, is that in rural Georgia by far, the most common model is that of a sole private physician practice in a rural community. The majority of these physicians are nearing retirement age. How will these small rural communities, who have few resources, make the transition? From my personal experience, in Georgia, it is clear that this is a very appropriate setting for nurse practitioners.

Education of Nurse Practitioners for Rural Practice

My years directing the family nurse practitioner program at Georgia Southern have helped me to understand how important it is to be able to recruit nurses from their rural home communities in the hope that they will return home to practice. This is especially true of nurses who have families and children. The mean age of our student FNP's is 35 years and it is very important that we focus on their adult learning needs if we hope to use them to fill our need for rural providers. We must be able to recruit and educate nurses within their home based rural community— to build rural, culturally sensitive curricula and to offer clinical experiences within the rural setting. All rural health care providers, including nurse practitioners, work in isolation and need strong preparation for their role.

There is a marked lack of access both for primary programs and continuing education. Distance learning models, especially interdisciplinary approaches to education for health care providers, and career laddering are some approaches that need to be considered.

I am cautious about the GME dollars. Although my understanding is that the sharing of GME moneys with advanced nursing education will be put back into the Clinton plan. we must he sure that these pass through funds are targeted to rural community hospitals and agencies that can offer rural clinical experiences to nurse practitioners.

The demand for clinically expert nurse practitioner educators is crucial. There is a serious need to re-tool nursing faculty, especially those who prepare rural based nurses to become nurse practitioners. In my own program, it takes me 2-3 years to recruit a nurse practitioner faculty member. Both recruitment and retention are a serious problem across the country and mirrors the pattern seen with all rural health care professionals. Existing nurse faculty need further training to become NP educators. Their role as role models in rural clinical settings is critical.

We know that there are more Associate Degree nurses in rural areas, so if we hope to prepare needed nurse practitioners, nurse anesthetists and certified nurse midwives for rural practice, we must make it easier for them to attain the Baccalaureate and go on to graduate study. This could be done through distance learning modalities. Minority and bilingual nurse practitioners are critically needed in the rural south and there needs to be initiatives to support this education.

NP's support the expansion of the National Health Service Corps with a 20% set-aside for non-physicians. There is concern that the model which is built for medicine does not meet the needs for nurses, predominately women, who are land locked to their home communities by family commitments but could be eligible with a change in criteria. CNM's—low number of placement sites for CNM's. Also, the number of placement sites for CNM's in the NHSC is very limited. CNM's payment limited to maternity cycle precludes offering full spectrum preventive care for women which is sorely needed in rural areas.

In terms of health care reform, our job as nurse educators is to teach our nurse practitioners to understand concepts associated with managed care, managed competition, risk management, marketing and how they can position themselves to be part of a managed care system. We need to ensure that we are building a collaborative system that supports both providers and consumers of health care.

Thank you for inviting me to speak before you today. I am happy to respond to questions or to assist the committee in any way that would be appropriate.

Senator HARKIN. Frances Hoffman, chief executive officer at Franklin General Hospital in Hampton, Iowa. Welcome.

Ms. HOFFMAN. Thank you for inviting me to come today, and thank you, Senator Harkin, for stepping in and helping us with a few regulation difficulties we have run into.

I come from a community of about 4,200 people, Hampton, IA. My hospital has 40 acute care beds and 52 nursing home beds, and we are half-owner with another hospital of two physician family practice clinics in the county. The county population is about 12,000.

I have been asked to give my thoughts on the effects of President Clinton's proposal on rural hospitals. I think there is a great deal that is very positive in that proposal—universal coverage, simplified paperwork. The concept of integrating health care providers I think is something that can work very effectively. I am part, my hospital is part of an integrated network in north central Iowa. We share equipment, we share staff, and I would be happy to describe that in more detail if you have questions later.

The emphasis of primary and preventive care is crucial to any kind of health care reform.

I do not in any way want to diminish the importance of those very positive aspects of the proposal, but my chief concern in coming today is with regard to the Medicare piece of it, or rather, the lack of a Medicare piece of reform.

My hospital serves a population of which 21 percent are over age 65, and the fastest growing piece of that population is over 85. These are big consumers of health care. Seventy-five percent of the patients who come to my hospital come under Medicare. We serve those patients at charge structures that are below the mean in a State that is the fifth-lowest charge State in the Union. So we are offering good quality care at a very reasonable price.

In addition to that, we offer people care by their neighbors. I think that is a very important aspect of people getting well quickly, that they feel the care and concern of the folks who are talking care of them.

If we are not able to keep our hospital open, we will be seeing 75, 85, 95-year-old people having to travel 60 miles roundtrip to the next local hospital where they can get care. They will probably put off that care until something reaches the crisis point, and then they will be a very expensive part of the health care system.

My board and I have taken significant actions this last year to try to assure that we will be able to continue to offer health care services in north Iowa and in our county. We have developed a joint venture, as I said earlier, with a private hospital to establish a clinic and to hire physicians so that we have more security that our physicians will stay with us.

We are working on assisted housing for the elderly in our community. We have an nursing home. We opened a rural health clinic to help an underserved area in our county.

All of these things are an effort to diversify and try to get into areas where we are not so heavily Medicare-dependent. But the reality is that we have a very elderly population, and there is no way to avoid a heavy dependence on Medicare.

Out of a $5 million budget for me this last year, nearly $1 million was written off as contractual allowances, the difference between what we charge and what Medicare was willing to pay to us. Two years ago, we lost Medicare-dependent status; that was $300,000. And while we have it back for an interim period, it cannot be budgeted because we will not have it for long. This last summer's budget cuts that took place, we translated into about another $400,000 of cuts at my hospital. I have working employees who are now on food stamps. So we are doing our bit; we are really trying, but there is a limit to how far we can go.

If you look at more money coming into the system as the result of coverage of uninsured people, the reality for me is that bad debt and charity care last year was only $58,000. So even if you covered all those people, $58,000 is not really going to make much of a dent.

We have reached the outer limits of what we are able to do within the confines that we have been given. We have taken positive action. We will continue to take positive action. There is no question that we need to have health care reform, and we are very supportive of that.

I think also, though, that all parts of the system have to be included to make this work. I think Medicare needs to be folded into any kind of health reform for this to work at all. Certainly, I would notice virtually no difference with the 75 percent population in my hospital if we did not include Medicare in the health care reforms.

So I guess my plea to you is to please fold Medicare into whatever proposals you plan to make, and help us to maintain very high-quality health care at a very reasonable price in rural areas.

Senator HARKIN. Thank you very much, Frances, for that fine testimony. I will have some questions for you.

[The prepared statement of Ms. Hoffman follows:]

PREPARED STATEMENT OF FRANCES HOFFMAN

Thank you for the opportunity to speak with you today.

My name is Frances Hoffman and I am the Chief Executive Officer of Franklin General Hospital in Hampton, Iowa—a community of 4200. My hospital has 40 acute care beds, 52 nursing home beds, and is half owner with another hospital of two family practice clinics. We serve a county with a population of 12,000.

I've been asked to give my thoughts on President Clinton's proposed health care reform and its impact on rural hospitals and the communities they serve. I think there is a great deal that is positive in this proposal.

First in importance is the emphasis on primary and preventive care. Health care is least expensive and most effective at the primary care level. My hospital emphasizes preventive screenings in addition to emergency services, surgery, and acute medical/surgical care. We recently purchased one of only a few mammography units in Iowa capable of visualizing dense breast tissue. We made this purchase because we want to provide the very highest quality of preventive care at reasonable prices close to home.

A second important positive step taken in the Clinton proposal is universal coverage. While very few people in my service area are without some kind of health care coverage, I believe this to be critical to health care reform.

Third is the concept of Accountable Health Plans or Integrated Delivery Systems. My hospital is part of a very effective regional, integrated system in north Iowa. The system includes eight hospitals, one community health center, fourteen primary care physician clinics, and one rural referral hospital. It covers 13 counties in north central Iowa. Recently, five of these hospitals developed a cataract surgery program where they jointly will purchase one set of equipment that will travel to each rural hospital with the surgeon on the day he comes to perform surgery. North Iowa Mercy Health Center, the rural referral hospital, made the initial investment and provided coordination of this service. It will be paid back as surgeries are performed over the next three years. Integration and cooperation work, especially in rural areas. I can now provide cataract surgery in my hospital and our older patients no longer have to travel 60 miles round-trip for this service. The network of hospitals also shares technical staff like physical therapists, laboratory technicians, and x-ray technicians. We share cost containment ideas and jointly develop policies for our hospitals.

Fourth is the need for simplified paperwork. We are all aware of how much money is wasted by the present multiple processing systems. I applaud the President's proposal to eliminate this area of waste.

These are all very positive aspects of President Clinton's proposal. The one very significant negative for rural health care is the proposal to reduce Medicare funding.

Of patients served by my hospital last year, 75% came under Medicare. Out of a $5 million budget, nearly $1 million had to be written off as Medicare contractual allowances, the difference between what we charge and what Medicare will pay. Well, you may say, it's just that your charges are too high. My charges are below the average in the fifth lowest charge state in the country. Last year, my hospital lost $300,000 as a result of Medicare Dependent Status being taken away. The budget cuts in Medicare enacted last summer resulted in another $400,000 reduction for us. That is $700,000 out of $5 million budget that already includes $1 million in Medicare contractual allowances. With these last cuts, some of my employees have had to go on food stamps.

Again, you may say, the coverage of uninsured patients will help make up for further reductions in Medicare. Last year, my hospital had only $57,596 in bad debt and charity care. And some of these people did have insurance but were unable or unwilling to pay copays or deductibles.

I want to encourage you to fold Medicare into any health care reform that is enacted. The reform proposal includes many positives. But if Medicare is not included, health reform will mean very little to my hospital.

My Board of Trustees and I have taken action to try to assure that Franklin General Hospital can continue to provide health care well into the future. We intend to survive. We are diversifying into clinic services that are not as dependent on Medicare reimbursement. We have rolled with every punch Medicare has dealt us—so far. But we are not able to do so without limit. Our population in Franklin County is 21% over the age of 65. The fastest growing part of the population is those 85 and older. We will be dependent on medicare funding whether we wish it or not. Loss of our hospital is a real possibility if further Medicare cuts are enacted. Hospital closure would result in a loss of emergency services. Without the ability to stabilize trauma and heart patients, there is a much increased chance that these patients won't make it alive to a referral center. Without a hospital, patients will have to travel 60 miles round trip to receive health care services. Many of our elderly citizens simply don't have the transportation to make such a trip, so they will go without health care services until they reach a crisis—usually an expensive crisis. Physicians prefer to work in communities with hospitals. We could very well lose our physicians if the hospital closes. Please held us to continue to provide high quality, low cost care to these elderly citizens. believe Medicare can and should be included in any health reform proposal. Thank you.

Senator HARKIN. Ron Nelson, a physician assistant at Cedar Springs Clinic in Cedar Springs, MI. Welcome.

Mr. NELSON. Thank you, Mr. Chairman and members of the committee.

Senator Harkin, like you, I also come from a rural community and was born and raised in a rural community. In that particular community, there was no hospital. We were delivered in a clinic and transported home by the local funeral home which ran the ambulance service. So I am sensitive to rural community issues.

I have had 16 years of experience practicing in a rural community, in a rural health clinic at this time, and currently serve as community services director for a community health center in a rural poor county in Michigan.

The focus of my remarks today is on the cost-based systems that exist in those rural communities. Specifically, the Rural Health Clinics Program, which as you know was enacted in 1977, was enacted to provide access to care in those rural communities. There were three basic criteria. They needed to be a nonurban or rural community. They needed to be staffed by physician assistants, nurse practitioners, or nurse midwives. And they needed to be designated as an underserved area.

The projection was that 2,000 clinics would occur. Of course, that did not occur; in the mid-1980's, there were less than 400 clinics. After several changes which occurred in the late 1980's, I am happy to report to you that today there are over 1,300 certified rural health clinics in the United States and an estimate of 1,500 will occur by the end of this year.

These clinics traditionally provide care to rural communities, which we all know have a high number of elderly and Medicaid-eligible individuals. The clinic that I work at in Cedar Springs provides care to a population of which 60 percent is Medicare or Medicaid-eligible.

One of the fastest growing areas that we have seen in this particular program has to do with small rural hospitals that are struggling with the inpatient census and declining utilization and who are recognizing this program as a mechanism to develop strong primary care-based programs to ensure health care delivery systems within their communities.

I have also been asked to comment on the rural outreach program which I serve as director for, with a community health center based in Baldwin, MI. This is one of the original community health centers based in a rural community. This program is funded under the rural outreach program through the Office of Rural Health Policy.

This particular program is a consortium model, using the local rural community hospital, the community health center and local public health, to deliver perinatal health care services to an underserved population of which the county where the family health center is located is the poorest in the State of Michigan.

This particular program uses the services of nurse practitioners, physician assistants, and nurse midwives to provide a range of services to individuals, focusing on perinatal health care. We are now providing approximately 40 percent of the obstetrical care in this rural underserved community. And I am happy to report that 90 percent of the women are entering into care in the first trimester of their pregnancies.

We are able to do this because of the cost-based reimbursement, and I think it is important as we look at the Health Security Act to consider the programs that exist there today. Specific to the Health Security Act, we are certainly encouraged by the "essential community provider" category. However, there are questions to be asked.

What happens after the 5 years? What happens to the cost-based methodology in this programs if I am in fact as a rural health clinic designated as an essential community provider?

The tax credit portion contained in the Health Security Act, we support. We believe this is important to maintaining recruitment and retention of quality-trained health care professionals in rural communities.

One of the areas that must be addressed and is addressed in the Health Security Act, however, that needs more specifics has to do with the supply of health care professionals in rural communities. We need to look at how we are going to provide additional training of other health care professionals, such as physician assistants, nurse practitioners, and certified nurse midwives. The focus needs to continue on primary care. However, as we have talked about with the graduate medical education dollars, there needs to be an opportunity to focus some dollars on training specifically in those rural communities.

We also support the bonus payment that is suggested in the program. However, it only affects physicians. It does not extend to other practitioners such as PAs, NPs, and certified nurse midwives.

We also heard from Dr. Lee about the National Health Service Corps expansion and a 20 percent set-aside to focus on nursing education. I do not see in that a focus on also addressing PA education or PA utilization within the National Health Service Corps in that category. We see the practice development initiative that talks about the write-offs for equipment, which is focused on physicians. There are many practices in rural communities today that are staffed, either community owned or owned by PAs and nurse practitioners, that could also benefit from similar tax write-offs for equipment. Is that going to be extended to them?

Finally, I would like to mention something that Senator Wellstone touched on earlier. There is a concern that stratification will occur. I am not convinced that the urban centers in an alliance plan have the sensitivities or the understanding of what happens in rural America to be able to effectively ensure that services are delivered in those rural communities. There are programs out there that are in fact providing that type of care. We currently have a total of about 3,000 programs between community health centers and rural health clinics that are providing care to underserved populations. The rural health clinics are all in nonurban and rural areas. That program needs to be preserved, and we need to look at the methodology as to how they are reimbursed to preserve its existence as a safety net in the rural communities.

I thank you for the opportunity to provide comments today, and I am available to answer questions.

Senator HARKIN. Thank you very much, Ron.

[The prepared statement of Mr. Nelson follows:]

Prepared Statement of Ron Nelson

SENATOR HARKIN AND MEMBERS OF THE COMMITTEE. AS A PHYSICIAN ASSISTANT AND RURAL HEALTH CLINIC PROVIDER WITH NEARLY 16 YEARS OF EXPERIENCE PRACTICING IN RURAL UNDERSERVED AREAS, I WANT TO THANK YOU FOR THIS OPPORTUNITY TO TESTIFY.

I AND MY COLLEAGUES IN THE RURAL HEALTH CLINICS COMMUNITY WELCOME THE HEALTH CARE REFORM EFFORT AND APPLAUD THE CLINTON ADMINISTRATION FOR BRINGING THIS ISSUE FRONT AND CENTER. FOR THOSE OF US WHO HAVE BEEN DELIVERING HEALTH CARE IN RURAL UNDERSERVED COMMUNITIES FOR MANY YEARS, THIS IS LONG OVERDUE.

MR. CHAIRMAN, IN ADDITION TO BEING A CLINICALLY PRACTICING PHYSICIAN ASSISTANT AT THE CEDAR SPRINGS RURAL HEALTH CLINIC, I ALSO SERVE AS THE PROJECT OFFICER FOR A PERI-NATAL PROGRAM FUNDED UNDER THE RURAL HEALTH OUTREACH GRANTS WHICH YOU HAVE CHAMPIONED AS CHAIRMAN OF THE LABOR-HHS APPROPRIATIONS SUBCOMMITTEE.

THE RURAL HEALTH CLINICS PROGRAM WAS ADOPTED BY CONGRESS IN 1977 AS AN EFFORT TO IMPROVE ACCESS TO HEALTH CARE IN RURAL UNDERSERVED AREAS THROUGH THE UTILIZATION OF PHYSICIAN ASSISTANTS AND NURSE PRACTITIONERS. FORMER SENATOR DICK CLARK FROM IOWA WAS THE LEADER IN THE SENATE, ALONG WITH SENATOR LEAHY, FOR THE ESTABLISHMENT OF THESE CLINICS. IN FACT, IT WAS THE SENATE AGRICULTURE COMMITTEE THAT HELD THE FIRST HEARINGS AND PROMOTED THE IDEA OF RURAL HEALTH CLINICS.

WHEN THE CONGRESS PASSED THE RURAL HEALTH CLINICS ACT, IT WAS EXPECTED THAT THERE WOULD BE NEARLY 2,000 FEDERALLY CERTIFIED RURAL HEALTH CLINICS UNFORTUNATELY, WE HAVE YET TO REACH THAT GOAL AND IT HAS ONLY BEEN WITHIN THE PAST FEW YEARS THAT WE HAVE EVEN BEGUN TO SEE ANY GROWTH IN THE PROGRAM. AND WHILE WE WELCOME THE HEALTH CARE REFORM EFFORT, WE ARE CONCERNED THAT IN THE DRIVE TO REFORM THE ENTIRE SYSTEM, THE RURAL HEALTH CLINICS PROGRAM WILL GET LOST IN THE SHUFFLE.

IN ORDER TO UNDERSTAND OUR CONCERNS, IT IS IMPORTANT TO UNDERSTAND WHY THE RURAL HEALTH CLINICS PROGRAM WORKS.

THERE ARE ESSENTIALLY THREE CRITERIA A CLINIC MUST MEET IN ORDER TO BE ELIGIBLE FOR RURAL HEALTH CLINIC STATUS:

1. THE CLINIC IS LOCATED IN A RURAL AREA (DEFINED AS 'NON-URBANIZED BY THE CENSUS BUREAU);

2. THE CLINIC IS LOCATED IN A MEDICALLY UNDERSERVED AREA, HEALTH PROFESSIONAL SHORTAGE AREA, OR GOVERNOR-DESIGNATED UNDERSERVED AREA

3. THE CLINIC HAS A PHYSICIAN ASSISTANT, NURSE PRACTITIONER OR CERTIFIED NURSE MIDWIFE ON-SITE AND AVAILABLE TO SEE PATIENTS AT LEAST 50% OF THE TIME THE CLINIC IS OPEN.

ONCE CERTIFIED AS A RURAL HEALTH CLINIC, THE CLINIC IS ELIGIBLE FOR COST-BASED REIMBURSEMENT FROM MEDICARE AND MEDICAID, RATHER THAN THE TRADITIONAL FEE-FOR-SERVICE.

WE BELIEVE THE COMBINATION OF RELYING ON PAs, NPs, OR CNMs AS A PRIMARY SOURCE OF HEALTH CARE DELIVERY AND PROVIDING COST-BASED MEDICARE AND MEDICAID REIMBURSEMENT RATHER THAN FEE-FOR-SERVICE IS WHAT MAKES HEALTH CARE DELIVERY VIABLE IN RURAL AREAS

AS YOU WELL KNOW, MR. CHAIRMAN, MANY RURAL COMMUNITIES, PARTICULARLY UNDERSERVED RURAL COMMUNITIES HAVE A DISPROPORTIONATE NUMBER OF ELDERLY AND POOR CONSEQUENTLY, MANY RURAL MEDICAL PRACTICES SERVE OVER 50% MEDICARE AND MEDICAID PATIENTS WITH MEDICAID OFTEN BEING THE DOMINANT OF THE TWO.

WE ALSO KNOW THAT TRADITIONALLY, MEDICARE AND MEDICAID PAYMENTS FOR PRIMARY CARE SERVICES HAVE BEEN QUITE LOW RELATIVE TO MORE TECHNICAL PROCEDURES FOR WHICH PAYMENTS ARE HIGHER. THE COMBINATION OF THESE TWO FACTORS HAS MEANT THAT IT HAS OFTEN BEEN VERY DIFFICULT TO SUSTAIN A RURAL PRACTICE USING A TRADITIONAL FEE-FOR-SERVICE PHYSICIAN MODEL.

THE REASON IS QUITE SIMPLE, MR. CHAIRMAN

WHEREAS A TRADITIONAL SOLO PHYSICIAN'S OFFICE IN AN URBAN OR SUBURBAN SETTING HAS THE POTENTIAL TO COST-SHIFT IT'S MEDICARE AND MEDICAID "LOSSES" TO PRIVATE PAYING PATIENTS WHO MAKE UP THE BULK OF THE PRACTICE, THIS OPPORTUNITY IS NOT AVAILABLE IN A RURAL UNDERSERVED PRACTICE BECAUSE THERE IS NOT A LARGE ENOUGH BASE OF PRIVATE PAYING PATIENTS TO SHIFT TO.

BY USING A COST-BASED APPROACH TO PAYMENT AND RELIANCE ON PHYSICIAN ASSISTANTS OR NURSE PRACTITIONERS, PRACTICES ARE ABLE TO MAINTAIN A LEVEL OF ECONOMIC VIABILITY THAT WOULD OTHERWISE NOT BE POSSIBLE.

HEALTH SECURITY ACT

THE HEALTH SECURITY ACT HAS MANY OF US CONCERNED ABOUT THE FUTURE OF THE RURAL HEALTH DELIVERY SYSTEM.

THE ADMINISTRATION HAS PROPOSED THE ESTABLISHMENT OF A NEW CATEGORY OF PROVIDER CALLED "ESSENTIAL COMMUNITY PROVIDER." A FEDERALLY CERTIFIED RURAL HEALTH CLINIC WOULD BE AUTOMATICALLY DEFINED AS AN ESSENTIAL COMMUNITY PROVIDER.

AS AN ESSENTIAL COMMUNITY PROVIDER, ALL HEALTH PLANS SEEKING TO SERVE PATIENTS IN AN ALLIANCE'S REGION WOULD BE REQUIRED TO CONTRACT WITH ALL RURAL HEALTH CLINICS IN THAT REGION FOR A FIVE YEAR PERIOD WE THINK THIS REQUIREMENT IS CRITICAL TO PROVIDING CONTINUITY OF CARE IN UNDERSERVED AREAS HOWEVER, WE ARE CONCERNED ABOUT WHAT HAPPENS AT THE END OF THE FIVE YEAR PERIOD

ACCORDING TO THE PLAN, AT THE END OF THE FIVE YEARS, CONGRESS WILL HAVE TO RECONSIDER THE WHOLE ESSENTIAL COMMUNITY PROVIDER ISSUE BASED UPON RECOMMENDATIONS FROM THE SECRETARY OF HEALTH AND HUMAN SERVICES. THIS LEAVES THE FUTURE UNCERTAIN FOR RURAL HEALTH CLINICS.

RURAL HEALTH CLINICS ARE ALSO CONCERNED ABOUT THE CONTINUATION OF COST-BASED REIMBURSEMENT UNDER MEDICARE AND MEDICAID. WE BELIEVE THAT COST-BASED REIMBURSEMENT FOR PRACTICES THAT ARE PRIMARY CARE ORIENTED AND PERFORM FEW PROCEDURES IS A VERY APPROPRIATE METHOD OF PAYMENT AND IS FAR PREFERABLE TO FEE-FOR-SERVICE.

UNDER COST-BASED PAYMENT, PRACTICES HAVE STRONG INCENTIVES TO PROVIDE PRIMARY CARE SERVICES. UNLIKE FEE-FOR-SERVICE, THERE IS NO INCENTIVE TO "UP CODE" OR ORDER UNNECESSARY TESTS BECAUSE IT DOES NOT CHANGE THE CLINIC'S PAYMENT. COST-BASED REIMBURSEMENT PLACES A PREMIUM ON PROVIDING CARE IN THE MOST COST-EFFECTIVE MANNER.

ALSO, GIVEN THE ATTITUDES OF SOME PRIVATE THIRD-PARTY PAYORS REGARDING PAYMENT FOR SERVICES PROVIDED BY PHYSICIAN ASSISTANTS AND NURSE PRACTITIONERS WE ARE CONCERNED THAT SOME ALLIANCE HEALTH PLANS WILL DISCONTINUE CONTRACTS WITH RURAL HEALTH CLINICS AT THE END OF THE FIVE YEAR PERIOD UNLESS SOME TYPE OF MANDATE CONTINUES.

I CAN TELL YOU FROM PERSONAL EXPERIENCE THAT THERE ARE MANY INSURANCE COMPANIES WHO REFUSE TO COVER THE MEDICALLY NECESSARY SERVICES OF PHYSICIAN ASSISTANTS AND NURSE PRACTITIONERS THAT ARE LEGALLY PROVIDED TO OUR PATIENTS. IN MY HOME STATE OF MICHIGAN, WE WERE FORCED TO GO TO THE LEGISLATURE TO MANDATE THAT BLUE CROSS/BLUE SHIELD OF MICHIGAN COVER PA SERVICES PROVIDED IN UNDERSERVED AREAS OF THE STATE. COLLEAGUES OF MINE IN IOWA TELL ME A SIMILAR SITUATION EXISTS WITH BLUE CROSS/BLUE SHIELD OF IOWA. INSURANCE COMPANIES COLLECT PREMIUMS FROM INDIVIDUALS THAT LIVE IN RURAL AREAS, BUT THEN DENY COVERAGE FOR MEDICALLY NECESSARY SERVICES PROVIDED BY THE ONLY HEALTH CARE PROVIDER IN THE COMMUNITY.

IT WOULD APPEAR THAT FOR THE FIRST FIVE YEARS OF THE HEALTH SECURITY ACT, THIS TYPE OF OUTRAGEOUS BEHAVIOR BY INSURANCE COMPANIES WOULD BE PROHIBITED. BUT WHAT HAPPENS AT THE END OF THE FIVE YEARS. WILL SOME HEALTH PLANS REVERT TO THEIR TRADITIONAL POSITION OF ONLY PAYING FOR PHYSICIAN SERVICES DELIVERED BY A PHYSICIAN? WILL FEDERALLY CERTIFIED RURAL HEALTH CLINICS BE DROPPED BY PLANS? IF THIS IS PERMITTED TO HAPPEN, HEALTH CARE DELIVERY IN RURAL AREAS WILL BE JEOPARDIZED MR. CHAIRMAN.

FUTURE OF RURAL HEALTH CLINICS

OVER THE PAST TWO YEARS, THERE HAS BEEN CONSIDERABLE INTEREST IN THE RURAL HEALTH CLINICS PROGRAM. MUCH OF THAT INTEREST IS BEING DRIVEN BY RURAL HOSPITALS. BY

ESTABLISHING HOSPITAL OWNED AND OPERATED RURAL HEALTH CLINICS, THE HOSPITALS ESTABLISH A STRONG, COST-EFFECTIVE PRIMARY CARE PRESENCE IN THE COMMUNITY.

I BELIEVE THE RURAL HEALTH CLINICS PROGRAM HOLDS THE ANSWER FOR MANY CHRONICALLY UNDERSERVED COMMUNITIES. WE HOPE HEALTH REFORM ENCOURAGES THE ESTABLISHMENT OF MORE RURAL HEALTH CLINICS AND ASSISTS IN STRENGTHENING THOSE ALREADY IN EXISTENCE.

MR CHAIRMAN, I WAS ALSO ASKED TO DISCUSS BRIEFLY THE RURAL HEALTH OUTREACH PROJECT I HELP RUN IN LAKE & NEWAYGO COUNTIES.

HEALTH BEGINNINGS WAS STARTED IN 1990 AS A COOPERATIVE EFFORT BETWEEN THE VARIOUS HEALTH CARE PROVIDERS, THE MICHIGAN DEPARTMENT OF HEALTH AND THE SCHOOL SYSTEM. THE LEAD AGENCY IS FAMILY HEALTH CARE,INC. A FEDERALLY CERTIFIED COMMUNITY HEALTH CENTER. THE GOAL OF THE PROGRAM IS TO IMPROVE ACCESS TO PERINATAL HEALTH CARE SERVICES IN THESE TWO RURAL COUNTIES.

LAKE COUNTY IS ONE OF THE POOREST COUNTIES IN MICHIGAN WITH AN AVERAGE PER CAPITA INCOME OF $9,996. NEWAYGO COUNTY, WHILE LARGER (POPULATION 39,000) AND AN AVERAGE PER CAPITA INCOME OF $11,693, IS NOT IN MUCH BETTER SHAPE ECONOMICALLY.

IN 1980, THERE WERE 12 PHYSICIANS DELIVERING BABIES IN LAKE AND NEWAYGO COUNTIES WHILE TODAY, THEY ARE SERVED BY ONE PRACTICING OBSTETRICIAN. LAKE COUNTY HAS A THREE-YEAR INFANT MORTALITY RATE OF 20.3 DEATHS PER 1,000 LIVE BIRTHS. THIS IS MORE THAN DOUBLE THE NATIONAL AVERAGE OF 10.3 PER 1,000. IN ADDITION, LAKE COUNTY RANKS FIRST IN THE STATE FOR PERCENTAGE OF POPULATION ON PUBLIC ASSISTANCE AND IN 1987, OVER 50% OF ALL DELIVERIES IN LAKE COUNTY WERE FINANCED THROUGH MEDICAID. FINALLY, THE TEEN PREGNANCY RATE IN LAKE COUNTY IS TWICE THE STATE AVERAGE.

BEGINNING IN LATE 1989, MANY OF US IN THE HEALTH CARE PROVIDER COMMUNITY BEGAN DISCUSSING THE PROBLEM OF TEENAGE PREGNANCY IN LAKE AND NEWAYGO COUNTIES AND THE ASSOCIATED PROBLEMS OF LOW BIRTHWEIGHT BABIES AND HIGH INFANT MORTALITY.

AT THIS PARTICULAR TIME I WAS ALSO VERY ACTIVE IN THE AMERICAN ACADEMY OF PHYSICIAN ASSISTANTS AND BECAME AWARE OF THE RURAL HEALTH OUTREACH GRANT PROGRAM. IN CONSULTATION WITH MY COLLEAGUES, WE DECIDED TO APPLY FOR AN OUTREACH GRANT.

I WANT TO TAKE THIS OPPORTUNITY TO THANK YOU, MR. CHAIRMAN, FOR YOUR EFFORTS TO ESTABLISH THIS RURAL OUTREACH GRANT PROGRAM. IF IT HAD SERVED NO OTHER PURPOSE, IT BROUGHT TOGETHER VARIOUS ENTITIES IN THE COMMUNITY THAT HAD LITTLE CONTACT OVER THE YEARS.

IN 1990, WE SECURED THE INITIAL FUNDING FOR THE PROJECT.

THE CORNERSTONE OF THE PROJECT IS THE FAMILY HEALTH CARE PERINATAL CONSORTIUM. WITH FAMILY HEALTH CARE AS THE LEAD AGENCY, THE CLINIC PROVIDES STAFF, INCLUDING A NON-PHYSICIAN PROVIDER, A MATERNAL AND CHILD HEALTH NURSE, CLINICAL SOCIAL WORKER AND OTHER ALLIED HEALTH PERSONNEL.

THE GOAL OF THE CONSORTIUM IS TO IMPROVE PRENATAL CARE RECEIVED BY THE TARGET POPULATION WITH THE END RESULT BEING A 50% INCREASE IN PRENATAL VISITS BY PREGNANT TEENAGERS, FEWER LOW BIRTHWEIGHT BABIES, IMPROVED ACCESS TO WELL-CHILD CARE IN THE FIRST FIVE YEARS OF LIFE AND PROVISION OF PARENTING EDUCATION TO PREGNANT WOMEN AND NEW MOTHERS

WE ARE CURRENTLY IN THE LAST YEAR OF OUR THREE YEAR GRANT AND WE BELIEVE WE ARE HAVING A POSITIVE IMPACT. HEALTHY BEGINNINGS IS CURRENTLY DELIVERING 40% OF THE OBSTETRICAL CARE IN LAKE AND NEWAYGO COUNTIES. IN COOPERATION WITH THE COUNTY SCHOOL SYSTEM, WE ARE HELPING TEENAGE MOTHERS TO COMPLETE THEIR HIGH SCHOOL EDUCATION AND, WHERE POSSIBLE, ASSISTING WITH POST-SECONDARY EDUCATION. 90% OF OUR TARGET POPULATION IS ENTERING CARE DURING THE FIRST TRIMESTER OF PREGNANCY AND AS A RESULT, WE HAVE ALREADY SEEN A DROP IN THE INCIDENCE OF LOW BIRTHWEIGHT BABIES.

MORE IMPORTANT THAN JUST THE STATISTICS, MR. CHAIRMAN, IS THAT BECAUSE OF THE COST-BASED REIMBURSEMENT THAT IS AVAILABLE THROUGH THE BALDWIN COMMUNITY HEALTH CENTER, THIS PROJECT WILL CONTINUE AFTER THE GOVERNMENT GRANT HAS DISAPPEARED.

HAD THE RURAL OUTREACH GRANT NOT BEEN AVAILABLE, WE MIGHT NEVER HAVE ATTEMPTED TO PUT THIS CONSORTIUM TOGETHER IF IT WEREN'T FOR THE AVAILABILITY OF COST-BASED REIMBURSEMENT, WE COULDN'T AFFORD TO CONTINUE THIS PROGRAM.

MR. CHAIRMAN, YOUR SUPPORT FOR COST-BASED REIMBURSEMENT AND THE RURAL OUTREACH GRANT PROGRAMS IS GREATLY APPRECIATED AND WE HOPE THAT SUPPORT WILL CONTINUE AS WE UNDERTAKE THIS EFFORT TO REFORM OUR HEALTH CARE DELIVERY SYSTEM

I WOULD BE HAPPY TO ANSWER ANY QUESTIONS.

Senator HARKIN. I have to go out and visit with Congressman Volkmer for just a second on some pending legislation that is up today. I am going to recognize Senator Wofford for questions, and I will return, hopefully, within 5 minutes.

Senator Wofford.

Senator WOFFORD. Thank you, Senator.

I am sorry I missed some vital testimony earlier. My presence was needed in the Foreign Relations Committee to make a quorum on some urgent business they had. I especially regretted missing the oral testimony, although I have read the written testimony, of Frank Trembulak from the Geisinger Medical Center in Danville. I have visited Geisinger and seen their good work, this past August and on other occasions with them around Pennsylvania. They have been heralded as a real model of the kind of health delivery system we need in rural America, and I want to herald them once again today.

Let me begin by asking Frank a few questions that I think were not covered in your written testimony, or covered adequately for me. Could you describe the ways in which Geisinger has attracted and retained doctors and health care professionals in their rural clinics?

Mr. TREMBULAK. Yes, Senator, and thank you for your comments.

Generally, we have been able to attract primary care physicians and other specialists to our rural area through the group practice model, having a core of physicians to which the primary care practitioners can relate, seek consultation, and so forth. A challenge for us is to enhance that communication vehicle through technology like telecommunications and other ways of tying in our rural sites into the specialists, and also be able to communicate generally, transporting patient information from site to site, as there is a continuum of care that we are trying to establish in those areas.

So it is providing that clinical collegiality as an overall group; although that group is spread through a very broad geographic area in Pennsylvania, that is key to that success.

Senator WOFFORD. You are in 30-some counties?

Mr. TREMBULAK. We are in 31 different counties. However, we are finding the ability to recruit primary care clinicians has become extremely difficult even in recent months, where we now have over 66 vacancies for primary care physicians.

Senator WOFFORD. Many have been arguing that it is very difficult to establish managed care plans in rural areas. Pennsylvania has a greater rural population than any other State, and you have done just that, organized a managed care plan in rural areas. Can you give us any more clues on what to do, and what is the source of your success in developing a larger rural patient base?

Mr. TREMBULAK. From the standpoint of the health plan, the health maintenance organization, that was originally established in 1972 under a grant from then HEW to see if actually, a health maintenance organization could be viable in a rural community. And we had that plan in operation for more than 13 years, primarily in the Danville area, a community of 7,000 people. We then expanded that program through our service area, which is now licensed in 25 of our 31 counties that we consider our service area. And again, the nucleus and the ability to spread that plan was through the integration of our physicians and our hospitals, as well as relating and being able to work with 13 other hospitals and over 400 other clinicians throughout the service area.

Developing that network and the integration of the network and the ability to service patients in a continuum of care provided that basis, and therefore allowed, if you will, the financing vehicle to be very cost-effective, in that we are the lowest-cost health plan in the areas we serve, and we enjoy a significant premium differential. So we are able to provide that service, work with the clinicians by providing information in a positive gatekeeper role—where the previous presenter talked about gatekeeping and the potential negative effects—providing information to help them enhance their practice.

Senator WOFFORD. One more Pennsylvania-focused question. From your experience, could you tell us about the ratio of primary care providers to specialists at Geisinger? Do you think that is about the right ratio, and what do you think about the President's recommendations for training more primary care providers? That is a question that other members of the panel may wish to comment on, too.

Mr. TREMBULAK. The Geisinger organization, since its founding in 1915, was founded as a regional medical center with a multispecialty group practice and grew up for the first 65, 70 years of its tradition as a tertiary care referral center. It was not until the late 1970's that we actually moved forward into developing primary care and alternative providers of care. We are now aggressively moving in this vein, as we feel that the primary care delivery is the key to successful delivery and also the key to education and preventive care.

Currently, our ratio is somewhere in the neighborhood of about 30 to 35 percent primary care physicians in our organization. That does not include the physician assistants, the midwives, and the nurse practitioners we have, who number somewhere in the neighborhood of 120 other staff members.

We really feel that that ratio is low; we would actually like to see the primary care delivery aspect of our organization reach somewhere in the neighborhood of at least 60 to 65 percent of our overall physician complement and delivery complement, and we are striving and pushing very aggressively to do that, although we are doing it not just from the standpoint of attempting to employ those individuals, but we are also doing that by relating and affiliating with other physicians who currently exist in rural communities and assisting them with their practices.

As far as training, we feel it is imperative to move the focus of physician training to primary care. We are somewhat skeptical of the receptivity of the academic medical centers to move quickly in this regard, but it is a challenge, and also, the aspect of the academic medical centers perhaps beginning to work with clinicians to provide retraining of currently practicing specialists to see if they are interested and willing to go back and brush up on primary care skills, and actually look at that as a method of also expanding the primary physician base.

So we encourage that activity. Right now, we are seeing—and I mentioned this in my verbal testimony—the fact that the competition is growing, the salaries, and the price competition to acquire primary care physicians is extraordinary. Even though there are incentives within the Health Security Act for physicians to locate in rural communities, if in fact the numbers are not there, there is still the potential that urban areas and urban organization health plans can still ante up the dollars to attract these people from rural areas.

So I think there are some good thoughts, but we need to work harder in refining those to secure that manpower.

Senator WOFFORD. Does anyone else in the panel want to comment on the ratio of primary to specialists?

Ms. HOFFMAN. I would not be able to give you a number, but I can tell you in north Iowa—I am guessing—it might be similar to Geisinger. It is not nearly enough, and it is extremely difficult to recruit physicians into rural areas.

Senator WOFFORD. I heard one of you talk about the question of folding Medicare into the alliances, into the proposed new plan. I may have missed the testimony of others, but I would be interested in any additional comments you may have on whether Medicare should from the beginning be folded into the alliances, whether it should be done faster than the President proposes, whether the gradual method of, as you turn age 65, having the election, whether that makes sense.

Mr. TREMBULAK. Senator, I would just say that I offered in my verbal testimony the fact that we do not believe that the financing of the Health Security Act, excluding Medicare beneficiaries and other beneficiaries for VA and other programs, is going to be at all viable. Therefore, we support the folding in of these other beneficiaries, particularly Medicare, and a way to perhaps transition that is to move quickly into the aspect of refining the current Medicare risk contracting rules and regulations, simplifying those, assuring more equitable payment, and allowing those beneficiaries to participate fully under this type of universal coverage program. To have multiple variations or tiers of a program just does not make sense.

Mr. NELSON. Senator, we are also concerned from the rural health clinic program standpoint that if the Medicare program is folded into the alliances, that we be concerned and careful as we look at the rural health clinic programs, which are currently receiving cost-based reimbursement, and how in fact those rural health clinics, which provide primary care services, will be able to continue to provide those services in the rural and underserved communities. Specifically, how do they interact with those alliances as Medicare is folded in.

That is a major concern that we believe is not yet totally addressed in the sole community provider category. So that is a concern that we see from the rural health clinic standpoint.

Ms. HANSON. One thing that I see as a patient provider, with the number of rural patients that I take care of, and that is a good thing in the plan, is the ability to reimburse for medications, because I see patients every day who cannot buy the medication after we prescribe it, especially hypertensive. So I think it is very important that we are going in that direction.

Ms. HOFFMAN. To speak specifically to the concept of phasing a program in, I think, at least for a lot of the hospitals that I am familiar with in Iowa, we will be dead and gone by the time Medicare is folded in if it takes any period of time at all.

Dr. THOMPSON. Senator, to add a comment, I asked my local hospital administrator before I came if he had any thoughts on this. He said please emphasize that the underinsured, as Frances said, are not our biggest problem. It is the underpaid Medicare and Medicaid patient. That is what is killing rural hospitals.

Senator HARKIN. That is right. I do not know how we are going to get that point through, but that is exactly right. That is the biggest problem we have.

Ms. HOFFMAN. If I might just give one example, on outpatient services for physical therapy, the formula used by Medicare to reimburse us guarantees that we will never have our costs covered. We are at about 85 percent of what it costs us to provide that service right now, according to the formulas that Medicare uses.

Senator WOFFORD. The other question I was going to ask is about the payment and reimbursement provisions of the fee-for-service plans in the alliance. There is to be a negotiated fee schedule by the alliances for fee-for-service plans.

Are you comfortable with this aspect of the plan, and will this control costs? Is this the best way to proceed?

Mr. NELSON. I think there is a concern, as a practitioner and as a physician assistant, that that plan cover all providers. Senator Harkin touched on that when Dr. Lee was testifying.

I had an experience recently in Michigan of having to work very hard to pass legislation to mandate that current insurance companies cover the services of physician assistants in practice settings. A concern is that those particular alliance plans, whatever fee schedule is developed, must cover all of the qualified providers in the delivery of service.

I was concerned in earlier discussion that there seemed to be a feeling that, well, all nurse practitioners and physician assistants work in group practices. That is not the case. As many of you know, in many rural communities, they may be the sole community provider out there. And that is where we have to be careful as we look at the health alliance, not to exclude those providers as a covered provider in those fee-for-service programs.

Ms. HANSON. And further, before this can even happen, even thinking about putting them in, we have to get the barriers removed that they are already trying to practice under. If we cannot prescribe, if we cannot get reimbursed, if we cannot have a mechanism to admit patients if they need to be admitted or referred to specialists if they need to be referred, then no matter how many people we put out, or how nicely we craft the system, if the providers that are being prepared to provide cannot provide, then we have not done our job.

Dr. THOMPSON. I have another addition to that. I certainly recognize the team approach. In fact, I have a physician assistant joining my practice in March. I would like to also speak to the counter of that. That is, some of the Federal programs that we have experienced actually penalize you if you have not yet been able to recruit a physician assistant or a nurse practitioner, which has made it very hard for us to work to recruit them further. Rural health clinic statutes and so on—we are not eligible for that until we have a PA or a nurse practitioner on staff. It is very hard to recruit for that when you do not have that status designated.

So it is kind of a Catch-22, which is the flip side of the problem they are discussing.

Senator HARKIN. I do not think I understand that.

Dr. THOMPSON. OK. As a physician in a practice, I am not eligible for rural health clinic status, even though the area is, the population is, and so on, until I have a physician assistant or a nurse practitioner in my employ.

Ms. HANSON. That is the way that legislation is.

Mr. NELSON. I would like to clarify that. That is based upon the fact that the requirement of the legislation is that a mid-level, i.e., a physician assistant, nurse practitioner or nurse midwife, staff the clinic 50 percent of the time. However, in OBRA 1989—I believe I have the year correct—there was an amendment that allows the physician to apply for a one-year waiver. And for the first year, you can apply for a waiver if you document within 90 days prior to the time you apply that you have been attempting to recruit a mid-level; for the first year, you can establish a rural health clinic with a waiver and not have a PA, NP, or nurse midwife. That is specifically in legislation and is being done every day.

Dr. THOMPSON. However, the fact of the matter is we were not granted that year waiver. We asked for it, and it was not granted. So there is some discrepancy, apparently, in how things are being applied.

Senator HARKIN. Did you say you brought on a physician assistant in March?

Dr. THOMPSON. We will be having one join us in March. I lost my other physician to a metropolitan network.

Senator HARKIN. I know; I remember that very well. I have since talked to him.

I apologize for having had to step out. It is the end of the session, and there are a lot of bills that we have to keep our eye on.

I understand that Senator Wofford asked you about folding into Medicare into the plan. I guess my comment, and then perhaps a question for all of you, is that this idea of one size fits all just is not going to work. I have been to Dr. Thompson's clinic. It is an interesting clinic. As he said, it is more than a doctor's office and less than a hospital. But what I liked about the idea is that in many rural areas, you do not need a full-time hospital, but you do have to have primary care services, which is what he provides, plus you have to have some emergency care services.

And I think it is a very cost-effective approach. I do not know of any others around like that. It is an interesting approach, and I am just wondering if some of our smaller rural hospitals, perhaps, those with less than 20 beds might evolve into something like that with some of our more metropolitan hospitals taking up the hospital care.

If you have looked, and I am sure you have, Dr. Thompson, at President Clinton's proposal and the alliances and so on, have you got a concept of how you will fit into this?

Dr. THOMPSON. I read the plan last week, and I have some question. Again, when you are unusual, and you cannot be pigeonholed, you oftentimes find that you are a place without a country. You do not fit the EACHs/PCHs program. You are a quote "for-profit entity" so you are not eligible for a lot of the community-based programs and grants and so forth. It is indeed very frustrating to try and evolve.

I think I would like to emphasize that it is not just my vision, but it is the vision of the nursing team that I have assembled and the other business personnel and medical assistants. They all share that dream that it is a doable job, and they could all be working somewhere else for more, too.

We can do it. It is a cost-effective method. The problem is your sanity falls into question when you could be working less hours less stressfully somewhere else for more pay. That is ultimately the problem in recruitment. But with appropriate modifications of that, without losing cost-effectiveness, that could be corrected.

And it has been especially borne out where we are at. Sure, there is a hospital 20 miles away—and by the way, I want to point out we work very synergistically with our hospitals. I have hospital privileges and deliver babies and so on there. We are not meant to be competitive or replace them. But there are people who will not make the grade 20 miles. They will arrive in a lot worse shape, or they will die before they get there. That is the role we play, that stabilization—or, as someone said earlier about gatekeeping, in a positive way, we figure out where they need to be, and if they need a neurosurgeon or a chest surgeon, we stabilize them and fly them out to the area that has that.

So I am not sure—the plan that I read is so general yet—I am not sure where we would fit. It would be nice if there were some allowance—they talk about the academic teaching centers developing networks, and perhaps we may fit into that, as we have trained residents before at our facility.

Senator HARKIN. Tell me about Geisinger. Maybe Senator Wofford already asked you this. How do you see yourselves fitting into this?

Mr. TREMBULAK. We are presently working with a number of hospitals and physicians throughout our service area. On the hospital side, there are several community hospitals that are just not able to continue to exist as full-service hospitals. Their communities are very concerned, and they have now agreed that they need to restructure those hospitals into kind of a full-service-type clinic or emergency center-type program. And we would work with them in doing that. The problems that we are encountering in trying to plan that is the capital necessary to make that conversion for that hospital, and the community is looking at how it can raise the funds, and also then organizing the existing staff—and in some communities, the staff is an elderly staff, so we are looking at how we can supplement that staff by recruiting other physicians to the community.

So we are trying to work where there are several examples where the hospitals can no longer make it—either their census is so low, or they are small hospitals to start with—and they need to try to create another type of delivery.

Senator HARKIN. The reason I am interested in your testimony, and I have read it over, is that obviously, you are an HMO, and you are strictly rural—how many counties do you cover?

Mr. TREMBULAK. Thirty-one.

Senator HARKIN. You cover 31 counties. And yet obviously, you are doing quite well. And yet we hear that managed care systems will not be able to operate in rural areas.

Obviously, it is viable, and not only are you providing the care, but you also provide health education, and conduct research as well.

Mr. TREMBULAK. Yes, sir.

Senator HARKIN. So what is your secret? Why are you able to violate the normally accepted concept that HMOs cannot operate in rural areas?

Mr. TREMBULAK. I think the foundation—and I addressed this somewhat for Senator Wofford—is that fact that at our base is trying to already integrate our physicians and our other services so we had the nucleus of a delivery system. We have continued to grow and work that that delivery system throughout our service area, incorporating other physicians who are non-Geisinger physicians and bringing them in affiliation, through the HMO in actuality, leading with the HMO, to enroll them, to capitate and take care of their populations.

Senator HARKIN. So are they similar to PPOs? Would they be preferred providers?

Mr. TREMBULAK. Yes; to that extent, we have a number of specialists and primary care physicians who join up as panelled physicians for our HMO. So they are, if you will, available and listed as preferred providers for us.

On the other hand, they do accept other coverages, and they participate with other plans that may be available. We have been successful. There have been numerous health plans that have been attempted in our area, primarily proprietary health plans, that have failed. The only health plans that have continued to thrive and, I believe, have been subsidized are the Blue Cross plans, and they have been subsidized through their indemnity programs.

So I think it ties back, again, to the efficient delivery of care and having the flexibility of having alternative delivery, alternative types of facilities of delivery, where you can then build your network.

Senator HARKIN. Go ahead, Charlene.

Ms. HANSON. I was just going to make a comment on that. In south Georgia, we have what we call the Woodpecker Trail Consortium, which is a group of hospitals that have banded together and, using some disproportionate care funds out of indigent care, are building ambulatory care and wellness centers and centers for the elderly. The key to that whole thing, as Mr. Trembulak says, is flexibility and the ability of the individual, unique community to do it the way it works in their area and not needing to make it fit into a specific structure, because we have different strengths in each community and different caregivers, so it has to be a very loose model that can fit for that particular area. But it does work.

Senator HARKIN. Finally, Ron, you mentioned in your written testimony the rural outreach grant program that you have utilized.

Are there outcomes that we have seen through this program? Do we want to incorporate or to use some of the things that we have learned in the rural outreach program in this health reform bill?

Mr. NELSON. I think that information is beginning to come in. We were in the first cycle of the rural outreach grant program, which is now in its third year, and those were 3-year grants. I believe there were over 100 grants awarded in that first cycle. And we are now beginning to see that information and data come in about the kinds of unique and creative methodologies that were used to provide rural health care. I believe that that is some information that may be beneficial and helpful as we look at the whole health care reform issue.

Senator HARKIN. Well, I am interested in looking at that data.

Mr. NELSON. I think this particular program is unique in that one of the things that we have established as a goal in that particular program is to deal with the poverty issue through education. So that we have set a goal for ourselves to have all of these young women complete a minimum of a high school education and vocational skills, or college-level courses. We have forged a partnership with the local community education program; we provide child care, transportation. And that has all really been facilitated through a coalition that was formed as a result of that rural outreach grant and using, then, the cost-based reimbursement methodology with the community health center to be able to have that program stand alone.

I am happy to report that at the end of the third year, it will be stand-alone in terms of supported by the fees that it generates on the cost-based methodology. Now, if health care reform takes away that cost-based methodology, I do not believe it will exist. In fact, I can assure you in its current scope, it will not be able to provide the range of outreach services because it will not have the revenue to support them.

Senator HARKIN. Interesting. Well, that is something that I want to look at through this committee as we continue to work on health care reform.

Mr. NELSON. Certainly.

Senator HARKIN. Harris, anything further?

Senator WOFFORD. No. Thank you.

Senator HARKIN. Thank you all very much for being here. We appreciate it. Thank you.

We will call the third panel to the witness table. We welcome Jim Bernstein, director of the Office of Rural Health and Resource Development in Raleigh, NC. I understand he will be commenting on the training, recruitment and retention of rural health care providers.

Carol Miller is the president of the New Mexico Public Health Association. She is from Ojo Sarco, NM, and last spring served on the White House Task Force on Health Care Reform.

And Mr. Steve McDowell is director of the Integrated Community Health Development Project in Lawrence, KS. He is a former director of the Office of Rural Health in Kansas.

Thank you all very much for being here today. As I have said to the other panelists, we have your written testimony, which will be made a part of the record in its entirety.

I will recognize you in the order in which I called your names. Mr. Bernstein, please proceed.

STATEMENTS OF JIM D. BERNSTEIN, DIRECTOR, OFFICE OF RURAL HEALTH AND RESOURCE DEVELOPMENT, RALEIGH, NC; CAROL MILLER, PRESIDENT, NEW MEXICO PUBLIC HEALTH ASSOCIATION, OJO SARCO, NM; AND STEVE MCDOWELL, DIRECTOR, INTEGRATED COMMUNITY HEALTH DEVELOPMENT PROJECT, LAWRENCE, KS

Mr. BERNSTEIN. Mr. Chairman, thank you for inviting me.

I have been working in rural health for 25 years. Our office in Raleigh, NC has helped to establish 55 community health centers in rural areas of North Carolina. Along with the Federal community health centers, we have a network or an infrastructure of over 80 centers in small communities around the State. We also recruit physicians, and we have recruited over 1,100 of them since we started our office in the 1970's.

I would like to hit upon eight issues very quickly, if I may, relating to health reform. First, I want to say that I am really supportive of the health plan. Universal coverage is essential in any meaningful health reform proposal, and as you pointed out, it is particularly important for rural areas where we have a disproportionate share of people who are uninsured.

The package developed in the plan I think is fair and equitable, and there is recognition of the special needs of rural and underserved areas.

Second, I support President Clinton's attempt to systematize the Nation's expensive and ever growing medical training expenditures. We put billions of State and Federal dollars into the system every year, and I do not think we are getting our money's worth in that investment right now.

I can say from my 25 years' experience in primary care that one thing we have learned is that just increasing the supply does not necessarily solve the problem.

We pioneered the use of physician assistants and nurse practitioners in community practice in the early 1970's, and as a matter of fact, all of our health centers were run exclusively by nurse practitioners and physician assistants in the 1970's. We used to identify local people, bring them back to the university, train them, put them back into their communities as providers, and that system worked very well.

Then, the schools, particularly the nursing schools, assumed the pattern of the medical schools, and in their entrance requirements, they emphasized GPAs and research and did not care particularly where the applicant came from or what the applicant was going to do when the applicant was through training. And as you can guess, we have the same problem with those schools as we do with the medical schools.

The push for greater use of PAs and NPs has created a strange alliance between groups that earnestly care about expanding PA and nurse practitioner practice, and subspecialists who would gladly hand over primary care to nonphysicians if that means they can keep the status quo and leave medical education unreformed and focused on specialties.

It is clear we need significantly more numbers of nurse practitioners and physician assistants. However, I would caution about how far we can go unless we have a good primary care physician base in rural areas. The physicians cannot take second call 6 nights in a row, even if they have five nurse practitioners or PAs working with them. So there is a balance, and it needs to be a team approach.

The third point I would like to hit on is loan repayment and other incentives. The bill has an extensive list, and I compliment them for putting them in the bill. But I think that the States and the Federal Government can go just so far in putting carrots in and sweetening the pot to get more nurse practitioners, physician assistants, and in particular, physicians, to practice in underserved areas. I think there is going to have to be some sort of a stick, and one of them might be what you were talking about earlier, Senator. It might be that a plan, in order to participate and have the middle class, wealthier people in the suburbs, and the more dense population as part of their plan, will have to provide good access in the rural areas that surround those cities. That could be one way to do it.

Another would be that we assess the plans that do not want to participate in rural areas some sort of a tax or risk assessment, and we put that money into rural networks.

The plan as it stands is not satisfactory. It does not define what sufficient access is at the Federal level. As you pointed out, it is not even clear whether the States could define it if they wanted to. It is very ambiguous. I think that piece needs a lot more work.

The fourth piece I would like to say something quickly about is the teaching hospitals. The teaching hospitals today that are turning out the family doctors, the primary care doctors, have changed their roles. They are now a player in a delivery system. Many of them are sort of like managing partners in competing delivery systems. Yet they control the supply of primary care doctors, and they are underwritten right now by DME and IME moneys and health profession moneys, and some States put State money into these programs. So what you have is a lot of public moneys underwriting training programs in hospitals where there is a tremendous incentive to retain those physicians in their own plan competing with the plan nextdoor.

So that piece needs to be looked at very carefully to make sure that everybody has fair access to the supply of physicians.

The next piece in the plan has to do with the role of academic medical centers. There is a small paragraph or some language about them providing TAs to develop networks. I have to say that I think academic medical centers are about the poorest choice we can pick to do that kind of work. So that needs to be looked at pretty carefully.

I also see that there is going to be a conflict of interest there because a lot of these academic medical centers are the same teaching hospitals I referred to earlier that have a vested interest in one or two particular networks.

Sixth, I am very concerned about the roles of the State and Federal Governments. The plan has some good ideas, but it is not consistent. It puts a lot of responsibility on the State Government to make sure everything works, and talks about what they will do if it does not work, cost containment and so on, but it does not transfer over the tools. It retains in its own hands at the Federal level the tools to effect some of the provisions in the plan.

For example, the moneys that Dr. Lee talked about for medically underserved populations, the $2.7 billion set-aside for the 5-year period 1995-2000, to develop consortia and qualified practice networks, does not say one word about the role of the States. If you want the States to participate in this, which you need to have happen in this kind of decentralized plan, you had better build a way for them to participate with the $2.7 billion.

The plan also has protection for essential community providers, but again gives no explicit role for the States in defining providers. To give you an idea of how far off I think they are right now, they define as areas that get special treatment medically underserved areas and medically underserved populations and designations. In North Carolina, 94 of our 100 counties are designed as MUPs. Well, I do not think we would decide that we want to put special emphasis on all 94 of our 100 counties in North Carolina.

So I would urge the Senate to look at the relationship between the Federal Government, the State Governments, the alliances, and the plans. It needs a little bit of work.

The seventh piece has to do with what Senator Wellstone brought up earlier, which has to do with the deductibles and copays for poor people. I personally feel like they are burdensome; they are obstacles to getting good care for people. Seventeen percent of households in North Carolina early less than $10,000 a year. We played out the sliding fee scale arrangement in the plan, and in terms of a family that makes $35,000, that would be the same as putting down $17 for each prescription, $33 for each doctor visit, $66 for dental care, and $83 for a mental health visit, proportionate to their income. I do not think that that is a fair plan.

And the last point was brought up by you, Senator Harkin, so I will not spend a lot of time on it. I think that taking the money from Medicare and Medicaid is going to disproportionately hurt rural areas, and the real reason for that is that they have a disproportionate share of Medicare beneficiaries in their service areas. Many of our hospitals, as you know, have 70 percent Medicare/Medicaid—mostly Medicare, actually—and if we start taking the money out of Medicare, they are going to be hurt the most.

I appreciate the opportunity to be here this morning and provide what I hope was constructive criticism, and I would be happy to answer questions later.

Senator HARKIN. Thank you very much, Mr. Bernstein.

[The prepared statement of Mr. Bernstein follows:]

PREPARED STATEMENT OF JAMES D. BERNSTEIN

I appreciate the opportunity to be here. My name is Jim Bernstein, and I serve as president-elect of the National Rural Health Association, a national membership organization that provides leadership on rural health issues and represents providers, consumers and academic centers working in rural health.

But I come here today not to speak for NRHA but to state a personal vision that I have formed since 1968, when I first began working in rural health as the director of a hospital and eight clinics in New Mexico.

I have served as the Director of the North Carolina Office of Rural Health and Resource Development since its inception in 1973. With modest state investment, through this Office, North Carolina has built a rural health infrastructure that utilizes physicians, physician assistants, nurse practitioners and nurse-midwives.

The Office staff have helped to develop 55 community-based, community-operated health care centers and has recruited more than 1,100 primary care physicians, nurse practitioners and physician assistants to rural and inner-city communities in our State. In the mid-1980s, we augmented our program to include technical assistance to small rural hospitals and we are currently the lead agency in North Carolina for the Essential Access Community Hospital Program.

Rural Health Problems

For more than 20 years, we have sought to address the many problems that continue to plague rural health today: significant barriers-financial, socioeconomic, and geographic-that block access to care; a fragmented system that impedes the development of sound health networks; shortage of primary care physicians, PAs, NPs and CNMs; a disproportionate share of fragile, vulnerable, isolated aged residents; lack of a sophisticated infrastructure for ancillary services, e.g. senior services; fragmented EMS services; difficult access to capital for bricks and mortar projects; and weak insurance markets.

There are many rural health success stories today, and health care access for rural people has greatly improved since the 1960s. But gaps and significant problems remain. Rural populations, which are complex and differ by region, cannot be ignored during this nation's important health reform debate.

I am supportive of the Clinton Health Reform Plan.

Universal coverage is essential in any meaningful health reform proposal. The Health Security Act marshalls a battery of resources to ensure the 37 million Americans not now covered will be covered.

The benefit package developed in the Clinton proposal is fair and equitable. Revaluing upward by 10% primary care work RVUs will help alleviate the disparity in specialist/generalist reimbursement.

There is recognition of the special needs of rural and underserved areas and the resources and incentives needed to help meet those special needs, e.g.: primary care workforce training and location incentives; consortia building and networking resources; premium subsidies for low income families; Medicare HPSA bonus program payments (refining the program and increasing the payments to 20% for primary care services are important actions and should create incentives significant enough to encourage primary care providers to locate in hard-to-recruit-for places); and tax credits for primary care providers locating in HPSAs.

Reforms in Workforce Issues and Medical Education

I support the Clinton Plan's attempt to systematize the nation's expensive and ever-growing medical training expenditures. Our nation's citizens pay billions in subsidies to schools that train physicians, nurses and other providers, yet this investment does not always address our needs. For example, students have increasingly by-passed primary health care in favor of higher-paying specialties, which tends to drive up costs. In the meantime, medically needy communities, both rural and urban, which could be best served by primary care providers, have severe shortages of medical personnel. In 20 years of experience in primary care, we have learned that merely increasing supply isn't enough.

Our office pioneered the use of PAs and NPs in community practice, and when we started centers in the early 1970s, they were exclusively staffed by NPs and PAs. We identified local nurses and others, and we helped to develop programs for them to obtain advanced training without leaving their home communities for extended periods of time. Today many of our nurse practitioner programs have assumed the pattern followed by our medical schools. Entrance requirements emphasize GPAs and interest in research rather than where the applicant came from and what type of practice he or she wishes to pursue after training.

The push for greater use of PA and NP practitioners has already created a strange alliance between groups that earnestly care about expanding PA and NP practice and subspecialists who would gladly hand over primary care to nonphysicians if that means they can keep the status quo and leave medical education unreformed and focused on specialties.

It is clear we need significantly more NPs and PAs providing primary care services. However, in the looming transition shortage of primary care providers I would be wary of becoming overly enthusiastic about future rural area expansions in primary care through a greater reliance on PAs and NPs. A critical mass of primary care physicians is needed in any area before PAs and NPs can be optimally utilized.

Like many states we have developed loan repayment and other incentives for NPs and PAs as well as for physicians using long and short term strategies. The Clinton Health Plan proposes a creative and comprehensive set of financial incentives to encourage providers to choose primary care and to practice in underserved rural and urban communities. However, simply providing more and more federal and state financial incentives will not in itself solve our distribution problem. The strength of the Plan's managed competition strategy to reform the delivery system is its emphasis on rational delivery systems. In order for rural areas to benefit from the strategy, the plans, as a condition of participation, must demonstrate that they can provide access to the entire health alliance population no matter where they reside. It appears to me that this issue is not dealt with satisfactorily in the Plan. Nor does the Plan provide sufficient direction to the states regarding "acceptable access."

Managed care has created an unexpected outgrowth in that teaching hospitals have become competing delivery systems. These hospitals have three important assets that will allow them great discretion in how local and regional health delivery changes under health reform. Many teaching hospitals: have sophisticated capacity to develop long-term, strategic planning; they have the money to allow them to sustain their long-term strategies; and they control the output of physicians.

The structure of DME and IME payments under Medicare or whatever new system is devised will determine the composition of the physician generalist/specialist production. Teaching hospitals thus by and large can develop their own feeder systems using their own graduates, subsidized by the federal government.

I am concerned about whether rural and underserved communities will be part of this system. Moreover, I am concerned about the integrity of the overall educational system.

I recommend that the Plan develop ways to evaluate and reward teaching programs based on how successful they are in producing generalists and in encouraging their graduates to practice in areas of need. Funding for medical education should be based on the performance of training programs using the above criteria. This performance-based rating should also apply for the training of physician assistants, nurse practitioners, and midwives.

Those training sites that do a good job of guiding graduates to serve in needy rural and urban communities should be rewarded for serving the needs of our nation.

State and Federal Roles

I am also concerned that the Plan remains inconsistent regarding the roles of State governments and the Federal government. In dividing responsibilities, the States are given heavy duties to insure that the Health Plans act equitably in covering all citizens. In assuring adequate access to a choice of Health Plans the State's responsibilities are quite significant.

Under Title III, Subtitle E., in the section on Medically Underserved Populations, the $2.7 billion set-aside (1995 to 2000) in grants and contracts are made through the Secretary's Office and are limited to 1) consortia of public or private health care providers and 2) qualified community practice networks. There is no role and no funding for the States indicated.

The Plan contains sound protection for "essential community providers," including CHCs, migrant health centers, and other public health service programs. Yet there is no explicit role for states to play in determining those providers.

The federal government retains, inappropriately I believe, important regulatory powers1 by being the sole designator of underserved areas that link local communities to important federal funding and by retaining discretion for funding the development of networks. Network participation is an essential activity for rural communities if they are to be fully and equitably integrated into the future health care system. States can and should play a big role in the development and support of local health systems.

In addition, I would like to see federal resources tied with greater priority to Health Professional Shortage Areas, a more restrictive designation than Medically Underserved Population (MUP). Medically Underserved Population (MP) designations are too broad and watered down to be the criteria for federal aid. Too many borderline communities would qualify. Ninety-four of our state's 100 counties currently are designated, in whole or part, as a MUP. In lieu of the MUP designation, I suggest the states be given the authority to designate additional underserved areas based on criteria approved by the Federal government.

Today in our unreformed health system, the roles of state and federal government agencies are for the most part clear and appropriate. As a former Governor, President Clinton undoubtedly would appreciate the desire and current role the States have to help local communities retain control over their health care systems. I urge the Senate to work with the President to eliminate inconsistencies and problems evident in the health plan that warp the relationship between the state and federal governments.

Copayments and Low- and Moderate-Income Families

I would like to comment on the deductible and financing issues of the Clinton Plan and how that impacts poor families. Most low- and moderate-income families are going to be forced into one or two low cost plans in their region. For example, about 10 percent of the households in North Carolina have annual incomes below $10,000/ and 27 percent have incomes between $10,000 and $25,000. These families will have no real ability to "vote with their feet" if the quality of their health plan is inadequate. Thus it is critical that if we are going to address the health care needs of the most vulnerable populations we must either provide additional premium subsidies to give everyone a meaningful choice of plans or we must stringently oversee the lowest cost plans to assure that they deliver high quality health care services.

Copayments under the plan may also be a burden for low and moderate income families. For example, based on the average N.C. household income, the $5, $10, $20 and $25 copayments of the low cost plan for a household living on $10,000/year are the equivalents for that household of paying $17 for each prescription drug, $33 for each doctor's visit, $66 for certain dental procedures and $83 for each mental health or substance abuse therapy session. These are costs that are obviously proportionately unaffordable for poor families stretching their monthly budgets.

The Plan must protect our State and our nation's most vulnerable populations if it is truly to be the American Health Security Act.

Medicare, Medicaid, and Rural Providers

Finally, I am concerned that the savings designed to be generated from the Medicare and Medicaid programs will disproportionately affect rural hospitals, physicians and other providers. In many rural practices and hospitals, 75 percent of the patients are covered by Medicare or Medicaid. Rural providers have struggled to survive in the 1980s. The $800M/year set aside as payments to hospitals serving vulnerable populations will surely assist many rural hospitals in need. However, the eligibility/entitlement methodology should probably be reviewed particularly for its impact on small, isolated hospitals.

I want to stress, that though I have expressed concerns about President Clinton's Health Security Act, I support this important and overdue legislation. President Clinton has done a wonderful job of balancing the extraordinary range of difficult issues involved in health care policy. However, this is an opportunity for constructive criticism, and I didn't want to give up my chance to put in some suggested changes. I would be happy to answer any questions.

Senator HARKIN. Carol Miller, welcome. Please proceed.

Ms. MILLER. Thank you, Mr. Chairman and Senators. I first want to thank you, Senator Harkin, because I served on the Health Care Task Force because of your staff who, when they went to work at the White House, noticed that there was no representation, or very little, from rural areas and insisted that there be some rural people actually brought in to work on it. I think that we would not have had any say on rural areas if it were not for your staff; so I want to especially thank you for that.

I really appreciate the opportunity to share my initial assessment of the President's Health Security Act of 1993 and how it is going to impact rural America. For the purposes of today, I am going to focus on a couple points, but there are a few other issues I want to raise that I hope I can add in later for written testimony—particularly problems with Title III, the public health initiatives, which are very disappointing, and I would be happy to answer questions about that later; Medicare and Medicaid—particularly Dr. Lee spoke this morning about incentives for rural physician recruitment, but when you actually read the section under Medicare, I cannot imagine who wrote it. I actually fell off my chair laughing when I got to that point, because it was ridiculous. It says that you can get an incentive for recruiting a physician into your community, but only if he is currently practicing less than a year in his current specialty and if he comes from more than 100 miles away and if he is not going to see more than 15 percent of his current patients. That takes away total incentives that some of us have. We are trying to create relationships with physicians in our State that we might be able to attract to our areas, and I do not know where this "more than 100 miles" comes from or what the purpose of it is.

It is interesting—the challenge of this bill to me is that the broad brush looks okay, but some of the details are just not going to work, and we really have to focus in on a lot of those details.

I also want to comment on the coverage of undocumented workers under the President's plan, which is not just a border issue. I feel it is something we have to take on as a nation what we are going to do, because this is a somewhat different situation. Many of these people are working and will actually be having payments for health insurance taken out of their pay checks, but they will not be able to access the system.

I think when we talked about moving to prepaid health care, this was not what we had in mind. We are talking about leaving millions of people prepaid with no access.

But because time is limited today, I am going to focus on two key issues for me. One is the development of the rural continuum, and the other is what I have called the ticking time bombs, which are the financing mechanisms for reform.

We are attempting to finance health care reform through cuts in Medicare. We are going to institutionalize historical spending and establishing our budgets, premiums, and subsidy levels, and we are capping the Federal subsidy.

I have been traveling around the United States quite a bait, and what I have been asking people to do is to identify the first image that they get when they think about "rural." Many people think about New England. It depends where they are from. Their image might be a New England commons, with a church with a white steeple. People from the Midwest think of that area. I think about places like New Mexico. I have been in Alaska a lot, and I think about Alaska.

How do we design a health care system that will meet the needs of so many different kinds of places? If we were Europe, these would be different countries. I mean, they are very far apart from each other, and everything about them is different—the kinds of people who live there and the kinds of health care systems that they have.

The reason I would like to talk about this continuum is that it allows these regional and community differences to be placed on the table and considered. I really do not think we want to have a generic shotgun approach to rural, because that will end up not meeting the needs of any rural community.

Actually, I mentioned to Dr. Lee this morning that I have coined a new word for the most populated rural areas, which is "ruburban," that I think we need on the other end of the spectrum, that is, the places that are not quite rural and not quite suburban.

And then we have rural the way we think of it—frontier and wilderness.

These are very different places, and the problems with the current same span the same continuum. The closer you are to an urban area, the more services you have, the better access, the easier it is to recruit providers.

I want to caution the committee and also all of us who are rural advocates, because there have been a number of us here today and there will be others of us at hearings, that when you hear someone talking about either in opposition to part of the plan or in favor of it, it is very important to find out where they are coming from, because they may have identified that in their community it will work perfectly just the way it is right now, whereas other people will have differences with it. I think it is going to be very hard to get a true rural consensus on this issue because the differences are there. And I do not think we should kid ourselves that it is going to be easy to achieve that. I can tell you that within some of the associations I am involved in, trying to achieve consensus on this health reform is a very painful process to go through. We are so different, and this is so important.

So I will tell you why my opinion is skewed on it and where I am coming from so you know, because I have worked in frontier New Mexico for a long time with clinics. We recently, to resubmit our Federal grant application, had to count our 2,900 patient records, and we found out that 76 percent of our patients had no insurance at all, and only 6 percent were covered by Medicaid. That is an extreme, but it is an extreme that exists in a lot of places.

When we talk about New Mexico, with 25 percent uninsured, we are talking about our urban areas having maybe 15 percent uninsured and our rural areas up to—no one has topped our 76 percent yet, so maybe we have got the worst.

And I want to say that even though I welcome the expansion of the National Health Service Corps, it took our community more than 5 years to recruit a physician even though that vacancy was a high-priority slot of the National Health Services Corps.

The Corps, when it was reauthorized a few years ago, provided more choice to physicians. And we did hear the case about—isn't it ridiculous—this woman wanted to work in a particular area, and the National Health Service Corps wanted to send her to Alaska. Well, I have to tell you that when people take Government money to get their medical education, I think there may be some obligation to actually go where they are most needed, even though I think maybe taking someone from a rural area and moving them to Alaska—I mean, I can see both sides of it, but I can tell you that in frontier New Mexico, frontier Wyoming, there are places where we would never get a physician unless the Federal Government told them that that was the last vacancy left and that that is where they are going. So we have to be very careful.

Just hearing about the numbers of increases does not assure me that the places I worry about will actually get any of the providers.

On the financing reform mechanisms, I think everyone in numerous hearings has already raised the issue of financing it on cutbacks on Medicare, so I am not going to go through that.

But I would like to talk about the use of historical cost factors, which is part of the Clinton plan, particularly Section 6006. What that section says is that in 7 years, a commission is going to somehow redistribute the financing in the country so that we can deal with the historical spending issue.

This was probably one of the only things that all of the task force members working on rural, in every policy paper and in every discussion, we had unanimous consent on. It was the only thing we ever achieved it on, was that we could not do the financing based on historical spending, that it would be absolutely deadly to rural areas.

So to open the plan, the legislation, and find that institutionalized in here——

Senator HARKIN. So you are saying your task force unanimously agreed on this, and yet it found its way into the plan anyway, on using the historical basis.

Ms. MILLER. Right. That is correct. We did not want it.

Senator HARKIN. I understand.

Ms. MILLER. It is here. We are stuck with it. And we are counting on Congress to correct that part of it, because what it does is it rewards the high-cost States. Their basic budget and their premiums are going to be set on that level. And actually, we need to turn the whole system upside-down. People talk about incentives that we are going to give rural providers, but we are not going to be given the financial resources to actually have those incentives. So I am very concerned about that, and we are really counting on Congress to help us with that.

We do not want to wait 7 years. Actually, by the end of the task force, we pulled all the rural people together into a rural cross-cutting group where we just looked at every issue. And we felt for an interim step that maybe we could average somehow or come up with a formula to take historical spending and look at a national per capita rate and blend the two as a way to equalize a little bit to get us where we need to go. I hope that Congress will definitely look into that, and I hope this committee will look at that as an interim step. Really, we have to turn the system upside-down. We need rural incentives and not urban incentives.

We did not do as good of a job as the academic medical centers in urban areas. They got special add-ons to help them. And yet all of the their rural advocacy, we lost this one, and I cannot stress it enoug .

It is a myth that rural spending is less—or, in fact it is less, because it is less because, as someone said, people get food stamps. Rural health care workers qualify for food stamps. Rural health care workers qualify for Medicaid, full-time workers.

We have a problem with low wages, and it is institutionalizing those wages in the system. At the same time that we are currently recruiting for a physician assistant, we have had people tell us they are expecting salaries of $90,000 to move to a rural area, because that is what they know they can make now in urban areas.

Rural providers are already at the edge of the financial cliff, and we have to have help, and we have to have it soon. The capping of the Federal subsidy is a serious concern. I discussed this with my congressional delegation before we even saw the legislation, because New Mexico, like other rural States, is a high subsidy States. We need the Federal subsidy for low-income families, unemployed, low-wage workers, seasonal workers, self-employed below 250 percent of poverty. And we are very worried that these subsidies are capped.

I guess I should have been suspicious in September——

Senator HARKIN. I am going to have to ask you to wrap up.

Ms. MILLER [continuing]. OK. Sorry about that.

Senator HARKIN. Go ahead and finish the point.

Ms. MILLER. In September, I asked Ira Magaziner at the final meeting of the Health Care Task Force how we could protect the subsidies. He told me they were going to be like an entitlement. And in the legislation, what they are is a capped entitlement, and I see what he meant. We really need to make sure that the subsidies are adequate. It is a very important issue.

I will conclude with that and be happy to answer questions.

Senator HARKIN. I appreciate that. Good testimony.

[The prepared testimony of Ms. Miller follows:]

PREPARED STATEMENT OF CAROL MILLER

Mr. Chairman and Members of the Committee, thank you very much for providing me this opportunity to share with you my initial assessment of how the President's Health Security Act of 1993 will impact rural America. I will be submitting additional concerns in writing later addressing problems with Title III. Public Health Initiatives, Title IV—Medicare and Medicaid, Section 4042.(f)(4) Physician Recruitment, and parts of Title I—Health Security.

Because time is limited today, I feel I must focus on only two key issues at this hearing: 1.) the development of an understanding of the rural continuum and 2.) what I call the ticking financing time bomb caused by the attempt to finance much of reform through cuts in Medicare, the institutionalization of historical spending in establishing budgets, premiums and subsidy levels for alliances and plans, and the capping of the federal subsidy.

The Rural Continuum

I would like to ask each of you to think about the first image that comes to mind when you think about rural America. Some of you will think about the idyllic small towns of New England, a green commons and a church with a white steeple. Others of you may think about the Midwest, green rolling hills covered by corn and dotted with red barns. Others will think of the west, open range, dry and made green in patches by irrigation, grazing cattle, mountains off in the distance. Since I have been traveling frequently to Alaska, I will think of the small isolated village hundreds of miles from anywhere. All of these—and even more that I haven't named—are part of what we commonly define as rural, each presents unique and very different challenges to the health care system and each will be impacted differently by health reform. Ours is a very large and diverse country and the challenge is in designing and supporting a health care system that provides all of us access to affordable, high quality health care.

The reason that like to talk about the rural continuum is that it allows these regional and community differences to be placed upon the table and considered rather than a generic, shotgun approach to rural with a capital "R" which ends up not meeting trip needs of any rural community. The way I define the continuum is a progression from rural to frontier to wilderness—moving from the most populated to the least populated. When I talk about rural health reform, I am speaking about the whole continuum and only using the generic term to save time. Problems with the current system follow this same continuum with more providers and access in rural areas, less in frontier, and almost none in the wilderness. One size fits all health reform will not work in rural America.

I must caution you, that when you hear rural advocates speaking in favor of or in opposition to various aspects of the Clinton and other health reform proposals, it is very important to find out where they are from because the rural movement spans the spectrum of opinion. For example, many rural advocates come from states which have good access even in rural areas, well established provider network and rates of uninsured as low as 10%. This is very different from my experience in frontier New Mexico where we have documented rates of uninsurance as high as 76% in a Community Health Center service area, where only 6% are covered by Medicaid, and where recruiting a doctor can take five years even when designated a high priority vacancy by the National Health Service Corps.

Reform Financing Mechanisms—Rural Friend or Foe

A. Financing reform through cuts in Medicare

Rural health care providers of Medicare Part A and Part B health services feel extremely threatened by the plans to finance much of health reform with cuts in the Medicare program. Because rural communities frequently have higher percentages of elderly residents, rural providers are more dependent on Medicare revenues than urban providers. Medicare recipients make up the majority of patients receiving inpatient care in rural hospitals and make up the majority of patients seen by rural health providers. Medicare already pays only 90 cents on the dollar. The plight of rural hospitals has been heard many times by this committee and other members of Congress. We must make sure that providers serving Medicare recipients are fairly compensated for the care. We can not afford a reformed system which continues cost shifting.

B. Institutionalization of historical cost factors in establishing budgets, premiums and subsidy levels for alliances and plans

I would like to ask this committee to carefully study Section 6006 (Health Security Act) Recommendations to Eliminate Regional Variations in Alliance Targets Due to Variation in Practice Patterns; Congressional Consideration. Every policy paper, tollgate, and meeting of the rural workgroups throughout the entire life of the Health Care Task Force unanimously rejected historical spending as a basis of establishing targets and budgets for the financing of health reform. Yet we lost this battle and Congress has been presented a bill which ignores our pleas for equitable payment.

Using historical spending as a starting point rewards the providers who have been the most costly in the past.

Differential payments based on historical spending already contributes to the shortage of health care providers in rural areas.

Using historical spending is double jeopardy for rural providers who have been paid less despite the fact that their unit costs are higher because they are not able to achieve volume savings or economies of scale.

Although rural historical spending has been lower than urban, it may need to be higher in order to assure geographic access to rural Americans. Recruitment and retention incentives will be necessary to expand the numbers of providers working in rural areas. Reimbursement in many rural communities will need to be cost-based rather than charge-based to fairly cover the cost of a rural practice and/or facility.

Section 6006. establishes a commission to report to the Congress on eliminating regional variations in alliance targets due to variations in practice patterns, historical variation among State Medicaid plans, State maintenance of effort payments for noncash assistance recipients and those that are attributable to historical differences. These differences will not be eliminated until the year 2002 and must remain budget neutral. Rural providers are already at the edge of the financial cliff. They cannot wait seven years for a Commission and Congress to compensate them fairly.

In order to assure the survival of the rural health care system during the transition to national health reform, a fair rate must be established before the implementation begins. One interim step may be to look at a transition formula which blends historical spending with a national per capita average.

C. Capping of the federal subsidy.

I come from New Mexico which is going to be a "high subsidy state," needing the Federal subsidy for low income families, the unemployed, low wage workers, seasonal workers, self-employed below 250% of poverty and the all of the other categories eligible for the Federal subsidy.

Title IX, Subtitle B, section 9102 Capped Federal Alliance Payments, describes a "Capped Entitlement" which sounds like an oxymoron to me. I am afraid that when health reform begins to cost more than anticipated and since the employer and individual shares are capped, that the only place to find additional funds will be through the Federal share—a ratcheting down of the subsidy and further cutbacks in Medicaid and Medicare, and the Public Health Initiatives.

I have worked in health care most of my life—as a provider, an administrator, and for County, State, and Federal government. While working on the Health Care Task Force wrote a paper entitled myth of Administrative Simplification. Based on more than 30 years of working in health care, I did not see any administrative simplification in the reform proposed by the President. More than 1000 pages of the Health Security Act create administrative complication, not simplification—establishment of alliances, certifications of plans, enrollment, collection of premiums and copayments, application for subsidies, end of year reconciliations for states, alliances, plans, providers, employers, and individuals. There are costs associated with all of these activities that could be used to pay for health care. I call on this committee and the Congress as a whole to simplify the steps. Let us think about how much structure we need between the person presenting a health security card to a provider and that provider being paid for the care.

I look forward to working with you to pass comprehensive health reform legislation—for all Americans—no later than 1994.

Senator HARKIN. Steve McDowell, project director of the Integrated Community Health Development Project in Lawrence, KS. Welcome.

Mr. MCDOWELL. Thank you, Senator. You have my written testimony, and I just want to try to highlight a little of that, in the interest of time.

The Integrated Community Health Development Project is a project funded by the Kansas Health Foundation, and it is working in 10 rural Kansas communities to build integrated systems of care to assure local access.

In each community, a cross-section of citizens have formed a working group to understand the changes in health care delivery, to try to come to a consensus on an appropriate scope of services for their community, and then to try to decide how to structure those services so that they can maintain access to care.

These rural communities have decided that, at a minimum, they need to have access to emergency services, primary care services, public health services, and community-based long-term care. Further, they have, after much struggle, come to the conclusion that they have got to integrate those delivery systems.

In planning for health reform in rural America, I think this point cannot be overstated, that the rural health care delivery system is not just a hospital or a practitioner or a public health department or an emergency service. Rather, a rural delivery system is just that—a system of care that coordinates and integrates local resources in order to minimize duplication, contain costs, and assure access.

I think that there are several specific problems with the Health Security Act. First, in an attempt to look at developing integration, there is the program called the Qualified Primary Care Network, or QPCN. However, the QPCN does not recognize the importance of integrating one of the most vital aspects of the rural delivery system, the emergency medical system, such as Dr. Thompson at Strawberry Point has been trying to do.

A second problem that I am concerned about, that has been addressed by some of the other participants here today, is that the Act, if you will, grandfathers in current categorical programs and existing delivery models and does not seem to recognize the need for any flexibility in the future for designing new systems. Development of alternative approaches has in many instances required exhaustive and often unsuccessful efforts to secure waivers of existing laws. Once again, Dr. Thompson said that in an attempt to become a rural health clinic, he could not get the waiver that he was trying for.

The Act's failure to allow positive change through innovative models, while in all probability an inadvertent oversight, places major barriers in the way of new programs to deliver health care more efficiently, and I believe should be corrected.

Another specific example is that in an attempt to be able to maintain care in rural areas, the plan proposes the concept of "essential community provider," and provides them with special protection in reference to payments they will receive from health plans. While this concept is an important one and does protect certain groups, especially the Federal investments in various programs, as currently proposed, the investment of dedicated private practitioners, as well as the investment of sole community provider hospitals and primary care hospitals is not protected.

In addition to these concerns about the Health Security Act, I have some specific concerns about the September 15th joint memorandum of the Federal Trade Commission. In the memorandum, mergers involving hospitals of fewer than 100 beds, with an average daily census of less than 40, are granted a safe harbor for merger. And while there are many situations in which mergers of small hospitals are obviously appropriate, I am concerned about the breadth of this safe harbor.

The breadth of this safe harbor leaves no checks and balances in place to assure ongoing access to care. Urban hospitals will be free to acquire the rural hospitals and their secondary market areas, d wnsize those hospitals, and import patients to their urban market.

As you know, research indicates that it is our most vulnerable populations for whom having to travel to access-based services can pose access problems, and who therefore are most dependent upon our rural hospitals.

A second concern is that because the safe harbor does not contain a process of checks and balances, it has the potential to run directly counter to the efforts that States are undertaking to form rural networks. As you know, the EACH/PCH program has included a State role in network formation and development. Such a role for States has been omitted under the breadth of this safe harbor.

Finally, because the FTC safe harbor only looks at the parameter of size, issues such as the quality of the merged institution and the choice of practitioners and patients as to whether the acquisition is appropriate have been totally left out of the loop.

In addition to these specific concerns about antitrust, I have several overall concerns about antitrust and rural delivery systems. In reading the Health Security Act, I was particularly concerned about the lack of antitrust protection for QPCNs, and as a former director of a State office of rural health, I am concerned about how States will be able to assure the development of effective networks under the State Action Doctrine, when so many market areas cross State lines.

In the past several months, I have been involved in beginning development of networks in the northeastern part of Kansas, which crosses into Missouri; a network in the northwestern part of the Kansas which involves Kansas, Nebraska and Colorado; and in the southeastern part of the State which crosses into Oklahoma. I fail to understand how the Health Security Act anticipates addressing this important issue of the role of markets which cross State borders in health care delivery systems in rural America.

Finally, I would like to comment on some of the perceived anti-rural bias in the plan that Senator Kassebaum had an opportunity to hear when she was in Garden City with Senator Dole last month, by using one small example.

One of the primary assumptions in the Integrated Community Health Development Project is that rural health care is not urban health care in miniature. We have learned over and over again that downsizing urban health care delivery models is not an effective solution to developing integrated systems of care.

Recognizing that lower costs of health care can begin by educating our youth in healthy activities, the plan correctly identifies school educational activities as a priority. But in establishing criteria for local education agencies to receive planning grants to build capacity for educational programs, the Health Security Act limits such grants to education agencies that involve a minimum of 25,000 students. No school district in any of the 85 rural counties in Kansas would qualify for any of these grants.

I urge the committee therefore to assure rural Americans that any health care reform plan passed by Congress and signed by the President will recognize their concerns and accommodate the unique issues facing the rural delivery system.

Thank you.

[The prepared statement of Mr. McDowell follows:]

Prepared Statement of Steve McDowell

Mr. Chairman, Distinguished Members of the Committee, my name is Steve McDowell and I am the Director of the Integrated Community Health Development (ICHD) project funded by the Kansas Health Foundation. Previously, I was the Director of the Office of Rural Health in Kansas.

I come before you today as a strong supporter of health care reform who believes in the necessity of containing costs, providing quality health care, and assuring that health care is a right available to all Americans. I also come before you today with serious concerns about what health care reform may mean to the fragile rural health care delivery system.

It is my belief that in order for health care reform to be effective in rural areas, it must provide appropriate encouragement for locally integrated delivery systems while appropriately protecting the fragile systems in our underserved areas. While it is beyond the scope of my testimony or this hearing to discuss whether managed competition can be effective in rural communities, I would like to address several specific concerns I have in reference to the Health Security Act as well as to other recent activities involving health care reform.

The Integrated Community Health Development Project funded by the Kansas Health Foundation is working in ten Kansas communities to build integrated systems of care which can assure local access to care. In each community a cross section of citizens have formed a working group to understand the changes in health delivery, come to a consensus on an appropriate scope of services for their community and then to decide how to structure those services. These rural communities have decided that at a minimum they need to have local access to Emergency Services, primary care services, public health services and community based long term care. Further they have come to the conclusion that the delivery system needs to be integrated. In planning for health reform in rural America, this point cannot be overstated, the rural health care delivery system is neither a hospital, a practitioner, a public health department or an emergency medical system. A rural delivery system is just that, a system of care that coordinates and integrates local resources in order to minimize duplication, contain costs and assure access to a comprehensive range of services.

The Health Security Act recognizes the concept of locally integrating services and creates a new program called the "Qualified Primary Care Network", QPCNs, to achieve that goal. Nevertheless the Act fails to recognize the importance of integrating one of the most vital aspect of the rural delivery system - prehospital and hospital emergency medical services

- within networks as well as omitting other important rural resources that must be integrated into networks such as sole community providers, essential access community hospitals and primary care hospitals. Moreover, the concept of QPCNs isolates primary care from public health. Our experience in Kansas is that effective integration for rural communities includes all of the services in a community, not simply primary care services.

I am also concerned that the Act "grandfathers in" current categorical programs and existing delivery models, and does not seem to recognize the need for flexibility in approaching the future. Public and private sector attempts to bring about more effective health care delivery in rural communities have identified the critical importance of alternative delivery models, including stepped-down hospitals, stepped-up primary care centers, and the participation of many different kinds of grass-roots-based community organizations. Development of alternative approaches has required exhaustive (and often unsuccessful) efforts to secure waivers of existing laws and regulations at many levels,

and this has inhibited their growth in many situations. The Act's failure to allow positive change through innovative models, while in all probability an inadvertent oversight, nonetheless places major barriers in the way of new programs to deliver health care more efficiently and effectively in rural communities, and I believe should be corrected.

Health care reform is likely to increase the demand for primary care practitioners in urban and suburban areas. In recognizing the added stresses this will place on rural underserved areas as they attempt to recruit and retain practitioners, the Health Security Act increases the differential payment for Medicare patients from ten percent to twenty percent. In addition the plan proposes the concept of "Essential Community Provider" and provides them with special protection in reference to the payments they will receive from health plans. The concept of "essential community providers" is an important one, and protects the federal investment in shortage areas through the community and migrant health center program, the maternal and child health program, the federally qualified health center program and the rural health clinics program. However as currently proposed the investment of dedicated private practitioners as well as the investment of sole community provider hospitals and primary care hospitals is not protected.

In addition to these concerns about some of the proposed provisions of the Health Security Act, I have some very specific concerns about the impact of the September 15th joint memorandum of the Federal Trade Commission and the Department of Justice on anti-trust safety zones in rural America.

In the memorandum, mergers involving hospitals of fewer than 100 beds with an average daily census of less than 40 are granted a safe harbor for merger. While there are many situations (such as the Ukiah case) in which mergers of small hospitals are obviously appropriate, I am very concerned about the breadth of this safe harbor. Those concerns come under the following headings:

A: Access

The breadth of this safe harbor leaves no checks and balances in place to assure ongoing access to care. Urban hospitals will be free to acquire the rural hospitals in their secondary market areas, downsize those hospitals and import patients to their urban market. As you know, research indicates that it is our most vulnerable populations for whom having to travel to access basic services can pose access problems, and who therefore are most dependent upon our rural hospitals. The breadth of this safe harbor is likely to serve to the advantage of urban hospitals and to the detriment of rural hospitals.

B: Interaction with State Plans

Because the safe harbor does not contain a process of checks and balances, it has the potential to run directly counter to the efforts that States are undertaking to form rural networks. As you know, the EACH/RPCH program has included a State role in network formation and development. Such a role for States has been omitted under the breadth of this safe harbor.

C: Quality and Choice

Because the FTC/DOJ safe harbor only looks at the parameter of size, issues such as the quality of the merged institution and the choice of practitioners and patients as to whether the acquisition is appropriate have totally been left out of the loop.

Given the large percentage of rural hospitals that fall under this safe harbor, unless these problems are addressed, we are likely to see major market shifts that limit choice, hamper the ability of States to do effective planning, and limit access, regardless of what happens with the Health Security Act.

In addition to the safety zone on rural hospital acquisition, I have several concerns regarding the safety zone on physician networks. This safety zone uses a very narrow definition of geographic market that will have the effect of prohibiting efforts to create systems of managed cooperation and instead force fragile rural provider systems to be divided and conquered by urban-based health plans.

In addition to those specific concerns about anti-trust, I have several overall concerns about anti-trust and rural delivery systems. In reading the Health Security Act, I was particularly concerned about the lack of anti-trust protection for QPCNs and, as a former Director of a State Office of Rural Health, I am especially concerned about how States will be able to assure the development of effective networks under the State Action Doctrine when so many market areas cross State lines. In the past several months, I've been involved in developing networks in the Northeastern part of Kansas crossing into Missouri, in the Northwestern part of Kansas crossing into Nebraska and Colorado and in the Southeastern part of the State crossing into Oklahoma. I fail to understand how the Health Security Act anticipates addressing this important issue of the role of border states in the health care delivery system of rural America.

Finally, I'd like to comment about some of the perceived anti-rural bias in the plan that Senator Kassebaum had an opportunity to hear when she was in Garden City with Senator Dole last month by using one small example. One of the primary assumptions in the Integrated Community Health Development Project is that rural health care is not urban health care in miniature. We have learned over and over again that downsizing urban health care delivery models is not an effective solution to developing integrated systems of care. Recognizing that lowering the costs of health care can begin by educating our youth in healthy activities, the plan correctly identifies school educational activities as a priority. But in establishing criteria for local education agencies to receive planning grants to build capacity for educational programs, the Health Security Act limits such grants to education agencies that enroll a minimum of 25,000 students. No school district in any of the 85 rural counties in Kansas would qualify for a grant.

I'd urge the committee, therefore, to assure rural Americans that any health care reform plan passed by Congress and signed by the President recognizes their concerns and accommodates the unique issues facing the rural delivery system.

Senator HARKIN. Very good. Thank you.

"The Health Security Act limits such grants to local education agencies that enroll a minimum of 25,000 students." Well, I just learned something new. I did not know that was in there.

Again, thank you all very much. I have been taking some notes. Again, Ms. Miller, would you go over again with me your concerns about a 7-year window to make adjustments to the financing to correct inequities between rural and urban areas? You suggested a blended rate to equalize urban and rural. Would you go over that again?

Ms. MILLER. One recommendation was to try to determine what the total budget is, and what if we had a per capita allocation of the total budget, and then adjusting that somehow—and I am unfortunately not a health economist, so I do not know—but then taking the historical spending issue and coming up with a blended rate, just as a first step to have some time to work on it.

I agree that it is a very difficult thing, and it is going to take some time. I am also sorry that the time was not taken in the development of the plan with all the economists that were available.

So I do not have a specific formula in mind, but there must be some way to shift some of that money among the alliances and among the States.

Senator HARKIN. And you say that this blended rate should go into effect when?

Ms. MILLER. Well, I do not see how we can get started in calling it national health reform if some States are going to be disadvantaged from the very beginning and yet are going to have all these mandates of universality and a comprehensive benefit package.

Senator HARKIN. So right away is what you are saying.

Ms. MILLER. An example of a State that is going to have a very difficult time they think is Alaska. I have been working with them. Sixty percent of their population is already covered by Federal programs directly, and only 14 percent have private insurance. If they get a rate that is based on something that is not going to work for them, and they do not get the subsidies, they are not going to have the money to even implement the reform.

That is the concern. How do we get up and going? How do we assure the access in rural communities, which we have all admitted need incentives—and recruitment cost is quite expensive—how do we do it if we are stuck in a budget that is based on what we have been allowed to spend in the past or had available to spend in the past?

Senator HARKIN. Well, in any system like that, we still have to be careful because if you have blended rates someone is going to get more and someone is going to get less. I am just concerned about how we set that up.

Ms. MILLER. Well, the way the decision was made was to actually protect those who have more now.

Senator HARKIN. But if you base it on historical spending now, then no one really gets hurt in the beginning, theoretically. Then, you go on for 3 or 4 years, 7 years, whatever it might be, and you re-examine it and make adjustments. But if you do it right off the bat, it seems to me that some areas might wind up getting hurt immediately, without being able over a period of years to establish perhaps different systems of delivery. For example, those who may have been in a higher cost area under the alliance program may bring those costs down substantially over 5 or 7 years. But to do it immediately would be very difficult.

I tend to agree with you, and I have argued long and hard that locking in these historical rates is going to penalize a lot of areas. I am just trying to figure out what we do in the beginning to make sure we do not unfairly penalize those areas that have been high-cost areas.

Ms. MILLER. It is a difficult problem, and the thing to me that is most interesting is that the areas with the most competition are also the highest spending areas. So there is a whole issue about where there is the least competition, like rural America, those are the low-cost places. The places with lots of academic medical centers and specialists, like Massachusetts, New York and Florida, those are the higher-cost places.

I do not really have an answer. I hope that with the staff we can work on something. I do not want to destroy a good health care system where it exists. But we are going to be mandated to create a health care system in rural America without the financial resources to really do it.

Senator HARKIN. Speaking of those areas, Mr. Bernstein, you were talking about how we evaluate and reward teaching programs that train more generalists, rather than specialists and are successful in getting these generalists to practive in rural areas. Isn't that what you were talking about, building in some kind of either incentives, or were you talking about mandating certain levels of generalists? Now, the bill does provide, I think by 2002, that in teaching programs, at least 55 percent of those entering residency programs must be primary care. That is not sufficient?

Mr. BERNSTEIN. No; I think that would be great. We could set it higher. Since they are probably not going to reach that one, it does not make any difference to me.

The issue is to put more emphasis on performance as we go along, of what they actually do, rather than to fund process, which means how many students spent 2 months in a rural area from the class, and more money for this, and more money for that. Those are all process issues, not that they do not need to be done, but the Government needs to look more at the end result each year and reward those institutions that do a better job of producing generalists.

Actually, I would not do the system the way they are planning to do it. I think they are missing a big point here, because the State Governments put a lot of money into medical education and nursing education, more so than undergraduate; they put all the money in, or a lot of the money. So the Federal Government needs to leverage the State money so you will have both moneys put in the same pool, going in the same direction.

If it were me, I would set my criteria like they do—50 percent generalists, or whatever you use—and I would say to the States that you will get this money on an historical basis—that is, all the health profession money, all the DME money, all the IME money—but you will have to pool your State money, which in a lot of States is a substantial amount of money. Then, they would have to come back with a plan on how they are going to meet the goals set by the Federal Government. That would force the deans of the different health professions schools to sit down and figure it out.

For instance, if Duke wanted to be all specialists, and they could work out a deal with the rest of the deans in North Carolina to produce more generalists, that is fine, but let them figure out how to do it. Then, you would have the State money and the Federal money all going the same way, and the States would not get the whole 100 percent of the Federal money unless they came up with a plan that was adequate to the Federal commission, let us say.

I think that would be much more effective. You would have much more leverage if you did it that way.

Senator HARKIN. Let me just ask you a question that has been asked of every panel. Basically, the incentives to attract providers to rural areas, the tax credits, the loan repayment provisions—are they adequate?

Mr. BERNSTEIN. Are they adequate?

Senator HARKIN. We have heard others say that it will be okay for the 5 years, and then people will leave. The concern is that once providers have finished their 5 year obligation they will leave.

Mr. BERNSTEIN. We find that physician, urban or rural, in North Carolina, 50 percent of them move by 5 years' time anyway, and it does not make any difference whether it is urban or rural. That is about the time frame. Five years, 50 percent move.

Senator HARKIN. You mean they leave their initial location after 5 years?

Mr. BERNSTEIN. Yes, their initial location. My point is that the incentives in there are not bad. The problem is you cannot win with those kinds of carrot incentives only. There is going to have to be some leverage on the plans either to put funding into the rural networks, extra funding, because they have the privilege of treating all of Raleigh-Durham and Chapel Hill, and then the rural areas, they would have to put some extra money up to help the rural networks. Or you are going to have to mandate those plans to cover those rural counties if they are going to also serve Raleigh-Durham and Chapel Hill. And I would make it a condition on all the plans, but let the plans come together. For instance, of Kaiser and Pru Care want to fund a rural network together so they both have a really good rural access system, that would be fine; but they would have to prove to either the State or the Federal Government that they could do that.

The problem with the plan is that the Feds are pretty silent about it, as you mentioned, and it is not clear that they are even instructing the States to do anything about it; it is not even clear to me that if the States wanted to do something about it that the Federal Government would think it was the right thing to do.

Senator HARKIN. Any other thoughts? Are these incentives enough—$1,000 a month for up to 5 years, loan repayments? How about out in Kansas?

Mr. MCDOWELL. I sure think they are a step in the right direction. My particular point is that those incentives are for new folks coming in. What about the doctors like Dr. Thompson, who has committed himself to stay? There are no incentives and no protections for him. He would not be at this point an essential community provider. He may be able to become a rural health clinic, which would make him one.

But there is a whole group—there are not enough—but there is a group of practitioners out there now for which there are no protections. So if you are incentivizing to bring some more people in, I think there ought to be some look at continuing to provide incentives or protections for that group who have decided, for a variety of reasons, to be there already.

Senator HARKIN. One last thing. The current ratio of one physician for 3,500 in the definition of a health professional shortage area—do we need to reexamine that?

Ms. MILLER. I think we need to look at it, but I do not want to see it part of the Health Security Act, because when we revise the HPSA designation, I do not want to have to open this thing. I would like to deal with it either in the core reauthorization—we do need to look at it, but we have to be careful how much we throw into this one piece of legislation. I mean, maybe we will want to change it in 5 years if there actually is an influx of providers to rural areas; maybe we would look at it again.

One thing that we have to be very careful of is that some people would like to start counting nurse practitioners and PAs in the shortage designation. I think we have to be careful to make sure that that does not make it impossible to get physicians in rural areas. Particularly if you are doing a lot of emergency medical service and a lot of after-hours calls, you still need physicians.

So I think yes, we need to look at it, but let us do it in a more studied way and not lump it into this particular piece of legislation.

Senator HARKIN. Thank you all. Just one last thing. Mr. Bernstein, thank you for this little bit of information you put in about the copayments. You say, "For example, based on the average North Carolina household income, the $5, $10, $20 and $25 copayments of the low-cost plan for a household living on $10,000 a year are equivalent of a middle-income household paying $17 for a prescription drug, $33 for each doctor visit, $66 for certain dental procedures, and $83 for each mental health or substance abuse therapy session." That is quite a bit.

Mr. BERNSTEIN. I hope those numbers are right. I am sure somebody will check them. That is just taking the formula that is in the plan and playing it out. So for someone who makes $10,000, someone who makes $35,000, paying the $2, $10 and whatever, that is how it looks to the $10,000 family, which is a lot of money.

Senator HARKIN. Yes, I know. That really puts it in perspective. Thank you all very much for coming a great distance. Carol thank you for your help on the task force; and thank you, Mr. McDowell and Mr. Bernstein.

The committee will stand in recess subject to the call of the chair.

[Whereupon, at 12:55 p.m., the committee was adjourned.]

THE HEALTH SECURITY ACT AND THE ROLE OF THE PHARMACEUTICAL INDUSTRY

THURSDAY, NOVEMBER 18, 1993

U.S. SENATE,
COMMITTEE ON LABOR AND HUMAN RESOURCES,
Washington, DC.

The committee met, pursuant to notice, at 2:33 p.m., in room SD–430, Dirksen Senate Office Building, Senator Kennedy (chairman of the committee) presiding.

Present: Senators Kennedy, Dodd, Simon, Wofford, Coats and Gregg.

OPENING STATEMENT OF SENATOR KENNEDY

The CHAIRMAN. The committee will come to order.

Today's hearing is the latest in the committee's consideration of President Clinton's Health Security Act. This afternoon, we will discuss the role of the pharmaceutical and biotechnology industries in health reform.

Large numbers of elderly Americans and many others with chronic illnesses are deeply concerned about the cost of prescription drugs. One of the most important aspects of health reform is to assure that those who need medications are able to get them at an affordable price. The key part of meeting this challenge is to do so without jeopardizing the research and development needed for new drugs.

President Clinton's Health Security Act proposes a fundamental overhaul of our health care system to provide comprehensive, affordable care for all. Under the President's plan, all Americans will be guaranteed coverage for their prescription drugs, regardless of their choice of health plan. The proposed Medicare prescription drug benefit will be particularly important to elderly Americans.

Today, many insurance policies exclude prescription drug coverage, or cover them only at additional burdensome expense. Drug prices have risen twice as fast in the United States as in any other industrialized country. Less than half of those on Medicare currently have adequate coverage for prescription drugs. Every day, families and retirees are confronted with the distressing choice between buying food or buying medicine. The Health Security Act will end these tragic choices.

But as we ensure access to prescription drugs and take steps to ensure that the drugs are reasonably priced, we must not jeopardize the pharmaceutical industry's capacity to innovate or impede research on new treatments.

(163)

This committee has dealt with the complex issues of prescription drug pricing and regulation for many years. Our experience has shown the importance of maintaining the conditions which have made the United States a world leader in biomedical research. This leadership is especially true for the biotechnology industry, whose extraordinary breakthroughs hold great promise for the future.

There is wide agreement that costs must be contained without the Government getting into the business of actually setting prices. We all want research and development to continue as rapidly as possible. We all agree that the Government should get good prices on the prescription drugs it purchases.

The administration has made a commendable effort to achieve these goals with a series of balanced measures to assure greater competition. Although there are no actual price controls, concerns have been raised that some of the proposals will have the effect of controls. It is clear that we must address these concerns and ensure that containing costs and providing access to affordable drugs can be achieved without sacrificing innovation. I look forward to working to reach an acceptable resolution of this vital issue.

O first panel consists of representatives who can speak to that subject.

I will recognize Senator Coats.

Senator COATS. I am just catching my breath, Mr. Chairman. Go ahead, please.

The CHAIRMAN. Senator Dodd.

OPENING STATEMENT OF SENATOR DODD

Senator DODD. Thank you, Mr. Chairman.

Let me begin by thanking you for holding this hearing today to give this critically important part of our health care industry an opportunity to be discussed, including the views of those who are from the industry and those who have been critical of the industry and its practice. I hope we will have a good chance to vent a lot of issues.

I would like to welcome all of the witnesses who are here with us today.

If I may, let me just share a couple of thoughts as we begin this process. The topic today, as we all know, is an important one because pharmaceuticals should and do play a critical role in both improving the quality of health care in the country and lowering health care costs.

The track record of this industry, I think, is pretty clear. Vaccines have prevented close to one million cases of polio in the United States. New prescription therapies have prevented more than 600,000 premature deaths from heart disease and nearly 500,000 premature deaths from stroke.

Prescription drugs have saved the lives of an estimated 90,000 Americans who, without them, would have died from tuberculosis. Those are not insignificant statistics.

In many of our hearings on health care reform, we have heard a great deal about the importance of disease prevention. As these examples demonstrate, the pharmaceutical and now biotechnology companies and industries have contributed, in my view, a great deal to this cause, and we should make sure that we craft a reform package that will enable these industries—new companies and older members of the industry—to redouble their efforts. We are going to have to confront the issue of costs in our health care system, but I hope we do not do that at the price of dealing with the quality of health care as well.

I hope that the hearing today will give us an opportunity to engage in some rational discussion on the impact health care reform will have on our Nation's drug companies. Discussions of this sort too often have been clouded by emotion and polemics.

I believe that all segments of the health care industry should be called upon to be partners in reforming our health care system and ensuring that all Americans have access to health care that is both affordable and of high quality—and they need not be inconsistent goals. We have got to confront the high cost of our health care system, and the drug companies and industries have got to be a part of solving that problem.

I would like to point out that much of the pharmaceutical industry has already agreed voluntarily to control their prices. And obviously, all of us are going to watch that carefully.

Many people, in my view, wrongly try to demonize the pharmaceutical industry—they are an easy target—and blame them for all of the high costs associated with health care. That is easy. This line of argument is overly simplistic in my view and does a great disservice to the consumers of this country and may end up in the long run hurting our ability to preserve one of the best aspects of our current health care system. With all of its flaws, there are good aspects to it.

We must not allow our zeal to sock it to the pharmaceutical industry to cripple our ability to develop new medicines that could benefit millions of people in this country and countless millions of others beyond our shores. We also ought to be able to save money at the same time.

We must remember here in Congress that it will probably be the pharmaceutical and biotechnology industries' research and development that will come up with cures for AIDS and cancer and lupus and other deadly diseases. I am sure that all of us can agree that we would not want to do anything that would put off the day when those cures can be developed.

While there has been a great deal of attention devoted to the high cost of some drugs—and rightfully so, I might add—what has been left out of the debate, far too often, is the fact that in many cases pharmaceuticals also save money. Drugs and vaccines generally lower the cost of health care by providing a substitute for higher-cost and far less effective treatments.

The treatment of ulcers is a case in point. Ulcer surgery costs roughly $30,000 in this country, while drug therapy for the same problem costs around $900—not insignificant in its cost, but certainly far less than surgery.

Because of this medically effective and cost-effective pharmaceutical alternative, from 1977 to 1987, there was an 80 percent reduction in the number of ulcer surgeries in the United States. That is not insignificant.

Much of the discussion about the high price of pharmaceuticals also ignores the high price of pharmaceutical research and development. In 1993, major American pharmaceutical companies will spend $12.3 billion on research. That equals the combined research of every other country in the entire world in that same area.

In fact, the American pharmaceutical industry spends an average of 16.7 percent of its sales on research and development. That is nearly twice what the computer industry spends and nearly three times what the electronics industry spends for its research. Much of this money goes to drugs that will never generate even a dollar in sales. Only one in 5,000 compounds screened ever reaches the market as a new drug and fewer than one-third of the drugs launched recoup the cost it took to develop them.

We also should not overlook the important role that the pharmaceutical industry plays in our economy. This industry employs 300,000 people all across the Nation, and the industry is a major exporter. More than one-third of its total sales are to other countries. In 1993, the industry will have a trade surplus of $1.35 billion.

While I believe many of the attacks on the industry are misguided, I do believe that we must examine such concerns as the impact of pharmaceutical prices on our Nation's individuals and families. I am pleased that the President's reform package includes a prescription drug benefit for all Americans. I know this is of great importance to our Nation's Medicare population.

I would note on this point that today, prescription drugs account for only 7 percent of health care spending, yet account for 40 percent of what people pay out-of-pocket for health care.

So prices and costs are a real concern that this committee, I know, and the full Congress are going to pay particular attention to. But I think it is also important that we keep our eye on the quality issues, the research issues, the development issues that are part of this debate.

Mr. Chairman, I hope that our witnesses today will improve our understanding of the important issues related to the pharmaceutical industry, that they appreciate the concerns reflected by many of our colleagues in various legislative efforts over the years to try to contain costs, and that the health care reform package must involve them. And I hope they will help us to inject some cool, reasoned insight into what has too often been an overheated subject.

Thank you, Mr. Chairman.

The CHAIRMAN. Thank you very much.

Senator Coats.

Senator COATS. Mr. Chairman, I cannot top that statement. If I tried to say what is on my mind, I would be accused of plagiarism.

Senator DODD. That is all right. That gets done around here. [Laughter.]

The CHAIRMAN. Not with my stuff. [Laughter.]

Senator COATS. The concerns expressed by Senator Dodd are my concerns, and I would add my name to those, Mr. Chairman, who thank you for inviting these individuals here to tell a side of the story that unfortunately has not been told in the health care debate to date. The drug industry has been made one of the chief villains of our Nation's health care problems, and I think unfairly so. They do have a story to tell, and it is an impressive one in terms of drug therapy and the costs that it has saved the American people by substitution of drugs that provide treatment for serious injuries, serious diseases, serious symptoms that, were it not for the provision of drugs to alleviate those symptoms, we would be spending a far greater amount of money in the health care system.

Their research and development has given Americans a quality of health care that no other country in this Nation, or on this planet enjoys, and we need to recognize that. We need to recognize what it takes to develop those drugs and the kind of profits necessary to plow the kind of money into research and development that brings us that remarkable record of success. So I am happy that we can explore that.

I also think it is important to explore ways in which the drug manufacturers can contribute to our maintaining the quality of health care in this country, but at a lower cost, a cost that Americans can afford. I know they have some initiatives in that regard, so I look forward to their testimony today.

I do not have a formal opening statement, Mr. Chairman, but thank you.

The CHAIRMAN. Thank you very much.

Senator Simon.

Senator SIMON. Thank you, Mr. Chairman. I regret that I have two meetings going on at the same time, and I am going to have to juggle them this afternoon.

I am sorry I just arrived for the tail end of your statement, Senator Dodd, and I do not know whether I agree or disagree with it, but you had great testimony to it from Senator Coats, and there is no question about the contribution that you have made and are making.

The cost factor has to be looked at, however, and if you saw the booklet the White House put out on health care and the costs in terms of pharmaceuticals compared to the inflation costs, it has been a contributor. The question is how do we get the right kind of balance, and how do we encourage the research that needs to be done, and how do we encourage you to continue to provide those cutting edge things that are so important to the future of all of us, and at the same time, have some lessening of the cost factor. That is not an easy one, and I do not know what the answer is, but I hope the hearings here can help provide it.

Thank you, Mr. Chairman.

The CHAIRMAN. Thank you very much.

Senator Gregg.

OPENING STATEMENT OF SENATOR GREGG

Senator GREGG. Well, let me simply add that I do not believe that we can address the issue of health care unless we address the issue of how we continue to have a vibrant research industry in the area of drugs, because you cannot improve health as we go into the 21st century unless you have a strong drug atmosphere, an atmosphere which allows those people who are willing to be entrepreneurs and willing to apply their imagination and creativity to uses in the area of production of drugs.

I guess one of my primary concerns with the President's plan is the fact that I think it will have a dramatic chilling effect on the willingness of people to invest venture capital in the drug industry. It will also, I believe, have a substantial chilling effect on those folks who wish to push the envelop of research in the area of designing new medical technologies not only in the drug field but in the physical technology field.

The Government has shown itself to be a very poor chooser of the winners and losers in the area of industrial policy. We have shown that time and time again, our most recent example being the decision of the Government not to pursue the supercollider, which was again an example of the Government trying to choose a winner and loser in the area of physics.

If the Government is going to take over the business of deciding who the winners and losers are in the area of drugs and what will be the right drug and what will be the wrong drug, what we are going to inevitably end up with is a system that picks a lot of losers and spends a lot of time in delay and bureaucracy.

What we need is a system that does just the opposite—allows the marketplace to drive the opportunities and puts the entrepreneur and the researcher at the forefront of the decision process rather than at the end of a long line of paperwork.

Thank you, Mr. Chairman.

The CHAIRMAN. Thank you.

We will include in the record statements of Senators Thurmond and Hatch.

[The prepared statements of Senators Thurmond and Hatch follow:]

PREPARED STATEMENT OF SENATOR THURMOND

Mr. Chairman:

It is a pleasure to be here this afternoon to receive testimony concerning the role of the pharmaceutical industry in health care reform. I would like to extend a warm welcome to our witnesses here today.

There is no question that all Americans need access to affordable prescription drugs. Unfortunately, too many Americans are having to make the choice between paying for their prescribed medicine or for their food.

Mandated government price controls or "price review boards" would penalize pharmaceutical research, and eventually drive companies out of the industry. Recent studies of the pharmaceutical industry would indicate that the free competitive market along with strong safeguards to ensure quality help contain price increases.

As you know, in 1993, the pharmaceutical industry spent an estimated $12.6 billion on research and development. The Office of Technology Assessment estimates that in 1990 the average cost of research and development for each new drug marketed in the United States was $359 million.

The best hope for treatment and possible cures for many of the health problems we face today is with the area of pharmaceutical and biotechnology advances. If we try to establish "price discipline", we will see a decrease in pharmaceutical research and development, and fewer pharmaceutical and biotechnology breakthroughs.

Again, I would like to welcome our witnesses here today, and I look forward to their testimony.

PREPARED STATEMENT OF SENATOR HATCH

Mr. Chairman:

Thank you very much for holding this important hearing on the President1s proposed health care reform legislation and the role of pharmaceuticals in health care.

As we attempt to frame a system that will provide, in the words of President Clinton, "health care that's always there," we need to make sure that innovative medicines will be there for our children and our children's children.

We need to make sure that, in our zeal to make health care more affordable, we don't inadvertently stifle the development of medicines that will save both money and lives.

That is why this hearing is so important. I hope it will help the Committee gain a clearer picture of the role of prescription medicines—and the industry that develops them—in health care reform.

Progress is very important to Americans, especially in medicine. Breakthroughs that help us lead longer, healthier lives win high praise.

It is deplorable to me that the very industry responsible for these research breakthroughs has been demonized and is constantly the target of attack.

I find this ironic, and perhaps dangerous. By putting this industry under attack, we compromise its ability to find cures for the deadly and costly diseases that plague us.

What is even more ironic is the fact that some critics of the pharmaceutical industry are attacking the industry of yesteryear. They are, in effect, beating a dead horse.

I wonder if the Committee is aware that, according to the Bureau of Labor Statistics, drug inflation for the 12 months ending in October was 3.4 percent?

This is barely above the rate of general inflation, in stark contrast to the 1991 figure for drug inflation of 9.4 percent.

I wonder if the Committee is aware that an April 1993 study by The Boston Consulting Group, concluded that market forces—particularly the growth of managed care—are holding down the prices of both existing and new drugs?

The study found that the introductory prices of products approved and launched during 1991 and 1992 were, on average, 14 percent.

I wonder if the Committee is aware that, at last count, 17 major drug companies, whose products make up 2/3rds of the market, have pledged to hold overall price increases to the rate of inflation?

The problem with the Health Security Act is that it would make matters worse.

According to a new study by Price Waterhouse, the Medicare rebate tax contained in the Health Security Act, will help raise the industry's effective tax rate to more than 55 percent. I guess this is the 90s version of tax reform.

That tax burden, plus the "breakthrough drug committee," plus the Medicare "blacklist" drugs from the Medicare program add up to some pretty powerful disincentives to invest in new cures.

The bottom line is that I think we have to put this "patient" on the examining table and make sure we aren't signing the death warrants of people who could be saved by medicines that may never be discovered. We want health care that's always there . . . but we also want to ensure that new medicines will be there for people who need them. That is my goal.

The CHAIRMAN. As our first panel, we welcome Dr. Charles Sanders, chairman and CEO of Glaxo, Inc.; Lodewijk de Vink, who is president and chief operating officer of Warner-Lambert; Judy Lewent, chief financial officer and senior vice president of Merck; Gerald Mossinghoff, president of the Pharmaceutical Manufacturers Association; and Mitchel Sayare, chairman and CEO of ImmunoGen, from Cambridge, MA. I have had the opportunity to visit the ImmunoGen plant.

As a final point I know many companies are developing real breakthrough drugs while others are developing "me-too" drugs. The problem, from my point of view is how to maintain the incentives for the ones that are truly innovative.

As Senator Simon has mentioned, there are numerous things happening this afternoon. So I will apologize for all of us, including myself, should we be forced to leave early.

We welcome all of you here, and we will start with Dr. Sanders. We are glad to see you.

STATEMENTS OF DR. CHARLES A. SANDERS, CHAIRMAN AND CEO, GLAXO, INC., RESEARCH TRIANGLE PARK, NC; LODEWIJK J.R. De VINK, PRESIDENT AND CHIEF OPERATING OFFICER, WARNER-LAMBERT CO., MORRIS PLAINS, NJ; JUDY C. LEWENT, CHIEF FINANCIAL OFFICER AND SENIOR VICE PRESIDENT, MERCK & COMPANY, INC., WHITEHOUSE STATION, NJ; GERALD J. MOSSINGHOFF, PRESIDENT, PHARMACEUTICAL MANUFACTURERS ASSOCIATION, WASHINGTON, DC; AND MITCHEL SAYARE, CHAIRMAN AND CEO, IMMUNOGEN, INC., CAMBRIDGE, MA

Dr. SANDERS. Thank you, Mr. Chairman. I am very pleased to be here to testify before you once again.

My name is Charles Sanders, and as you noted, I am chairman and CEO of Glaxo, Incorporated, which is a research-based pharmaceutical company.

I have spent my entire professional life in health care. I started off as a cardiologist at Massachusetts General Hospital, a professor of medicine at Harvard, and then became general director of that hospital, leaving there in 1981 to join the pharmaceutical industry.

I am deeply interested in health care reform, as I am sure you know. I believe very strongly that we should have access for all Americans. I am very concerned about the cost issues which have been increasing and are acute as far as our health care system is concerned. I am deeply, deeply concerned about our ability as we address costs, and that in our zeal to contain costs that we do not erode quality; and, very importantly, that we maintain innovation in our system because it really is the key to the future, as all of you have pointed out.

Pharmaceuticals are the most cost-effective means of providing health care. I think we all would much prefer to take a pill to prevent or to cure a disease rather than go into a hospital and incur thousands and thousands of dollars of expense, often not reaching the same definitive end point of a cure that you might have from a pharmaceutical. Pharmaceuticals obviously contribute tremendously to the quality of our lives.

Now, we, as the research-based pharmaceutical industry, really depend upon our whole drug discovery process. Innovation is our life blood. If we are successful in that, we have done our job, if our products are accepted by the market and improved therapies result. We can come back to the "me-too" drugs later on, but I think at this particular point in time, Senator Kennedy, the marketplace is demanding a very high standard in terms of the introduction of new drugs. If you do not have a significant therapeutic benefit when you introduce a new product, then you do not have a commercial success, and you will not recoup your investment. That is the law of the marketplace, so be it.

Let me give you three examples of some compounds that have come to the marketplace in the last 3 years that have really made a tremendous difference in terms of not only quality of life, but in terms of saving money. The first of these is a compound called Exosurf. Exosurf is surfactant. Premature babies are born with a deficiency of surfactant. Exosurf, which is developed by Burroughs Wellcome Company, is inhaled; it essentially provides surfactant to the respiratory-distressed premature babies until such time as the babies can build their own. This has made a tremendous difference in terms of the technology of treatment of neonatal units.

The CHAIRMAN. Is that hyaline membrane disease?

Dr. SANDERS. Yes, very much the same type of thing. Hyaline membrane disease results as a deficiency of surfactant. And of course, we did not have that many years ago, and infants had to be supported respiratorially for months at a time, at a very, very high cost, and often with a baby who might be significantly impaired as a result.

What has happened, of course, is that not only has mortality gone down, but in the case of the Children's Hospital in Minneapolis, a $4 million project was scrapped simply because they did not need it; Exosurf had made that much difference.

The second example that I would like to give is the example of people who have received autologous bone marrow transplants because they have cancer, and they get total body radiation, and then they have bone marrow implantation. At Duke, the average cost of those procedures, which was usually many weeks in a sterile facility until such time as the implanted bone marrow could take over, was $140,000.

With the advent of something called granulocyte colony stimulating factor, which stimulates white cells, the bone marrow takes up much quicker, and the average cost now is $75,000, with shorter hospitalization and less technology used.

The third example that I would like to give is one of Glaxo's own products called Zofran, which controls the nausea and vomiting associated with chemotherapy. As you know, about 95 percent of the people who receive chemotherapy will have significant nausea and vomiting, often unremitting, keeping them in the hospital for a longer period of time simply because of that complication.

Zofran has controlled that in almost 100 percent of the cases now, and as a result, people get out of the hospital faster, and obviously, there is tremendous cost saving. But from the human point of view, if I went into the wards of the Massachusetts General Hospital, particularly the pediatric wards, 20 years ago, with children who had received chemotherapy, it would just be a terrible scene. Kids would be throwing up; they would be curled up in bed; they were essentially miserable, and there was not anything much that could be done except to just give them fluids and try to wait it out.

You go into that ward today, and you see kids up, playing, because they have received Zofran. They are eating hamburgers or whatever they eat in hospitals these days—I have not been to Mass General lately—but I am told by my colleagues that it has just rejuvenated the way that we treat cancer. So it has been of tremendous benefit.

Those are three examples of where, clearly, it is cost-effective and enhances quality of life.

Now, there are a number of health care reform proposals before the Congress, of which you are much more aware than I. I think from the point of view of building on the present system, really trying to maintain the incentives and preserve the incentives for innovation, that the proposal which has been put forth initially by The Jackson Hole Group and is best reflected, I think, in the Breaux-Durenberger and in the Chafee bills, is the one which I would personally favor.

On the other hand, the administration bill has many, many good things in it. But there are two concerns that I have about it as far as its ability to promote or to impede innovation. The first of these, of course, is the Breakthrough Drug Committee, the advisory committee to the Secretary which can determine whether or not a drug is excessively priced. And the corollary to that is the Secretary's authority to essentially blacklist a drug as far as Medicare reimbursement is concerned. While both are not directly fixing of prices, they certainly do put the Government into a very primary path as far as pricing is concerned.

Admittedly, it is attractive, perhaps, in order to keep prices and costs down, to take a very short-term approach; and while there might be some benefits by using this particular mechanism in the short term, I would argue that the long-term costs are unacceptable.

Specifically, if I as a fiduciary of a pharmaceutical research-based company am charged with setting the research strategy which will yield the returns of tomorrow, I would be very reluctant to commit us to a high-risk strategy which at the end of the day might be very expensive, but which would be disallowed or blacklisted by the Secretary simply because the price was deemed excessive. And that is a concern that I think we should all have as we move through the issues relating to health care reform.

Specifically, if there were a drug which was directed to the elderly population, and I knew it might get blacklisted, and I had a competing research project that was going to another population, I might not embark upon the elderly population.

Let me give you another specific example. Twenty years ago, in 1972-73, Glaxo embarked upon a program in serotonin research, which is a ubiquitous substance in the brain. We did not know where it was going. It was strictly basic research. We knew that serotonin was present in large amounts and must have something important to do with the brain. But it took us 17 years to bring Zofran to the market.

If I had to make that decision right now, in the face of the constraints proposed by the Breakthrough Committee or the blacklisting of the Secretary, I am not really sure I would make that decision. I just do not know the answer to that. Fortunately, I do not have to make that decision.

But the important thing, of course, is that we do not want to do anything which will impede innovation, which will lead to the obstruction of research that will lead to the cures of the drugs of tomorrow. I think we all share in that particular mission.

I hope that as we move down the road, that 10 years from now we can look back upon this particular time and say, yes, we did something for access, we did something for cost containment, we did something for quality, but we also did something for innovation.

Thank you.

The CHAIRMAN. Thank you very much.

[The prepared statement of Dr. Sanders follows:]

PREPARED STATEMENT OF DR. CHARLES A. SANDERS

Mr. Chairman, I am Charles A. Sanders, M.D., chairman and chief executive officer of Glaxo Inc., the second largest research-based pharmaceutical company in the United States. Glaxo Inc. is a subsidiary of British-based Glaxo Holdings p.l.c., with U.S. headquarters, including a 1.5-million-square-foot research and development center in Research Triangle Park, N.C. Glaxo employs more than 6400 people in the U.S.

Like all pharmaceutical companies, Glaxo has a keen interest in the ultimate shape of health care reform. We are interested because it obviously will affect our business, but more importantly, we are interested because it will affect our mission. We exist to discover and develop innovative pharmaceuticals to treat unmet medical needs, an effort to which Glaxo will devote $1.4 billion worldwide this fiscal year.

Today I will explain how our mission is consistent with the health care needs of this country, and in fact serves as the foundation for solutions to many of the problems that continue to vex our current health care system. I also will discuss how we might achieve the goals of health care reform in a manner that preserves the vital role of biomedical innovation. Finally, I will point out some concerns with the Administration's reform plan that might diminish innovation in the medical sciences and, along with it, the hopes of thousands of people suffering from diseases, like Alzheimer's, osteoporosis and cancer, that are inadequately treated now.

As a participant and observer of the health care system for 35 years, I have gained a broad-based perspective on both the problems facing our health care system and on some of the potential pitfalls we may encounter as we seek to reform it. First as a practicing cardiologist, and later as a professor of medicine at Harvard University, general director of Massachusetts General Hospital and now CEO of a major pharmaceutical company, I am convinced that health care in this country is second to none. However, I am also convinced that reforms are needed.

It is plainly unacceptable to allow 35 to 40 million uninsured Americans to live an ambulance ride away from financial ruin. It is plainly unacceptable to ration health care based on an individual's ability to pay. But it is also plainly unacceptable to compromise the quality of the health care services we have come to depend on and can look forward to in the future.

So it is beyond question that we must contain costs, expand access and preserve and improve quality, and I commend the efforts of President Clinton, Senators Chafee, Breaux and Durenberger, and others, to address these important issues.As we grapple with them, however, it is equally unacceptable to overlook the role of biomedical innovation in providing solutions.

Whatever direction we take, we must recognize and encourage innovation, because innovation impacts every point of the cost-access-quality triangle.

As pharmaceutical companies make strides in unlocking the secrets of disease and in designing more effective medicines, innovation will enhance quality. As these new medicines keep more people out of the doctor's office, out of surgery and out of the hospital, innovation will help contain costs. As technological advances improve efficiencies in health care delivery, innovation will help expand access.

Recent history provides us with abundant examples, but I would like to focus on three that originate close to home in North Carolina. The first involves Burroughs Wellcome Co., which, like Glaxo Inc., has its national headquarters in Research Triangle Park, N.C. The second involves work at Duke University Medical Center in Durham. The third involves an innovative medicine produced by Glaxo.

In 1990 Burroughs Wellcome launched a lung surfactant that helps premature infants and other newborns with underdeveloped lungs breathe easier. For thousands of infants suffering from respiratory distress syndrome (RDS), this medicine, along with a similar one later produced by Ross Laboratories, has meant the difference between life and death. While it's impossible to measure what these medicines have meant to scores of worried and fearful parents, an important measure of their effect on public health comes from the federal Centers for Disease Control.

In 1990, the same year as the launch of the Burroughs Wellcome product, CDC reported an infant mortality rate of 9.2 deaths per 1,000 births, a 6% decrease from the year before and the lowest rate ever recorded in the United States. According to the CDC, this overall drop in infant mortality is largely attributable to the decrease in deaths from RDS as a result of the availability of the new lung surfactant therapies. The credit for this achievement must go to the innovative research first by scientists in academia, supported in part by the National Institutes of Health, and later by scientists at Burroughs Wellcome, who licensed the compound and guided it through an expensive and time-consuming development process involving more than 6,700 babies. In addition, 10,000 infants in more than 400 hospitals received the drug free through an expanded access program.

Not only is this new therapy saving lives, but it also is saving money by reducing hospitalization and the use of other resources formerly devoted to treating these children. For example, Minneapolis Children's Medical Center in Minnesota was planning to build a new unit for care of children born with chronic lung disease. According to Dr. John Fangman, head of the neonatology unit, use of the new lung surfactant drugs allowed them not only to scrap their plans for the new unit, but also to close their existing unit because the population of babies needing chronic care decreased so dramatically. By canceling the building project, the hospital saved at least $4 million and was able to use their existing unit for other purposes.

Similar cost savings are being achieved at Duke University in a bone marrow transplantation program where the use of a new therapy has had a dramatic impact on the lives of many cancer sufferers. Use of this new therapy has also turned what was a high-mortality, inpatient procedure into a highly successful procedure performed largely on an outpatient basis.

The Duke program has performed autologous bone marrow transplants on more than 850 patients. Undo the earlier approach to bone marrow transplant, patients were required to spend weeks in isolation units while their bone marrow engrafted and began producing new blood cells. The cost per patient was about $140,000 in 1990 and rising.

Today, largely because of a product of biotechnology that stimulates the growth of bone marrow—a compound called granulocyte colony stimulating factor, or GCSF—most patients are able to be hospitalized for only 4-5 days, and the median per-patient cost has dropped by $75,000. Improved drug therapies also are contributing to decreasing mortality rates, which in the program's first decade ranged from 21 to 25% in the first 100 days of treatment, compared to about 2 to 3% now. The value of biomedical innovation in this area was summarized by no less an authority than Dr. William P. Peters, director of the Duke Bone Marrow Transplant Program, who has cited his experience as "an example of where a new technology not only improved outcomes but decreased costs."

Improved outcomes and decreased costs are also being realized by hospitals using one of Glaxo's recent drugs, Zofran (ondansetron hydrochloride), an innovative medicine that prevents the severe nausea and vomiting caused by cancer chemotherapy. While oncologists and cancer patients quickly realized its benefit, hospital officials concerned with cost containment are appreciating it for another reason spelled out in a Wall Street Journal article on November 3.

The article reported on efforts by a Michigan hospital to develop a treatment plan for cancer patients that would reduce costs without compromising the quality of care. The difficulty lay with patients taking a particular anti-cancer drug that, because of the violent retching associated with high doses, often left patients severely dehydrated and their kidneys subject to damage. A three- to four-day hospital stay was typically required to ensure the patient was sufficiently hydrated before his or her release.

By re-examining its treatment protocol, however, the hospital was able to reduce hospital stays to one night for 80% of their patients receiving the high-dose chemotherapy. Central to the success of the shorter stay, the article said, was Zofran. The drug proved so much more effective than other therapies, "it's not even ethical to withhold it," said the physician in charge of the hematology/oncology unit. The article also noted that, at a hospital cost of about $130 a dose, the drug "is much cheaper than a day in the hospital."

Each of these cases stands as a dramatic example of the payoff of biomedical innovation. But none is unusual. Each joins a host of other achievements demonstrating the same effect: cardiovascular drugs that allow patients to avoid $40,000 coronary bypass surgery; psychotropic drugs that reduce schizophrenia patients' need for institutionalization and other treatment, saving costs of $25,000 a year; ulcer drugs that have made expensive and uncomfortable gastric surgery largely a thing of the past.

My purpose here is not simply to provide a laundry list of solutions to health care problems made possible by pharmaceutical industry innovation, although the effects of the innovations are clear. Rather it is to point out that these innovations were not coincidence. They were the direct result of significant investments undertaken with innovation as the goal, with the clear expectation of reward should innovations result.

It is not coincidental that of the 97 new drugs marketed worldwide in the 15 years ending in 1989, 47 originated in the U.S. It is not coincidental that a 1992 General Accounting Office report examining global competitiveness of 11 major U.S. industries cited the pharmaceutical industry as the only one that had maintained its leadership position throughout the 1980s. It is not coincidental that industry analyst Heinz Redwood concluded that "the American pharmaceutical industry has a clear and outstanding lead in developing major, medically innovative, globally competitive and therapeutically accepted new drugs" and that there exists "an indisputable link between pricing freedom and successful innovative research and development in the pharmaceutical industry."

To the extent prescription pharmaceuticals are part of the solution to the health care issues we face today, they have achieved that status because we operate in a free market that rewards the high-risk enterprise of pharmaceutical discovery and development. So if we accept, first, that this country's free market system has allowed the U.S. industry to become the world's leader in the discovery of innovative medicines, and, second, that we must achieve the cost-containment, access and quality goals of health care reform, the question becomes how to reconcile these sometimes competing agendas.

Mr. Chairman, we have a model for reform that does this. It is the concept of managed competition originally advocated by the Jackson Hole Group, in which I have been an active participant. It is an approach that would call for the government to play an appropriate role in establishing an overall framework that allows the best of the current free market system to widen access and further contain costs. Importantly, because market forces would not be substantially impeded, it also would preserve the incentives for innovation that will be the key to overall cost savings in the future.

This is a particularly appealing reform strategy because it builds on the market forces at work today. Already these forces are reducing costs by moving more and more toward managed care. They are requiring pharmaceutical companies and other providers to re-examine their operations with an emphasis on increasing efficiencies and decreasing costs. They are demanding proof not only of a medicine's clinical effect, but also of its economic effect on the total costs of disease management.

Enactment of health care reform legislation based on the Jackson Hole Group model of managed competition would accelerate this trend and lead to further significant adjustments in the way the pharmaceutical industry approaches its discovery, development and business practices. We recognize, however, that under meaningful reform all players in the health care industries must accommodate change. The status quo is unacceptable. While the changes required by a market-based system of managed competition would be challenging, they are reasonable if we are to reach our health care reform goals.

Among the changes would be a further refinement in the standards of success in the research-based pharmaceutical industry, a situation requiring sharper decisions in the boardroom, higher quality in the laboratory, and increased competitiveness throughout the industry. Without question, these new standards will be good news both for patients waiting for medicines to cure or ameliorate the effects of disease, and for the companies who can deliver on their promise of providing the medical innovations meeting those needs.

Our ability to deliver on that promise is less certain, however, under some of the provisions of the Administration's version of managed competition. Especially concerning are the price controls, both implicit and explicit, that would fundamentally change the economic equation in health care delivery. They also would change fundamentally the nature of the industry's decisions about what sort of research and development to pursue. It is a sad fact of scientific and economic life that companies simply will not be able to continue their current approach to investments in biomedical R&D when their ability to realize returns on their successes is uncertain.

Contributing to the uncertainties are the enormous anti-competitive powers given to various offices and entities in government. Among the most concerning is the authority given to the health alliances to establish global budgets through control of premium rates. Such budget caps would inevitably lead to a cost-focused line-item approach to-medical decision-making, forcing trade-off costs vs. quality.

An example of the effect is the 30-year-old patient with high cholesterol, but who is vigorous and otherwise healthy. A formulary committee may argue that it can't justify coverage of lipid-lowering medications. Such coverage would only add to this year's expenditures, with no discernible improvement at year's end in the patient's health. He still suffers from high cholesterol; he still must take the medication. Unexamined are the questions of how the lack of coverage today will affect this patient in 10 years. Will coronary bypass surgery be required? How much greater will his health care costs be over his lifetime?

As a developer of innovative drugs, we recognize that formularies will remain part of the health care landscape for some time to come. However, the interests of patients, physicians, budget directors and pharmaceutical companies all would be served by formularies that consider not just acquisition costs, but also overall economic and quality-of-life outcomes. Artificial budget caps force a distortion in health care decisions that may well lead to higher costs over time.

Similar concerns are presented by the proposed Advisory Committee on Breakthrough Drugs. This is a panel that would be empowered to examine the launch prices of new drugs that represent significant advances over existing therapies. It would determine the "reasonableness" of the price by studying, among other things, projected prescription volume, manufacturing costs and research expenditures.

Putting aside the difficulties associated with arriving at a fair definition of "reasonable," putting aside the terrible precedent of a committee of this sort rummaging through a company- books, the power exercised by this so-called advisory committee would be extraordinary. While it would not have price-setting powers, it would be putting a government imprimatur on a specific pricing level. It would prevent the health plans and individual physicians from considering the benefits of a new medicine objectively and arriving at their own opinions of its value.

Perceptions of value are at the heart of another troubling aspect of the Administration's proposal, the provision that gives the Health and Human Services (HHS) Secretary power to blacklist a drug for the Medicare population. If the Secretary deems a new drug "inappropriately priced," he or she may exclude it from Medicare coverage, or negotiate an extra discount in addition to the one that would be mandated for all pharmaceuticals.

This provision conceivably could discourage research into pharmaceutical treatments for diseases of the elderly. These diseases—Alzheimer's, for example—are among the most puzzling to understand, and therefore are among the most costly to explore in terms of drug discovery and development. They also are among the most expensive in terms of costs to society. If, however, a drug company knows that after its huge investments of time and resources the resulting compound may not be available to the very people for whom it was designed, it would have to consider carefully whether it can afford to invest the time and money to begin with. Indeed, it may be the case that the entire market for some compounds lies within the Medicare population, making the negotiation with HHS not a true negotiation at all because of the unilateral leverage the Secretary would bring to the table.

The same considerations apply to the proposed Medicare rebate scheme, which adds an element to the R&D decision-making process that may tilt the balance further toward conservatism. The rebate seems to be predicated on the idea that companies will see a windfall of revenue from the increased use of pharmaceuticals in the Medicare population. Based on Glaxo's analysis, however, the induced demand will be far lower than that estimated by the Administration, largely because Medicare recipients as a group are already using pharmaceuticals. The Administration proposal would simply change the method of payment.

It's entirely possible, as our findings suggest, that the revenue realized by increased demand will be offset by the rebate, resulting in a net negative financial impact. Indeed, independent securities analysts have already recognized this. A September 1993 report from Lehman Brothers, for example, asserts that "a 15% discount off this segment of drug sales [the proposed rebate amount has since increased to 17%] would completely negate the volume gains generated in the initial years, and in the out years, the pricing discounts would outweigh any volume gains."

Again, if a company must subject the revenues it receives from medicines developed for diseases of the elderly to a minimum 17% tax—a tax that could apply to more than 40% of its business—that company would have to ask itself whether it makes financial sense to invest the hundreds of millions of dollars and staff hours such a project requires.

Despite these and other provisions that would discourage investments in innovation, this does not mean the research-based pharmaceutical industry would end its research. Research is what we do. It defines us. It is central to our mission.

At the same time, we would not be blind to the environment in which we do our research. We would not be blind to the marketplace forces and economic realities that would determine our success' and stability as a company. The ultimate effect, then, may well be a bias away from long-term, high-risk projects to shorter term, lower-risk projects. The probable result would be a stream of new products that may advance the pharmaceutical sciences, but only incrementally. They will be products representing small refinements and improvements in medicines in familiar therapeutic categories. This is not to diminish the value of incremental gains, which are an important way science progresses. It is only to point out that in a highly regulated environment, the big stretch in R&D would be the exception rather than the rule.

My company, Glaxo, may provide a glimpse of how these forces would be translated into realities. Earlier, I talked about the success of one of our newer products, Zofran0. If, however, a drug company knows that after its huge investments of time and resources the resulting compound may not be available to the very people for whom it was designed, it would have to consider carefully whether it wants to invest the time and money to begin with, which has quickly become a standard therapy in oncology wards across the country.

Zofran is the result of basic research into the role of the neurotransmitter serotonin that Glaxo began in 1972. It was not until 1990, when Zofran was introduced into the market, that we were able to realize a return on our investment in research and development that spanned approximately 20 years. It is easy to forget the internal debates that occurred when the effort encountered seemingly insurmountable obstacles and the soul-searching discussions on whether to continue its funding. Given the significant difference the medicine is making in patients' lives, it seems almost unimaginable that anything could have sidetracked it. Yet we have to ask ourselves, if the project were beginning in an environment dominated by regulation and cost containment, would we pursue it? Fortunately I don't have to answer that question. Yet the fact remains, many similar questions are around the corner.

Some of those questions will be basic ones involving choice. Recently Glaxo announced a five-year $15 million international research collaboration to find better treatments for tuberculosis. This initiative was launched because the company realized that although modern medicines and vaccines have done much to control the disease, TB remains a major health risk in much of the world. The new effort, in which Glaxo scientists will work with scientists from three academic institutions in the United Kingdom and one in South Africa, will attempt to discover novel targets for new drugs, using the techniques of biochemistry, molecular biology and genetics.

In planning this venture, Glaxo had a choice: Should we invest in a therapeutic area in which well-defined drug regimens already exist? Should we be satisfied with existing therapy, or should we attempt to take the therapy to the next level?

Our answers might have been different in an environment dominated by regulation and cost containment.

In another collaboration, Glaxo is investigating some exciting, promising and somewhat futuristic work in anti-sense research, which involves blocking the genetic messages that actually cause disease. This research has a potential to one day prevent herpes, cancer, the common cold, and even AIDS. This is an area of science that has wondrous potential, yet it will be years—some say as many as 15 years or more—before we know whether we can successfully translate anti-sense research into medicines.

Again, our choice was clear: Do we embark on what is clearly a long-term, high-risk project? Or do we play it safe, investing in discovery efforts in which the research pathway and the possible product are more well-defined? While we are firmly committed to our anti-sense project, an environment in which our potential for return is limited would make these questions far more difficult.

Such an environment would force yet other, perhaps more fundamental choices as well. If the exigencies of a regulated marketplace and the realities of business cause investments in innovation to slow or shrink, which project gets the funding? Would it be the one offering hope to cancer patients whose vomiting is so severe that many choose to forego the chemotherapy treatments that may save their lives? Or would it be the one holding the potential to wipe out tuberculosis worldwide? Or would it be the one that might save thousands of lives otherwise lost to AIDS? Or would it be the one that might save billions of dollars of lost productivity costs associated with the common cold?

If society is to continue to realize the benefits of innovation, free market forces must be allowed to work. Market-based managed competition as embraced in the Breaux/Durenberger bill and the Chafee bill provides an excellent framework for reform, and may well be the solution we all are looking for. However, in a highly regulated setting such as the one proposed in the Administration's plan, we may see short-term cost-containment, but some very significant long-term costs.

What will those costs be? If the pharmaceutical industry must become more conservative in its R&D decision-making, what will be the costs to the thousands suffering from arthritis and osteoporosis? What will be the costs for thousands more Alzheimer's sufferers, diabetics and heart disease victims?

As a physician, a former hospital administrator and pharmaceutical CEO, I'm convinced the costs of curtailing pharmaceutical research—both in economic and human terms—would be tremendous. But how do we as an industry or we as a society quantify that cost? How do we count expenses associated with a medicine that might have been discovered, but wasn't?

Clearly it is impossible to peek into the future and arrive at adequate answers. Nevertheless, before we enact health care reforms that diminish the promise of continued biomedical innovation, it is our duty to at least consider the questions.

The CHAIRMAN. Mr. de Vink.

Mr. DE VINK. Thank you, Mr. Chairman.

I appreciate having the opportunity to testify today. My name is Lodewijk de Vink, and I am president and chief operating officer of the Warner-Lambert Company.

I am testifying today on behalf of my colleagues at Warner-Lambert, a worldwide company devoted to quality health care and consumer products. Parke-Davis, our pharmaceutical division, has been in business for some 127 years.

My testimony today will focus on the changing marketplace in prescription drugs in the United States. I have submitted my written testimony for the record and would like to take this time to highlight four points.

First, market changes are forcing companies to rethink their long-term strategies. Third-party coverage of prescription drugs in the private market is increasing dramatically. The percentage of the United States population with some form of prescription drug benefit grew from 30 percent in 1987 to approximately 50 percent today; and as a result, large, sophisticated buyers are exerting increasingly important market power.

Already, approximately 68 percent of the pharmaceutical products are sold to hospitals, HMOs, and other managed care organizations.

This institutionalization presents a tremendous challenge. It requires dealing with aggressive managed care organization, capitation, formulations, and many other market changes. With or without legislative health care reform, the market is changing for good.

Second, generic competition is further changing the market. Ten years ago, this committee helped write the Hatch-Waxman Act. The legislation established a fundamental pharmaceutical cost containment strategy for the United States. The strategy ensures certain and immediate reward for innovation through market exclusivity, followed by equally certain and immediate price competition from generic manufacturers.

Clearly, the explosive growth of the generic sector since the enactment of the Act is evidence that competition works.

Third, a result of this changing market is cost-cutting. As you know, many companies have restructured, and regrettably, approximately 30,000 jobs in the pharmaceutical industry have been eliminated since the end of 1991. These companies have taken a charge against earnings of approximately $4.8 billion to pay for the restructuring.

Research will not be spared in the current round of cost-cutting. A recent analysis of the U.S. pharmaceutical industry by Bear Stearns & Company predicted that research will fall both as a percentage of sales and in absolute dollars. Our ability to continue investing more in research is clouded by the many uncertainties surrounding the pharmaceutical market.

Let us not forget that it is today's investment in research that will provide future generations with new cures and indeed new hope.

Finally, the hallmark of the American health care system has been its global leadership and commitment to progress, technological advancement, and constantly higher standards of quality.

Isn't it ironic, Mr. Chairman, that the European Community is presently drafting an industrial policy for the pharmaceutical industry that moves away from price controls at the same time that the American system is even considering moving forward to it?

On a personal note, I want to State to this committee that I am proud to be a member of this successful industry. It has made innumerable contributions to reduce or even eliminate devastating effects of crippling diseases. I am proud to be part of an industry that has shown global leadership in the advancement of health on a worldwide basis. And indeed, I am proud to be part of Warner-Lambert.

Two months ago, we launched the first pharmaceutical product that deals with the effects of Alzheimer's disease. It is not a cure, but it offers the first ray of hope to 4 million Americans who suffer from this disease and millions more struggling to provide daily care.

In conclusion, Warner-Lambert supports efforts to improve the health care system, but only if that change does not impede our basic vision to discover innovative pharmaceuticals that advance the health and well-being of people throughout the world.

Mr. Chairman, I look forward to working with you and the members of your committee on these important issues, and I am pleased to answer any questions you may have.

Senator DODD [presiding]. Thank you very much for your testimony.

[The prepared statement of Mr. de Vink follows:]

PREPARED STATEMENT OF LODEWIJK DE VINK

Thank you Mr. Chairman. I appreciate having the opportunity to share with the Committee our thoughts regarding the role of the pharmaceutical industry in health care reform.

My name is Lodewijk de Vink and I am President and Chief Operating Officer of the Warner-Lambert Company. I have worked in the pharmaceutical business for 24 years, in a variety of capacities, both in the U.S. and overseas. I am testifying today on behalf of my colleagues at Warner-Lambert.

I hope that my testimony will reflect my strongly held view that the business in which I am engaged advances the health and well-being of people throughout the world.

1. WARNER-LAMBERT COMPANY

Warner-Lambert is a worldwide company devoted to discovering, developing, manufacturing and marketing quality health care and consumer products. The members of the Committee may be familiar with some of our brand name products, such as Listerine, Benadryl, Schick and Wilkinson Sword shaving products, Rolaids, Halls cough drops, Trident, Dentyne, and Certs. Our Pharmaceutical Sector is comprised of three divisions: Parke-Davis, which has been engaged in the pharmaceutical business for 127 years; Warner-Chilcott, our generic drug division; and Capsugel, the world leader in manufacturing empty, hard-gelatin capsules. These businesses represent approximately 40 percent of Warner-Lambert revenues.

Last year, Warner-Lambert's total sales for all products, worldwide, was $5.6 billion and the Company ranked in the Fortune 100. Warner-Lambert employs approximately 34,000 colleagues worldwide and has significant operations in locations represented by several members of this Committee, including: Milford, Connecticut; Rockford, Illinois; Lititz, Pennsylvania; and Greenwood, South Carolina.

Unlike many other companies in the pharmaceutical industry, Warner-Lambert's health care business has always reached beyond prescription drugs. We believe that today's changing health care market confirms the importance of this approach: it requires equal attention to continued research and development, self care through over-the-counter medications, and vigorous price competition through expanded use of generic drugs.

2. SUMMARY AND OVERVIEW OF TESTIMONY

My testimony today will focus on the changing marketplace for prescription drugs in the U.S. The pharmaceutical industry faces a challenge unprecedented in its history as aggressive managed care organizations, the institutionalization of pharmaceutical care, generic competition, and other market changes force companies to reduce costs and rethink their long-term strategies. The result is an industry that is searching for ways to provide better and more cost-effective medicines to Americans in a more efficient and rational manner.

We support the notion of universal coverage and appropriate reform of the U.S. health care system. We believe both can complement the market forces that are already permanently changing our businesses. Warner-Lambert agrees with much of the health care reform plan proposed by President Clinton, but we must take exception with a few specific provisions. The U.S. pharmaceutical industry cannot continue to lead the world in research and development if research is made riskier by government involvement in new drug pricing and our resources are further strained by huge rebates to Medicare. It is ironic, Mr. Chairman, that the European Community is presently drafting an industrial policy for the pharmaceutical industry that will likely reject price controls and separate pricing from reimbursement decisions.

In our view, appropriate reform of the health care system will ensure high quality care, delivered in a timely manner. That is what has distinguished the U.S. system historically from European and other systems, and it should not be abandoned. The hallmark of the American system is its commitment to progress, technological advancement, and constantly higher standards of quality. This should not be compromised.

Mr. Chairman, my testimony will begin by discussing the changing marketplace for pharmaceutical products. Then, it will discuss how this change is reflected in business strategies. Finally, I will share with the Committee the views of Warner-Lambert generally on health care reform. I would be pleased to discuss specifics in response to any questions from the Committee.

3. THE MARKETPLACE FOR PHARMACEUTICALS IS CHANGING RAPIDLY AND DRAMATICALLY

It is no secret that the pharmaceutical industry today measures change in months rather than years. One can hardly pick up a morning newspaper without reading about restructuring, aggressive managed care organizations challenging manufacturers for better terms or conditions, adjustments in predicted earnings, or new alliances in the form of mergers, acquisitions, or joint ventures.

Some argue, Mr. Chairman, that the pharmaceutical marketplace is broken and should be fixed. We submit that this ongoing change reflects a responsive marketplace that is causing the pharmaceutical industry to produce better and more cost-effective medicines for Americans in a more efficient and rational manner. More importantly, just as it has contributed greatly in the past, the pharmaceutical industry offers tremendous hope to victims of disease.

a. The Institutionalization of Care

The change we are experiencing is a function of several market forces. Third-party coverage of prescription drugs is increasing dramatically. The percentage of the U.S. population with some form of prescription drug benefit grew from 30 percent in 1987 to approximately half today. With or without legislated health care reform, managed care is expected to grow further over the coming years.

And as more Americans are covered by third-parties, large, sophisticated buyers are playing an increasingly important role—and exerting increasingly important market power. Already, approximately 68 percent of pharmaceutical products are sold to hospitals, health maintenance organizations ("HMOs") and other managed care organizations. That figure is expected to grow to 77 percent in two years. Some have labeled this the "institutionalization" of the pharmaceutical marketplace.

A consequence of institutionalization is increasingly aggressive cost containment. A variety of cost containment mechanisms are becoming commonplace, such as mandatory drug utilization review, generic substitution, formularies, step therapies and related strategies to manage pharmaceutical benefits.

Warner-Lambert believes it is in the public interest that all Americans have coverage for prescription drugs, even though this coverage will result in the use of many of the cost containment strategies in the private sector mentioned above. We believe the demands on pharmaceutical manufacturers to meet the challenges posed by third-party payors will continue to moderate the actual cost of pharmaceuticals. These market forces help shape our business strategies at Warner-Lambert.

But the development of managed care is not the only significant change we are facing.

b. Generic Competition

Ten years ago, this Committee and the Committee on the Judiciary debated, and ultimately enacted into law, the Drug Price Competition and Patent Term Restoration Act of 1984. That legislation, commonly known as the Hatch-Waxman Act, established the fundamental pharmaceutical cost containment strategy for the U.S. The theory was simple: Ensure certain and immediate reward for innovation through patent and Food and Drug Administration-enforced market exclusivity, followed by equally certain and immediate price competition from generic manufacturers upon expiration of the patent or exclusivity period.

The explosive growth of the generic sector since enactment of the Hatch-Waxman Act is evidence that competition works. Prior to that law, generics represented less than four percent of total prescriptions. In 1986, that figure had grown to approximately 23 percent. Last year, the generic industry's market share was 40 percent, and it is expected to exceed 60 percent by 1997. Wall Street analysts assume an annual growth rate of 18 percent for the generic market, but less than five percent for brand name products.

This growth is fueled in part by the expiration of patents on several major pharmaceutical products in the next few years. From 1992 through 1995, more than 60 drugs with combined sales of $13.5 billion will lose either patent protection or market exclusivity in the U.S. In the second half of the decade, at least 40 additional major pharmaceutical products will lose protection of exclusivity. Few therapeutic categories are, or will be, immune to generic competition.

c. European Co-unity and Pharmaceuticals

Another factor creating pressure in the marketplace is competition from Europe. As I mentioned above, it is ironic that the European Community ("EC") is drafting an industrial policy for the pharmaceutical industry that moves away from price controls and separates pricing from reimbursement decisions. While this policy is only in draft form, an official of the EC has stated publicly their conclusion that national price control systems for pharmaceuticals have failed to contain health costs and have not helped encourage the flow of new drugs.

Europeans recognize the importance and value of the pharmaceutical industry both to the health care system and to their economy. Thus, they are developing a program to facilitate the development of their domestic industry. They have reviewed intellectual property laws, and intend to encourage more research and development in Europe, discourage direct price controls, and rationalize distribution systems and other impediments in their domestic market. Their goal is clear: to help the European pharmaceutical industry become a dominant force in the global market.

d. *The Financial Impact of Existing Federal Laws*

As the EC is moving toward a freer market, several recently enacted federal laws in the U.S. have created significant financial burdens for the industry.

A Price-Waterhouse study documents that the average annual cost of four public laws—Medicaid rebates, Food and Drug Administration user fees, discounts to the departments of Veterans Affairs and Defense, and four tax provisions of the Omnibus Budget Reconciliation Act of 1993 ("OBRA-93")—will be $2.9 billion for each of the next five years. This is approximately 30 percent of the pharmaceutical industry's 1992 after-tax profit of $9.5 billion.[1]

It is worth noting that the General Accounting Office ("GAO") reported that the effective tax rate for the pharmaceutical industry was no better than most industries,[2] and that report was issued before OBRA-93.

4. CHANGE IN THE MARKETPLACE IS CAUSING CHANGE IN BUSINESS STRATEGIES

Most pharmaceutical companies have already formulated and are now executing strategies to respond to this changing marketplace. Generally, strategies are two pronged: reduce costs and accelerate top line growth through new products and markets.

a. *Cost-Cutting*

Warner-Lambert is among those companies that took action to reduce costs and our experience serves as a good example of the tough decisions ahead. In 1991, we globalized our businesses to reflect the new realities of worldwide trade. This involved a reduction in our work force of 2,700 jobs. We began the process of eliminating as many as twenty facilities worldwide, made redundant by the new rules of global trade.

As you know, many companies have taken similar action. Regrettably, approximately 28,000 jobs in the pharmaceutical industry have been eliminated since the end of 1991. These companies have taken a charge against earnings of approximately $4.8 billion to pay for restructuring. For your information, Mr. Chairman, I have attached to my testimony a list of restructurings announced by companies in the pharmaceutical industry that includes the impact upon jobs and associated charges.

Equally worrisome to this Committee and others concerned about health policy is the likelihood that research and development activities will not be spared in the current round of cost cutting. A recent analysis of the U.S. pharmaceutical industry by the investment banking firm Bear Stearns & Co., Inc., argued that,

> Although still the lifeblood of the industry, research and development expenses, we believe, will fall not only as a percentage of sales but also in absolute dollars in the 1990s . . . . Just as the oil industry decided it was cheaper to buy than to discover oil reserves in the 1980s, so too could the drug industry opt to buy products rather than discover them.[3]

Cost cutting is necessary to withstand the immediate economic pressures of the changing market as well as the impact of recently enacted public laws that have drained substantial revenues out of the industry. Clearly, research and development is vital both to the public health and the future success of pharmaceutical companies and we cannot ignore it. But that investment is clouded presently by the many uncertainties surrounding the pharmaceutical market.

b. *Top-Line Growth*

Companies are seeking ways to enhance top-line growth with more certainty. Traditionally, top-line growth meant new medicines. Today, it means this and many other things. It can mean greater emphasis on over-the-counter medicines, including the conversion of products from prescription-only to over-the-counter use. The joint ventures recently announced by Warner-Lambert and two partners, Wellcome, p.l.c., and Glaxo Holdings, p.l.c., are premised on this notion.

Top-line growth can also mean increased activity in the generic market, such as the announcements by nine research-based pharmaceutical companies over the past year that they would enter the generic market in one form or another, joining Warner-Lambert and two others already in the generic business. The search for new

---

[1] Price Waterhouse, Financial Trends In The Pharmaceutical Industry and Projected Effects of Recent Federal Legislation, October 21, 1993, E-2.
[2] General Accounting Office, Tax Policy: 1988-1989 Company Effective Tax Rates Higher in Prior Years, Washington, D.C., August 1992, p. 36.
[3] Bear Stearns & Co., Inc., "Purge and Surge", October 15, 1993, p. 21.

products has led many pharmaceutical companies to more licensing arrangements, strategic alliances, and greater financial involvement in biotechnology.

c. *Impact of Market Changes on Profitability*

And finally, Mr. Chairman, our bottom-lines have been altered dramatically as a result of these changes. Critics of the pharmaceutical industry often point to the historic levels of profitability that existed in the 1980s to support notions that are inconsistent with today's marketplace realities. An examination of profitability today paints a different picture.

A composite of some of America's leading pharmaceutical companies [4] for the post-Hatch-Waxman Act period, 1984-1993, shows a ten year earnings per share ("EPS") compound annual growth rate of approximately 13.2 percent. In and of itself, this is an impressive statistic. However, when you narrow the window of time—to five years, three years and one year—growth rates fall to 12.2 percent, 10.8 percent, and 4.6 percent, respectively.

The average EPS growth rate for the Standard & Poors 500 companies ("S&P 500") was 10.9 percent for the same ten year period. The profitability of the pharmaceutical group was better by 2.3 percentage points. But the difference shrinks to 1.4 percentage points when five year data is compared. The S&P 500 actually outperforms the pharmaceutical group in profitability over the past three and one year periods.

The more current growth rates are a direct result of competitive and market pressures that have evolved in the marketplace during this period. Managed care has been a major driver in this process; the move to managed competition will only accelerate this change.

But it is a widely accepted notion that risky ventures such as pharmaceutical research and development must pay a premium in the capital markets to attract financing. The Office of Technology Assessment ("OTA") explained,

> Pharmaceutical R&D is an investment, and the principal characteristic of an investment is that money is spent today in the hopes of generating even more money in the future. Pharmaceutical R&D is a risky investment; therefore, high financial returns are necessary to induce companies to invest in researching new chemical entities. Changes in Federal policy that affect the cost, uncertainty and returns of pharmaceutical R&D, may have dramatic effects on the investment patterns of the industry. Given this sensitivity to policy changes, careful consideration of the effects on R&D is needed. [5]

It is fair to ask why pension funds, institutions and other investors would assume more risk by investing in research-based pharmaceutical companies when much safer investments offer comparable—or better—growth. The answer is that many won't. As other witnesses have explained in more detail, approximately $100 billion in capital has been taken out of the pharmaceutical industry since the beginning of 1992.

That is not a good sign for those who look to this industry to continue advancing biomedical science. The changing marketplace presents a tremendous challenge to those of us in the pharmaceutical industry. But as the OTA warned, Congress should be careful and recognize the sensitivities of the pharmaceutical industry to public policy.

5. WARNER-LAMBERT POSITION ON HEALTH CARE REFORM

Warner-Lambert supports efforts to improve the U.S. health care system to allow the free market to operate more efficiently; universal coverage, including prescription drugs, recognizing that it will intensify competition in the marketplace; and efforts to encourage research to find more cost-effective treatments and cures. With that in mind, there are several specific concerns that we would like to bring to the attention of the Committee.

a. *Outpatient Drug Benefit*

While the uninsured and Medicare beneficiaries would receive a federally-mandated outpatient prescription drug benefit under the President's plan, this does not mean that 72 million new patients will be brought into the pharmaceutical market. Most already use medicines, including those who have medigap prescription drug insurance coverage. Health care reform may cause prescription drug unit volume to

---

[4] Warner-Lambert, Johnson & Johnson, American Home Products, Bristol-Myers Squibb, Schering Plough, Pfizer, Eli Lilly, Upjohn and Marion Merrell Dow.
[5] U.S. Congress, Office of Technology Assessment, Pharmaceutical R&D,: Costs, Risks and Rewards, Washington, D.C. U.S. Government Printing Office, February 1993, Foreword.

expand, yet, net revenue will not rise significantly, if at all, due to increased discounting and the many other cost containment elements of managed care.

Warner-Lambert has some concerns about the Medicare outpatient prescription drug benefit, specifically the proposed rebate tax and the "blacklisting" of new drugs. Warner-Lambert opposes the creation of an Advisory Committee on Breakthrough Drugs to analyze price. I would be pleased to discuss these, and any other issues, in response to questions from the Committee.

b. Research as Cost Containment

In a more general sense, we are concerned that the debate on health care reform and prescription drug pricing ignores the overriding importance of research as a long-term overall cost containment strategy. The system is not static and can be improved by the development of new, cost-effective technologies and greater understanding of science. Yet, less than $25 billion is spent annually on biomedical research by the National Institutes of Health and the pharmaceutical industry, while the Nation spends $900 billion annually for health care. Eliminating all private research funding in the U.S. would have little if any impact on today's health costs. But new innovations offer tremendous cost savings for tomorrow.

We are also concerned that too little attention is paid to the central purpose of health care: the treatment and curing of disease. Pharmaceuticals are a tremendously cost-effective part of our health care system and should be viewed as part of the solution to managing the total cost of quality health care.

6. CONCLUSION

At Warner-Lambert, we view the marketplace challenges ahead as opportunities to better fulfill the basic vision of our enterprise: to advance the health and well-being of people throughout the world. Warner-Lambert supports efforts to improve the health care system. Even though managed competition would intensify forceful market pressures on the Company's research and development, pricing, marketing, and other business practices, Warner-Lambert stands ready to compete in the radically new marketplace. Moreover, whatever happens legislatively, managed care is already dramatically reshaping the pharmaceutical environment.

Pharmaceutical Restructuring Announced

Year	Company	Pre-Tax Charge (millions)	Employee Reduction
1991	Warner-Lambert	$544	2,700
1992	Syntex	320	2,200
	Bristol-Myers Squibb	890	4,600
	Eli Lilly	720	
1993	Merck & Company	775	2,100
	Marion Merrell Dow	180	1,200
	Upjohn	255	1,500
	Pfizer	750	4,000
	Johnson & Johnson	200	3,000
	American Cyanamid	175	2,500
	Eli Lilly	TBD	4,000
	Total	$4,809	[1] 27,000

[1] Represents 8% of total workforce

Senator DODD. Ms. Lewent.

Ms. LEWENT. Good afternoon, Senators.

My name is Judy Lewent, and I am chief financial officer and senior vice president of Merck.

Two years ago, Merck adopted its own principles and responsibilities on health care reform which in most respects parallel the six principles underlying the President's Health Security Act.

We believe, however, that a seventh principle—innovation—must be woven tightly into the fabric of America's reform legislation, because new and better medicines are the best chance we have for conquering disease and lowering health care costs.

For pharmaceutical research and development, a free market allows innovation. Conversely, price controls and other forms of top-down regulation stifle incentives for R and D investment.

We have seen this economic principle at work in today's market. The U.S. pharmaceutical industry contributes almost half of the important new drugs introduced throughout the world. While our share of market contributions has continued to increase, contributions from European countries have decreased.

The International Trade Commission attributes our industry's strong global condition to a relatively unencumbered economy which has not implemented price controls on pharmaceuticals.

Free market dynamics lead to competitive prices. Specifically, marketplace competition has driven down annual drug price inflation in the years since 1990, and the market impact probably has been understated. A recent study estimates that for almost a decade, the Bureau of Labor Statistics' price index for pharmaceuticals has systematically overstated drug price movements by a margin of over 40 percent. We anticipate that current market trends will soon bring this index in line with CPI.

Merck supports and has been fighting for constructive health care reform, but proposals that repress pharmaceutical innovation are in no one's interest. We would urge that price controls, excessive regulation, and other shortsighted constraints be set aside as we discuss long-term policy solutions.

Keep in mind a few basic facts about the R and D process, which we heard earlier. First, for every 5,000 to 10,000 substances examined, only one will prove safe and effective enough to market for human use.

Second, a child entering first grade could graduate from high school in the average time—that is, 10 to 12 years—it takes to complete the careful and costly research and development required for a new drug.

Finally, only three out of 10 marketed prescription medicines recoup the average cost of R and D. We do not know at the outset if our investment will yield a major success or a dismal flop. But the burden is on the successes to recoup their own costs, cover the costs of those that do not, and fill the financial hole left by the total failures.

Restricting returns to some arbitrary standard of reasonableness will signal that even a major new drug may not earn back its cost. Reasonableness is best determined by the marketplace, the ultimate arbiter of value.

Industry needs more than market incentives to pursue innovative research and development. There must be the financial resources to do so as well. It is cash flow—the profits remaining after expenses, capital investment and taxes—that drives our ability to fund R and D.

Numerous academic studies have documented the responsiveness of R and D to changes in cash flow. Specifically, for every $100 decline in cash flow, R and D investment declines by $30 to $40. This symmetric relationship is particularly relevant today, since recent Federal legislation has already tightened the tourniquet on industry by a projected $14.5 billion hit to cash flow through 1998.

Revenue reductions of this magnitude will take their toll on R and D. Based on the studies I just referenced, industry R and D could fall by at least $2 to $3 billion over the next 5 years. To try to put this in some perspective, this is equivalent to shutting down Merck's research labs for the better part of 3 years. Why would that matter? I think it is interesting to keep in mind that to reverse that process, to rebuild a productive research organization, to reactivate innovation, would take an estimated 10 years. This represents a decade of lost opportunity for medical breakthroughs.

The pharmaceutical industry has already been reducing expenses and streamlining operations in response to market dynamics. If cash flow is constrained by regulatory pressure and price controls as well as by the changing marketplace, firms are likely to make draconian cuts in their R and D budgets. Path-breaking research and development will be significantly diminished.

The real bottom line is that heavy-handed regulation always has unintended effects. The unintended effects of price controls on pharmaceuticals will cause suffering for everyone—providers, patients, and future generations. I would urge you to allow the marketplace to work.

I thank you for the opportunity to testify today and look forward to any questions.

Senator DODD. Thank you very much.

[The prepared statement of Ms. Lewent follows:]

PREPARED STATEMENT OF JUDY C. LEWENT

Good afternoon, Mr. Chairman and members of the Committee. My name is Judy Lewent. I am Chief Financial Officer ad Senior Vice President of Merck & Co., Inc., positions I have held since 1990 ad 1992, respectively. I joined Merck in 1980.

Two years ago Merck adopted its own Principles and Responsibilities on Health Care Reform, which in most respects parallel the six principles underlying the President's Health Security Act. To the extent that his objectives are access to quality health care for all Americans, with security in coverage and choice, and appropriate savings through shared responsibility, we warmly applaud his efforts. Merck appreciates the opportunity to testify today on the role of pharmaceutical research and development because we believe a seventh principle—innovation—is critical to the success of national health care reform.

For research-based pharmaceutical companies, innovation means the discovery and development of new medicines. Innovation must be woven tightly into the fabric of America's reform legislation because new and better drugs are the best chance for more effective and lower-cost solutions to disease.

Innovation requires the economic incentives of a free market environment to flourish. In fact, Mr. Chairman, Merck believes that it is only in a market-based system that America can retain adequate incentives for both forward-looking pharmaceutical research and development and competitively priced drugs. I will provide examples that the marketplace is already working and that more regulation is not needed.

These are the principles underlying my comments to the Committee today. On the details of the President's proposal, Mr. Chairman, Merck has a number of very specific concerns and I will touch on them briefly at the conclusion of my testimony.

MERCK'S COMMITMENT TO INNOVATION

For more than a century, Merck & Co., Inc., has been committed to a tradition of pharmaceutical innovation. Researching the mysteries of disease and discovering important medicines is what the Company does best. Towards this goal we have dedicated billions of dollars to mesh the best scientific minds with the most modern engineering and manufacturing facilities. In 1993, for example, Merck expects to spend some $1.2 billion on research, more than double what we spent just five years ago in 1987.

We recently opened a $65 million R&D facility in Pennsylvania that houses 210 researchers and staff. Part of this structure is dedicated to complying with a new

FDA requirement to do scale up testing of products at one-tenth the normal size of a production run. Previously, FDA only required testing on laboratory-size batches before manufacturing began.

Over the course of this century, investment in innovative research and development by Merck and other U.S.-based companies has significantly improved our quality of life. Americans live longer, healthier lives today and a major factor contributing to this improvement is the control or cure of disease. Many diseases that once crippled or killed millions each year have gone the way of the iron lung.

In 1919, for example, influenza killed more people worldwide than did all the battles of World War I. In 1920, 11 diseases, including tuberculosis, influenza, colitis, syphilis, diphtheria, whooping cough and measles killed more than 540,000 Americans—four times the population of Hartford and almost equal to the population of Boston. Pharmaceuticals have played a major role in essentially eliminating deaths from most of these diseases. Merck alone made breakthrough contributions with vaccines for measles, diphtheria and pneumonia, and with broad base antibiotics.

In the 1960s, the industry tackled and produced major pharmaceutical advances against arteriosclerosis, hypertensive heart disease, intestinal obstruction, peptic ulcers, hypertension and active rheumatic fever.

Some may tell you that the pharmaceutical industry does not do its own research—that it "steals" research done by the government. There is considerable conclusion over what—and where—research and development is done in this country. Innovative R&D is a multi-stage process. The preponderance off efforts are in early-phase, basic research—which focuses on disease etiologies and human biological processes. Merck and other pharmaceutical companies also do basic research, but in addition, we collectively spend billions annually on applied research and the development of new drugs. In fact, over 90 percent of the new medicines introduced in America since World War II were discovered by the pharmaceutical industry.

The diseases of earlier decades, caused predominately by external agents such as toxins and bacteria, were easy research targets for prevention compared with the diseases that have more complex etiologies. The degenerative diseases of the 1990s—heart disease, cancer, dementia, emphysema, peptic ulcers, arthritis, not to mention AIDS—will test our skill at molecular and chemical engineering and require future commitments to research and development of enormous magnitude.

INNOVATION EQUALS COST SAVINGS

Mr. Chairman, innovation to produce medical advances, especially through new medicines, is the long-term key to conquering disease and improving health and quality of life. And as such, it also is the ultimate weapon in controlling health-care costs.

For example, some $10 to $12 billion is spent every year in the United States for the care and treatment of older women who suffer serious bone fractures as the result of osteoporosis. For a victim of this disease, nothing more strenuous than opening a jar can break a wrist; rolling over in bed can produce a fractured spine.

Merck currently has a drug in the late stages of development—FOSAMAX—which is being studied to determine its ability to reverse the bone density loss that leads to these fractures. First Lady Hillary Rodham Clinton, in a recent article in the dies Home Journal underscored the financial and social values of targeting just this one disease for prevention and treatment. If Merck's product makes it to the market, the America taxpayer may save billions in Medicare and Medicaid costs for nursing home admissions and other medical care necessitated by osteoporosis. As significant, millions of older women will be living independently at home, not sitting gowned and alone in institutions.

Similarly, there are more than 900,000 hospitalizations each year in the U.S. for congestive heart failure, at a average cost of $10,500 per stay. In clinical studies, Merck's VASOTEC reduced the number of hospitalizations by 30 percent in patients with symptomatic heart failure and left ventricular dysfunction—which is a weakening of the heart's main pumping chamber. If just 1,000 such patients took VASOTEC, we could realize net savings of over $2.1 million.

An experiment in New Hampshire, where the State set a three-drug limit on prescription use among Medicaid recipients over age 60, resulted in a 35 percent decline in pharmaceutical expenditures over a 11 month period. Unfortunately, any savings were more than offset by an increase in nursing home admissions, up by more than 10 percent. When the cap was discontinued, the use of medications returned nearly to base-line levels and nursing home admissions returned to previous levels. The ultimate losers here were those elderly patients who were forced to trade independence and quality of life for pound-foolish spending policies.

Merck and other American pharmaceutical companies have active, aggressive research projects underway in the areas of Alzheimer's, cancer, arthritis, diabetes, osteoporosis and cardiovascular disease. The estimated annual cost of treating these diseases is $360 billion, over one-third of total expenditures on health care in the U.S. in 1992. Pharmaceutical products to treat or prevent these diseases could result in significant reductions in spending. But at Merck alone it will take thousands of scientists, working millions of hours to examine tens of thousands of substances and conduct increasingly numerous clinical trials to try to discover and develop the rare compound that eventually becomes a prescriptive treatment.

A vibrant research and development environment also yields important benefits for society in the form of advanced understanding of both normal and disease processes. Pharmaceutical industry scientists contribute equally with their colleagues in academia to articles published in peer reviewed journals. More over, recent studies provide strong evidence that competitive research—undertaken by competitor firms in comparable therapeutic areas, using diverse approaches—produces valuable spillovers and enhance the productivity of R&D. (Spillovers are the sharing of knowledge so common among scientists.) Research leading to the synthesis and development of today's antihypertensive drugs illustrates this point. In the 35 years between 1945 and 1980, over half-a-dozen companies developed pioneer agents, each contributing important new advances along the spectrum of discovery in the control of hypertension.

INNOVATION REQUIRES SUSTAINED INVESTMENT

For several reasons intrinsic to pharmaceutical research and development, a sustained, long term investment of resources is required to maximize the potential for innovation. First, the odds against getting a compound to market are tremendous: about 10,000 to 1. This means that for every 10,000 substances examined by private pharmaceutical firms, only one will prove safe and effective enough to be marketed for human use. The converse of this is that without examining all 10,000 compounds, that one would not be found.

Second, is the time factor. A child entering first grade could graduate from high school in the average time—10 to 12 years—it takes to complete all the necessary, careful and costly research required to ensure that the product will benefit patients. This same student will have passed 40 by the time this average drug will have recovered its developmental costs.

Third, market success is concentrated in a small number of prescription products. Duke University economists Grabowski and Vernon, looking at product introductions in the 1970s and early 1980s, found that 70 percent of marketed prescription medicines in this period did not recoup the average cost of R&D. Highly successful breakthrough products must earn a return that permits them to "carry more than their own weight": they must recoup their own R&D costs; cover the costs of those that don't; and fill the financial hole left by all the R&D failures. Obviously, these odds leave no room for indecision in investment—we must constantly strive for winners.

A note on the issue of failures. Critics of the industry accuse us of "waste" and reference the number of dead-end projects that do not produce drugs. On this issue, the Office of Technology Assessment (OTA), in a study released this spring, recognized that these failures may be an inevitable function of aggressive research. Study director Judith Wagner recently told the Wall Street Journal that OTA assumes "drug companies don't throw money down a sinkhole purposefully."

Fourth, a research gulf once spanned may have to be traversed again and again. Antibiotics are a good example of this point. A study underway at the Center for Strategic and International Studies (CSIS) on sustaining innovation in America finds that continuing R&D in the area of antibiotics is "absolutely essential" since the capacity of bacteria to mutate and develop resistance is outstripping the ability of research to invent new therapies. The best and most frightening example: today's strain of tuberculosis.

Finally, the pharmaceutical industry is highly competitive. Today's research pipeline includes over 4,000 drugs in varying stages of development, reflecting a cumulative investment of over $50 billion by the industry. And just as importantly, even where firms' research overlaps in a therapeutic area, their unique approaches to solving today's and tomorrow's medical problems mean that the resulting products will provide valuable therapeutic alternatives for patients. The industry has been described as one where "past achievements buy little respite from the need for innovation as a condition of survival." The paradox of this high risk business is that the road sign to success reads, "invest".

A case study in point on the inseparable link between sustained investment and innovation is the discovery and development of lovastatin, Merck's breakthrough drug for patients with high cholesterol. An abbreviated chronology begins in the early 1950s, when Merck researchers undertook an investigation of the biosynthesis of cholesterol. By the mid-50s, our scientists were testing over 100 resins to find one that would bind bile salts in the intestine. They found one, but with several unpleasant side effects. Research programs in the 1960s shifted focus to fibrate compounds; in the early 1970s yet another lead—oxygenated sterols—proved unsuccessful and it was not until 1979 that we had isolated our target, lovastatin, and filed for a patent. Then began a start-stop-and-start again process of clinical trials. Finally, on 31 August 1987, some 30 years after we began our effort, lovastatin was given FDA approval for patients with high cholesterol levels that could not be reduced by diet.

But the story of investment continues. Since the early 1980s, Merck researchers have worked to uncover possible benefits of lovastatin for patients with atheriosclerosis, which is a leading cause of heart attack and stroke deaths in this country. As a result of this research, Merck expects to receive the FDA labeling change which states that lovastatin can actually cause regression of atheriosclerosis in some patients.

This is a major advance, because it is the first time that a single drug will actually be proven to reverse the clogging of arteries. Our research in this area, which involves over 6,000 patients, will continue through 1998 to determine if this regression can actually be linked to a clinically demonstrable reduction in deaths from heart attack and stroke. While this research is not related to producing a new product, it is precisely the type of innovative investment which can dramatically benefit patient health by discovering new uses for our products.

In strict economic terms, lacking the investment incentives of prices, profits and market access, we might not have undertaken the research at all. If Merck had shut off permanently—or screwed too tightly, or too soon—the investment valves during this long, tortuous and risky process, the world still might be waiting for a lovastatin.

A FREE MARKET FUELS INNOVATION

America's free market system historically has worked to position the U.S. pharmaceutical industry as a global leader, maintaining a strong share of the world wide prescription drug market and responsible for 43 percent of important new drugs introduced worldwide in the years the 1970s and 1980s. U.S. contributions to global innovation have increased in this decade to 47 percent; while contributions from European Commonwealth countries decreased in this two-year period, from 31 percent of new drugs to 19 percent.

Research and development by America companies dominated at least eight critical therapeutic categories of major global drugs, including anti-infective, neurological, respiratory, cardiovascular and blood/clotting. The General Accounting Office studied 11 high-technology industries and in a report released last fall cited the pharmaceutical industry as the only one in which U.S. firms maintained their international competitiveness in the 1980s. The International Trade Commission attributed the U.S.'s strong position in the world market primarily to a "relatively unencumbered" economy "which has not to date implemented price controls on pharmaceuticals."

At a time when other sectors of the U.S. economy have leveled off or actually reduced their commitment to innovation, PMA reports that member firms have increased the average percent of revenues spent for R&D to 16.7 percent, up from 11.7 percent in 1980. A report released last month by Price Waterhouse on financial trends in the pharmaceutical industry concluded that American research-based companies have "maintained their commitment to research despite an increasingly difficult economic environment."

We can attribute our position in the world market to a climate that combines a sophisticated scientific infrastructure with a market offering the incentives and rewards necessary for innovative research and development. We have seen what a change in one of these two climate controls can mean for the pharmaceutical industry in Canada and Australia. Both countries have the necessary technology and talent but R&D progressively has been switched off in both with the implementation of price controls.

Professor Lacey Glenn Thomas of Emory University has extensively studied Europe and Japan in order to identify the policies adopted by nations with respect to fostering an innovative, competitive pharmaceutical industry. His findings highlight the importance of stringent safety and quality regulations and pro-innovation pricing.

Using a standard of product acceptance in a critical mass of major markets, Professor Thomas identified the U.S. as producing the greatest number of "globally" important drugs during the period 1965 to 1985. In countries like Japan or France, which adopt protectionist policies and which actively control prices, the home-based pharmaceutical industry has focused on minor, "local" products which cannot compete on the world market.

A survey by the Pharmaceutical Manufacturer's Association (PMA), on the other had, determined that by far the lion's share—approximately 80 percent—of R&D expenditures in this country are devoted to developing New Chemical Entities (NCEs), rather than to modifying/enhancing existing compounds. Clearly, a market driven system in the U.S. has acted as a potent incentive for genuine innovation in therapeutic areas where the risks of pioneering failure are at their highest.

Two points are worth developing here on the issue of so-called "me-too" drugs. Focus on "me-too" products disguises the true value of many of the new chemical entities brought to market by the industry. For example, Merck's VASOTEC, was the second ACE inhibitor for the treatment of hypertension. While some might consider this a "me-too", it has contributed significantly to patients' health. VASOTEC was the first product to demonstrate reduced mortality and decreased hospitalizations in symptomatic heart failure patients and is the only product indicated for decreased rate of heart failure development in asymptomatic patients whose medical histories include myocardial infarction, angina, long standing hypertension and ischemic heart disease.

Second, the concept of "me-too" exists in retrospect only. Up until two years ago, for example, Merck's experimental drug FOSAMAX was expected to run second or even third in the race for approval for treatment of osteoporosis. Our competitors' compounds have failed and now FOSAMAX leads the field.

A FREE MARKET ENGENDERS CHANGE

Mr. Chairman, it is the inherent responsiveness of free market industries to public demands that has yielded a new decade of radical reforms in the pharmaceutical industry. Just as tough, persistent messages on pollution prevention have caused industry to self regulate to improve the environment, market demands for high quality medicines, at competitive prices, have irreversibly changed the dynamics of the pharmaceutical industry in the 1990s.

Specifically, marketplace competition has driven down annual drug inflation in the years 1990 to 1993. And the impact probably has been underestimated. A recent study estimates that bias in the construction of the Bureau of Labor Statistic's (BLS) price index—the pharmaceutical PPI—has systematically overstated manufacturers' drug price movements, back at least to 1984, by a margin of over 40 percent.

Part of the overstatement arises from the failure to incorporate new products in the BLS's market basket. Compounding this problem, but more difficult to quantify, is the fact that most firms reported catalogue prices to BLS, rather than the typically lower transaction prices.

The net effect, however, is that instead of the 9 percent average annual growth rate reported by the BLS for the late 1980s, the actual rate of growth in the pharmaceutical PPI was just over 6 percent. This compares to overall CPI growth of 3.6 percent. Pharmaceutical prices clearly have not exceeded general inflation by the factor of three that is so commonly quoted. Moreover, current trends in voluntary price restraint are likely to bring the two indices into line.

Beginning in January 1994, the BLS will update its sample market basket of drugs every two years, rather than every 5 to 6 years, in an attempt to better capture the positive effects of new product introductions. BLS is further interested in measuring the actual transaction prices that reflect the intensity of discounting, rebate transactions, and price competition that is prevalent today.

Increased competition and consolidated purchasing have a direct impact on market place dynamics. Just eight years ago, large customers, including HMOs and the government, accounted for about 30 percent of Merck's sales; today about half of our drugs go to that market. For the past two years, 87 percent of new drugs entered the market at prices lower than those for existing competitive products, including Merck's entries, MEVACOR, PLENDIL, and PEPCID. Since 1990, the annual growth of industry revenues has decreased by over 6 percent, from 17.7 to 11.1.

Exacerbating the impact of this new era of tough market forces are increased costs of doing business. The most frequently cited average cost of R&D per new drug marketed in the U.S. in 1990 is $359+ million. This actually is a lower-bound figure for several reasons: the underlying data only runs through the early 1980s; the research-related capital expenditures are understated; and the hefty costs of concluding mandated, post-approval clinical trials is potentially excluded, and at best, understated. Lengthening development times and higher out-of-pocket costs, caused in part by greater clinical testing requirements, will continue to drive this upward trend.

In Merck's own experience, targeted R&D on complex, chronic illnesses is increasingly costly and despite substantial investments, we have not seen improvements in clinical success rates—i.e., the likelihood that a product candidate will clear the hurdles of human testing before submission for FDA approval. For years, Merck has invested heavily in asthma research. Although we now may have a good compound in late stage research, time will tell—we have had more than our share of failures. Venzair, a receptor antagonist, was about to begin phase III trials and showed promising signs of efficacy—but was discontinued as a development project because it was not well tolerated.

Merck's AIDS initiative project, ongoing since 1986, is the largest research project we have ever waged. We have studied thousands upon thousands of compounds. Some have failed in the test tube, others in animal studies and four, to date, have failed in human trials. But we continue to invest because of the tremendous medical and social need.

CASH FLOW DRIVES R&D

In addition to market incentives needed to pursue innovative research and development, there must be the financial ability to do so. It is cash flow—the profits remaining after expenses, capital investment and taxes—that drives our ability to fund R&D. Whereas R&D project decisions are based on expectations—like the probability of a breakthrough drug—R&D investment decisions are based on cash flow. Internally-generated cash flow in the form of company profits is less costly and more practical than raising external equity every time an investment is to be made. For growth firms with high intangibles—the profile of a successful pharmaceutical firm like Merck-cash flow is a real operating concern.

Numerous academic studies have documented the responsiveness of R&D to changes in cash flow: for every $100 drop in cash flow, R&D investment declines $30 to $40. This symmetric relationship of cash to commitments for research is particularly relevant today, Mr. Chairman, since dramatic market changes and federal legislation already have tightened the tourniquet on industry cash flow. Price Waterhouse estimates that combined, OBRA'93, the Medicaid rebate of OBRA '90, the price discounts mandated in the Veteran's Health Care Act of 1992 and the prescription drug user fee implemented in 1992 will impose $14.5 billion of costs and lost revenue on the pharmaceutical industry over a five-year period 1994-1998.

Revenue reductions of this magnitude will take their toll on industry R&D. That is inevitable. The pharmaceutical industry has been reducing expenses and streamlining operations for several years now; we cannot simply shield R&D while looking elsewhere for savings.

What kind of cuts are we talking about? In response to the $14.5 billion revenue loss and expectations of future reductions in the potential for adequate returns on investment, R&D will fall by at least $2 to $3 billion over the next five years. This is the equivalent of shutting down Merck's research labs for the better part of three years.

If cash flow is constrained by regulatory pressures and price controls as well as by the changing marketplace, firms are likely to make far more draconian cuts in their R&D budgets. I will revisit this issue later in my testimony. Suffice it to say now, though, that when reductions in private research, applied research, and development are layered upon the existing slowdown in public biomedical spending, society is the ultimate loser.

Keep in mind, Mr. Chairman, that to reverse the process—to reactivate innovation—would take an estimated 10 years. That's the time required to rebuild our research organization. We cannot just flip on the lab lights and resume productive research.

Some critics would argue that if we reduced our promotional expenses, R&D could be spared cutbacks. Promotion of prescription pharmaceuticals primarily is a process of educating physicians on the indications, benefits, risk and side effects of new therapeutic approaches and new information about old products. Surveys show that physicians rely heavily on pharmaceutical companies' representatives for this information.

. An example of the medical and social value of educational activities is the story of diuretic antihypertensives. Until the early 1960s, many physicians were unconvinced of the importance of treating hypertension and opposed routine use of antihypertensives. With the discovery of diuretics, including a major research breakthrough by Merck, the educational activities associated with these therapies helped physicians realize the benefits of controlling high blood pressure.

To the extent that we could do so without inducing reductions in our sales volume—which would reinforce the negative cash flow—a reduction in educational efforts could be an actual disservice to the public.

Unfortunately, these dramatic shifts in pricing and market behavior—and the hard management decisions they create—too often are obscured by outdated rhetoric about obsolete patterns of operation. Yet it is critical to recognize that change is happening and that the momentum for further change is embodied in free market reform initiatives, not top-down regulatory controls.

HIGH RISK REQUIRES POTENTIAL HIGH REWARD

The industry's responsiveness to market changes underscores our fragility. Intense competition for a consolidated block of buyers, who demand demonstrated economic and clinical value for the dollar, more and more drives the way we do business. And yet, we must balance our social obligations to our customers and patients with our fiduciary responsibility to the firm's owners. Because of the enormous and constant risks associated with innovation, pharmaceutical firms cannot afford to rely on debt financing, which constrains cash flow by placing a fixed obligatory draw on it. Firms such as Merck rely on equity as the source of long-term financing and equity is more risky, and costly, than debt.

For the shareholder, investment in the potential for a breakthrough pharmaceutical is similar to any high risk venture: you would not bother without the prospect of a substantial prize to compensate for all the failures and marginally successful attempts. The bottom line economics here are quite basic: if research cannot ultimately provide returns, shareholders will make investments elsewhere. A chilling case in point: a nearly $75 billion decrease in market capitalization of 12 major drug firms over the period December 1991 to October 1993 reflects concerns about the future viability of returns from the industry under the cloud of potential cost regulation by government.

The economic axiom of risk and reward has been distorted for the public, however. Two points need to be addressed here, Mr. Chairman.

First, accounting reporting methods inflate performance levels.

Returns on R&D investments have attracted considerable attention for decades, most recently in the Office of Technology Assessment report, "Pharmaceutical R&D: Costs, Risks and Returns," published earlier this year. Academic studies investigating industry profits have found, and a thorough reading of the OTA report would bear this out, that pharmaceutical profits are not excessive; that in fact, industry returns equal its cost of capital. However, profits are perceived as too high for several reasons.

First, the public looks only at the big winners. Unfortunately, as the Grabowski and Vernon study shows, with the majority of products below or just on the profit horizon, the breakthrough products are highly visible, and their success obscures the performance of the vast majority of products. Focus should be on an entire portfolio of products, since without the breakthroughs most portfolios would never break even.

Further, Generally Accepted Accounting Principles, the rules that define accounting practice, do not appropriate measure the economic performance of firms that invest heavily in research and development. Company performance calculated from financial statements in an Annual Report—the book rate of return—is overstated and makes a successful firm appear more profitable than it truly is. How is this?

A pharmaceutical company's most important asset is patents, the scientific knowledge that results from research and development investment. That is why Merck's value is approximately eighteen times its annual income. However patents, which are intangible assets, are not reflected on our financial statements, unlike investment in machinery and equipment. This treatment of our most productive asset causes an upward bias in our returns; if you compared two firms with identical revenues and expenses, but one invested heavily in research and development and the other in capital equipment, the first firm would appear more profitable.

As a financial practitioner, I note the dichotomy between what the financial markets are assessing about the industry's current and future challenges and what the public may conclude by reading the accounting data in our annual report, which reflects the past.

In addition, the measurement issues inherent in the accounting approach are flawed because they do not reflect a market-based assessment of industry returns when drawing conclusions about our profitability. But a recent report from the Office of Technology Assessment (OTA) did just that, i.e., it looked at industry returns versus shareholder requirements. OTA concluded that industry's returns are in line with costs.

A second point deals with straw men and public policy.

Merck believes that pharmaceuticals are a natural component of structural reform of our nation's health care system. Properly prescribed and administered, pharmaceuticals are the most efficient health care intervention, one that produces real savings for the overall health care system. Already we see an increased concentration of buyers and an increased cash flow squeeze on providers as the buyers wield their clout for more price concessions. Yet despite all the evidence that the market is working, there is intense political pressure to "do something" in particular to rein in pharmaceutical costs.

All of the issues cited—profits, prices, promotion—are straw men. The problem really is lack of coverage, in relative and absolute terms. If you are wearing a coat with a hole in it, Mr. Chairman, that's where you will feel the draft. Many Americans typically have not been covered for pharmaceuticals in their health plans. Prescriptions drugs represent a noticeable out-of-pocket expense for many patients, while physician visits and hospital costs do not. Elderly Americans, many of whom are on fixed incomes and use more pharmaceuticals more regularly, are particularly sensitive to drug costs. The unreimbursed $1,000-a-year prescription for angina pectoris seems burdensome; the $41,000 for bypass surgery is virtually invisible to the patient. The $10,000 hospitalization for congestive heart failure will make less of an impact on a patient's wallet than $600 annual cost for a prescription of VASOTEC.

The real point here is that alternative therapies should be covered equally to encourage most appropriate use and that the marketplace will control costs by allocating resources to the most effective therapy.

Through a myopic focus on drug prices, Congress risks short-sighted policy development and could sacrifice the legitimate role of pharmaceuticals in reducing overall health care spending. I am afraid that as currently drafted, the Administration's Health Security Act sends exactly the wrong signals to research-based firms and will damage the incentive and reward system that motivates innovative R&D.

CONCERNS WITH THE CLINTON PLAN

Of primary concern with the Administration's proposal are the implicit and explicit controls on pharmaceutical utilization and prices. For example, the Health Security Act establishes an Advisory Council on Breakthrough Drugs that would be charged with examining the "reasonableness" of launch prices on drugs representing breakthroughs or significant advances over existing therapies. The Act also specifies criteria by which "reasonableness" should be determined, including manufacturing cost information, expected sales volume, R&D costs and prices of drugs in other countries.

To the average citizen, these criteria may appear logical; to the practitioner of innovation they are a recipe for disaster. Attempts to artificially control introductory prices will have a chilling effect on R&D because the incentive to do pioneer R&D will have been removed. Keep in mind that firms do not know at the outset of their research whether their work will yield a major success or a dismal flop. Restricting returns to some arbitrary standard of "reasonableness" will signal that even a major new drug may not earn back its cost.

As a concrete example, Merck secured final FDA approval for PROSCAR for the treatment of symptomatic benign prostatic hyperplasia (BPH)—or benign prostate enlargement—after 16 years of research and development; PROSCAR is a breakthrough. No other drug has ever been able to act on a major cause of BPH. Without the expectation of adequate cash flow based on market driven or "self-imposed" cash flow constraints, we will look long and hard at future research in disease areas which require R&D resources that we might not currently possess. PROSCAR was introduced at a price of $1.40 per day.

"Reasonableness" is best determined by the marketplace—the ultimate arbiter of value; today's marketplace is working to ensure that unreasonably priced products will not be used.

REVERSE RELATIONSHIP OF REGULATION TO RESEARCH

As regulations roll out, Mr. Chairman, research rolls up. The cash flow constraints contained in the proposed new marketplace provide enormous challenges for the management of firms and a tremendous threat to R&D. To the extent that challenges evolve from the market itself firms retain the ability to adapt their business and to manage these new uncertainties.

I will outline for you a likely scenario for R&D given growing cash flow constraints from a nonregulatory-oriented reform package. Please bear in mind that this considers primarily the ability to fund R&D; the adverse impact on incentives that we see in the Administration's plan carry far more onerous implications.

First stage response to consistent downward pressure on cash flow would be cuts in the rate of growth of R&D, followed eventually by reductions in the absolute amount. Firms are likely to begin with a scale back in intensity, which they will accomplish through attrition or outright reduction of the workforce over time, elimination of research programs, and so on.

What programs will feel the knife first? Perhaps early-phase research, where marketable products remain a long shot, to avoid large upfront costs.

These reductions will not happen overnight, but the effect will be pernicious. Cutbacks in early-phase research will reduce patenting activity and the beneficial "spillovers," or knowledge-sharing, that enhances R&D productivity. Reduced investment in capital equipment, and lower demand for scientists, will damage the very infrastructure that is critical to future R&D growth.

Industry consolidation also is a possible outcome. Firms require a critical mass in order to undertake risky R&D that occupies years. If cash flow no longer will support a portfolio with a broad enough base, then a merger or similar alliance with a stronger company is the only road to survival. Like reductions in basic research, consolidation reduces opportunities for competitive research which gives rise to spillovers.

What if a regulatory filter—such as a bureaucracy to set prices on breakthroughs—is placed over an already constricted cash flow?

I assure you that the incentive to do pathbreaking research and development will be destroyed. Firms do not know at the outset of their research whether their work will yield a major success of a dismal flop. Controlling prices removes the "prize" to which I referred earlier, so why would a firm tackle a new and risky disease if management could foresee only an inadequate reward? And, since historically, pharmaceutical returns have just covered costs—because of a handful of breakthrough products—restricting returns on those breakthroughs will guarantee that the broader product line will never break even.

If industry steps back from the plate, who will step forward? Who will generate the epidemiological knowledge that emanates from the R&D process? And who, at the end of the process, will shoulder the responsibility and the expense for the massive clinical trials to demonstrate product value and generate further information about disease management? And who will disseminate information to physicians about new products?

Nor will these adverse consequences be restricted to the pharmaceutical industry and its customers. The Chair of President Clinton's Council of Economic Advisors, Laura D'Andrea Tyson, has written that high-technology-intensive industries are associated with higher compensation, higher productivity, and higher value added per employee than are other manufacturing sectors. Merck believes that these benefits, and their contribution to American standards of living, are seen in the pharmaceutical industry's global competitiveness, pre-eminence in the discovery of breakthrough products, and excellent export performance. American society thus stands to lose more than "just" some undiscovered products if innovation dies.

The Act contains numerous other stringent cost containment mechanisms, including a mandated minimum Medicare rebate of 17 percent and the ability to blacklist drugs from coverage under Medicare.

It is striking how little we have learned from the experience of Canada and European countries that have exercised stringent price controls without exorcising overall spending increases. What these policies have accomplished is an influx of pharmaceutical investment to the U.S., where it is now threatened as well.

CONCLUSION

Merck supports and has been fighting for constructive health care reform. But reforms that threaten medical advance through innovation are in no one's interest. We would urge that price controls, excessive regulation and other short-sighted constraints not dominate the blackboard as we work through long term policy options.

For the pharmaceutical industry specifically, ill-conceived reforms add new, unnecessary risk to what has always been a complex and unpredictable environment. We will have to cut the rate of growth in our total R&D spending. I can assure you that this is not a scare tactic.

The real bottom line is that regulation always has unintended effects and that the unintended effects of price controls on pharmaceuticals will cause everyone to suffer, providers and patients and future generations. Let the market work.

I thank you for the opportunity to testify today and look forward to any questions.

Senator DODD. Mr. Mossinghoff.

Mr. MOSSINGHOFF. Thank you, Mr. Chairman.

America's research pharmaceutical industry commends the administration for proposing a comprehensive health care reform plan that addresses all of the extremely complex elements of the health care system. We support strengthening consumer choice among competing private plans rather than mandating a single payer. We support providing comprehensive benefits, including prescription drugs, for all Americans. We support continuous coverage regardless of illness. We support greater emphasis on prevention and medical outcomes and think that our industry has a lot to contribute there.

We are also pleased that the administration has indicated that it will remain flexible and open to constructive suggestions on ways to improve the proposals. We believe there must be greater reliance on free market competitive forces in a reformed health care system.

Mr. Chairman, with your permission, I would like to use a few illustrations that are included in my prepared statement to kind of summarize the positions made by my colleagues.

This shows something that you indicated earlier on, that is, the out-of-pocket burden to help pay for outpatient prescription drugs. This chart is for 1991, the last year for which HCFA has data, and it shows the $289 billion in hospitals, and $10 billion of that is paid out-of-pocket, as compared with the $36 billion for outpatient prescription drugs, where more than half is paid for out-of-pocket. I think it is a pretty dramatic illustration of the point you made in your opening statement.

The next chart shows health care expenditures as a percentage of gross domestic product, and it uses numbers from the President's speech. In 1965, 6 percent of GDP went to health care; by 1992, it was up to 14 percent. But prescription drugs are shown in green there, and it shows that in 1965, prescription drugs were about one-half of one percent of GDP, and 27 years later, were about 37 percent of GDP. If all elements of the health care system during those 27 years had been as constant a percentage of gross domestic product as prescription drugs, health care expenditures would today command about 7.5 percent of gross domestic product, and you would probably not have the crisis that the Congress needs to address.

This chart shows the effect on the marketplace, which has already been outlined, plus the voluntary restraints in the industry. The green is the manufacturers' prescription prices. The yellow is the CPI medical, and the red is the general inflationary rate for all items. You can see that in 1990, it was about 8.7 percent for prescription drugs, but there has been a constant and steady decrease to 7.3, to 5.5, and finally, second quarter to second quarter, we are just about at the average inflation level. The marketplace does work, and the voluntary restraints of 18 companies that represent about two-thirds of the market are working to restrain price increases.

This is the chart that shows the research growth in the industry—from 1980, $2 billion, to 1993, $12.6 billion, in research and development. The blue bars are the PMA companies. The yellow bars are NIH for comparison, and you can see that early on, they spend more on research and development—basic research, in their case—than the industry; but during the 1980's, we gradually passed them by and are now moving away.

Now, PMA and our industry fully support increased funding for NIH. They are the world's premier basic biomedical institution. But the fact is we spend far more on research and development than NIH does.

This next chart shows that we are the source of new drugs, and that is not widely understood. We do a lot of polling, and a lot of people think drugs come from the Government, or they think drugs come from universities. Of the 100 most prescribed drugs in the United States last year, 94 drugs came from private industry, 2 were patented by individuals, and a total of 4 came from universities and Government.

A confirming study done by Tufts University looked at all of the new chemical entities approved during a 10-year period, and there, 93 percent came from industry and the remainder from Government and universities.

Finally, my last chart. We hope as we proceed—and we appreciate your opening remarks and others—this is the graphic showing the cost of just eight uncured diseases. The estimates are not PMA's; they are the major associations that watch those diseases and care about the patient with those diseases. Those eight uncured diseases alone, not including AIDS, add up to over $400 billion a year. There are pharmaceutical sales during that same period of $51 billion a year, and we submit that those sales are going to pay for the research and the cures for that enormous amount of expense that goes into the uncured diseases.

Finally, I would just say there has been a lot of talk about windfall sales and windfall profits——

Senator DODD. Could you read what those eight diseases are? Which ones are we talking about?

Mr. MOSSINGHOFF. They are osteoporosis, diabetes, stroke, depression, arthritis, Alzheimer's, cancer, and cardiovascular diseases. And the chart does appear in our prepared statement.

And Mr. de Vink mentioned the drug that his company has come on the market with. Just Alzheimer's alone is a $90 billion a year cost, according to the Alzheimer's Association. It is enormous cost, and that has nothing to do with the cruelty of that disease to the elderly who suffer from it.

Finally, in closing, I will say there has been a lot of talk about the windfall sales and windfall profits if drugs are covered. And obviously, everyone is going to have their projections, but we had a major conference Monday, and one of the most respected health economists in Washington, a former senior official of the Congressional Budget Office, estimates that there will be increased volume if a drug benefit is included in health care reform. But there will be so many biases against the research side of the industry, with Medicare rebates, with generic substitution. And his estimate is that the net loss of the administration's plan to the research side of the pharmaceutical market will be somewhere between 6 and 11 percent of revenues. The net gain to the generic side of the market will be significant—anywhere from 33 to 50 percent.

So we hope you will keep those numbers in mind as you proceed in deciding what is going to be provided in terms of prescription drugs for this industry.

Mr. Chairman, that completes my statement.

Senator DODD. Thank you very, very much.

[The prepared statement of Mr. Mossinghoff follows:]

PREPARED STATEMENT OF GERALD J. MOSSINGHOFF

Mr. Chairman and Members of the Committee:

I am Gerald J. Mossinghoff, President of the Pharmaceutical
Manufacturers Association. PMA represents more than 100
research-based pharmaceutical companies -- including more than 30
of the country's leading biotechnology companies -- that
discover, develop and produce most of the prescription drugs used
in the United States and a substantial portion of the medicines
used abroad. I appreciate the opportunity to appear today at
this important hearing on the role of the pharmaceutical industry
in healthcare reform.

Our companies support President Clinton's goal of assuring
healthcare security for all Americans without sacrificing quality
of care. To accomplish this goal, comprehensive healthcare
reform is needed. Total healthcare costs are rising too fast.
And too many people lack coverage for necessary medical care,
including prescription drugs. These problems must be addressed.

The Administration is to be commended for proposing a
comprehensive healthcare-reform plan that addresses all elements
of an extremely complex healthcare system. We support
strengthening consumer choice among competing private plans,
rather than mandating a single-Government payer. We support
providing comprehensive benefits, including prescription drugs,
for all Americans. We support continuous coverage regardless of
illness. We support greater emphasis on prevention and medical
outcomes. And we support strong safeguards to ensure quality
care. We also are pleased that the Administration has indicated
that it will remain flexible and open to constructive suggestions
on ways to improve its proposal. We believe that there must be
greater reliance on the free competitive market in a reformed
healthcare system.

As Congress begins work to achieve comprehensive healthcare
reform, we believe three overriding principles must be kept in
mind.

(1) ALL AMERICANS SHOULD HAVE PRESCRIPTION-DRUG COVERAGE

o The first principle is that coverage for prescription
drugs must be provided to all Americans just like coverage for
other medical treatments. Drugs not only prevent disease and
save lives -- they save money. They keep patients out of
hospitals, out of nursing homes, out of emergency rooms, out of
doctors' offices and out of surgery. And to ensure that there is
no disincentive to the use of drugs, we urge that they be
included in a common deductible with other medical services. The
industry takes this position with the full knowledge that
expanded drug coverage, as defined in the Administration's
proposal, would result in a net loss for many companies.

Under the Administration's plan, millions of people who now
lack drug insurance -- including older Americans -- would be
covered for the first time. Because so many people currently
lack such coverage, the cost of medicines is a particular burden
to patients compared to the cost of other, more expensive
healthcare services that are normally covered by insurance. In
1991, the most recent year for which the Government has published
actual healthcare expenditures, the country spent $289 billion on
hospital costs -- about eight times what was spent on
pharmaceuticals. Yet Americans paid twice as much on drugs out
of their own pockets -- $20 billion -- as they spent out-of-
pocket on hospital bills -- $10 billion -- as shown in Figure 1
below.

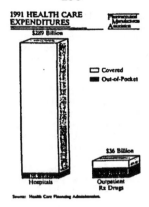

Figure 1.

Drugs are not only the most cost-effective form of medical treatment -- they represent a small share of national healthcare expenditures. Outpatient prescription drugs as a percentage of national healthcare expenditures have declined from 8.9 percent in 1965 to just 4.8 percent in 1991. While healthcare costs have increased rapidly, the share of Gross Domestic Product spent on prescription drugs has remained relatively constant for the past three decades -- at just over one-half of 1 percent, as shown in Figure 2 below.

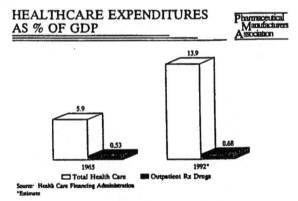

Figure 2.

(2) COMPETITION CAN AND MUST BE RELIED ON TO CONTROL COSTS

   o The second principle is that market competition can and must be relied on to control costs, without Federal Government price regulation or other unnecessary and anti-competitive Government intrusion in the market.

   Competition is working in today's pharmaceutical market. Radical changes have occurred and are continuing to occur in that market -- and these changes already are restraining drug prices for existing and new drugs. As reported in the May 3, 1993 edition of _Fortune_ magazine:

"No matter what happens in Washington market forces are already bringing the lower drug prices that politicians and consumers seek. Two factors have converged to change the prognosis for the industry: The onset of managed care has altered demand, and a profusion of low-cost alternatives to high-priced drugs has increased supply."

According to an April 1993 study by The Boston Consulting Group (BCG), "Managed care grew explosively in the 1980s.... Managed care organizations use a number of tools to reduce drug budgets, including formularies, drug utilization review, generic substitution, aggressive discount negotiations, and demands for demonstration of the economic value of the products. Their success, particularly in more active therapeutic areas where several competitive compounds are available (e.g., H2 antagonists, ACE inhibitors), has put intense pressure on the pharmaceutical industry to deliver high value for low cost."

Unlike European Governments, the U.S. Government decided to rely on generic competition to control prescription-drug costs with the enactment of the Drug Price Competition and Patent Term Restoration Act of 1984. The law accelerated the approval of generic products by the Food and Drug Administration. As a result, the generic share of the prescription-drug market doubled from 15 percent to 30 percent during 1983-1989. By next year, more than 50 percent of all new prescriptions in the U.S. are expected to be filled by generics. Continued strong growth in the generic industry is anticipated as more than 200 drugs with $22 billion in 1991 sales will come off patent during the 1990s.

In addition, 18 PMA companies, representing about two-thirds of the U.S. market for prescription drugs, individually and voluntarily are keeping their average price increases at or below the inflation rate.

The major market changes -- spurred by the growth of managed-care programs, generic competition and concerns about possible price regulation -- have had an enormous impact on pharmaceutical companies. Twelve leading companies have announced job cuts of more than 27,000 employees in just the past year. And, according to an October 21, 1993 report by Price Waterhouse, "The 13 pharmaceutical companies tracked by Standard and Poor's lost $90 billion in market value over the 18-month period ending June 30, 1993."

As a result of these powerful market forces and voluntary company actions, price increases for existing and new drugs are dramatically slowing during the 1990s. In its study, Price Waterhouse reported that, "Drug manufacturers' prices increased at a 3.5 percent rate during the year ending with the second quarter of 1993 -- 2.6 percentage points less than the Consumer Price Index for medical care and only slightly more than the CPI for all items," as shown in Figure 3 below. The Price Waterhouse comparison was based on a more comprehensive and accurate producer index for pharmaceuticals than that used by the Bureau of Labor Statistics (BLS). In response to academic criticism that its Producer Price Index for pharmaceuticals significantly overstates the actual rate of price increase, the BLS has announced that it will substantially revise its index beginning in January.

201

PRICE INDICES, 1989-1993
PERCENT CHANGES

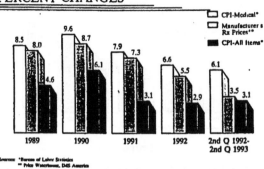

Figure 3.

The prices for new products also show a moderating trend.
Prices for new products approved and launched during 1991-1992
were on average 14 percent lower than the leading product in the
same therapeutic category, according to the BCG study.

In testifying on November 16 before the Senate Special
Committee on Aging, Judith L. Wagner, Ph.D., Senior Associate of
the Health Program at the Office of Technology Assessment (OTA),
concluded that growing market competition in the pharmaceutical
industry will continue to restrain drug price increases:

"Together, these developments have created a new market
place in which employers and insurers have both strong incentives
and the power to contain the costs of prescription drugs by
forcing drug companies to compete more vigorously on the basis of
price....Thus, over the next few years, growing price competition
can be expected to provide a strong moderating influence on the
rise in prescription drug expenditures."

(3) THE DISCOVERY OF NEW <u>CURES</u> MUST BE ENCOURAGED

o The third principle is that the discovery of new cures
must be encouraged as the best way to maintain and improve the
quality of care for patients and to contain healthcare costs, now
and for future generations.

Unlike many other U.S. industries, the research-based
pharmaceutical industry continues to increase its investment in
research and development. The industry has doubled its R&D
expenditures every five years since 1970 and, for several years,
has been spending substantially more than the entire Federal
Government spends on all biomedical research. This year, the

industry will spend $12.6 billion on R&D -- a 13.2 percent
increase over 1992 and almost $3 billion more than the Federal
Government will spend on biomedical research, as shown in Figure
4 below. The industry will spend 16.7 percent of its sales on
research and development in 1993 -- compared to an average of 3.7
percent for all industries engaged in R&D.

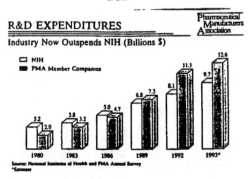

Figure 4.

The research-based pharmaceutical industry not only spends more than the Federal Government spends on biomedical research, it is the source -- not the Government, as many people believe -- of almost all new drugs discovered and developed in the United States. As shown in Figure 5 below, private industry was the source of more than 92 percent of the new chemical entities approved in the U.S. during 1981-1990 -- while the Government accounted for just 1 percent. And of the 100 most prescribed patented drugs in the U.S. in 1992, 94 were patented by private industry -- compared to just 4 by Universities and the Federal Government.

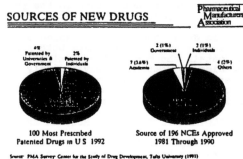

Figure 5.

In the Briefing Book on its healthcare-reform proposal sent to Members of Congress on October 13, the Administration discussed the value of biomedical research generally in terms that eloquently describe the value of pharmaceutical R&D: "The history of American medicine is in large part the story of tremendous advances in medical research that has saved lives, improved the quality of care and helped reduce health care costs. Advancing research and technology increases the potential for more effective, low-cost treatments. Small investments in research have historically paid billion dollar dividends in decreased costs and restoration of productivity."

Just as medicines have conquered diseases of the past, including tuberculosis, polio, syphilis and diphtheria, the industry's new therapies will succeed in combatting the diseases of the present -- if the incentives for pharmaceutical innovation are preserved. Pharmaceutical breakthroughs, including those from biotechnology, provide the best hope that new cures and treatments will be developed. The rise of biotechnology follows earlier scientific advances that also led to better understanding of diseases and ultimately more effective medicines. Pharmaceutical innovation has followed a pattern in the treatment of

disease -- from the relief of symptoms, to control of disease
mechanisms and finally to cure or prevention. Products now in
the pipeline could provide more cures and better controls for
many of today's most intractable and costly diseases.

For example, the industry has almost 300 medicines in human
clinical trials or awaiting approval at the Food and Drug
Administration for just eight diseases that afflict older
Americans. These eight diseases alone -- osteoporosis, diabetes,
stroke, depression, arthritis, Alzheimer's, cancer and
cardiovascular disease -- cost the United States more than $430
billion a year, as shown in Figure 6 below. A cure for just one
of these diseases would produce enormous benefits by improving
patient health and cutting healthcare costs.

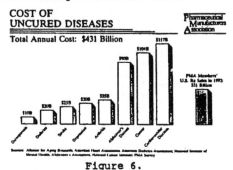

Figure 6.

New Laws Already Cost $14.5 Billion

The three principles just discussed, applied to the
Administration's healthcare-reform bill, raise several serious
concerns. One major concern is the financial effect the bill
would have on pharmaceutical companies -- particularly when added
to the cost of recently enacted Federal legislation. In its
study, Price Waterhouse calculated the combined impact on
pharmaceutical companies of:

o Medicaid rebates on prescription drugs mandated by the
Omnibus Budget Reconciliation Act (OBRA) of 1990.

o Rebates to the Veterans Administration and the Defense
Department required by the Veterans Health Care Act of 1992.

o User fees specified by the Prescription Drug User Fee Act
of 1992.

o The revenue-raising provisions provided under OBRA 1993.

The financial impact of this legislation is shown in the
chart below:

**Economic Impact of Recent Legislation on the
Pharmaceutical Industry, FY 1994-1998**
[Billions of dollars]

Provision	1994	1995	1996	1997	1998	1994-98
1. Revenue-raising provisions of OBRA 1993	$0.484	$0.724	$0.726	$0.697	$0.667	$3.298
2. Medicaid rebates (OBRA 1990)	$1.547	$1.752	$2.018	$2.373	$2.518	$10.208
3. VA and DoD price discounts (Veteran's Health Care Act of 1992)	$0.105	$0.109	$0.114	$0.120	$0.125	$0.573
4. Prescription drug user fee (Prescription Drug User Fee Act of 1992)	$0.054	$0.075	$0.078	$0.084	$0.090	$0.381
Total	$2.190	$2.660	$2.936	$3.274	$3.400	$14.460

The costs to pharmaceutical companies as a result of the four new Federal laws will total $14.5 billion from 1994 through 1998. The average annual cost of the legislation -- $2.9 billion a year -- represents almost 25 percent of the industry's total investment in research and development in 1993.

Huge Increase In Tax Burden Rate

If the four new Federal laws mentioned above had been in effect in 1992, Price Waterhouse has calculated, the pharmaceutical industry would have faced a tax burden rate of 41.4 percent of pre-tax income. The "burden rate" includes Medicaid rebates, veterans' discounts, and FDA user fees, plus Federal income taxes. The industry's actual tax rate in 1992 was 31.2 percent. Price Waterhouse also calculated the additional impact of the Administration's proposed Medicare rebate as if it had been in effect in 1992:

"If the Administration's Health Security Act were enacted, the combined tax burden rate would initially rise to 55.3 percent of pharmaceutical industry income due to the proposed Medicare rebate, and then drop down to 44.2 percent in 1998 when Medicaid rebates are scheduled to terminate under the Administration's plan."

At either 44.2 percent without the Medicaid-rebate tax or 55.3 percent with it, the enormous additional financial burden on pharmaceutical companies inevitably would siphon away funds available for the research and development of new life-saving, cost-effective medicines. Any healthcare-reform plan must fully recognize the profound financial impact of these four new laws and the proposal for a Medicare-rebate tax on research-based pharmaceutical companies.

We believe that several provisions in the Administration's healthcare-reform bill -- including the provision for a Medicare-rebate tax -- would adversely affect patients, the prospects for saving healthcare dollars and one of America's most internationally competitive high-technology industries. These provisions would undermine the incentives for pharmaceutical research and development -- the best hope for improving patient health while reducing healthcare expenditures.

Medicare-Rebate Tax

As noted, pharmaceutical manufacturers would be required to pay billions of dollars in Medicare-rebate taxes to the Federal Government. Such a rebate would reduce revenues to pharmaceutical companies in precisely the same manner as an excise tax. A Medicare rebate would constitute an additional tax on an industry that already pays income taxes at about the average rate for all U.S. industries. The proposed Medicare-rebate tax would apply to a third of the total U.S. pharmaceutical market. As discussed, a Medicare-rebate tax would raise pharmaceutical companies' tax burden rate to 44.2 percent or 55.3 percent, depending on whether the Medicaid-rebate tax is terminated in 1998 as proposed by the Administration. Either way, substantially less money would be available to fund the industry's investment in research and development, slowing the development of new cures.

Government Blacklisting Of New Drugs

The Administration proposes to empower the Secretary of Health and Human Services (HHS) to blacklist a new drug -- i.e., deny coverage for Medicare patients -- if the Secretary determines the drug is "excessively priced." This would give the Federal Government broad power to regulate pharmaceutical prices.

We fear that such power would be used principally to address
budgetary pressures, not the medical needs of patients. And it
could very well stifle the development of new life-saving, cost-
effective medicines. The Wall Street Journal, in a May 25, 1993
article, reported, "Ever since the administration started talking
about health-care changes, the fear of price and cost controls
has hurt the biotech business. On Wall Street, stock prices of
biotech companies have plummeted. Financing has dried up. And
plans for expansion, including hiring, new construction and new
projects, have been put on hold."

What company would be willing to invest the necessary time
(about 12 years) and money (an average of $359 million) to
discover and develop a new drug with the prospect that Federal
Government regulators might blacklist the drug because they feel
its price is "excessive"? And those new medicines that are
developed and are blacklisted would be available to all patients
except those elderly who could not afford to purchase the drugs
on their own.

Public Utility-type Price Commission

A public utility-type Price Commission -- the so-called
"Advisory Council on Breakthrough Drugs" -- would have the power
to "examine the reasonableness of launch prices of new drugs that
represent a breakthrough or significant advance over existing
therapies." This would not only be unwise and unnecessary, it
also would be virtually impossible to implement, as was pointed
out by Dr. Wagner of the OTA in her testimony on November 16:
"It is extremely difficult, if not impossible, to know what the
'right' price for a breakthrough drug is. Every criterion for
evaluating the entry price of a new drug is problematic."

The Advisory Council would not be the only one charged with
monitoring drug prices. The HHS Secretary also would be required
to monitor price increases in each sector of the healthcare
system and report the findings periodically to the President.
There is no need or reason for an Advisory Council to duplicate a
function to be performed by the Secretary -- especially when the
Council would concentrate solely on just one segment of the
healthcare system. Further, while the Council would only have
the authority to publicize prices, a structure would be in place
whose powers could easily be expanded to include the power to
regulate the price of drugs. The Council would thus be the first
major step to reducing the industry to a public utility, chilling
precisely the kind of research the Government says it wants to
encourage -- high-risk R&D against the most intractable diseases.
The competitive marketplace -- not the Federal Government --
should determine the value of new medicines to patients.

Prior Approval

The power of the HHS Secretary to require "prior approval"
before a prescription is prescribed or dispensed was not included
in the bill released by the Administration on October 27, but
such power was in the September 7 Working Group Draft of its plan
and is expected to be included in the Administration's bill when
it is introduced in Congress. In the Working Group Draft, the
HHS Secretary could require physicians or pharmacists to obtain
prior Federal Government approval before prescribing or
dispensing a medicine under Medicare if the Secretary believes
the drug is "not cost effective."

Two of the Administration's major goals in healthcare reform
are to achieve simplicity and reduce costs. Federal prior-
approval requirements would have exactly the opposite effects.
In practice, such a system would create a huge bureaucratic
roadblock -- with doctors from all around the country jamming

Federal switchboards trying to get through to Federal operators so their patients can receive the medicines they need. Prior-approval requirements also would subject elderly and disabled Medicare patients to unwarranted Federal bureaucratic intrusion and limit the access of these patients to needed medicines. Other patients would properly receive the medicine their physician determines is most appropriate to treat their particular condition, without having to obtain prior Federal Government approval.

Medical Liability

Disappointingly, the Administration would attempt to cover doctors, nurses and hospitals in medical-liability reform, but not the manufacturers or suppliers of medical devices and medicines. Provider-malpractice reform without product-liability reform would shift the cost of litigation and liability from physicians and hospitals to manufacturers and suppliers -- at the expense of healthcare innovation.

Anti-Discount Requirement

Pharmaceutical manufacturers, as a condition of partici-pating in Medicare and Medicaid, would have to agree to severe limitations on their right to offer discounts to selected purchasers. Such an anti-competitive prohibition would be inconsistent with the Administration's overall attempt to stimulate competitive market forces. Price competition is central to any market-based effort to restrain healthcare costs.

The ability of a healthcare plan to offer higher quality healthcare within a fixed premium would depend in part on the plan's ability to negotiate with product suppliers as well as service providers.

In analyzing the Administration's plan, Merrill Lynch, in an October 7, 1993 analysis, stated, "In total, the [Administra-tion's] proposals, if adopted, would place the drug industry into a quasi-public utility structure, in our judgment."

Price Regulation Of Drugs Would Slow Innovation

Price regulation of pharmaceuticals would be particularly harmful. Studies show that price regulation of pharmaceuticals stifles innovation -- which harms patients and increases overall healthcare costs. The U.S. International Trade Commission, in a 1991 study of the pharmaceutical industry, stated, "The enactment of cost-containment programs, price controls, or both, on a national level often results in decreased levels of R&D spending in that these programs reduce revenues that can be reinvested in R&D programs. Several countries that have implemented such programs have seen their pharmaceutical industries weaken or shift outside their borders."

Regulation of drug prices would be especially harmful because it would bias research towards low-risk, low-benefit new products. Heinz Redwood, an industry analyst, wrote in a recent study, "Price regulation causes drug industry decisionmakers to shorten their time horizons and to reduce the scientific risk inherent in their research projects. The search for relatively quick, predictable results safeguards a satisfactory, if uninspiring, financial performance. In the long run, such policies produce an industrial formula that seeks to imitate rather than innovate."

An editorial in the April 2, 1993 edition of Science magazine summed up the impact of drug price regulation in this way: "The major casualties of excessive price pressure on drugs would be the small biotechnology companies, the rate of development of new drugs to relieve human suffering, and global leadership of the United States in creating new pharmaceuticals."

World Leader

For many years, the pharmaceutical industry's success in developing new and better medicines has made it one of the country's most innovative and internationally competitive industries. The industry has a good chance to remain innovative and competitive -- if the incentives for pharmaceutical innovation are preserved.

In its 1991 study of the industry, the ITC reported that

U.S. firms accounted for nearly two-thirds of the new drugs introduced in the world market during 1940-1988. In his recent study, Heinz Redwood stated, "The American industry has a clear and outstanding lead in discovering and developing major, medically innovative, globally competitive, and therapeutically accepted new drugs...Perhaps the most important finding is that the American lead includes all but one of the therapeutic classes."

The General Accounting Office, in a September 1992 study, concluded that the pharmaceutical industry maintained its competitive position and strong international leadership during the 1980s, while most other high-technology industries experienced some decline in their position. A report in the March 9, 1992 edition of Fortune magazine placed the pharmaceutical industry at the very top of the list of the country's most internationally competitive industries.

As a result of its competitive strength, the industry has consistently maintained a positive balance of trade, even with Japan. The industry's positive trade balance is expected to be $1.3 billion this year.

In conclusion, we believe the three principles outlined earlier in this statement -- coverage, competition and cures -- are fully consistent with the six goals specified by President Clinton for his healthcare-reform plan. Our industry firmly believes we can contribute significantly in helping to meet these worthy goals. We look forward to working with this Committee in your efforts to achieve healthcare reform in a way that will accommodate our major concerns.

Mr. Chairman, that concludes my prepared Statement. I will be pleased to respond to any questions that you or other Members of the Committee may have.

Senator Dodd. Mr. Sayare.

Mr. Sayare. Thank you, Senator.

My name is Mitch Sayare, and I am the CEO of ImmunoGen, a biotechnology company in Cambridge. There are 185 people in our company. What we do is develop cancer therapeutics, innovative products to treat a very, very difficult disease, one which incurs, as Mr. Mossinghoff just said, huge costs to the American health care system.

What we have done with our technology is to create an opportunity for patients who take our drugs to have a period of disease-free survival in which they are not treated and not imposing costs on the health care system.

Our most advanced product is designed to treat lymphoma, but that product is not yet on the market. In fact, the product is now in multicenter phase three clinical trials and is probably 2, 3, even 4 years away from the market.

Yet we are alive. All 185 of us are paid every day for doing the work that we are doing, the innovative research. That money obviously does not come from sales of products, since we have none that are yet in the marketplace. Where that money to fund our payroll and the innovative research that we undertake comes from is from investors.

Now, you may have noticed in the last 8 or 9 months a slide in the value of the stocks of the companies in our sector. In fact, ImmunoGen's stock has gone from around $25 to about $10. Most of the other companies in my sector have gone 30, 40, 55 percent decline. Why is that?

Well, there may be a number of reasons, and as a scientist, I am not willing to accept, without solid data, what those reasons are as proof. But the suggestion has been made that the prospects of health care reform and the components of health care reform that were talked about by my colleagues here on the panel have scared those investors away.

Our industry, the biotechnology industry, distinguishes itself from the pharmaceutical industry by virtue of its need for investor funds to carry out our operations. Since we do not have sales, we must have investors. They are not there. They are scared away. What are they scared of?

When an investor looked at ImmunoGen to make an investment in our company—and I use my company as an example—what he saw in the product development cycle were basically three risks. There was the technology risk, the possibility that our technology would not prove out to be sufficient to treat a disease that we had targeted. The second is the FDA risk; the possibility certainly exists, and there is good evidence of this, that the drug may not be able to transit the process of regulatory approval through FDA. The third risk is the market risk; will the drug be accepted in the marketplace? Will there be competition? Will we be able to get the price that we need to get? Our investors were willing to take on that risk when they put money into ImmunoGen.

Now there is a fourth risk. The fourth risk is will we be able to price our product in a way that gives us and them a return on their investment. That is the question that is in our investors' minds, and I think it is the reason why our investors turned away from our industry and went and put their money into other industrial sectors. This is a real problem for us. We need to cover our operating expenses, and the investors are not there to permit us to raise that capital.

So what do we do? We have to survive. Our products yet are not in the marketplace. We have no choice but to turn away from the investment community, since they are not there for us, and to look at the big pharmaceutical companies or other sources, and say, look, this is what we have—we have a lot of promise, and we have products in the pipeline. Can you give us the funds to cover our operations in return for certain rights to our products?

Clearly, that diminishes the return to ImmunoGen's investors of the value of those products, but nevertheless it is the only way we have to survive. So we went out and hired a banker, and the banker is out on the street, looking for opportunities for ImmunoGen's products with pharmaceutical companies.

And interestingly enough, because we have built up the infrastructure that we have with our investors' money, the primary interest in our products comes from offshore companies. Most of the local companies, or domestic companies, have the infrastructure that we have built, whereas some of the foreign companies do not have that infrastructure in the United States, so they see us as an opportunity.

So in summary, let me just say that we find ourselves in the awkward position of not being able to fund our operations with the help of the very group of people we had counted on being there in the future, because of the prospects of this health care reform, because they see it as an additional risk that they are not willing to take on.

Thank you very much.,

[The prepared statement of Mr. Sayare follows:]

PREPARED STATEMENT OF MITCHEL SAYARE

Mr. Chairman and Members of the Committee, I am Mitchel Sayare, President and Chief Executive Officer of ImmunoGen, Inc. My testimony is presented on behalf of ImmunoGen, as well as on behalf of the Biotechnology Industry Organization (BIO). I appreciate the opportunity to share my experience and views on the extremely important issue of the pricing of breakthrough drugs. As you know, "breakthrough drugs" are defined in the President's proposed Health Security Act as those that present a "significant advance over existing therapies"[1]. These drugs are essential to the lives of many patients and also to the effort you have undertaken to improve the nation's health care system and contain its cost.

Let me describe what biotechnology is. In addition to being the name of our industry, it is also a way of conducting research by using the tools of modern biology, be they cellular, molecular, or genetic. As I am sure you are aware, its products have generated major advances in human health.

The industry is also characterized by its origins. Most biotech companies were founded on research or technology developed in an academic setting. ImmunoGen is an example. Our research began as a venture capital-funded project at Harvard University's Dana Farber Cancer Institute. I was the company's first employee outside of Dana-Farber when we opened our own laboratory in 1986. Since inception, we have spent $11 million at Dana-Farber covering the costs of basic research, in addition to funding our own operations.

ImmunoGen directs its research toward substantially improving the long-term survival of cancer patients, an extremely important goal of U.S. health care. One in three Americans will contract cancer and one in five will die of it. Our first two products—both in advanced human clinical trials, but not yet approved by FDA—

[1] Sec. 1572(a), Health Security Act.

are expected to increase periods of disease-free survival for people with lymphoma and small-cell lung cancer. If successful, these drugs will alter the course of diseases for which survival rates are poor and have improved only slightly in the last thirty years. They hold the promise of improving the quality of life for patients, increasing their productivity and, because the drugs can be given on an outpatient basis, greatly reducing the cost of treatment. Although our expectations have been bolstered by results in the first 300 patients in clinical trials, I must emphasize that we are still several years away from the market. That is, the development of an effective biotechnology product is not a simple exercise, but requires considerable time and substantial financial investment. In this respect, too, ImmunoGen is typical of the biotechnology industry.

Biotechnology's Importance for Individuals and the Health Care System

American biotechnology has already yielded rich rewards for medicine. Among them are effective treatments for Gaucher's disease and dwarfism, for the anemia associated with renal failure, and for immune disorders induced by chemotherapy, among others. There is even greater hope for the future. We believe that recent discoveries in biotechnology will produce cures for cystic fibrosis, hemophilia, Parkinson's disease, lymphoma and other forms of cancer, AIDS, and Alzheimer's disease. If this hope is realized, even partially, the benefit to the people of the United States—and the world[2]—will be incalculable.

The strengths of the industry are its youthful agility and its willingness to take on substantial risk. Again pointing to ImmunoGen as typical of our industry, we have brought four products from the research bench to the clinic in five short years. We are now conducting 17 different human clinical research protocols on these products in an effort to understand how best to use them. These accomplishments and the many others of BIO's member companies could not have occurred in an environment that does not richly reward investment.

The industry holds great promise, too, for making a direct contribution to the United States' economy. Besides the skilled and well-paid jobs it creates and the American products it brings to the world market, the biotechnology industry promises to lengthen the working life and quality of life of individuals and to reduce health care expenses. Although biotechnology products can be expensive, they are typically highly cost-effective. For example, certain patients with multiple sclerosis ordinarily must be hospitalized one to four times a year, at an approximate cost of $10,000 per admission. With the use of the drug Betaseron, however, admissions in this population are expected to fall by one third—more than compensating for the annual cost of the drug.

The Financing of Biotechnology

I have already noted the considerable time between investment and the initiation of research, on the one hand, and clinical trials, FDA approval and marketing, on the other. A second fact about drug pricing needs to be emphasized. Once research has paid off and an exciting biotechnology product reaches the market, it is subject to imitation and back invention, without violating its patent. In other words, the period in which a return on investment can be realized is often very short. Thus, biotechnology companies take great risks in hopes of a return usually long delayed and, when it arrives, brief in duration.

Until now, the risks—and they are considerable—have been these: (1) Will a given research program yield an effective technology? If so, (2) will the product gain the necessary regulatory approvals? Finally, (3) once available to the public, will the drug gain market acceptance? Now a fourth risk looms—that government will have a say in whether a company can charge enough to produce a return on investment that is acceptable to the company and its investors. This last risk, when added to the others, gravely threatens the viability of the industry.

The Current State of the Industry

Because some in the private sector have been willing until now to accept the first three risks noted above, private investment has supported biotechnology. At least 90% of our industry's research and development capital comes, not from drug profits, but from investors—mostly, middle-income citizens participating in the stock market through mutual funds and pension funds. Last year the industry spent $4.7 billion on research and development, 90% paid for by these investors. ImmunoGen alone, since its beginning, has spent $85 million.

---

[2] The United States is currently the world's leader in biotechnology, though Japan "has targeted biotechnology as an industry [it] wants to dominate by the year 2000." Henri A. Termeer, "The Cost of Miracles", Wall St. Journal, November 16, 1993.

Even with this support, and despite its demonstrated successes, the biotechnology industry as a whole is not yet profitable. Since its inception it has lost $10 billion— $3.6 billion in 1992 alone.[3] Fewer than 1% of the 1,300 biotechnology firms in the United States are profitable. With very few exceptions, biotechnology companies are small and under-capitalized. 99% have fewer than 500 employees and 58% of the companies are unlikely to survive more than two years on currently available resources.

This situation is worsening. The industry's value as perceived by the market (its stock prices) fell by 30 percent in the first two quarters of 1993. There are reasons for this besides the draft health legislation you are considering, including the failure of products in clinical trials and profit margins that have disappointed investors. There is little doubt, however, that a major factor in the fall of our stock is investors' reaction to the Administration's proposal to regulate the pharmaceutical and biotechnology industries. The proposal adds another, major risk to the product development process that has frightened investors and severely impairs our ability to raise operating capital.

The Health Security Act would, if enacted in its present form, impose beat pressure on the price of drugs, which cannot fail to make the industry less attractive to investors. Yet, without continued ability to attract private investment, this essential; life-saving and extraordinarily productive segment of the economy cannot survive.

The Industry's Concerns about the Health Security Act

Three provisions of the Act strongly discourage investment by companies and private investors: (1) reviews by an Advisory Council on Breakthrough Drugs and the Secretary of Health and Human Services of the reasonableness of a drug's initial price[4] (2) the requirement that drug manufacturers discount by at least 17% all drugs sold to Medicare patients[5] and (3) the Secretary's authority to negotiate, for new drugs sold to Medicare patients, a special rebate and to deny reimbursement for a drug if she is unable to negotiate "an acceptable rebate amount".[6]

What are our concerns? Certainly not that we will lose a 'right to be unreasonable' at the expense of the sick and the elderly. Rather, we are concerned that government officials, to whom the Act gives crushing authority over our industry, will not understand the financial incentives that sustain investment in biotechnology. As an illustration of this, let me point out how low a priority the drafters of the bill seem to place on research—the life blood of our industry and our primary expense by an overwhelming margin. Research costs are last in the list of eight factors that the Breakthrough Drug Advisory Council and the Secretary are told to consider in reviewing prices[7] and they are not mentioned at all as an element the Secretary is to consider in negotiating Medicare rebates.[8]

Our broad concern is this. The nature of government is conservative, not risk-seeking. Successful business, on the contrary, must be innovative, flexible and quick to respond to opportunities, and its investors must be willing to reward this behavior by assuming risk. Regulation has a long history—and that history does not suggest that it will nourish the entrepreneurial spirit of our industry. We are deeply troubled by the Act because we know that imposing regulation on an industry—especially regulation that may limit economic returns—discourages private investment. In our case, for the reasons noted previously, an expected return on long-term investments must not be overshadowed by fear of government power to influence prices at the end. (The mere announcement of the possibility quickly and drastically depressed the market in our stocks, which are only now beginning to recover.) If fear causes investors to turn away at this crucial time, the industry will be in grave danger, and so will be our best hope of cures and lower health costs.

The Issue Congress Must Address in Its Final Health Reform Enactment

Although the Administration finds managed competition and global budgets sufficient for all other sectors of health care, Congress has been asked to enact a troubling price mechanism for the drug industry. This mechanism establishes in the pharmaceutical market alone, a role for the Secretary of Health and Human Services. This committee must decide whether this is advisable. A thoughtful article by one of our members well described the central question you must answer. "If we alter market mechanisms . . . on breakthrough drugs, will we continue to get

---

[3] Ernst and Young survey, note 4 supra.
[4] Sec. 1572, Health Security Act.
[5] Sec. 2003(c)(1), Health Security Act.
[6] Sec. 2003(c)(3), Health Security Act.
[7] Sec. 1572(b)(1)(D), Health Security Act.
[8] Sec. 2003(c)(3)(C). The list ends with the term "other relevant factors"

breakthrough drugs?" His answer was, in part, that "Congress should be less concerned about the possibility that a company might someday charge a high price for its AIDS vaccine for the two or three years before a competing product is available than about that company's ability to obtain the research-and-development funds needed to develop the vaccine in the first place."[9] I concur, and I thank you for the opportunity to discuss today our convictions on this important subject.

Senator DODD. Thank you very much, Mr. Sayare, for your testimony.

I am going to ask that the clock be turned on here, so that we can keep an eye on ourselves. This marvelous piece of technology was designed in the 17th century, with the bells and whistles on it. We will reset it every 5 minutes, so we can move through the committee members with questions.

Senator COATS. Is that designed by the people who are designing the health care plan? [Laughter.]

Senator DODD. Now, now, now.

First, thank you all for your testimony, and we will include any additional information that you may want to supply to the committee for the purposes of considering your testimony.

Let me begin with the question that a lot of us get, who do not necessarily understand this issue with sophistication. We have recently seen a voluntary effort to control prices. The average question I will get from a constituent of mine is, well, of course, they did that. There is a health care bill coming along, and they are frightened to death in the pharmaceutical industry. If it had not been for the fear of some price control mechanism, these characters would have gone out and just let those prices continue to rise. You scared the hell out of them, and they dropped their prices. Once you get through this health care debate, Senator, they are going to raise those prices again as fast as they can.

What possible assurances can you give the constituent who raises that question with me, that what we are seeing here is just an aberration, in a sense, to get through the political difficulties faced by what people perceive, rightly or wrongly, as an excessive increase in the prices charged generally by the industry?

Dr. SANDERS. Let me take a shot at that. I cannot speak for the industry; I can just speak for my own company. As Mr. de Vink said, this marketplace has changed very substantially in the last 3 years. We are having to compete in ways in which we never had to compete before, and actually, the marketplace does in fact work, because that is the most important restraining influence in prices as far as your constituents are concerned. We have certainly taken the pledge. Having the threat of price controls certainly does focus one's attention on that.

But suffice it to say, I think the answer to your constituent is that it is a different day in terms of provision of health care. Everybody is very concerned about cost containment. We have to compete in a very tough marketplace, Senator. As I said earlier, breakthrough drugs, while they may be very cost-effective, are going to have to be priced in a very reasonable fashion. The marketplace will in fact demand that.

One of the points I did not make, by the way, is that the breakthrough drugs, so-called, only account for one five-hundredth of

---

[9] Henri A. Termeer, note 2 supra.

total health care expenditure. Yet when you think about it, those are the ones that have the greatest potential to be cost-effective and improve quality of life.

Ms. LEWENT. Mr. Chairman, I might add again from Merck's perspective, we initiated this policy of adhering to price increases no greater than CPI over 3 years ago because we recognized that business should try to recover the inflationary costs in their business, no more and no less. At that point in time, we felt that our price increases over the 1970's and 1980's, with the actions of that period, had recovered the increases in the effects of CPI on our business, and that going forward, the responsible thing to do is just to match CPI with our underlying cost structure and our price increases.

So I would absolutely endorse the comment made earlier that the first and foremost arbiter of what is going to happen in the market is the marketplace; but in addition, I think it is a rational business practice to cover no more than, but to try to recover inflation. And that is what Merck tried to State well over 3 years ago in their policy.

Mr. MOSSINGHOFF. Mr. Chairman, I would add, reinforcing what has just been said, that the Boston Consultant Group did a study, and the pledge that has been made by 18 companies has to do with the price increases on existing products. I think the fact that the market works is pretty well demonstrated by the fact that over the past 2 years, new drugs entering therapeutic classes are discounted 14 percent below the leader in that class, and the pledge did not cover new drug pricing at all. The fact is the marketplace forced that to happen. There was a 14 percent decrease.

So I think the effort of the administration to move toward managed care and managed competition is the right approach to take, and if anything, that is going to increase the competition, which our companies are fully well able and willing to compete in without any Government price controls.

Mr. SAYARE. Senator, the Biotechnology Industry Organization, an industry group which I am representing, also has pledged to maintain a CPI cap. We find that to be fair and no reason to consider it otherwise.

Senator DODD. Let me just put the question to you very directly, then, all of you here at the table—and Mr. de Vink, you, too should comment on this, since I am going to ask all of you to respond.

Mr. DE VINK. Well, I do not think I can add much more, other than that I do believe that the marketplace works, and the statistics are clearly that over the last 3 years, it has come down dramatically, and it is not just something which has happened due to this legislation.

Senator DODD. But are you satisfied that tying this with the CPI is a fair way to proceed?

Mr. DE VINK. That is a question of debate and the degree to which the CPI reflects the true cost of doing research.

Senator DODD. What I want to know, I guess, and I am going to ask you—because we are going to be around for some time on all these questions—is here today: do I have your assurance, those of you who are present at this table today, that when this debate is over with, and we have a health care plan, if price controls are not part of it, do I have your assurance, testifying before this committee on the 18th of November, 1993, that you are going to stick with the exact plan that you have talked about here today?

Dr. SANDERS. Yes.

Ms. LEWENT. Yes.

Mr. MOSSINGHOFF. I think I am going to not answer that because the Department of Justice told us to stay out of this area of activity, that we cannot predict what our companies are going to do. If I were guessing, I would say absolutely yes, but I am really not in a position to commit.

Senator DODD. We are two to one here now.

Mr. SAYARE. I would say yes, definitely.

Mr. DE VINK. The only reason why I cannot commit to that, Senator, is the fact that I cannot predict what the new environment will be and what it will take to get new compounds onto the marketplace. I do not know whether there will be additional regulation or more difficulties being put in front of getting a product on the marketplace.

I think CPI is not an index which necessarily relates to the cost of getting products. All I can pledge is that we will relate it to the cost of doing business, and not anything else.

Senator DODD. I appreciate that.

Let me turn to Senator Coats.

Senator COATS. Thank you, Mr. Chairman.

I am curious about a couple of things. I missed the statistics on the revenue reductions and the impact in R and D. I think, Mr. de Vink, you gave those, or actually, both of you addressed that.

Ms. LEWENT. Yes.

Senator COATS. Those revenue reductions cover what period of time?

Ms. LEWENT. That was a 5-year period.

Senator COATS. The last 5-year period of time?

Ms. LEWENT. The future 5-year period.

Senator COATS. That is what your projection is, then?

Ms. LEWENT. That was a projection, yes, of potential——

Senator COATS. If the President's plan is enacted?

Ms. LEWENT. No. The projection was based on the fact that if we just take the result of the recent initiatives, including OBRA and new rebates in the marketplace, and look at the total cost to the industry through 1998, that aggregates to $14.5 billion.

Senator COATS. And of that, what percentage would R and D be reduced?

Ms. LEWENT. What we then estimated was to say that a large portion of that—not all of it, of course—would be taxable. So we reduce that amount by taxes and then say of that which would be the cash flow reduction, about 30 to 40 percent of that would be the factor that research would be cut. That is how we get to the $2 to $3 billion that we would see being reduced from those actions alone, before other marketplace initiatives, but taking the macroeconomic studies that we have seen and the results that show this basically 100 reduction in cash flow to a $30 to $40 reduction in R and D spending and translating that to the impact of these recent initiatives of $14.5 billion.

Senator COATS. So that in the next 5 years, we are already going to see a significant decrease in funds available for R and D?

Ms. LEWENT. That is right.

Senator COATS. And have you done the same analysis relative to the President's health plan, and what additional changes would occur if that plan were enacted as presented?

Mr. MOSSINGHOFF. I can respond to that, Senator. The four provisions that are existing law—it is OBRA 1990 and the Medicaid rebates, it is the VA discounts, it is the user fees, and it is the section 936 Puerto Rican tax credit—those things add up to the $14.5 billion.

We can get you an answer for the record in terms of money, but in terms of percentage, Price Waterhouse estimates that if those four laws plus the Medicare rebate proposed in the administration's plans were in effect, we would have an effective burden tax rate in our industry alone of over 55 percent. It would be an enormous financial burden to the industry—some applying across the board, but a lot of it applying directly to this relatively small pharmaceutical industry.

Senator COATS. So the result is going to have to be fewer drugs coming to market, less research and development into new breakthrough drugs.

Mr. MOSSINGHOFF. I would think that is the inevitable result, but obviously, these officials would be the ones who would make those decisions.

Senator COATS. Have any of you suggested or communicated to the administration tying whatever health care reform takes place in with reform of FDA and the FDA approval process, linking that to health care reform, because many of you have indicated both today and in previous testimony the delays in getting these drugs to the market and the increase in costs relative to bringing the final product to the consumer because of unnecessary FDA approval time.

Mr. MOSSINGHOFF. Well, we have not really tied the two together at this point, but I would volunteer to say that we are pleased with the efforts of the FDA in implementing the user fee bill that you played a key part in. We are now 6 weeks into fiscal year 1994. This is the year that they have pledged to have all applications that are received this year acted upon—or, 55 percent of the applications received this year acted upon—in 12 months, and next yea , they say 75 percent of the applications will be acted upon. Ther proof of the pudding is to see whether or not that really happens, but there certainly is no lagging on the part of FDA in trying to use the authority and the money you gave them through the User Fee Act that we agreed to totally, to speed the approval of new drugs.

Senator COATS. I wonder if I could ask a little bit about unitary pricing. My understanding is that the Clinton plan would mandate the specific criteria under which pharmaceutical company manufacturers would give discounts to wholesalers or retailers. Is there a mechanism which ensures that that discount is passed along to the consumer?

We know the discount goes to the manufacturer, but does that pass on all the way through?

Mr. DE VINK. Well, I guess we give the discounts to the Government when it comes to that. I think there is certainly volume discount with HMOs and drug chains. That is the Robinson-Pattman Act fair trade competition here. There is nothing else which I think I would say favors one customer over another. I think it is performance-related, whether it is volume or whether it is information, and as such we have applied these practices for as long as I have been here.

Mr. MOSSINGHOFF. Senator, I would add that the provision that is in the 1,340-page bill, we had a major activity trying to dissect and understand that very complex piece of legislation. It does provide on our side, I think, some changes in the Robinson-Pattman Act, but none of our antitrust counsel can yet tell me what those changes will do. But as near as I can tell, there is absolutely nothing in that act which would say that if we are forced to give discounts to community pharmacists, that they would have to pass those on to the ultimate consumer. I just could not find it. In may be in there, but I could not find anything.

Senator COATS [presiding]. I think we will have a chance to pursue that with the next panel. I do not know the answer to that, either.

My time has expired.

Senator GREGG. I will give you more time.

Senator COATS. Senator Gregg and I have been waiting for a long time to take over this committee. [Laughter.] And it occurs to me this might be the opportunity here. I will run over and get the gavel, and we will see how fast Senator Kennedy's staff can get him back here before I undo a few of the things that we have been doing this past year.

We are in a real time crunch, and I want to apologize to the second panel, because I will not be able to stay, even though I am very interested in your testimony. It is my understanding that Donald Moore, who is a former president of the National Association of Retail druggists, is here, and he is an Indiana native, and I regret that we have so much going on—there he is—we were about ready to take over——

Senator DODD. What did you try to get away with? It is dangerous to leave. [Laughter.]

Senator COATS. My time has expired, and I thank the witnesses for their testimony.

Senator DODD. Senator Gregg.

Senator GREGG. Thank you.

First, I want to put this in the context—because I am not sure anybody really understands what the full proposal is—but as I understand the President's proposal, it is that the national health board will create a subcommittee called the Drug Breakthrough Committee, which will evaluate new drugs, and the Secretary of HHS will also have a committee called the Advisory Council on Drug Breakthrough, and that these two new committees will then take a look at whatever drugs you folks are able to find enough money to develop, and that may be hard, because as I understand it, about $80 billion has flowed out of the drug industries since the announcement of the President's plan, the effect of which, of course, is to take a lot of capital out of your system, which capital,

I presume, a significant part of it, goes to R and D. But presuming you are able to still produce drugs which are new and which are going to aid people in addressing sicknesses, whether it is Alzheimer's or heart diseases or cancer or whatever, it looks to me like under the President's program, you are going to have at least two major new—on top of FDA, which you have already talked about—review groups to deal with. Have you given any thought to that and what impact it might have on, first, your capacity to get the drug to market, and second, your capacity to get investors? I think that was addressed by some of you, but I would be interested in any specifics relative to the specific pl n, the two-step committee that has been created here which is, I suspect, more than two committees. I suspect there will be literally hundreds of subcommittees formed by these two committees.

Dr. SANDERS. If I could respond to that, Senator, the Drug Breakthrough Committee is really one of the greatest concerns that I as an individual and a CEO have in terms of the innovative process here. You can use the example of Alzheimer's, a perfectly good reason for expressing concern here, in the sense that if we are going to have to spend $250 million or $300 million on the process of developing a drug in this particular area and know at the end of the day, we are going to have to jump the hurdle of a Breakthrough Committee, which has the right to say it is excessively priced, and an HHS Secretary who would have the right to essentially delete that drug from reimbursement of the Medicare system, I think we would really think twice about whether or not we would go off into a very high-risk investment.

Senator GREGG. If I understand you, you are saying that basically, when you are making your investment decision, there is going to be an inherent tendency to want to knock off review by as many of these committees as possible. So that since one of these committees is directly related to reviewing drugs which would benefit senior citizens under Medicare, and you had a choice between investing in something that might go to that generation of citizens or the younger generation of citizens, you are probably going to choose the younger generation, because you can skip a committee of review.

Dr. SANDERS. Yes, particularly with the Secretary's ability to just blacklist the drug on the Secretary's initiative.

Senator GREGG. So their language may end up discriminating against senior citizens.

Dr. SANDERS. That is possible—an unintended effect.

Senator GREGG. Is that a leading question?

Dr. SANDERS. Pardon?

Senator GREGG. Nothing.

Yes, Mr. Sayare?

Mr. SAYARE. I just wanted to also respond by saying that there is pretty good evidence in my industry that that is one of the principal causes of the departure of our investors to other areas, and as you point out, with the capital flight that has occurred, raising more money for purposes of conducting innovative research on the part of my industry has been jeopardized. That puts not only innovative research at risk; it also puts our very survival, that is, the survival of my industry, at risk. And I think the proposal of having a Breakthrough Drug Committee has done a lot to create that problem for us.

Senator GREGG. Are you familiar with Mr. Termer, who runs Genzyme?

Mr. SAYARE. Yes.

Senator GREGG. He said, and I quote: "We raised $100 million for our new cystic fibrosis gene therapy product last year. If we had to try to hold an offering today, we could not do it. The threat of price controls has done more to damage the biotechnology industry than anything else that has happened in this industry's history."

Would you agree with that statement?

Mr. SAYARE. Oh, absolutely. The dimension of the problem is just as big as Henry says, even larger. There have been a number of companies that have tried to raise that kind of capital to conduct their research, and been unable to in this environment. That is precisely the problem we face.

We have a somewhat smaller scale. In our lifetime, we have raised $110 million. We need at least that much more to get our first product into the marketplace, and the markets just are not there for us; the capital markets are just not there.

Senator GREGG. So you cannot to continue to expand and take on new technologies because of the fear of price controls over your head?

Mr. SAYARE. Precisely. We cannot do that. We have to look at other sources.

Mr. DE VINK. I would like to add to that that I think there are perfect examples within the marketplace that the marketplace can take care of the situation. As I mentioned earlier, we just launched a new product for Alzheimer's. It is the only product which is indicated for that disease at this time, for certain effects of Alzheimer's. And we have to go through the process of getting from one formulary to another formulary, and it is the marketplace which determines that.

If this were determined by a committee 10 years later, by reasonableness, I do not know whether you would make that decision to invest $380 million, whatever it is, the average cost to put a new compound on the marketplace.

Second, I do not understand what we are trying to do. Are we trying to make the market more efficient or less efficient? Europe has gone through years of price controls, trying to move away from it. They are saying it is not working, that it is stifling innovation. And it seems kind of odd that we want to reinvent the wheel and go downhill. I think it is a lesson we can learn.

Senator GREGG. If I can ask just one more question on this point, because what I am concerned about is not only the quality and the capacity to bring these drugs on the market, but the fact that we have an industry here which has really been on the point and on the crest of the wave in America as far as producing jobs and giving us an economy that has been technology-driven. This is especially true in my part of the country in New Hampshire. We have a couple of biotech companies, but we would like to have more. And certainly Boston is a center for a tremendous amount of biotech activity.

I am just wondering what effect does this have on whether you invest to produce in the United States, or whether you invest to produce in some other country? Is it affecting investment decisions as to where you do your manufacturing and where you do your research?

Mr. MOSSINGHOFF. I would say that from a general point of view that the U.S. has absolutely the lead in biotechnology. In 1992, more than three-fourths of the patents granted by the U.S. Patent Office were assigned to U.S. inventors in biotechnology. But the industry has been targeted by MITI, the Japanese Ministry of Industry and Trade. They have said that they will have the lead at least by the turn of the century. And there are very active—and maybe Mr. Sayare can comment—efforts going on now to provide the capital that U.S. biotechnology needs by Japanese investors, who sometimes take a longer view of their investment.

Mr. SAYARE. Precisely. Two things in that regard. The person who was supposed to be here—not me, but Lisa Kanti, whom I am replacing, who is the CEO of a company on the West Coast—is in Japan right now. Actually, she is scouring the world, looking for capital to fund her operations.

Let me point out that one of the ways that MITI endorses innovative research, or that the Japanese industrial policy does, is not by putting a constraint on pricing, but rather by rewarding innovation with higher prices—higher prices, much, much higher than the prices that are being charged in this country—for brand new pharmaceuticals that are introduced into the marketplace.

That is just the exact opposite of what this health care reform proposal is doing. It is stifling innovation by not permitting pricing to take place in an open market environment, and it is the thing that is scaring our investors away.

Senator GREGG. My time is up. Thank you.

Senator DODD. Thank you, Senator Gregg.

Let me pick up on a couple of these points. I presume one of the concerns we are going to hear from the next panel and that we have heard from others—and I note that I have expressed my concerns about price controls—but their argument is that the mechanisms in this plan have absolutely no teeth at all, and that everyone knows it.

I mean, except for this ability to be able to pull a drug out of the Medicare system, beyond that we are getting a lot of reports, possibly, advisory opinions of one kind or another. And I realize those can have some effect, but from those on the other side of this question we are hearing the complaint that this is a lot of talk signifying nothing when it comes down to trying to do something about this. So why are you worried? The discussion goes on all the time. There are people out there complaining about you. We have colleagues who give long speeches. There are amendments offered every year. You know they are going to come. Your investors know it. The markets know it. This is not going to end. You are constantly under the fear and threat that there is going to be some challenge to a scheme that presently arranges the prices and that is what presently is being talked about. This is not going to go away. Despite some of the speeches that have been given and statements that have been issued, no one that I know of at this juncture, and no proposal that I have seen being offered talks about putting in place price controls. They talk about backup authority, they talk about reports, they talk about issuing statements, but nothing that would indicate that they are going to sit and determine exactly what your price is.

What is the worry?

Mr. MOSSINGHOFF. I would comment that as far as the Medicare side of it, it really is a lot more than just jawboning and publication.

Senator DODD. I appreciate that. I understand. That aside, though.

Mr. MOSSINGHOFF. OK, fine. I think the position that members of PMA would take is that once you put a Government bureaucracy in place with auditors and economists, and you have got to have your necessary lawyers, once you begin to operate this way, there is going to be a virtually irresistible temptation, given budget crunches that are going to come every year I think probably for the rest of our lives, there is going to be an irresistible temptation to move from deciding whether a drug is unreasonably priced to simply deciding it is unreimbursable.

And it seems to me that if you put the infrastructure in place of a public utility-type price commission, which is what that provision would do, that the danger of——

Senator DODD. Well, there is a difference, by the way. There is a difference. There, they have the authority to actually set rates in a public utility.

Mr. MOSSINGHOFF [continuing]. That is right. But I am saying once you set the bureaucracy in motion, it would be very——

Senator DODD. It is the nose of the camel under the tent.

Mr. MOSSINGHOFF. Absolutely, Mr. Chairman.

Senator DODD. Dr. Sanders.

Dr. SANDERS. Mr. Chairman, there is also a very good example of that in the Medicare system, in the sense that when they were first introduced, we paid "usual and customary" as far as the physicians were concerned, and we paid reimbursable costs to the hospitals. We are now paying 80 percent of cost, and we are reimbursing physicians by RBRBS. So what was well-intended at the very beginning has been now tailored to what budgetary constraints are.

So that is a concern that I would have. It just seems to be a natural progression in terms of governmental regulation.

Senator DODD. Mr. Sayare, let me ask you this. I have heard you today, and I appreciate that you have clearly pointed out the problems of attracting capital, the inherent risks of biotechnology, and finally, this new element that we have briefly discussed here.

Have there been any studies done that would in fact indicate specifically the risk that you have associated with the general discussion about price controls and standby authorities—that might indicate that capital is going the other way. Or is it just generally believed because there are a lot of questions being raised, and we are doing something very different after 60 years of talking about health care reform? There is a clear understanding now that we are going to do it. What it will look like is a matter of debate and discussion, but I hear no one saying we are not going to do it any longer. That was the threshold question for years. But now, we are clearly going to do something.

And I appreciate that out there, whether from hospitals or doctors or anybody in the provider fields—and obviously your industry and others—there is a great deal of unease about what the administration and what the Congress are likely to come up with.

Aren't we really talking more about that generally, the overall question of what is likely to come out of this? Isn't that a better focus of what is happening in the marketplace in terms of capital?

Mr. SAYARE. I think in looking at what has an impact on our investors' thinking, one has only to look at an incident that occurred last spring in which Secretary Bentsen announced on a Friday, I believe it was, that price controls were no longer being considered. And the whole health care sector popped. We went up a couple percentage points. Investor enthusiasm turned around because we had been discounted tremendously for the uncertainty of what was in this package; it was before it was published.

There was a clarification of this point on Monday or Tuesday of the following week, and we went right back down to where we were before. This is not proof. That is the closest I can come to any specific evidence that there is a cause and effect relationship. But in our minds, the specter of price controls, even if they are not price controls, regardless of what we call them, there is a mechanism in here that increases the risk. And if you increase risk, Senator, the discount rate that analysts use to evaluate how much your company is worth is increased, and the more they discount the less value you have, and here we are.

Senator DODD. Two last points, quickly, and I think we can disregard the clock now.

One question that comes up—and I am not asking something here that you have not heard before—is that, while we appreciate all the arguments about the cost of research and development, the risks involved, and so forth, why is the industry—and I am speaking generically here—spending as much as it apparently does on the promotion of its products? If something is good, given that 60 percent of your products are sold to hospitals and the like and not sold out there in the general public, why is it every time I open a magazine or turn on some television program, there are very expensive promotional vehicles? What cost is the consumer paying for basically a Madison Avenue approach for something that ought to be able to sell itself? And again, I am not asking you a question you have not heard, but we get asked all the time about those aspects. I am going to ask—and I do not expect you to have it with you today—but I would like to get some sense of your budgets in terms of the cost, generally, of promotion and advertising a product so we can have some sense of what that is.

[The information referred to is retained in committee files.]

Dr. SANDERS. The major expense of promotion really is in the sales force and the detail reps. What is happening in those areas, as you are already familiar with, is that there has been a lot of downsizing. But there is a higher premium now being put upon what a sales rep or detail rep has to do. They have to really assume a primary educational function with the user of a particular pharmaceutical.

For example, Ematrex is a drug we just recently introduced to treat migraine. You have to administer by subcutaneous injection. It has to be administered correctly, and it has to be administered to the right patient, and there are certain contraindications for it. So you do not want it to go into the patient that does not have migraine headache on the one hand, or has a condition which that is specifically precluded.

So I will justify the two-thirds of the expenditures that we make in so-called promotion to support those detail reps and various educational enterprises.

To your question, 3 percent of total sales goes to magazine advertising, direct mail, to leave-behinds, to the so-called glitz of advertising. And I can assure you we are looking very carefully at that expenditure right now.

Ms. LEWENT. Mr. Chairman, if I might add to that, we have exploded a copy of the patient package circular for one of our drugs, Vasotec, just to try to convey the complexity of the message that Dr. Sanders was trying to talk about earlier.

We are not trying to get across a very simple message——

Senator DODD. What is this that I am looking at here? It looks like a prescription instruction.

Ms. LEWENT [continuing]. It is everything you need to know and the FDA wants you to know about how to prescribe Vasotec, one of our antihypertensives.

[The information referred to is retained in committee files.]

Senator DODD. I thought it was the Congressional Record for a moment. [Laughter.]

Ms. LEWENT. And a representative has to be sure that he conveys that information to the physician. So I think that just as a point of emphasis, you can see that we have to worry about adverse reactions and contraindications as well as appropriate dosing. This is not a simple product to get across. This is a complex product to administer properly.

And I guess I would just add to the earlier comments the fact that what we are doing is educating, and in that process what we are really talking about is a major undertaking of diffusing knowledge to a very broad physician and patient base. And that is not as simple a task as it looks to be. In fact, even today, when we look at major diseases like hypertension, I believe something like only about one-quarter of the population that really should be treated is still treated. So we still have a long way to go to get the message out. It is not a simple process. And that is the backdrop of where we are spending our money and what the objectives are.

Senator DODD. How much of Merck's budget is spent in what we call the "glitz" area, putting aside the detailing?

Ms. LEWENT. I do not have a number like that. We have adhered very strictly to the American Medical Association's rules in terms of what the appropriate ways to promote products are. So we feel that we are spending our dollars effectively and appropriately to get that message across.

Senator DODD. I would expect the chief financial officer of the company to say nothing less. [Laughter.] But I would still like to get the number if we could.

I apologize to you and to the audience for asking this question, because I know many of you in the audience are far more familiar with the industry and the issues involved, but there is an audience here broader than just those of us sitting in this room. Tell me the difference between the biotechnology and pharmaceutical companies. And is there a danger of us lumping everyone together? And if so, what are the dangers involved in that?

Dr. SANDERS. Let me give an answer to that. I think that biotechnology is just that. It is a technology by which you are really using DNA and gene sequencing and technologies to carry on your research. And it is something without which we could not do in the 1990's in terms of carrying on a modern research program.

What we do in terms of our biotechnology is we use that as means to define a biological system. And then, in the more traditional way in the pharmaceutical companies, that research base that I represent, we try to find a chemical molecule that will mimic an action that is really expressed as a natural substance, such as insulin or growth hormone or whatever—something that you can take by mouth. Biotechnology products are generally proteins which have to be administered intravenously because they are digested if you absorb them orally.

But there is almost a seamless interface here in the sense that we cannot do without biotechnology—we could produce biotechnology products, but our orientation is trying to make oral compounds for the most part. Biotechnology is, as Mr. Sayare expresses it, an individual, small start-up company which depends upon venture capital to pursue a particular research enterprise in the natural substance area.

Mr. DE VINK. Could I add that at Warner-Lambert/Parke-Davis, we consider biotechnology as enabling technology to help us in the drug discovery area. As a matter of fact, half of our discovery research program is done through biotechnology science, so it is an integral part of our discovery program.

In addition, we do support not necessarily your company, but a number of companies with investment, with alliances, where screening technologies are being shared. So there is a lot of interaction between the biotechnology as it was defined a minute ago versus the technology we use in the pharmaceutical side.

Mr. SAYARE. Let me just say that they are absolutely right; there is a big difference between the biotechnology industry and biotechnology. The industry is comprised of about 1,300 companies with about $20 billion in losses, so it is in clear distinction to the pharmaceutical——

Senator DODD. If anyone wants to know why you are having trouble getting investors. [Laughter.]

Mr. SAYARE. It has lots of medications that have been approved by FDA for sale. Actually, that was an excessive number. The number is actually about $3.5 billion in losses.

We spent last year about $4.7 billion on R and D. If you could describe—and I think both of the gentlemen are absolutely right—we are an industry that primarily depends on investors to cover our operating expenses, so in that way we also distinguish ourselves.

Most of the biotechnology companies of which I am aware were founded around academic research organizations. Some technology that came out of the university setting went to seed the technology of a biotechnology company. So that is another distinction between it and academia. That is not to say that we are any closer to academia, but our roots are much more closely aligned with academia than pharmaceutical companies are.

Senator DODD. And finally—though I think you made the point, but just to emphasize it—obviously, as we look at the health care reform package, there are issues here that have a far greater significance for you than for the rest of the witnesses here, except to the extent, Dr. Sanders, that you are involved in this directly. But would you highlight the areas you are particularly concerned about here as opposed to or distinguishing your industry from the pharmaceutical industry?

Mr. SAYARE. We are fragile. We are fragile in the sense that the capriciousness of the investment community directly affects our future. It is very difficult for us to sit down and create a 5-year strategic plan because we do not know if we are going to be around in 5 years, because we depend so much on the investment community.

My thesis has been that this health care reform act has components in it which are wondrous, which will have an impact on the American population that is very, very positive. But there are three components of it that are negative for my industry, and they all relate to mechanisms that are created that do not currently exist for having an influence on what introductory drug prices will be.

That influence and the attendant risk with that influence of a company not being able to set its own price, the price it needs to not guarantee, but offer a return to its investors, compounds the risk that the investors walked into the deal thinking that they faced.

One more risk is enough to cause them to turn away and go into other industrial sectors to make their investments, and that is exactly what has happened. It is hard to get their attention. Why should we invest in you now? Why should we put money in you when you cannot tell us whether or not your product, if and when it reaches the market, can recover your costs?

Senator DODD. I understand that. Now tell me why that is different from what their concerns are.

Mr. SAYARE. Because they do not depend on those investors to fund their operations. They depend on their cash flows to fund their operations. Those cash flows come from sales. We do not have any sales.

Senator DODD. Mr. de Vink.

Mr. DE VINK. I think we differ here a little bit.

Senator DODD. That is what I wanted to get to. I knew I could get you fighting each other. [Laughter.]

Mr. DE VINK. I can hardly believe you can run or continue to run a company on investments which are never going to give any return, and you can forever run in the red. Neither can we think that our investors are not interested in what is happening to our shares. I mean, if we talk about eduction in the value of the American pharmaceutical industry, we are talking about a reduction of 25 or 30 percent. One hundred billion dollars has been taken out of the value of this industry by our investors, which are our shareholders. And they are tremendously concerned.

You can argue about how long has one oxygen while this is going on, and you may have fewer tanks than we have, but the concept is identical. I mean, we are spending research in the same way, and we need to have a return, and our investors, our shareholders, want to have that.

So I do not think there is that dramatic difference at all.

Senator DODD. Any further comment on this?

[No response.]

Senator DODD. Finally, let me ask you—and I realize it is in litigation, but I am curious just looking at the issue from a layman's perspective—about the suit that has been filed by the pharmacists, complaining about what they see as the increased cost to them—if I remember correctly from looking at the memo, I think the number was something like 1,200 percent—as opposed to the HMOs and hospitals and the like. Distinguishing between groups, that is a pretty healthy difference.

First of all, are those numbers accurate at all, and if so, how do you justify that?

Dr. SANDERS. I am not sure I can speak to the accuracy of the numbers, Senator, and I cannot really comment on the specifics of the litigation. But one thing I would say is that we, as a matter of course in our industry, or at least as far as my company is concerned, do charge different prices to different classes of customers and have been doing so for a long time. The VA, for example, gets a much better break than other classes of customers, simply because of the fact that the VA will take your product and handle all of the distribution and administrative costs; you just deliver it to the door, and they take care of it from there. Whereas if you have to service an individual account, well down the chain, it is going to cost somewhat more.

The FTC looked at this issue as far as differential pricing about 4 years ago, I think, and said at that particular point in time that this practice of differential prices to different customers was pro-competitive. It is just the American way of doing business, and it always has been.

Senator DODD. Is that 1,200 percent figure accurate?

Dr. SANDERS. I am not sure. I am not sure what you are referring to.

Senator DODD. I am not sure I am remembering the number correctly.

Dr. SANDERS. In any event—I really could not speak to that. I am not sure that is right.

Senator DODD. Is there any other comment on this?

Mr. MOSSINGHOFF. Just the fact that the Robinson-Pattman Act does address exactly this issue. There is now litigation, so presumablyk the plaintiffs understood how the Robinson-Pattman Act wor s.

A major problem that PMA has with the p visi n that is in the health care reform Act is that despite the fact that we have some pretty high-priced antitrust lawyers, no one has quite told us what the difference is between that provision and the Robinson-Pattman Act.

I testified on Tuesday with an official of the FTC who indicated—and it was a surprise to me—that there was already an ongoing investigation in the FTC to look into the same thing under the Robinson-Pattman Act. So I would submit that it is probably not the right thing to do to change the law in some unknown or unspecified way while you have both FTC taking a look at it, and you have very active litigation in process.

Senator DODD. I did find the memo, and the suit claims that community pharmacies, in some cases, my memo says, pay as much as 1,200 percent more for the same drugs that manufacturers are selling to hospitals, HMOs, and so on. Now, I point out that none of the companies included in the suit are represented here that I know of at this table, except to the larger extent you are in the PMA.

Mr. MOSSINGHOFF. And we stay far away from pricing issues.

Senator DODD. It was just of interest to me, that 1,200 percent. I understand the differential, but that number jumps out at you. And I realize that plaintiffs filing lawsuits do not necessarily reflect what is absolutely the case.

Glaxo is in the suit. I apologize.

Mr. Sanders. We are in the suit.

Senator DODD. OK.

I am sure there will be additional questions from my colleagues. I appreciate your testimony here today. I really believe so firmly that you play a critical role in this debate and discussion. You obviously play a critical role in health care delivery in this country, but I want to emphasize the important role I think you can play in this debate.

And I do not like hearing some of the statements I hear coming out of certain places. And certainly those of us on this side of the table ought to be more sensitive to those kinds of statements that indict a group generally because of the actions of some. We ought to be more sensitive when those same vehicles and techniques are used against industries and groups of people.

I would just hope that despite your legitimate anger, in my view, in some cases where language and rhetoric have been excessive, to put it mildly, that you will not be tempted to withdraw from the health care reform effort, because we really need you to be a part of this debate and discussion.

I have raised some of the questions you will hear. There are many more. And we apologize if some of them seem naive, but they are consumer questions we get every, single day. If nothing else, I hope that in the last couple of years, because of the attention to some of these issues, there is a heightened degree of sensitivity about consumer reactions.

A lot of it has to do with the fact that people are paying out-of-pocket for a lot of this. I wish there were the same consumer reaction to some of the costs that they are paying indirectly, through higher taxes and the like, for items that are covered under the system. If people were more aware of how much those cost increases were affecting them, I think we would have similar reactions from the public. That is not the case. But nonetheless I think it is important that you take the criticism in the spirit that it is offered from most sources and that you stay at the table as we try to fashion an intelligent, thoughtful, responsible health care reform plan.

So I look forward to working with you in the coming months in that regard, and I thank you for your testimony. I am confident my colleagues will have some additional questions, and would ask you to respond to them as quickly as you possibly can.

Thank you for being here.

Senator DODD. Our second panel of witnesses includes Patricia Johnson, president of the Lupus Foundation; Donald Moore, former president of the National Association of Retail Druggists, representing the Community Retail Pharmacy Health Care Reform Coalition; Dr. Eugene Schonfeld, president and CEO of the National Kidney Cancer Association; and Judy Waxman, director of government affairs, Families USA Foundation.

We thank all of you for being with us today. We appreciate immensely your presence here today, and you have heard my colleagues' references to their comings and goings, so I apologize in their behalf for not being present here.

We are going to take all of your testimony, supporting documentation and other pertinent information you think the committee ought to have as part of the record today.

Ms. Johnson, we will begin with you, please. Welcome.

STATEMENTS OF PATRICIA A. JOHNSON, PRESIDENT, LUPUS FOUNDATION OF AMERICA, INC., ROCKVILLE, MD; EUGENE P. SCHONFELD, PRESIDENT AND CEO, NATIONAL KIDNEY CANCER ASSOCIATION, EVANSTON, IL; DONALD L. MOORE, FORMER PRESIDENT, NATIONAL ASSOCIATION OF RETAIL DRUGGISTS, REPRESENTING THE COMMUNITY RETAIL PHARMACY HEALTH CARE REFORM COALITION, ALEXANDRIA, VA; AND JUDY WAXMAN, DIRECTOR OF GOVERNMENT AFFAIRS, FAMILIES USA FOUNDATION, WASHINGTON, DC

Ms. JOHNSON. Thank you, Mr. Chairman.

I am Patricia Johnson, president of the Lupus Foundation of America and executive director of the Lupus Foundation of New Jersey. My testimony today will be in behalf of the national foundation.

I want to thank you for this opportunity to appear before you to express our views about the pluses and possible dangers of President Clinton's proposal to reform the health care system.

I am speaking today for the concerns of millions of people who could be dramatically affected by this plan. It appears that the Clinton health care plan focuses heavily on preventive health care and cost containment. Our biggest fear is that this legislation does not address the needs of the more than 100 million chronically ill people in this Nation who require continuing access to quality medical care and vital medicines.

When I speak of chronically ill, it is different from preventive care for healthy persons or people who have acute problems such as appendicitis. These are ongoing problems, and these are not preventable. But they have to be treated.

For committee members and others of the general public who may be less aware of lupus, let me tell you a little about it. It is a disease that afflicts as many as 500,000 Americans and an estimated one-half million yet undiagnosed. And it is not only the patient who is affected. This is a family affair. The whole family is touched by this disease, both financially and emotionally.

Lupus is a chronic inflammatory disease of the connective tissue caused by an overactive immune system. It can affect any vital organ or part of the body. There is no cure for lupus. People with lupus must live with the pain, fatigue, and medication side effects for their lifetime.

It is a disease with an unpredictable prognosis and very difficult symptoms. Among the symptoms are extreme ongoing fatigue, low-grade fevers, debilitating joint pain, among many others. In some cases, lupus is fatal.

It is intermittent, recurrent, and difficult to cope with and often causes many family problems. It is a lifelong battle.

For unknown reasons, more than 85 percent of lupus patients are women in their childbearing years, but men, children, and older people also have lupus.

It is one of 67 severe and often debilitating chronic autoimmune disorders which together affect an estimated 8 million Americans. These diseases include multiple sclerosis, rheumatoid arthritis, and Addison's disease, which affected the late President Kennedy.

Many lupus patients also suffer from other autoimmune conditions. Most people with autoimmune diseases share one thing in common—their disease is controlled only by daily medications. It is important to keep in mind that research breakthrough for any of the above conditions could prove critical for those with lupus.

Let us talk about medications. In the past, I have heard arguments that too much money has been spent on research for so-called "me-too" drugs. Let me make it very clear—there is no such thing as a so-called "me-too" drug for lupus patients, and there is no such thing as a "me-too" patient. The truth is that a drug that works for one patient may not work for another, even if they share the same condition. And giving lupus patients the wrong drug can cause them great physical distress or even kill them.

Let me point out a few other critical and related concerns. Appropriate medication is often determined only through trial and error. Patients frequently require combinations of medicines to bring their symptoms under control. Lupus patients also are apt to be extremely allergic; therefore, they can often tolerate only one or two specific drugs in a given therapeutic class. And since they often take so many other medications—from 9 to 20 pills a day is not unusual—they must be concerned with drug interactions and dangerous side effects. Long-term use of some steroids, for example, can cause softening of bones and require some patients to undergo costly hip and knee replacements.

What lupus patients desperately need are more medicines, more choices, more options, that can help them cope with this affliction. The one hope they have is that advanced medical research may bring a cure.

What concerns me most about the President's proposals as I understand them is that I fear they may curtail the options available to these people with lupus and other chronic diseases.

My first concern is that without continued and increased research and development, there may never be a cure. It would be tragic to create a new health care system that discourages cost-saving medical research and denies patients new therapies and cures.

The most likely source of any future lupus care is the biotech industry, either by itself or in partnership with an established pharmaceutical firm. Recent news that a small biotech company in California plans to start human clinic trials on a vaccine therapy for lupus was most heartening to us.

However, price restrictions, either direct or indirect, could stop that research dead in its tracks. Biotech venture capital, as you have heard from the prior panel, has already dried up with the talk of price controls. Clinical trials are also being postponed.

As you know, the President's proposal contains a number of provisions that could inhibit research. Although the phrase "global budget" does not appear in this legislation, there are indirect price controls on these companies which we need to produce a lupus cure.

Nor will price controls achieve long-term savings for the health care system. Improper treatment of patients such as lupus patients can result in costly hospitalization, which certainly is more expensive than if they had received proper treatment in the first place.

We are also concerned about provisions in the proposal that could eventually force all but the wealthiest of our citizens into HMOs or other managed care systems. These may be very cost-effective for preventive care, but they can be devastating for people with serious chronic disease who require the high-quality care and continuing one-on-one attention that only knowledgeable specialists can provide.

We are deeply concerned about any proposal that would take decisions about appropriate medical care away from doctors and give them to bureaucrats. Who is going to make the proper judgment as to who will get treatment and who will not?

Prior authorization of medications also can hamper and delay access in a timely manner to proper treatment modalities. It is just more bureaucracy and paperwork, and the patient is at risk.

Further, since lupus is a multisystem disease, we are also very disturbed by aspects of the bill which would reduce the number of specialists in favor of primary care physicians. This is exactly the wrong prescription for people with lupus who depend on the proper care and treatment of knowledgeable physician specialists. And you all note that I note in here many times "knowledgeable," because you can have specialists, but they are not necessarily knowledgeable for the particular disease which needs to be treated.

Limiting access to these specialists will cause more costly hospitalizations and even deaths. It will not be cost-effective. Diagnosing lupus is very difficult even for the rheumatologists who normally treat patients, let alone for general practitioners.

I want to make it clear that we do not oppose all aspects of the Clinton administration's reform proposal. On the contrary, we believe the plan contains several very positive components. We strongly agree with the concept of universal coverage and portability of insurance. No one should be denied coverage because of a prior condition, and no one should be afraid to leave a job for fear of losing their insurance.

I hope you will also remember that universal coverage would be worthless if chronically ill patients are denied access to their specialists and proper therapies, however.

To sum up, I do believe we are at a crossroads in history. The attention of the Congress is focused on the need for health care reform. We have what may be a unique opportunity to improve the lives of billions of people with chronic debilitating diseases.

America has long been the leader in providing quality health care and developing new and effective medications for treating the serious diseases of our time. Let us not adopt policies that would hurt or delay research or access to proper treatment for the millions of Americans who suffer from lupus and other chronic diseases.

I would like to say that I have worked in the health care field for many years, for American Heart, for Cystic Fibrosis, for all kinds of health care agencies, and I have been very involved. It is of great concerned to me that we not—and this is not only my concern but the concern of my organization—that we not diminish the strides that we have made in the past just for cost containment, or put any patients in jeopardy. I think this is a very, very dangerous thing, and we must be most careful of that. We need to keep our leadership role.

I sit on an institutional review board, and I would like to say that I already have knowledge of the fact that people are being trained in foreign languages to go abroad for research. So this is a concern that I have. I am very, very interested in this whole process, and I shall continue to be very active in my State of New Jersey and also in the region and also on the national level, for as long as I have a breath to draw.

I thank you very much for inviting me to share these views.

Senator DODD. Thank you very much, Ms. Johnson.

Dr. Schonfeld.

Mr. SCHONFELD. Thank you, Senator.

I am a kidney cancer patient, and I am a big time health care consumer. "Big time" is when you enter the hospital, and the bills run into the thousands and tens of thousands of dollars. So I know first-hand what the cost of care is in our system.

I woke up in intensive care. Let me tell you what it means to be a cancer patient after they take your kidney out. You wind up with an i.v. in both arms, one in your neck, a tube in your mouth, tubes up your nose and your stomach. They cut a hole in your chest to drain out the cavity in your body. They cover you with electrodes, and then they put a few tubes where I will not even mention. And you wake up, and God has got your attention.

I would like to tell you a little bit about kidney cancer. There are 27,000 new cases a year in the United States; 11,000 deaths in the United States. Up until 1987, there were more cases of kidney cancer in the United States than AIDS, and during the 1980's, more people died of kidney cancer than died of AIDS.

Kidney cancer, though, is a very small subset of the total cancer population. It is only about 2 percent of all cancer cases. This year in the United States, there will be close to 1.2 million new cancer cases. There are over 8 million cancer patients alive today in the

United States. Those patients are either getting care or they are getting regular follow-up while they are in remission.

Cancer is one of the single most expensive diseases in the U.S. economy. It is also one of the most difficult to stop. Despite all the money that has been spent on cancer research over the years, progress has come very slowly. And only within the last few years, really since the development of biotechnology, have we gotten a grip on how to deal with cancer effectively.

I testified before the FDA about a drug called Interleukin-2, which was the first biotech drug to come before the FDA. It is a relatively expensive drug, by the way. It costs about $30,000 to be treated with that drug. That is the drug cost, never mind the hospital care. And the FDA took 18 months to approve that drug from the time of the first hearing and review of the drug to the second hearing, when the advisory committee actually approved the drug.

I testified at both hearings. During the 18-month period, 16,000 Americans died of kidney cancer. That drug produces a complete remission in about 8 to 10 percent of patients. That means roughly 1,500 to 1,600 Americans died needlessly while the FDA debated the drug.

Also during that period of time, the company which produced that drug, Cedus, the price of the stock fell; the company fired 10 percent of its employees to cut its cash flow and losses. In addition, the company was eventually acquired entirely. Patients were suing their insurance companies because they had received the drug in clinical trials, and in some cases, the insurance companies were saying we are not going to reimburse for that because that is experimental. And there was tremendous turmoil because of this advisory committee at the FDA.

By the time the drug first came up for review before the FDA, by the way, it had been approved in nine European companies; the company had spent over $100 million developing it. That 18-month window added significantly to the cost of the drug. What is the interest on $100 million for 18 months? That interest cost eventually wound up in the price of the drug.

I have read the President health care plan very carefully, but more than that, I have really tried to study all aspects of the health care system since I had cancer. And I have looked at all kinds of issues—insurance issues, malpractice issues, hospital costs, all different aspects of this problem. And one of the things that concerns me is this whole Breakthrough Drug Committee, this whole advisory system that has been discussed here.

Unfortunately, I have seen up close how the Government works when it has an advisory committee, and frankly, I am a little scared. I have watched capital be redeployed in the health care industry. We heard about that today from some of the other witnesses, so I will not go into detail about that. The prices of drug stocks have fallen; biotech companies cannot get funding, and there is an enormous chilling effect that has set in because of what we see in this plan.

If the plan goes through, and we have advisory committees now looking at, quote-unquote, what things cost, I am really concerned that companies will not make the investment in R and D that will save my life. If my cancer comes back, the single most effective drug has a chance of helping me only 8 to 10 percent of the time; I have a 92 percent probability of dying of my cancer.

We desperately need new and better drugs. And it is not just a question that we need new and better drugs. When a patient does not have a really good drug for his disease, what happens is he takes the first drug, and if that does not work, he goes on to a second one and a third one, adding every step of the way to the cost to the health care system.

So it is very important that the first therapy that the patient gets be effective. And in kidney cancer, we have no therapy. Not only do we not have a therapy, but we do not have any diagnostic. There is no blood test, no mammogram, no urine test; there is nothing to tell a patient or a doctor that he has kidney cancer.

So we are in a very serious problem area when it comes to kidney cancer as well as many other kinds of cancer. If we have a review committee looking at the breakthrough aspects and the economic aspects, I am not so sure I really trust them to make the right decision, and I am afraid that the companies will reallocate capital to other areas.

For example, if I am in human pharmaceuticals, I can redirect my R and D to animal pharmaceuticals. If I am in biotech, I can go into agriculture with my biotechnology. I do not have to produce human pharmaceuticals. Or, if I am like Bristol-Meyers, and I own Clairol, I can put my money into cosmetics.

So I think there is an enormous threat here, and I think the Congress should be very concerned about it.

Thank you.

Senator DODD. Thank you very much.

[The prepared statement of Mr. Schonfeld follows:]

Prepared Statement of Eugene P. Schonfeld

Thank you for allowing me to talk with you today. I share your concerns about health care reform. I am particularly concerned about research, cancer, and the economic effects of health care reform.

Introduction

By way of introduction, I am a kidney cancer patient. I am also President and Chief Executive Officer of the National Kidney Cancer Association. Before I founded the Association, I started five high tech companies. I hold a Ph.D. in Management from Northwestern University and I have been on the faculty at Northwestern and at the University of Illinois.

One of my companies, Schonfeld & Associates, tracks research and development expenditures and publishes statistical reference works on corporate financial performance. These publications are sold to corporate research centers such as Bell Labs, to Wall Street, and to government agencies such as the IRS, the Department of Defense, and others.

I have no financial interest in any health care company. The National Kidney Cancer Association is supported by patients, families, and doctors, and by individual charitable donations. Besides providing information to patients and doctors, the Association also has a small research program of its own.

Initial Comments

Research has played an important role in the evolution of our health care system. Many of us would not be alive today if it were not for the success of past research.

However, medical research is now threatened by health care reform. As shown in Figure 1, health care R&D as a percent of health care costs peaked in 1982 and has declined consistently since then. This graph shows one reason health care costs have not been contained.

The United States has not invested enough money in medical R&D to control rising costs. If health care reform reduces research as a percentage of total cost, the U.S. will fall farther and farther behind its health-care-cost curve. The reason is that research not only produces new drugs which cure disease and better medical devices for diagnosing and caring for patients, research also produces innovations which reduce costs.

For example, the development of laparoscopic surgery means less invasive and less expensive surgery, shorter hospital stays, and less risk to patients. A new drug may keep a patient out of the hospital, and newer more sensitive X-ray film may uncover tumors when they can be removed without intensive chemotherapy or other treatments. Research also reduces the cost of making many products used in our health care system.

Much has been written about new medical technologies which are "expensive" while everyone has ignored the technical advances which have dramatically reduced costs. I think one of the problems is that CAT scan machines are highly visible capital expenditures for hospitals, while new surgical staples and pharmaceuticals are supplies. Financial accounting has steered many people to the wrong conclusions about the cost of health care technology.

Sources of Health Care R&D Investment

How much does the U.S. spend on health care R&D and where does the money come from? As shown in Figure 2, research spending has risen consistently. However, the leading source of R&D investment dollars has switched from the Federal government to private industry.

Health care reforms which reduce the rate of return on R&D by private industry will reduce total health care research. Some projects are not viable when rates of return drop. Also, the Federal government has already reduced its own share of R&D spending. Moreover, the Federal government cannot make up for any cutbacks in corporate research. The government faces huge deficits and has no money for long term research investments. The recent termination of the super collider project by Congress underscores this lack of funds.

In Figure 3, R&D as a percent of sales for seven major drug companies is compared to Federal health care research spending as a percent of health care costs. This graph shows that major drug companies have doubled their R&D spending as a percentage of sales while Federal government R&D has barely kept pace with costs. In fact, real Federal spending has declined if you take inflation into account.

Cancer

One of out of every three living Americans will die of cancer. Currently, there are over 8 million cancer patients in the U.S. You can think of them as having tested positive for cancer.

I talk with hundreds of cancer patients every year. I get phone calls every day and I know their problems with the health care system. First, and foremost, they haven't got a cure for their disease. The next time someone complains about the high price of drugs for a rare disease, remember that they are fortunate that they have a drug at all. Many of us don't have any effective therapy, and we are paying the highest price of all. We are literally paying with our lives.

Figure 4 shows that this year, almost 1.2 million new cases of cancer will be diagnosed in the U.S. and over 500,000 deaths will be due to cancer. About 28 percent of health care costs are consumed during the last year of life. As a killer, cancer is the single most expensive disease in the U.S. economy.

Through research by companies as well as by the National Cancer Institute, we are about to see some major breakthroughs in the diagnosis and treatment of cancer. For example, conventional chemotherapy has been replaced by immunotherapy in kidney cancer. Gene therapy is a reality and it is now possible to have a patient's body produce the chemicals needed to fight his own disease.

The President's health plan calls for reimbursement of care during NIH sponsored clinical trials. This part of the plan will speed research and help patients get state-of-the-art care.

However, as shown in Figure 5, we have a long way to go. The R&D budgets of General Motors and IBM have grown much faster than the budget of the National Cancer Institute... and these two companies are no longer competitive or meeting the needs of world markets. In fact, both companies have lost billions of dollars and their boards replaced their CEO's during the past year. The combined R&D budgets of just these two companies exceeds the total NIH budget.

Unfortunately, the National Cancer Act has not been enforced. Figure 6 shows that taking into account inflation and the number of new cases, Federal spending for cancer research actually declined 37 percent during the 1980's.

As a cancer patient, it is very clear to me that I should not count on the Federal government to find a cure for my disease. The Federal government has not been investing sufficiently in cancer research and it will not do so in the era of huge deficits.

Therefore, I must look to the private sector to provide for technical advances, new cures, lower cost treatments, and other innovations. If health care reform damages private sector research, costs will go up, quality of care will be less than it could be, and many people will die needlessly.

Price Controls

Price controls are the single biggest threat to the private sector, particularly pharmaceutical companies, medical equipment companies and other R&D intensive suppliers.

Price caps will be especially detrimental to R&D investment. As shown in Figure 7, biomedical research prices have been growing faster than the Consumer Price Index. Drug and equipment prices reflect costs, and this inflation index explains, at least in part, why consumers are seeing drug prices increase faster than other things.

If prices of drugs and equipment are capped at the CPI, the cash flows won't be sufficient to support the real costs of research and development. The amount of research done will be less.

Also, price controls discourage risk taking. No corporate manager or venture capitalist or company will put money at risk in an R&D investment program and develop products which may come to market 5 to 10 years in the future when a National Health Board of government bureaucrats will determine prices and profit margins.

Managers and investors are willing to take business risks and financial risks. They are unwilling to take a political risk, particularly when they can make investments in other opportunities where there is no political risk.

The reason is that R&D for new products is only one type of investment opportunity. Instead of risking capital on research, companies can make acquisitions, such as Merck buying Medco. Companies can expand marketing and move into more countries. Companies can launch new product lines which are free from price controls such as cosmetics or over the counter drugs. They can repurchase their own stock. They can modernize their manufacturing plants for existing products. Etc. Etc.

In this regard, Congress and the White House must understand that the laws of economics are more powerful than the laws you enact. Companies will respond and adjust to whatever you do. If you reduce the rate of return on R&D investments through price caps, capital will be devoted to other, less risky or more profitable opportunities. Health care reform can produce unwanted, even dangerous, economic side effects.

If the role of the National Health Board is to set prices or cap prices, it will destroy health care R&D and patients will feel the impact.

Those patients who have a drug for their disease would pay lower prices, such as patients who are on chronic high blood pressure medicine. However, patients who don't have a drug for their disease may never get a drug which helps them. Diseases such as cancer and AIDS will go right on killing Americans.

For example, I have kidney cancer. I had my kidney and tumor removed four years ago, but I have a 50 percent chance of recurrence. The most effective therapy currently available produces a complete remission in only 8 percent of patients. If my disease comes back, I face a 92 percent probability of death.

Will there be a drug for my disease if the National Health Board has the power to control prices? And if it won't have the authority to set prices, why do we need to spend $ 2 billion on a new Federal bureaucracy? Our deficits prove that we can't pay for the bureaucracy we already have.

The irony of this foolishness as shown in Figure 8 is that pharmaceuticals account for only 8 percent of total health expenditures. If all drugs were free, it would barely matter to the overall cost of health care in the U.S.

Private capital is already moving away from health care research. As shown in Figure 9, the market values of research intensive drug companies have dropped significantly. To produce this graph, I added up the monthly closing stock prices of seven research intensive drug companies: Abbott, Bristol, Lilly, Merck, Schering, Smithkline, and Upjohn, and divided the total by the S&P 500 Stock Market Index. These companies have lost almost 25 percent of their value relative to the overall market.

These companies compete for capital in the financial markets. Lower market values mean that the cost of capital is going up and less capital is available. Ultimately, capital flows are reflected in research budgets as well as in prices.

As I mentioned, I have been involved in several high tech ventures. Currently, "word on the street" is that capital for biotech start-ups has become basically unavailable. Entrepreneurs can't get money for new research-based health care companies.

Large companies are also responding. Managers are redirecting capital to non-research investments, such as acquisitions. Besides buying Medco, Merck is investing in building a new generic drug division to make low-priced, me-too products.

Recently, in India where the government has capped drugs prices for some time, Roche withdrew from the market. American companies are cutting back on their operations in India. Capital is being redeployed to other, more profitable areas. There have also been massive layoffs at major drug companies.

My fear is that we are seeing the future of health care research right now. Let this be an early warning sign to the Congress and to the White House.

Closing Comments

We need health care reform and there are many things which Congress can do to improve the situation. Let me mention several of the most important changes you can make, such as:

1. Make R&D tax credits permanent to encourage the development of innovations which reduce health care costs.

2. Enact a capital gains tax for long term investments so capital is readily available to fund new health care companies and more new products.

3. Repeal of the McCarren-Ferguson Act so we have competition and innovation in insurance, and pass a law prohibiting pre-existing condition exclusions.

4. Extend Robinson-Patman to services so unfair price discrimination is illegal in health care service markets.

5. Enact a uniform pricing law making it illegal for a hospital or doctor to charge different patients different prices for the same service.

6. Enact legislation overturning state laws which prohibit price advertising by retail drug stores so retail markets are more competitive.

As you consider these recommendations, think about price controls and the National Health Board. Washington has already helped the railroads, the airlines, the S&L industry, and the poor. Now it wants to help all of us, starting in the womb right up to death.

Under President Clinton's plan, health care expenditures would rise from about 14 percent to 17.4 percent of Gross Domestic Product. Is this what we want? Is this an improvement? Many other financial assumptions of the plan are equally questionable.

In particular, I'm concerned that under the President's plan we will boost expenditures for Federal and state bureaucracy while we cut spending on research. When I hear that the National Health Board will cost as much as the National Cancer Institute, I think Washington has its priorities all screwed up. Do you really want to allocate the next Federal dollar to support administrators rather than scientists?

237

In my view, the only way to change the fundamental cost of health care is through research and development which leads to innovations which change the true, underlying cost of curing and treating patients. I urge you to support reforms which encourage R&D and competition through innovation.

In closing, consider Figure 10 which shows a partial list of publicly owned bio tech companies in Senator Kennedy's state of Massachusetts. I have also enclosed a list of all publicly owned medical technology companies in Senator Pryor's state of Arkansas. Think about these states and these companies as the Senate debates health reform. If you were a patient, which state is more likely to help you?

I'm happy to answer any questions you have on health care reform. Thank you.

TOTAL HEALTHCARE R&D AS %
TOTAL U.S. HEALTHCARE COSTS

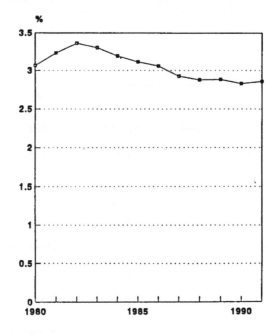

Fig. 1: NIH Data Book, 1992

U.S. SPENDING FOR HEALTH R&D
AND % SHARE OF SPENDING BY SOURCE

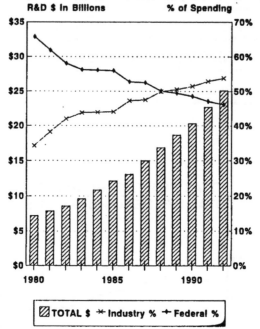

Fig. 2: NIH Data Book, 1992

R&D AS % SALES FOR 7 DRUG COMPANIES
vs. .
FEDERAL R&D AS % TOTAL HEALTH COSTS

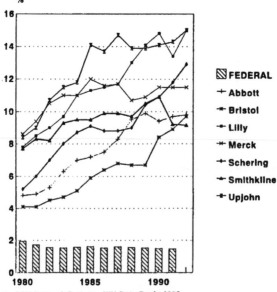

Fig. 3: R&D Ratios & Budgets, NIH Data Book, 1992

CANCER IN THE U.S.
NEW CASES DIAGNOSED AND DEATHS

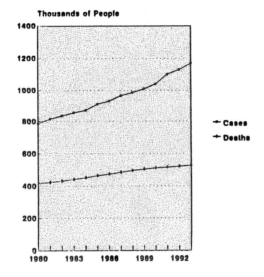

Fig. 4: American Cancer Society, 1993

NCI APPROPRIATIONS vs.
R&D $'s of GM and IBM   –

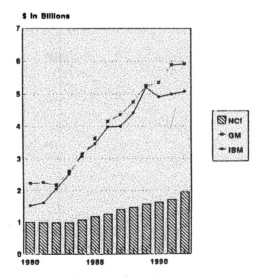

Fig. 5: R&D Ratios & Budgets, NIH Data Book, 1992

FEDERAL RESEARCH SPENDING PER NEW CANCER CASE

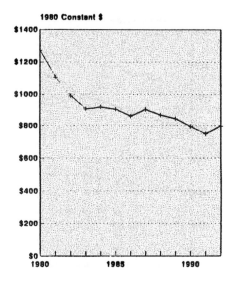

Fig. 6: NIH Data Book, 1990; ACS, 1991

NIH BIOMEDICAL R&D PRICE INDEX
vs.
CONSUMER PRICE INDEX

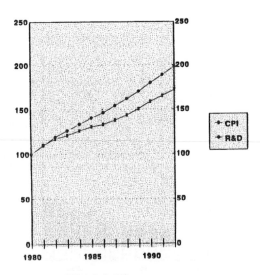

Fig. 7: 1980 = 100, NIH Data Book, 1992

SPENDING ON PHARMACEUTICALS
AS A % OF HEALTH EXPENDITURES

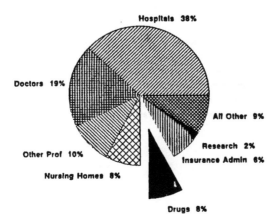

Fig 8: Bureau of Labor Statistics, Congressional Budget Office, 1992

STOCK PRICES OF 7 DRUG COMPANIES
AS A % PERCENT OF THE   –
S&P 500 STOCK PRICE INDEX

Fig. 9: Standard & Poor s Compustat Services
Sum of monthly closing prices for 7 companies
divided by monthly closing S&P 500 index

A PARTIAL LIST OF MASSACHUSETTS BIOTECH FIRMS WITH AN ESTIMATED 1,500 R&D JOBS ANNUAL SALES POTENTIAL OF $ 1.2 BILLION

	1992 R&D BUDGET $ In Millions
Biogen	60.4
Cambridge Biotech	9.2
Cambridge Neuroscience	12.2
Genzyme	15.7
Immulogic Pharmaceutical	13.5
Immunogen	16.1
Interneuron Pharmaceuticals	10.2
Neozyme	15.5
Repligen	13.7
Scigenics	10.4
Seragen	15.3
TOTAL	**192.2**

Fig. 10: Standard & Poor's Compustat Services

PUBLICLY OWNED MED TECH COMPANIES IN ARKANSAS
A COMPLETE LIST

	1992 R&D BUDGET $ In Millions
Professional Dental Tech	0.991

TOTAL

Fig. 11: Standard & Poor's Compustat Services

Senator DODD. Mr. Moore.

Mr. MOORE. Thank you, Mr. Chairman.

My name is Don Moore, and I am president of Moore Drug Store, Incorporated, in Kokomo, IN. I have a very large geriatric patient population, and I have been very interested in health care over the last several years. I am also the immediate past president of the National Association of Retail Druggists, and in that job, I have seen pharmacists and have worked with them all around the world as well as across the United States.

I am appearing before the committee today on behalf of Community Retail Pharmacy Health Care Reform Coalition, which was created in February of this year by NARD and the National Association of Chain Drug Stores. The Coalition represents 112,000 community pharmacists in more than 60,000 pharmacies, the totality of community retail pharmacy.

Community pharmacists employ more than one million people and annually dispense more than $2 billion, or 93 percent, of all outpatient prescriptions. To date, 47 State pharmacy associations, including Connecticut, representing 96 percent of all licensed pharmacists in the Nation, have endorsed the Coalition's health reform agenda, as have other national, local, and regional pharmacy organizations, retail associations, and 25 State chain drug associations.

NARD and NADS agree that the following concepts are fundamental to any reform of current health care delivery systems. The provision of pharmacists' services are essential to any basic health care plan. As the most accessible health care professionals, pharmacists are in a key position to ensure improved and appropriate medication use resulting in decreased overall health costs.

Current health care delivery systems suffer from redundant and nonstandardized administration. Often, unnecessary layers of intermediaries are involved in claims management systems. Uniform standards should be established for the management of health care that utilize electronic claims systems and eliminate unnecessary administrative layers.

Ensuring the public's free access to community pharmacy and community pharmacy's free access to the marketplace are the best ways to provide pharmacists' services and preserve the competitive market that exists for the provision of those services.

Also essential to the preservation of a competitive community pharmacy marketplace is the elimination of discriminatory pricing practices, which was mentioned earlier, by the manufacturers of prescription products. All pharmacies, irrespective of practice setting, must be able to acquire prescription drugs at the same price, subject only—and we want to make this clear—to the economies of scale, including volume.

With regard to President Clinton's Health Security Act, the leaders of the Coalition have endorsed the President's health care reform legislation, and we will actively promote the merits of the plan to the Nation's community retail pharmacists. The President and Hillary Rodham Clinton are to be commended for their efforts to bring about meaningful health care reform that has been talked about for decades.

In particular, we strongly endorse the provisions of pharmacy services and prescription drugs as basic benefits in the standard benefits package to be offered to all Americans.

Numerous studies have documented the cost savings of comprehensive community pharmacy services. When properly utilized, community retail pharmacists save the health care system billions of dollars by reducing the need for much more costly medical services, including emergency room visits, hospitalizations, and nursing home admissions.

I would like to add that I have heard all kinds of comments about the millions and billions being spent on medicine. But on these high-tech medicines, if you do not have the people at the bottom explaining to the patients, such as the pharmacists making sure that compliance is there, drug utilization review, making sure they are not allergic to it, that the two medicines can be worked together, this is where there is a big savings. I think I heard pharmacy mentioned once or twice in the previous panel. too many people are overlooking the work that we do and the work we do for the patients, especially those in the geriatric field.

In addition, the President's plan offers the American public relief from the needless and arbitrary cost-shifting that occurs through drug manufacturers' discriminatory price practices, which increases prescription drug prices to consumers. The elimination of discriminatory pricing practices by drug manufacturers will bring about a level playing field in all types of cost-shifting. This will lead to lower retail prices for consumers——

I would like to add here, especially the elderly; if they are not buying in an HMO, they are paying top dollar, and this is where the drug manufacturers are having a lot of their money coming from. The senior citizens are almost the cash cow.

In addition to advocating inclusion of pharmacy services in all health plans and elimination of drug manufacturers' discriminatory pricing practices, the Coalition also strongly supports other key provisions in the President's plan, including establishment of a Medicare prescription drug benefit with an equitable reimbursement formula; inclusion of a realistic professional dispensing fee that recognizes the value patient care services provided by the Nation's community retail pharmacists; a modification of antitrust laws to enable providers to join together to negotiate with health benefit plans and to ensure consumer access to community retail pharmacy services; also, repeal of the health insurance industry's exemption from antitrust laws; the reduction of costly and bureaucratic health benefit plan administrative procedures; prohibition of physician self-referrals, including physician ownership of pharmacies, and continuation of a pharmacy marketplace that utilizes the highly efficient community retail pharmacy infrastructure.

President Clinton's health care reform plan, which calls for universal access to prescription drugs and pharmacy services, will lead to lower overall health care costs for the health care system. In the new marketplace, the President's plan calls for drug makers to end cost-shifting to the retail consumer. Providing equal access to prices for all pharmacy providers regardless of setting will not jeopardize the research capabilities of the Nation's prescription drug manufacturers as they have claimed.

According to a February 1993 staff report by the Senate Special Committee on Aging, titled, "Earning a Failing Grade: A Report Card on 1992 Drug Manufacturer Price Inflation," in 1991 the net profit for the average Fortune 500 company was 3.2 percent, while average net profits for drug manufacturers were 12.8 percent. At the same time, the committee reported, net profits for retail pharmacies was 2 percent.

The President's legislative proposal will enable community retail pharmacy to maintain control over its infrastructure of 60,000 community retail pharmacies and would allow community pharmacy providers to negotiate with health benefit plans to provide access to high-quality pharmacy services to consumers without relying on third-party brokers.

Manufacturers, third-party administrators, and wholesale drug companies, planning for the future prescription drug marketplace, should keep in mind that no third-party middlemen or brokers can offer full pharmacy services and care to payers without utilizing the community pharmacy infrastructure.

We look forward to working with the committee to provide additional information on the Coalition's provision on the Health Security Act, and on the role of the Nation's community retail pharmacists in providing consumers high quality, cost-effective pharmacy care.

Also, Mr. Chairman, with your permission, would it be possible for our counsel, John Recter, to explain the lawsuit that is going on and the differences in pricing?

Senator DODD. I will get to that in a minute.

Mr. MOORE. Thank you.

[The prepared statement of Mr. Moore follows:]

PREPARED STATEMENT OF DONALD L. MOORE

Mr. Chairman, Members of the Committee

My name is Donald L. Moore, and I am president of Moore Drug Store, a community retail pharmacy in Kokomo, Indiana. I am also the immediate past-president of the National Association of Retail Druggists.

I am appearing before the Committee today on behalf of the Community Retail Pharmacy Health Care Reform Coalition, which was created in February of this year by NARD and the National Association of Chain Drug Stores.

The Coalition represents 112,000 community pharmacists in more than 60,000 pharmacies—the totality of community retail pharmacy. Community pharmacies employ more than one million people, and annually dispense more than two billion—or 93 percent—of all outpatient prescriptions. To date, 47 state pharmacy associations including CT. representing 96 percent of all licensed pharmacists in the nation, have endorsed the Coalition's health reform agenda, as have other national, local, and regional pharmacy organizations, retail associations, and 25 state chain drug associations.

NARD and NACDS agree that the following concepts are fundamental to any reform of current health care delivery systems:

The provision of pharmacists' services are essential to any basic health care plan. As the most accessible health care professionals, pharmacists are in a key position to ensure improved and appropriate medication use resulting in decreased overall health care costs.

Current health care delivery systems suffer from redundant and nonstandardized administration. Often, unnecessary layers of intermediaries are involved in claims management systems. Uniform standards should be established for the management of health care that utilize electronic claims systems and eliminate unnecessary administrative layers.

Ensuring the public's free access to community pharmacy and community pharmacy's free access to the marketplace are the best ways to provide pharmacists' services and preserve the competitive market that exists for the provision of those services.

Also essential to the preservation of a competitive community pharmacy marketplace is the elimination of discriminatory pricing practices by manufacturers of prescription products. All pharmacies, irrespective of practice setting, must be able to acquire prescription drugs at the same price, subject only to economies of scale, including volume.

With regard to President Clinton's Health Security Act, the leaders of the Coalition have endorsed the President's health care reform legislation, and we will actively promote the merits of the plan to the nation's community retail pharmacists.

The President and Hillary Rodham Clinton are to be commended for their efforts to bring about meaningful health care reform that has been talked about for decades. In particular, we strongly endorse the provision of pharmacy services and prescription drugs as a basic benefit in the standard benefits package to be offered to all Americans.

Numerous studies have documented the cost savings of comprehensive community pharmacy services. When properly utilized, community retail pharmacists save the health care system billions of dollars by reducing the need for much more costly medical services, including emergency room visits, hospitalizations, and nursing home admissions.

In addition, the President's plan offers the American public relief from the needless and arbitrary cost shifting that occurs through drug manufacturers discriminatory pricing practices, which increase prescription drug prices to consumers. The elimination of discriminatory pricing practices by drug manufacturers will bring about a level playing field and end all types of costs shifting. This will lead to lower retail prices for consumers, especially the elderly who stand to gain much through the President's proposed expansion of Medicare benefits.

In addition to advocating the inclusion of pharmacy services in all health plans and the elimination of drug manufacturers' discriminatory pricing practices, the Coalition also strongly supports other key provisions in the President's plan, including:

Establishment of a Medicare prescription drug benefit with an equitable reimbursement formula

Inclusion of a realistic professional dispensing fee that recognizes the valuable patient care services provided by the nation's community retail pharmacists

Modification of antitrust laws to enable providers to join together to negotiate with health benefits plans and to ensure consumer access to community retail pharmacy services

Repeal of the health insurance industry's exemption from antitrust laws

Reduction of costly and bureaucratic health benefit plan administrative procedures

Prohibition of physician self-referrals, including physician ownership of pharmacies, and

Continuation of a pharmacy marketplace that utilizes the highly efficient community retail pharmacy infrastructure

President Clinton's health care reform plan, which calls for universal access to prescription drugs and pharmacy services, will lead to lower overall health care costs for the health care system.

In the new marketplace, the President's plan calls for drug makers to end cost shifting to the retail consumer. Providing equal access to prices for all pharmacy providers regardless of setting will not jeopardize the research capabilities of the nation's prescription drug manufacturers, as they have claimed.

According to a February, 1993 staff report by the Senate Special Committee on Aging titled "Earning a Failing Grade: A Report Card on 1992 Drug Manufacturer Price Inflation," in 1991 the net profit for the average Fortune 500 company was 3.2 percent, while average net profits for drug manufacturers were 12.8 percent. At the same time, the Committee reported, net profits for retail pharmacies was only 2 percent.

The Pharmaceutical Manufacturers Association has reported that U.S. drug makers collectively have increased their investment in research and development by 16 percent over 1992 levels.

The President's legislative proposal will enable community retail pharmacy to maintain control over its infrastructure of 60,000 community retail pharmacies and would allow community pharmacy providers to negotiate with health benefit plans to provide access to high-quality pharmacy services to consumers without relying on third-party brokers.

Manufacturers, third-party administrators and wholesale drug companies, planning for the future prescription drug marketplace, should keep in mind that no third-party middlemen, or brokers, can offer full pharmacy services and care to payers without utilizing the community pharmacy infrastructure.

We look forward to working with the Committee to provide additional information on the Coalition's positions on the Health Security Act, and on the role of the nation's community retail pharmacists in providing consumers high quality, cost effective pharmacy care.

Thank you.

ENDORSEMENTS OF COMMUNITY RETAIL PHARMACY HEALTH CARE REFORM COALITION PRINCIPLES

As of November 18, 1993

State Pharmacy Association Endorsements:

Alabama Pharmaceutical Association, Alaska Pharmaceutical Association, Arkansas Pharmacists Association, California Pharmacists Association, Colorado Pharmacists Association, Connecticut Pharmaceutical Association, Delaware Pharmaceutical Society, Florida Pharmacy Association, Georgia Pharmaceutical Association, Hawaii Pharmaceutical Association, Idaho State Pharmaceutical Association, Illinois Pharmacists Association, Indiana Pharmacists Association, Iowa Pharmacists Association, Kansas Pharmacists Association, Kentucky Pharmacists Association, Louisiana Pharmacists Association, Maine Pharmacy Association, Maryland Pharmacists Association, Massachusetts State Pharmaceutical Association, Michigan Pharmacists Association, Minnesota Pharmacists Association, Mississippi Pharmacists Association, Missouri Pharmacists Association, Montana State Pharmaceutical Association, Nebraska Pharmacists Association, New Hampshire Pharmacists Association, New Jersey Pharmaceutical Association, New Mexico Pharmaceutical Association, North Carolina Pharmaceutical Association, North Dakota Pharmaceutical Association, Ohio Pharmacists Association, Oklahoma Pharmaceutical Association, Oregon State Pharmacists Association, Pennsylvania Pharmaceutical Association, Pharmaceutical Society of the State of New York, Rhode Island Pharmaceutical Association, South Carolina Pharmaceutical Association, South Dakota Pharmaceutical Association, Tennessee Pharmacists Association, Texas Pharmaceutical Association, Utah Pharmaceutical Association, Vermont Pharmacists Association, Virginia Pharmaceutical Association, Washington State Pharmacists Association, West Virginia Pharmacists Association, Wisconsin Pharmacists Association.

State Retail Association, and Chain Drug Committee Endorsements:

Alabama Retail Association, Arizona Retailers Association, Arkansas Grocers & Retail Merchants Association, California Retailers Association, Colorado Retail Association, Delaware Association of Chain Drug Stores, Florida Retail Federation, Georgia Retail Association, Illinois Retail Merchants Association, Indiana Retail Council, Inc., Association of Iowa Merchants, Kentucky Retail Association, Louisiana Retailers Association, Michigan Merchants Council and Associates, Inc., Minnesota Retail Merchants Association, Retail Association of Mississippi, Missouri Retailers Association, Montana Retail Association, Retail Merchants Association of Nebraska, New Mexico Retail Association, North Carolina Retail Merchants Association, Ohio Council of Retail Merchants, South Carolina Merchants Association, Tennessee Council of Retail Merchants, Texas Retailers Association/Texas Federation of Drug Stores.

Other Endorsing Organizations:

American Associated Druggists/United Drugs, American College of Apothecaries, Baltimore Metropolitan Pharmaceutical Association, Boston Association of Retail Druggists, Food Marketing Institute, Garden State Pharmacy Owners, Gateway-East Pharmacy Association, Indo-American Pharmacy Association, Metro-East Pharmacists Association, Philadelphia Association of Retail Druggists.

The Community Retail Pharmacy Health Care Reform Coalition of NARD and NACDS represents 112,000 community pharmacists in more than 60,000 pharmacies—the totality of community retail pharmacy. Community pharmacies employ more than one million people, and annually dispense more than two billion—or 93 percent—of all outpatient prescriptions.

PRINCIPLES OF PHARMACY SERVICES AND PHARMACY CARE IN HEALTH CARE REFORM

In recognition of strong evidence that pharmacy services and pharmacy care add value to patient care and reduce overall health care costs, the Community Retail

Pharmacy Health Care Reform Coalition endorses the following principles as critical factors necessary to maximize the role of pharmacy services and pharmacy care in a reformed health care system:

1. Pharmaceutical products and pharmacy services and care should be a basic core benefit under health care reform.

2. Enhanced pharmacy services and the proper management of patient drug use can generate significant overall savings.

3. Professional pharmacy services go beyond merely dispensing a pharmaceutical product and include the following professional services: Establishment and maintenance of a Patient Profile System; Drug utilization review DUR) and screening; Patient monitoring; Patient counseling and offering to counsel patients; Intervention and problem resolution; and Drug product selection.

4. Pharmacy services ensure that patients receive the maximum benefit from drug therapy and that drug-related problems are identified, resolved and prevented.

5. Pharmacists must be empowered and encouraged to exercise their professional expertise in making medication-related judgments in collaboration with other health care providers to maximize patient outcomes.

6. Pharmacists must have access to relevant patient information to support their professional judgment and provision of patient services.

7. Mandatory use of the uniform national electronic transmission standard will maximize the ability of pharmacists to provide thorough drug utilization review and determination of appropriate patient pharmacy services to achieve both service quality and cost containment goals.

8. Development of quality assurance programs, designed and implemented at local levels through a collaborative process, will enhance the quality of pharmacists' services.

9. Evaluation studies should further document the added savings pharmacy services contribute to patient drug use therapy.

10. Continued assurance of patient confidentiality is essential in the provision of pharmacy services and pharmacy care to individuals.

THE COSTS AND CONSEQUENCES OF DRUG NONCOMPLIANCE

Noncompliance with drug therapy costs 20 million workdays and $1.5 billion in earnings annually in the United States.

Drug noncompliance is the cause of: 10 percent of all hospital admissions, 25 percent of hospital admissions among the elderly, 23 percent of all nursing home admissions, $8.5 billion in excess hospitalization costs annually, Significant outpatient costs, Absenteeism from work and decreased job productivity.

An estimated 39 percent of adverse drug reactions requiring hospitalization are caused by improper medication use.

As many as half of all patients fail to take their medications as directed.

Approximately 10 percent of patients fail to have their prescriptions filled; as many as 30 percent fail to have their prescriptions refilled.

Studies show that, by the time patients get from the doctor's office to the pharmacy, they have forgotten half of the doctor's instructions about their prescribed medication.

Noncompliance includes failing to have a prescription filled or refilled as instructed by a physician, failing to take all of the medication when instructed to do so, failing to take the medication when scheduled, taking more or less than prescribed, or taking a drug in combination with food, medications, or under conditions warned against by the physician or pharmacist.

As many as 50 percent of patients with high blood pressure stop taking their medication during the first year, and after three years, only a third are still compliant with their prescribed drug regimen. In one study, one in four patients who had difficulty complying with antihypertensive therapies were hospitalized as a result of noncompliance.

The cost of the medication is small compared to the cost of treating the results of noncompliance. In one study the cost to treat noncompliance was four times the annual drug cost to the patient.

Senator DODD. Ms. Waxman, thank you for being here.

Ms. WAXMAN. Thank you very much for inviting me today.

Families USA is a nonprofit, nonpartisan organization working on behalf of families for health care reform. As you may know, Families USA has been concerned about the growing burden of rising health care costs on families. In that regard, next week we have a report coming out entitled, "Skyrocketing Health Inflation: 1980, 1993, and 2000," in which we will document what the high cost of not doing health care reform will be.

In particular, we have also been concerned about the rising cost of prescription drugs and how that makes us especially vulnerable to losing our ability to get the drugs we may need. The United States represents the world's largest market for pharmaceuticals. Unfortunately for consumers, the industry's strength has often been a bitter pill to swallow.

Last year, we issued a report entitled, "Prescription Costs: America's Other Drug Crisis," and we found a number of disturbing findings.

First of all, prescription drug use had increased in the 10-year period between 1977 and 1987, so that the average number of annual prescriptions increased by about 13 percent. However, consumer spending for p esc ipti n drugs greatly outpriced increased consumption, and the average American spent 3-1/2 times more for prescriptions during that time period.

And, as we have heard already, and I am happy to say we heard today, the drug companies are now saying their inflation has been high, but that in the last quarter, it is down to CPI or close to CPI, and that is wonderful. We hope that continues. But of course, that has not been true. In recent years, we have seen that the inflation rate for pharmaceuticals has far outpaced the CPI, in fact, to the tune of three to four times as much.

Also we heard before that this has directly hit on the pocketbooks of families. About half of all costs currently do come directly out of the pocketbooks of families, and for the elderly that is really closer to two-thirds of all prescription drug costs come directly out of their pockets.

We heard a lot, too, about return on investment and so forth, and we think, of course, profits are a good thing—and yet what are the profit margins that American pharmaceutical manufacturers have seen? In the study, we showed that they enjoyed profit margins that were two to seven times higher than average Fortune 500 companies. In 1991 alone, we looked at the companies that made the 20 most frequently prescribed drugs, and we found that they enjoyed profits of over 15 percent of their total sales. That is in comparison to the Median Fortune 500 company, which saw only a 3.2 percent profit. That is five times as high a profit.

The United States stands in marked contrast to other industrialized countries in the world. For example, a report by the Senate Committee on Aging showed that prescription drug costs on average were one-third less in Canada and 40 percent less in the European market. Why is that?

We did an other report called "Crossing to Mexico: Priced Out of American Health Care," because we had heard of many American citizens that actually go to Mexico to get medical care and, in particular, their prescription drugs. We found that along the border there were many little towns that were dotted with pharmacies and medical clinics just so Americans could come over to get their services met.

Our research found that it was very common for Americans to travel to Mexico to get their drugs at reduced prices. In fact, we compared the costs of six of those 20 most frequently prescribed brand name drugs that were sold in the United States to what they cost in Mexico, and we found on average that the drugs cost three times as much in the United States as they did in Mexico, some drugs costing over six times as much.

What is the lesson to be learned? We know that prescription drugs help Americans live longer, healthier, and more productive lives. However, as consumers, we feel that we must pay careful attention to the pricing practices and whether or not these drugs are going to be affordable.

Turning to President Clinton's Health Security Act, Families USA believes it gives us hope that America's other drug crisis can be brought under control. First of all, all Americans will have universal coverage, including coverage for prescription drugs. I did not hear so much about this this morning. I assume all of us are in agreement that that is a wonderful thing. That, too, will increase the pharmaceutical market considerably because so many people will have coverage for drugs.

Additionally, it seems like we are all in agreement that including drugs within the market-based system and capital and premiums at CPI will be another way that we can control the overall growth in the cost of drugs. Everybody seemed to feel that that was an agreeable way to go about it.

It seemed to me the main disagreement was on this Advisory Council on Breakthrough Drugs, and I have to say it really is surprising, as you yourself said, Senator—it is advisory only. It serves as kind of a conscience or, it seems to me, a way to look at whether or not the price is going to be reasonable. And it is kind of amazing to me that all the manufacturers seem very concerned about having to meet a reasonable standard. Nobody is saying there should not be profits, but if the drugs are not affordable then they are really not good for anybody.

Also, looking at the Medicare population, we are very pleased that a prescription drug benefit will be included for that population. It is clearly way overdue. We are also mindful that there must be meaningful cost containment for the Medicare population. We do believe that the lack of cost containment in the Medicare Catastrophic Coverage Act contributed to the estimated premiums for drug coverage and its eventual demise. We do not want to see that happen again.

With all the talk this morning about how much money went to profits, how much money will go to R and D, I think it is important to refer to the Senate Special Committee on Aging and emphasize that they did conclude in their report that in 1992, only 16 percent of the manufacturer's price of a drug went for research and development, as compared to about 35 or 36 percent that went to profits, marketing and advertising.

An anecdote I would like to share on how much money is actually spent on marketing is on which I was fortunate enough to be asked to speak to the pediatricians at their annual conference here in Washington a few weeks ago. As a registered participant, I was sent an invitation to one of the pharmaceutical company's dessert parties. Unfortunately, I was not able to go, but I wonder how much of the money I spend on prescription drugs went to this dessert party for the thousands of pediatricians, who prescribe to those drugs, of course, who were in town for the annual convention.

I hope, Senator, that you will share with us the information that you requested from the companies on how much of the drug price does go for marketing.

In conclusion, I would like to say that many times in the current market, we see the pharmaceutical industry simply pricing drugs out of reach of the consumer. We hope that the Health Security Act will assure that all Americans will get affordable drugs and that they will be part of insurance coverage that can never be taken away.

Thank you.

[The prepared statement of Ms. Waxman follows:]

PREPARED STATEMENT OF JUDITH WAXMAN

Mr. Chairman and Members of the Committee:

Thank you for inviting me to testify before you today on this important issue of prescription drugs. Families USA is a nonprofit, nonpartisan organization working on behalf of families for health care reform.

As you may know, Families USA has been concerned about the growing burden of rising health care costs on families. We have issued a number of reports that document the magnitude of the increase in expenditures on both families and businesses. In fact, next week we are releasing a new report which is entitled Skyrocketing Health Inflation: 1980, 1993 and 2000 which will analyze the total burden of health care payments on American families and businesses nationally and state-by-state. Our conclusion is that without health care reform, health care will become farther and farther out of reach for all of us.

The rising burden of prescription drugs makes us all especially vulnerable to losing our ability to get the drugs we need. The United States represents the world's largest market for pharmaceuticals. The demand for prescription drugs, coupled with their rapidly growing cost, has led the pharmaceutical industry toward the top of American industry. Unfortunately for consumers, the industry's strength is a bitter pill to swallow.

Last year, we issued a report entitled Prescription Costs: America's Other Drug Crisis. It examined the rising costs of pharmaceutical drugs in the United States by analyzing data provided by the 1987 National Medical Expenditure Survey.[1]

Our study uncovered a number of disturbing findings. Prescription drug use increased in the ten-year period between 1977 and 1987. The average number of annual prescriptions increased by 13 percent in that period. However, consumer spending for these prescription drugs greatly outpaced increased consumption. The average American spent almost three and one-half times more for their prescription drugs from 1977 to 1987—a 237 percent jump.

The costs of prescription drugs directly hit the pocketbooks of America's consumers. Over half of all drug costs (53.5%) are paid directly out-of-pocket, not through insurance or other payers. Private insurance picked up the cost of only one-third (31%) of consumers' drug bills. And for the elderly, almost two-thirds (63.7%) is paid directly out-of-pocket.

Pharmaceutical cost inflation has been three to four times the general inflation rate in recent years. While the Consumer Price Index increased only 21 percent from 1985 to 1991, prescription drug prices rose 66 percent. The average price of, the 20 most frequently prescribed drugs increased 79 percent over the same period. These 20 drugs account for over one-quarter (27%) of all expenditures on prescription drugs for people under age 65 and over one-third (37%) of all drug expenditures by the elderly.

These price increases result in large profit margins for American pharmaceutical manufacturers. In the same period, pharmaceutical companies enjoyed profit margins that were two to seven times higher than the average Fortune 500 company. In 1991 alone, manufacturers of the 20 most frequently prescribed drugs enjoyed profits of 15.1 percent of total sales. By comparison, the median Fortune 500 company saw only a 3.2 percent profit margin in 1991. In other words, pharmaceutical

---

[1] Families USA Foundation, Prescription Costs: America's Other Drug Crisis (Washington, D.C.: Families USA Foundation, 1992).

companies manufacturing the top 20 drugs in the United States enjoyed profits that were almost five times the median for Fortune 500 companies.

Pharmaceutical companies frequently increase the prices of the most commonly purchased drugs. Between 1985 to 1991, the price of Naprosyn (used to treat arthritis) increased ten times and the price of two other top 20 drugs increased nine times. Another eight of the 20 most frequently prescribed drugs increased eight times in the same period.

Pharmaceutical manufacturers argue that their pricing practices are necessary in order to recoup their high costs for research and development (R&D). The profit margins of the drug companies, however, are computed after all expenses, including industry R&D, are taken into account. Furthermore, pharmaceutical industry investment in research and development has not kept pace with profits. From 1989 to 1990, 30 of the top 50 pharmaceutical firms marketing in the United States increased their R&D expenditures by less than 10 percent. At the same time, industry profits rose over 16 percent. Pharmaceutical companies say they spend about 15 percent of their income on R&D. Since most companies raised their R&D budgets by less than ten percent, only 1.5 percent of prescription drug price inflation can be attributed to R&D investment. Approximately half of the price increases have gone to marketing, increased profits and other administrative expenses. [2]

The United States stands in marked contrast to other industrialized countries in the world. Not only are Americans more likely to pay for their prescription drugs out of their own pocket, but Americans are forced to pay much higher prices for these drugs. For example, a report issued by the Senate Committee on Aging reports that prescription drugs cost on average, one-third less in Canada and 40 percent less in the European market than in the United States. [3] The rate of drug price inflation is also lower in other countries as well. For example, drug prices have increased only 4.5 percent in Canada and only 2.5 percent in Europe. [3]

Last year, we also released a report entitled Crossing to Mexico: Priced Out of American Health Care. [4] In the process of conducting our research, it became obvious that Americans are getting their prescription drugs all along the border. In any Mexican border city, there is a striking number of pharmacies and medical buildings, with imposing signs in neon and steel, calling to the American consumer. As customers walk into the pharmacies, their medicines of all kinds are piled high on the counter the way breath mints are displayed in drugstores in the United States.

But the most interesting place we found was a little town called Algodones. Algodones is near an area of the southwest United States that is home to thousands of older people from the colder climates who winter in warmer weather—the "snowbirds" who populate acre upon acre of the desert in huge RV communities.

Algodones is a little oasis in the desert, about 30 miles west of Yuma, Arizona. Algodones is not really a town. It's more like a movie set of a community established for one purpose: to cater to the dental, optical, and pharmaceutical needs of older American consumers. Interstate 8 out of Yuma is dotted with billboards beckoning travelers to buy candy, perfume, and drugs across the border in Mexico. Algodones itself is almost entirely made up of pharmacies, optical stores, and dentist offices. It is a couple of streets deep, but you don't have to walk very far to get what you need. Thousands of older Americans meet their pharmaceutical needs during their winter stay, and then stock up for the rest of the year. The pharmacies of Algodones, along with the other pharmacies all along the border, are a major way American senior citizens afford their prescription drugs.

Our research found that it is common for Americans to travel to Mexico in order to purchase prescription drugs at greatly reduced prices. We compared the cost of the six of the 20 most frequently prescribed brand name drugs sold in the United States to the cost of these same drugs in Mexico. On average, these drugs cost over three times as much in the United States as they do in Mexico. Some drugs cost over six times as much.

The lesson to be learned here is simple. Pharmaceutical pricing practices in the United States are a symptom of an ailing and failing American health care system. We know that prescription drugs help many Americans live longer, healthier, more productive lives. However, many consumers are being hurt by these egregious pric-

[2] Stephen W. Schondelmeyer, "Statement on the Public Health Clinic Affordable Drug Act," Statement before Committee on Labor and Human Resources, U.S. Senate, October 6, 1991.

[3] Staff Report to the United States Senate Committee on Aging. "Earning a Failing Grade: A Report Card on 1992 Drug Manufacturer Price Inflation." (Washington, D.C.: Senate Special Committee on Aging, February 1993), p. 8.

[3] Ibid.

[4] Families USA Foundation, Crossing to Mexico: Priced Out of American Health Care (Washington, D.C.: Families USA Foundation, 1992).

ing practices. Unfortunately, the drug companies are making profits the new-fashioned way-by price gouging. The people who can travel to Mexico or Canada to buy their drugs are the fortunate ones-they have a safety valve. For the sake of all Americans, we need national health reform that ensures that affordable drugs are available to all.

President Clinton's Health Security Act gives us hope that America's drug price crisis can be brought under control. The first and most important reason for hope is that the Health Security Act requires that all Americans have universal coverage including coverage for prescription drugs. Currently, coverage for prescription drugs is not guaranteed, even if the family has coverage. And we are all at risk of losing the coverage we have at any time. Giving all Americans the security of knowing that they will never lose there health insurance and that it will always include prescription drug coverage is a giant leap towards making drugs accessible for everyone who needs them.

Secondly, the inclusion of drugs within the cap on premiums, we believe will go a long way toward controlling the overpricing we experience today. Drug manufacturers simply cannot be allowed to continue to charge us what they do today. The cap on the growth of premiums that is proposed by the Clinton bill will force manufacturers to negotiate with health plans on their prices. The beneficiaries of these negotiations will be the consumers who will gain access to more reasonably priced pharmaceuticals.

The Advisory Council on Breakthrough Drugs is another positive step toward controlling drug prices. While the council will not actually have the power to limit prices, the process of review and subsequent publication of their findings will help make manufacturers justify the prices they will charge for new drugs. The council will act as a gentle reminder, a conscience to the manufacturer to act responsibly when pricing new drugs. Consumers will benefit from this process.

We also appreciate that the President's plan includes prescription drugs for Medicare beneficiaries with effective cost containment mechanisms. Older Americans, under our current system, are faced with the need for high utilization of prescriptions, high prices and inadequate or nonexistent insurance. As a result, this population often goes without needed prescriptions which in turn results in the need for more extensive more costly care. A prescription drug benefit for Medicare beneficiaries is long overdue.

Meaningful cost containment, such as what is included in the bill is crucial to keep the benefit affordable to both taxpayers and beneficiaries. We believe that the lack of cost containment in the Medicare Catastrophic Coverage Act contributed to the estimated premiums for drug coverage and its eventual demise. We do not want to see that happen again.

The pharmaceutical industry will tell you that research and development will suffer if drug prices are restrained. But the price of drugs includes much more than legitimate research costs. A recent report by the Senate Special committee on Aging concluded that only 16% of the manufacturer's price of a drug goes toward research and development as compared to 36% that goes toward profits, marketing and advertising. Drug manufacturers have significant leeway to moderate their prices without interfering with their research and development. In fact, within the last year a few pharmaceutical manufacturers have committed to cutting marketing expenses and investing more in research. We think this is a positive outcome of the current trend to make manufacturers more responsible.

In conclusion, the pharmaceutical industry has been pricing drugs out of reach. Left unchecked the day will come when only the wealthiest Americans will have meaningful access to the prescription drugs they need. The Health Security Act will assure all Americans that affordable drugs will be part of insurance coverage that can never be taken away.

Senator DODD. Thank you very much for your testimony, and I thank all of you for being with us today.

And by the way, I meant to raise the issue, and I will do it in writing, of the differential in pricing between Mexico and the United States, since Mexico is very much on everyone's minds these days with the adoption of NAFTA in the House last night. There is great interest. I meant to inquire this afternoon, and I will do that t g the submission of a written question to our first panel. hrou h

But let me come back, Ms. Waxman, and raise the issue that I suggested in my opening statement. And tell me if you think these numbers are wrong, and if they are wrong, I would like to know what your numbers are. And by the way, I have not seen anyone really contest the numbers. When you are looking at a range of 5,000 compounds—and I have heard as high as 10,000, but more often 5,000 compounds—that for every 5,000, only one actually makes it to market. That is a staggering statistic. So is the number of years, 8 to 14, that it takes to go through the process. You have heard a couple of our witnesses, including Dr. Schonfeld, talk about a delay of 18 months in some cases.

I would say, by the way, Dr. Schonfeld, that I am sad to hear about the number of lives lost. I always think that one of the great things about our country and our products, and the reason they do as well as they do internationally, is because there is such reliability. There is a tremendous faith that when we approve a product, it is damned good. I think marketing may have something to do with it, but I suspect the fact that a pharmaceutical product with the label, "Made in U.S.A." on it, approved by the FDA, really means a great deal even in countries that may put out products more quickly than we do. And we all get frustrated with the FDA. I must get one constituency inquiry a week about the FDA, and I can get in line and bellow as much as anybody else, but part of me also wants them to do their job. I mean, I would be screaming at them were they to rush and put something out, and I would be the first one to be acting like a hypocrite, screaming, "How did you let that thing get out on the market?" and someone would say, "Senator, it was your phone call." So we all get a little caught up in these things, and we have got to be careful.

But that is a pretty overwhelming set of statistics. I do not know of anything quite like it. I remember a decade and a half ago, the whole battle over price controls on energy. I was in House of Representatives then. It was a nasty battle up here that almost rivalled what we have seen on the NAFTA issue. Then, the issue was over the dry wells. I do not recall a single member of the Texas, Oklahoma or Louisiana delegations even remotely coming close to suggesting the number of dry wells before they would get one that would produce.

I am not part of the industry, and I do not understand all aspects of it. But as just a layman sitting here with those kinds of statistics, it is stunning to me that there is that much of an effort made before something actually ends up on our shelves. Don't we run some risk with price controls—and I gather you are advocating price controls. Although you like the Clinton bill, it is not in there. If you could write it, you would put a price control vehicle in there—is that correct?

Ms. WAXMAN. Well, I really have not considered that. I am supporting what President has done.

Senator DODD. But would you support price controls? Would you like to see price controls?

Ms. WAXMAN. Well, I am really not an expert on how price controls work or not, but I suppose if it were in, I would be favorably inclined. I would want to learn more about it, but I really have not done that kind of research.

Senator DODD. When have those ever worked?

Ms. WAXMAN. Well, I am not here to advocate that. I am here to say that——

Senator DODD. Yes, but it is important because we listen to folks like you, because you bring a lot of knowledge to the table, and a bunch of us up here are going to vote on some of these things pretty quickly. Do we include this or not include it? Backstop or not backstop?

I was just listening to the man who was sitting in the chair you are in talking about how much of a chilling effect the measures have on investors in the biotechnology industry.

Ms. WAXMAN. Right. I cannot really talk about what is in the investor's mind, obviously, and if we knew what was in people's minds and what ran the stock market, we could do a whole lot better personally, I am sure. But the point is that all this bill is doing—and that is really what I am here today to support—the difference in opinion seemed to be over whether or not there should be an advisory committee that looked at what would be a reasonable price and published that information. It is not price controls. And "reasonable" does not mean that we do not acknowledge that arduous path that they have to go through.

If an investor is scared off because he cannot get five times the profit he could by investing in another Fortune 500 company, I cannot really address that and take care of that problem. But I could say that because of the necessity of the consumer getting that drug, it should be reasonably priced. And this bill does not even make it be reasonably priced.

Senator DODD. I do not disagree with that.

Ms. WAXMAN. I really do not see why there is such objection to having this advisory committee, and in fact, it seemed to me that the answers to your question—what I heard them say was that they were not really so opposed to the advisory committee, but they were just afraid of what it might become in the future. We can deal with that down the road.

Senator DODD. Let me go back to the original question for you. Do you argue at all with the numbers of the amount of compounds or the amount of years that it takes?

Ms. WAXMAN. I have no idea. I have no knowledge of that. That is not within my expertise. That may be correct. I do not know.

Senator DODD. Would that have any influence on your thinking if it were correct?

Ms. WAXMAN. Not really, because what I am saying is I understand it is an arduous process; I understand it takes a long time, and maybe it does not have to take that long. But all that can be taken into account when the committee decides what is reasonable, and it should be taken into account. But to me, the word "reasonable" means that it is fair, and "fair" means what it took to get there. But "fair" does not mean that just because it has been long, they can price-gouge the American public.

Senator DODD. No, and I do not think anyone was saying that.

Ms. WAXMAN. Well, I use that as an extreme term just to make the difference. There is reasonable and there is not reasonable. To me, reasonable should include what it takes to get there, but it should not mean we should therefore, because it is a hard process, not be allowed to look at and make some determination of what really is reasonable within that realm.

Senator DODD. I appreciate that.

Mr. Moore I raised the issue earlier about this, I do not want to get into a discussion here on the litigation. I raised the issue with the industry in that regard just in terms of those prices. Obviously, suits have to be run out, and I appreciate your willingness to have your counsel here. And I have an inquiry about that 1,200 percent figure in terms of what the differentials are, and I would like to find out what it is because I think it is a legitimate question.

But let me ask you this question, because there are allegations raised against pharmacists particularly in chain stores about pricing and differentials within the same chain stores, depending on where the store are located. Are there differentials that you charge customers based on where a chain store is located?

Mr. MOORE. I have one store only, and we have our own plan to work with.

Senator DODD. Well, for instance, People's Drug here in town; they are all over town. Do you think there is any differential in pricing that, say, a People's Drug Store would charge in one part of Washington as opposed to, say, up in Georgetown?

Mr. MOORE. I am not familiar with how that chain charges, Senator.

Senator DODD. OK. Are there any stores like that that you are aware of where there are differentials?

Mr. MOORE. The only thing that some of them use, the same as grocery stores and so forth, is they have different zones that they use, depending upon how competitive the situation is.

Senator DODD. And the price would vary accordingly?

Mr. MOORE. The price would vary, right, to some extent.

Senator DODD. And you are opposed to price controls?

Mr. MOORE. I am opposed to price controls, although probably 50 percent of my business now, I am told what I am going to get, either through Blue Cross, Medicaid, or whatever. And on the Blue Cross, it is take it or leave it.

Senator DODD. But you would not want to see price controls?

Mr. MOORE. I do not think price controls work.

Senator DODD. How about the advisory panels and so forth on getting information; does that worry you at all? Ms. Waxman's point here is they are just getting some information, and why is everybody getting up-tight; while the industry is saying, you know, when you start asking that stuff, you scare everybody, because they think all of a sudden you are going to start coming out with a bunch of——

Mr. MOORE. I cannot give you a good answer on that, Senator.

Senator DODD [continuing]. What would you recommend?

Mr. MOORE. Do you mean for the prices on the pharmaceuticals?

Senator DODD. Yes, as part of the bill. Should we have that advisory panel, or is that going to have a chilling effect? What do you think the result would be?

Mr. MOORE. I cannot give you an answer. I do not know.

Senator DODD. Dr. Schonfeld, I have got the feeling you have got an opinion on this.

Mr. SCHONFELD. Oh, yes. Well, as I said, I have tried to look at all aspects of the health care issue. One of the things I did after Senator Pryor came out with his report last February or the end of January, called "A Failing Grade," was that I decided to check his numbers. I went to Standard and Poors' Compustat, which is a statistical service used by Wall Street, and I ran out all the net income numbers for all of the publicly owned pharmaceutical and biotech companies that had sales over $10 million—in other words, people who had actually gotten a drug to market. The profit margins of those companies on average are not nearly as large as an analysis of only the Fortune 500 companies would suggest.

You have the big drug companies like the Bristol-Meyers who are diversified in all kinds of things, they have economies of scale, and they are doing very nicely. But you also have a lot of medium-sized pharmaceutical companies that are doing rather modestly. And then, in fact—and this might come as a surprise—one-third of all the companies actually showed losses last year.

So not everyone is making a humongous profit. That is number one. So you really need to look at all of the data, all of the industry, not just a few big guys.

The next thing—and I think this goes to your comments about Canada, for example, or Mexico—we actually have international burden-shifting in kind of an interesting way. There is a commission up in Canada that does influence drug prices very directly. If they decided that U.S. consumers should bear 100 percent of the R and D costs, they can push down the price of those drugs in Canada. That commission is very popular with Canadian voters. We wind up bearing 100 percent of the R and D cost in our market.

I think it would be interesting to ask where was the Commerce Department when some of these trade things were going on in the past. Hopefully, NAFTA will address that kind of a problem.

Senator DODD. Well, it should.

Mr. SCHONFELD. We hope so. But the other aspect of it is when we talk about price controls, would we put in a commission in the United States to cap the price of Arkansas chickens if Canada put in a commission to cap the price of Arkansas chickens? Or if they put in a commission to cap computer prices, would we put in a commission to cap computer prices?

The fact that it is drugs does not really matter when it comes to international trade like that, and I think what we are seeing is international burden-shifting.

Also in Mexico, as we know, the FDA has the highest regulatory standard of any such regulatory agency in the world, and you mentioned the reliability of American pharmaceuticals. Is the generic drug you buy in Mexico equivalent in terms of reliability to what you might buy here in the United States? I do not know.

Ms. WAXMAN. Pardon me. I think the drugs we looked at, anyway, were not generic drugs. They were the exact same drugs made by the same manufacturers.

Senator DODD. I assumed that is what you were saying.

Let me ask both you and Ms. Johnson—and I will address the question to you, Ms. Johnson, first—and you have lupus as well, do you not?

Ms. JOHNSON. I do not. I have cancer. But I work with lupus people, and I am the president of the organization, so I see the patients daily.

Senator DODD. Well, we do not have cures either for lupus or cancer. We have treatments, and they can make a difference. To what extent are you aware, and I presume you are, of where the most efforts are being made in regard to both lupus and cancer? Are they being made at NIH, or in the private sector? Where are the bulk of the efforts being made as you are tracking things and watching in terms of possible cures here?

Ms. JOHNSON. I would say it is diversified. NIH is certainly working on it. But NIH works on a lot of these things in conjunction with the pharmaceutical companies. It is not in isolation. And then, of course, there are private research dollars that are going into the large university research centers. So my opinion is that it is a mix.

Senator DODD. Dr. Schonfeld.

Mr. SCHONFELD. I think that is true. The NCI has made enormous contributions. However, the real rate of growth in the NCI's budget has been modest or almost nonexistent. I actually did an analysis, and I have charted it with my little home computer here so that you can see it. This shows Federal research spending in constant 1980 dollars divided by the number of new cancer cases every year. So this is how much they are spending per capita in 1980 dollars per new case.

Senator DODD. Is that a legitimate way to look at this?

Mr. SCHONFELD. I think so. The new case issue——

Senator DODD. We have just a handful of people with a really serious disease.

Mr. SCHONFELD. Well, everybody is talking about inflation and the CPI. The inflation index I used here was the Federal Government's own inflation index for biomedical research from the NIH; and then I divided it by the number it by the number of new cancer cases, which says how serious is the problem. This is a 37 percent decline in real cancer funding.

There is another chart here which compares the budget of the NCI to the R and D budgets of General Motors and IBM. Those are in just billions of dollars.

Senator DODD. We will include those charts as part of the record.

Mr. SCHONFELD. But the NCI budget has not grown as fast as many other companies, both in the pharmaceutical industry and outside of the pharmaceutical industry. In fact, these two companies together spend more money on R and D than all of NIH. And General Motors and IBM, as you well know, are not doing so well these days.

Senator DODD. They are doing better.

Finally, let me just ask, do all of you agree that pharmaceuticals ought to be included under the legislation?

Ms. WAXMAN. Absolutely.

Mr. MOORE. Yes.

Senator DODD. Do you support that as well, Ms. Johnson? You may have said so, and I apologize if I did not hear you.

Ms. JOHNSON. Yes.

Mr. Schonfeld. I think the Medicare benefit is particularly important to many people.

Senator DODD. So you all support that. And you all support the universality aspects of the Clinton proposal?

Ms. JOHNSON. Yes.

Ms. WAXMAN. Absolutely.

Mr. SCHONFELD. Yes. There are a couple of other things in there that apply directly to cancer patients, by the way, such as the——

Senator DODD. I am just trying to get some answers from everybody. Do you agree with that, Ms. Johnson?

Ms. JOHNSON. Yes.

Senator DODD. Mr. Moore.

Mr. MOORE. Yes.

Senator DODD. Ms. Waxman.

Ms. WAXMAN. Absolutely.

Senator DODD. OK.

Mr. SCHONFELD. There is a provision which says insurance coverage must include drugs that are in clinical trials that are NIH-sponsored. That is a tremendous boon to cancer patients, by the way.

Senator DODD. I am glad to hear that. Thank you.

All of your testimony and your thoughts on these subjects have been very helpful, and we will obviously be in continuing touch with you as we look at these issues.

We thank you for coming today and being a part of the hearing and expressing your views and thoughts.

[Additional material follows:]

ADDITIONAL MATERIAL

PREPARED STATEMENT OF PATRICIA A. JOHNSON

Mr. Chairman, and Honorable Members of the Committee:

I am Patricia Johnson, President of the Lupus Foundation of America and Executive Director of the Lupus Foundation of New Jersey. My testimony today is on behalf of the national foundation.

Thank you for this opportunity to appear before you to express our views about the pluses and possible dangers of President Clinton's proposal to reform the nation's health-care system. I am speaking today for the concerns of millions of people who could be dramatically affected by this plan.

It appears that the Clinton health-care plan focuses heavily on preventive health care and cost containment. Our biggest fear is that this legislation does not address the needs of the more than 100 million chronically ill people in this nation who require continuing access to quality medical care and vital medicines.

I know, Mr. Chairman, that you have long been a champion in the fight to increase research to find a possible cure and better treatments for lupus, as well as for increasing public understanding of this difficult disease. We want to express our deep and very sincere thanks for your continuing efforts.

For Committee members and others of the general public who may be less aware of this disease, I'll start by telling you a little about lupus, a disease that afflicts as many as 500,000 Americans and an estimated one-half million yet undiagnosed. Family members and loved ones are also touched by this devastating disease both financially and emotionally.

Lupus is a chronic inflammatory disease of the connective tissue caused by an overactive immune system. It can affect any vital organ or part of the body.

There is no cure for lupus. People with lupus must live with the pain, fatigue and medication side effects for their lifetime.

Lupus is a disease with an unpredictable prognosis and difficult symptoms. Among those symptoms are extreme fatigue, low-grade fevers and debilitating joint pain. In some cases, lupus is fatal!

Lupus is intermittent, recurrent and difficult to cope with. Therefore, it often causes family problems. It is a lifelong battle—for those who have it and for their families and loved ones.

For unknown reasons, more than 85 percent of lupus patients are women in the childbearing years, but men, children and older people also have lupus.

Lupus is one of 67 severe and often debilitating chronic autoimmune disorders, which together affect an estimated eight million Americans. These diseases include multiple sclerosis, rheumatoid arthritis and Addison's disease, which affected the late President Kennedy.

Many lupus patients also suffer from other autoimmune conditions. Most people with autoimmune diseases share one thing in common: Their disease is controlled only by daily medications. It is important to keep in mind that a research breakthrough for any of the above conditions could prove critical for those with lupus.

In the past, I have heard arguments that too much money has been spent on research for so-called "me-too" drugs. Let me make it very clear: There is no such thing as a "me too" drug for lupus patients. And there is no such thing as a "me-too" patient. The truth is that a drug that works for one patient may not work for another—even if they share the same condition. And giving lupus patients the wrong drug can cause them great physical distress or even kill them.

Let me point out a few other critical and related concerns. Appropriate medication is often determined only through trial and error. Patients frequently require combinations of medicines to bring their symptoms under control. Lupus patients also are apt to be extremely allergic, therefore they often can only tolerate one or two specific drugs in a given therapeutic class. And since they often take so many other medications—from nine to 20 pills a day is not unusual—they must be concerned with drug interactions and dangerous side effects. Long-term use of some steroids, for example, can cause a softening of bones and require some patients to undergo costly hip and knee replacements.

What lupus patients desperately need are more medicines, more choices—more options—that can help them cope with their painful affliction. The one hope they have is that advanced medical research may bring a cure.

What concerns me most about the President's proposals as I understand them is that I fear they may curtail the options available to people with lupus.

My first concern is that without continued and increased research and development, there may never be a cure. It would be tragic to create a new health-care system that discourages cost-saving medical research and denies patients new therapies and cures.

The most likely source of any future lupus care is the biotech industry—either by itself or in partnership with an established pharmaceutical firm. Recent news that a small biotech company in California plans to start human clinical trials on a vaccine therapy for lupus was most heartening.

However, I fear that price restrictions, either direct or indirect, could stop that research dead in its tracks. Biotech venture capital has already dried up with the talk of price controls. Clinical trials also are being postponed.

As you know, the President's proposal contains a number of provisions that could inhibit research. Although the phrase "global budget" does not appear in the legislation, there are indirect price controls on the very companies that we need to produce a lupus cure.

Nor will price controls achieve long-term savings for the health-care system. Improper treatment of lupus patients can result in costly hospitalization, which certainly is more expensive than if they had received proper treatment in the first place.

We are also concerned about provisions in the Clinton proposal that could eventually force all but the wealthiest of our citizens into HMO's or other managed-care systems. These may be very cost effective for preventative care, but they could be devastating for people with serious chronic diseases who require the high-quality care and continuing one-on-one attention that only knowledgeable specialists can provide.

We are deeply concerned about any proposal that would take decisions about appropriate medical care away from doctors and give them to bureaucrats. Who is going to make the proper judgement as to who will get treatment and who won't? Prior authorization of medications also can hamper and delay access in a timely manner to proper treatment modalities—its just more bureaucracy and paperwork.

Further, since lupus is a multi-system disease, we are also very disturbed by aspects of the Clinton bill which would reduce the number of specialists in favor of primary care physicians. This is exactly the wrong prescription for people with lupus who depend on the proper care and treatment of knowledgeable physician specialists. Limiting access to these specialists will cause more costly hospitalizations and even deaths! Diagnosing lupus is very difficult even for rheumatologists, who normally treat the patients, let alone for general practitioners.

I want to make it clear that we do not oppose all aspects of the Clinton Administration's reform proposal. On the contrary, we believe the plan contains several very positive components.

We strongly agree with the concepts of universal coverage and portability of insurance. No one should be denied coverage because of a prior condition, and no one should be afraid to leave a job for fear of losing insurance.

But I hope you will also remember that universal coverage would be worthless if chronically ill patients are denied access to their specialists and proper therapies.

To sum up, I do believe we are at a crossroads in history: The attention of the Congress is focused on the need for health-care reform. We have what may be a unique opportunity to improve the lives of millions of people with chronic debilitating diseases.

America has long been the leader in providing quality health care and developing new and effective medications for treating the serious diseases of our time. Let us not adopt policies that would hurt or delay research or access to proper treatment for the millions of Americans who suffer from lupus and other chronic diseases.

Thank you very much for inviting me to share my views on this extremely important topic.

Senator DODD. The committee will stand adjourned.

[Whereupon, at 5:01 p.m., the committee was adjourned.]

HEALTH CARE REFORM AND MEDICAL RESEARCH

WEDNESDAY, DECEMBER 8, 1993

U.S. SENATE,
COMMITTEE ON LABOR AND HUMAN RESOURCES,
Washington, DC.

The committee met, pursuant to notice, at 10:10 a.m., in room SD–430, Dirksen Senate Office Building, Senator Harkin presiding.
Present: Senators Harkin and Simon.

OPENING STATEMENT OF SENATOR HARKIN

Senator HARKIN. The committee will come to order.

We welcome you all here today to the first of what I hope will be a series of hearings that will begin today and stretch into next year on one portion or aspect of the Health Security Act and health care reform that I do not believe is getting enough attention. That aspect is medical research and the role that biomedical research will play in our health care reform bill that hopefully we will pass next year.

At the outset, I might just say that I believe that unless and until we address the issue of health research and how we fund it and how much we fund it, any form of health care reform will simply rearrange the deck chairs on the Titanic. It is still going to cost us more money, and it is going to bust the bank. And yet no one is looking at the one item that can save us more money than anything else, and that is medical research.

"We cannot be a strong Nation unless we are a healthy Nation. And so we must recruit not only men and women and materials, but also knowledge and science in the service of national strength."

These are the words of President Franklin Roosevelt, taken from his address at the dedication of the National Institutes of Health in October 1940. It is remarkable that even as war was raging in Europe and as the United States stood on the brink of entering that conflict, that President Roosevelt had the foresight to recognize the importance of our Nation's investment in medical research to its national security.

Today, 53 years later, America is about to embark on another historic challenge, the overhaul and reform of our $1 trillion a year health care system. The question now is whether President Clinton and the Congress have the vision and wisdom to recognize the vital role played by medical research in the health security of our Nation.

The purpose of today's hearing is to lay the framework for strengthening the role of medical research in the health care reform proposal and the debate that will be ensuing over the next year.

I firmly believe that a strong medical research program must be a fundamental priority of health care reform. Medical research is the key to eliminating disease and disability and making our health care system less costly and more effective.

Last year, nine of the leading ten causes of death among women were attributable to disease as were seven of the top ten among men. Heart disease and cancer, the two leading causes of death among Americans, will constitute fully one-fifth of America's health care bill next year.

Government costs for Alzheimer's disease, which devastates 4 million Americans and costs at least $90 billion a year, are expected to increase dramatically while baby boomers get older. If we do not do something about finding a cause, a cure, and more effective treatment of Alzheimer's, it is going to sink our ship. It is going to cost us more money than we can imagine.

The long-term savings from a cure or a preventive measure would be enormous. Progress is being made. Just last week, researchers announced that they had identified the genetic flaw that is linked to as many as one in seven cases of colon cancer. Equally exciting is news last month that researchers may have linked a genetic risk factor for Alzheimer's disease. If confirmed, this finding could lead to a simple diagnostic blood test, saving over $250 million a year, and could ultimately lead to a treatment for the disease, potentially saving as much, as I said, up to $90 billion in long-term care costs.

Moreover, funding medical research is an investment in our economic growth. Medical research has spawned the biotechnology industry which, by the year 2000, could be a $50 billion a year American enterprise.

Yet despite its promise, medical research is "threatened by inadequate funding of research and its infrastructure." This is the conclusion of the newly confirmed Director of the National Institutes of Health, Dr. Harold Varmus.

The United States devotes less than 2 percent of its total health care budget to the study of disease. In fact, in back of Senator Simon, who I am going to recognize shortly, the chart shows that NIH funding as a percent of health care expenditures in 1988 was a little over 1.2 percent; and last year, in 1992, it was less than 1.1 percent as a percent of health care expenditures. Then you add in the other health care research that we have beyond NIH, and you get up to just about 2 percent.

In contrast, defense spends 15 percent of its budget on research. Funding for approved NIH grants has fallen below 25 percent, compared to rates of 30 percent or more just a decade ago.

And if you look at the other chart on the far left, NIH funding compared to health care expenditures—the funding for NIH, along the bottom, is basically static from about 1988 to 1992. That is the green line that just goes along the bottom. Health expenditures is the red line, going up, as you can see, now up to $1 trillion. So health care expenditures keep going up, but the funding for NIH stays basically static compared to other health expenditures.

Unfortunately, these trends are likely to worsen. Because this year's budget agreement freezes discretionary spending for the next 5 years, our investment in medical research through the NIH is likely to decline in real terms unless we take action.

That is why Senator Mark Hatfield and I have proposed the creation of a Fund for Health Research as a component of health care reform. We propose that a portion of all health premiums would be placed in a fund dedicated to supplementing existing appropriations for the NIH. Once in effect, this fund would provide an additional $5 to $6 billion a year for the NIH and raise the grant success rate to 33 percent at a minimum.

I intend to pursue all of these questions during the course of today's hearings and hearings to follow. I hope to gain the support of this committee for incorporating the Fund for Health Research into the health care reform package passed by Congress and sent to the President hopefully by the end of next year.

Before beginning today's hearing, let me offer a parable to illustrate another important point. According to this story, a doctor while jogging around a lake spotted someone drowning. The doctor dove in, pulled out and resuscitated the victim and saved his life. He continued his jog until confronted by another drowning victim, whereupon he jumped in, pulled him out and resuscitated him, and saved his life. He then continued his jog until confronted with several other drowning people.

At the same time, the doctor spotted a researcher contemplating the situation. The doctor confronted the researcher, asking: "Why aren't you doing something?"

The researcher replied: "I am doing something. I am trying to figure out who is throwing all these people in the lake."

Unfortunately, the health care reform bill that we are talking about is focusing on rescuing the people without trying to figure out why they are in the lake in the first place.

The debate so far has focused almost entirely on treating, curing, and helping those who are already sick rather than conducting research and finding cures or preventing the diseases before they strike.

One of the goals of the President's Health Security Act is to change the incentives and reward providers for keeping people healthy and not reward them for simply doing more tests and providing more care. The Health Security Act authorizes more research on the appropriateness and effectiveness of clinical care and the development of clinical practice guidelines. And having already read Dr. Lee's testimony, I know he will cover that.

This is the direction we need to be heading in, and this type of research will help ensure that the care that is delivered is both cost-effective and appropriate.

In the pursuit of cost savings, however, we must not sacrifice quality and research that hold the promise of cure and treatment for millions of Americans.

I started off my statement with a quote from President Franklin Roosevelt. His words should give us direction even today, but his personal fight with polio also demonstrates the benefits of medical research. The polio vaccine was the direct result of both basic and applied research, and it has saved countless lives and dollars. According to a study being conducted by the Centers for Disease Control and Prevention, the cost to the United States Government if there were not a p li vaccine would be $900 million to $1 billion in direct costs and anoadditional $2 billion a year in indirect costs.

I hope this hearing contributes to expanding the debate on health care reform beyond the current discussion of delivering care to patients with illness to finding the causes and contributing to the elimination of those diseases.

[The prepared statement of Senator Harkin follows:]

PREPARED STATEMENT OF SENATOR HARKIN

The Committee on Labor and Human Resources will come to order.

"We cannot be a strong nation unless we are a healthy nation. And so we must recruit not only men [and women] and materials but also knowledge and science in the service of national strength."

These are the words of President Franklin Roosevelt, taken from his address at the dedication of the National Institute of Health in October 1940. It's remarkable that even as war was raging in Europe and as the United States stood on the brink of entering that conflict, President Roosevelt had the foresight to recognize the importance of our nation's investment in medical research to its national security.

Today, fifty-three years later, America is about to embark on another historic challenge—the overhaul and reform of its $1 trillion a year health care system. The question now is whether President Clinton—and the Congress—have the vision and wisdom to recognize the vital role played by medical research in the health security of our Nation.

The purpose of today's hearing is to lay the framework for strengthening the role of medical research in the health care reform proposal and the debate that will be considered by Congress over the next year.

I firmly believe that a strong medical research program should be a fundamental priority of health care reform. Medical research is the key to eliminating disease and disability and making a heals care system less costly and more effective.

Last year, nine of the leading 10 causes of death among women were attributable to disease, as were seven of the top 10 among men. Heart disease and cancer, the two leading causes of death among Americans will constitute one-fifth of America's health care bill next year. Government costs for Alzheimer's disease—which devastates four million Americans and costs at least $90 billion each year—are expected to increase dramatically while baby boomers get older. If we could discover cures, preventive measures and cost-effective treatments for any of these diseases, the long-term savings would be enormous.

And progress is already being made. Just last week, researchers announced they had identified the genetic flaw that is linked to as many as one in seven cases of colon cancer, as well as a number of other fatal cancers. Equally exciting is news last month that researchers may have linked a genetic risk factor for Alzheimer's disease. If confirmed, this finding could lead to a simple diagnostic blood test, saving over $250 million a year, and could ultimately lead to a treatment for the disease, potentially saving as much as $90 billion in long-term care costs.

Moreover, funding medical research is an investment in our economic growth. Medical research has spawned the biotechnology industry, which by the year 2000 could be a $50 billion per year American enterprise.

Yet, despite its promise, medical research is "threatened by inadequate funding of research and its infrastructure." This is the conclusion of the newly confirmed Director of the National Institutes of Health, Dr. Harold Varmus.

The United States devotes less than 2 percent of its total health care budget to the study of disease. In contrast, the defense spends 15 percent of its budget on research. Funding for approved NIH grants has fallen below 25 percent, compared to rates of 30 percent or more just a decade ago.

Unfortunately, these trends are likely to worsen. Because this year's budget agreement freezes discretionary spending for the next five years, our investment in medical research through the NIH is likely to decline in real terms without action.

Health care reform offers a great opportunity to reverse this course. First, we must recognize medical research as an essential underpinning of quality, cost-effective health care and provide a constant source of additional funding to support it.

That's why Senator Mark Hatfield and I have proposed the creation of the Fund for Health Research as a component of health reform. We propose that a portion of all health premiums would be placed in a fund dedicated to supplementing existing appropriations for the NIH. Once in effect, this fund would provide an additional $5 billion a year for the NIH, and raise the grant success rate to 33 percent at a minimum.

I intend to pursue all of these questions during the course of today's hearing. I hope to gain the support of this committee for incorporating the Fund for Health Research into the health reform package that will be passed by Congress and sent to the President by the end of next year.

Before beginning today's hearing let me offer a parable to illustrate another important point. According to this story, a doctor while jogging around a lake, spotted someone drowning. The doctor dove in, pulled out and resuscitated the victim. He continued his jog until confronted by another drowning victim. He saved this one, and continued his journey until confronted with several other drowning people.

At the same time, the doctor spotted a researcher contemplating the situation. The doctor confronted the researcher, asking her, "Why aren't you doing something?" The researcher replied, "I am doing something, I'm trying to figure out who's throwing all these people in the lake."

Unfortunately, the debate on health care so far has focussed almost entirely on treating, curing, and helping those who are already sick rather than conducting research and finding the cures for diseases before they strike.

The reaction to the Harkin/Hatfield proposal has been very positive. Over 100 organizations have endorsed the establishment of a medical research fund. We expect, however, that there will be some critics. They will charge that medical research leads to the development of expensive new technologies and therapies which add little to either the length or quality of life. I do not deny that new medical technology and new therapies are often expensive. However, what is driving costs up at an unacceptable rate is the inappropriate use of technology and new treatments.

It is the financial and other incentives in our health care system that drive up costs and result in inappropriate care. The problem is not the existence of innovative treatments but a delivery system where financial and other incentives encourage providers to run more tests and provide more care—regardless of whether it is appropriate or not.

One of the goals of the President's Health Security Act is to change the incentives and reward providers for keeping people healthy and not reward them for simply doing more tests and providing more care. The Health Security Act authorizes more research on the appropriateness and effectiveness of clinical care and the development of clinical practice guidelines. This is the direction we need to be heading in and this type of research will help ensure that the care that is delivered is both cost-effective and appropriate. In the pursuit of cost savings, however, we must not sacrifice quality and research that hold the promise of cure and treatment for millions of Americans.

I started off my statement with a quote from President Franklin Roosevelt. His words should give us direction even today but his personal fight with polio also demonstrates the benefits of medical research. The polio vaccine was the direct result of both basic and applied research and it has saved countless lives and dollars. According to the preliminary results of a study being conducted by the Centers for Disease Control and Prevention the cost to the U.S. government if there was not a polio vaccine would be $900 million to $1 billion dollars in direct costs and an additional $2 billion in indirect costs annually.

I hope this hearing contributes to expanding the debate on health care reform beyond the current discussion of delivering care to patients with illness to finding the causes and contributing to the elimination of those diseases.

I will recognize Senator Simon, and I thank you for being here, Senator Simon. After your opening statement, I want to introduce Dr. Micozzi to talk about the iron lung and why we have it here. But first, I will recognize Senator Simon for any opening statement.

OPENING STATEMENT OF SENATOR SIMON

Senator SIMON. Thank you. The iron lung is not for members of the committee who are here, I trust.

Senator HARKIN. It depends on whether you are going to support our bill or not. [Laughter.]

Senator SIMON. First, I want to commend my colleague Senator Harkin for his leadership in this field, as well as Senator Hatfield. We have to do better. I remember on the floor of the Senate, Senator Harkin, when you mentioned that in the last 7 years, we have done as much in military research as we have done in health care research since the beginning of the century. That is an astounding figure when you think about it.

I have just seen in recent days that two children of friends of ours have died. One of them, our colleague Senator Byron Dorgan, had a 23-year-old daughter who died. What if we had reversed those research figures? I know you cannot rerun history, but we can do better.

Research has lengthened life. When Social Security passed, the average American lived to be 58 years old. At that time, on the floor of the House, there was a discussion, and a Congressman from Minnesota whose name I do not remember said, "What if Americans turn out to live an average of 75 years?" And the sponsor of the bill said, "It will never happen. You are living in a dream world."

Here we are today with an average lifespan of 75. And it is not only that the lifespan has increased; the quality of life has improved. And that is because of research.

I am interested in this topic—and unfortunately, I am not going to be able to stay to the end of the hearing. As I look at this health care reform proposal—and I am pleased to be a cosponsor of it—the one area that troubles both supporters and opponents is the cost area; how solid are our figures?

I think the honest answer is that no one knows for sure. I think that Hillary Clinton and Ira Magaziner and the others, together with the people at HHS have put together the best figures that are available. But no one really knows what happens when you permit 37 million Americans to have access to health care.

My own instinct is that we are in some way going to have to do something that we are not accustomed to doing, and that is to build some flexible revenue into the health care bill so that we authorize the President, after consultation with the Senate Finance Committee and the Ways and Means Committee, to increase revenue in certain areas.

If we do not do that, and in fact the costs exceed the estimates, then I think there will be a squeeze somewhere on the benefits. And as I look at the total picture, the three areas where that squeeze might come are, one, in mental health, where frankly we just have not done the kind of job that we ought to be doing; second, long-term care, where the bill—and it is a good bill—does not go as far as we really ought to be going; and third, research. It is always easy to squeeze those dollars, but we do it at the peril of the future.

What we ought to be doing is looking to the future. We ought to be doing that in our fiscal house. This is the reason I favor a constitutional amendment saying you have to have a balanced budget unless there is a 60 percent vote of Congress to the contrary. We are the first generation of Americans who have not followed the practice of taking care of today and investing in the future. We are taking care of today and borrowing from the future.

I fear we may do the same in the field of health care, and that is why I think these hearings are so important. I look forward to working with you, Senator Harkin, and others in the administration and in the research community, to see that we do the kind of job that we ought to be doing.

Thank you, Mr. Chairman.

Senator HARKIN. Thank you very much, Senator Simon, for a very thoughtful, very eloquent statement. I appreciate it very much. And thank you for being here.

I also want to mention that Senator Hatfield could not be here today. He had to be in his home State, so he could not be here today.

I want to thank the National Museum of Health and Medicine of the Armed Forces Institute of Pathology for arranging to have this iron lung brought into the hearing room today. The iron lung is a dramatic reminder of how far we have come and how much progress we have made because of medical research.

I have asked Dr. Marc Micozzi, who is the director of the museum, to briefly explain how the iron lung works and how it was used to treat polio victims.

I wanted an iron lung brought in today because I can remember when I was a young kid, the fear of polio was something that struck terror in our hearts. And I remember as a young kid—I must have been in 6th or 7th grade, and the nuns took us to a hospital, and we saw all these people in iron lungs on one floor. That image has just always stuck with me, all my life. People were lying in these iron lungs, almost like in a coffin. It was a very terrifying thing.

I think it is a great example of how far we have come, and I appreciate your bringing it here.

Dr. MICOZZI. Yes, Mr. Chairman, thank you. One of the salient points about medical research is that in the 1940's and 1950's, that image that you saw was repeated in hospitals and communities and in some homes around the country. It is a tribute to research that today these devices are found only in historical collections in museums, and not in clinical practice.

I am here today with Mr. Alan Hawk of our Historical Collections to briefly demonstrate this device. This is what medical technology had available to deal with some of the acute outbreaks of paralytic polio, as well as some individuals who had long-term paralysis and inability to breathe from that disease.

As you said, it much resembles a coffin. This particular device is a lightweight, portable model, compared to the original device. The principles were pretty well worked out in the late 1920's in terms of the principles of physics that allowed the air pressure to be changed inside the compartment, which allows the patient to breathe in and then breathe out with the changes in pressure. And that could be controlled electronically through the air pump, which I will show you in a moment.

But right now, the way the patient got in here was to open up this lid; the patient went in, the head went through the far end so that the individual could breathe in the open air and communicate with others. And then this device was sealed up. There was an airtight seal, and the only way of access into that device then became through these little portholes in the sides. Hoses could be introduced into these holes to wash the patient. This larger port was opened up to allow the bedpan to be changed and to have access for other purposes.

Thousands of individuals spent time in these; hundreds of individuals spent their entire lives in a contraption like this.

In the summer of 1952, there were over 20,000 children stricken with polio. The wards were full of devices like this. Doctors and nurses were on standby in the event of a power failure. If the power went down, if there was an equipment failure, the air pressure could be controlled manually by this pump. And there are many retired doctors and nurses today who can describe to you what it was like running up to the polio wards during the power failure to man these pumps and keep them going until something else could be done.

That is what we had available to deal with polio in the 1950's. Medical research, of course, led to the polio vaccine in the 1950's, and we all remember in my generation getting the shots and then the sugar cubes with the oral polio vaccine in the schools.

Today, school children come to the museum, thousands of them each year, and they see this device or others like it, and to them it is something that seems like a time capsule or a time machine or something from outer space. And I think in some ways, it really is, compared to where we have come with modern medicine.

Often, in addition to the intended consequences of medical research, as the development of the polio vaccine to eliminate these, there are also unintended benefits. I spoke with Jim Watson this morning, and when he did his work to discover the structure of DNA, he was working under a polio grant when that work was done.

So I would like to welcome you all later today, if you have a chance, to come up and take a look at this device. Mr. Hawk can give you a white glove if you want to actually touch the artifact, and we are happy to be able to show this to you today.

Senator HARKIN. I appreciate your taking the time and the trouble to bring it here. When I talked to my staff about this hearing, I asked is there anything that we could visually use to show just how far we have come in the last year and what medical research has done for us, and I cannot think of a better visual representation than what you have right here.

Dr. MICOZZI. They are in museums today instead of hospitals.

Senator HARKIN. Where they belong.

Thank you very much, Dr. Micozzi.

Senator HARKIN. Well, Dr. Lee, can you top this? [Laughter.] Phil Lee is Assistant Secretary of Health for the Department of Health and Human Services. He is well-known to our committee and was just here a few weeks ago to testify at a hearing that I held on rural health issues.

Dr. Lee, it is good to see you again. Your statement will be made a part of the record in its entirety. Please proceed.

STATEMENT OF DR. PHILIP R. LEE, ASSISTANT SECRETARY FOR HEALTH, U.S. DEPARTMENT OF HEALTH AND HUMAN SERVICES, WASHINGTON, DC

Dr. LEE. Thank you very much, Mr. Chairman and Senator Simon.

I am pleased to have the opportunity to discuss the Health Security Act, which is now S. 1757, and to discuss how the National Institutes of Health is an integral part of the President's plan to improve the health of all Americans.

I am pleased, Mr. Chairman and also Senator Simon, that both of you are cosponsors. I also greatly appreciate that you have both been steadfast supporters of NIH and of biomedical and behavioral sciences research, as well as other public health and health care programs.

The iron lung, Senator Harkin, recalls very vividly when I was both a medical student and a resident, and as a young faculty member, actually, at New York University in the 1950's, I did research with a lawyer who was living in an iron lung. He was at Goldwater Hospital. It was, of course, a lifesaving device, but fortunately, basic research and then that basic research being applied in a very effective way, transformed the lives of millions of people in preventing polio.

We do have a job to do still in eradicating polio, not only in this hemisphere, but also throughout the world. And of course, WHO is now in a leadership position. We are as the United States supporting that program financially in significant ways, and hopefully we will be able to achieve the same objective that was achieved with smallpox eradication when D.A. Henderson, who is now my deputy for science and is directing our domestic immunization program, led that program worldwide—and again, with untold savings in terms of human suffering.

Senator HARKIN. I was down visiting CDC last year, and they told me that by the year 2000, they believe they will have eradicated polio from the face of the earth.

Dr. LEE. We are hopeful that that will be the case. And that is the best source of information on the subject.

The central role of NIH in the prevention research initiative becomes clear when the objectives of reform are viewed from a health perspective, from a quality of care perspective, and from a cost containment perspective, and you have mentioned all of those, Senator Harkin, in your opening statement.

The Health Security Act, S. 1757, is unique among the proposals before the Congress currently to reform the health care system. It emphasizes prevention more than any other proposal. It makes health plans accountable to achieve prevention and public health— that is, population-based health objectives. And it fosters a close working relationship between research, clinical medicine, and public health.

Prevention research is the foundation for both clinical preventive services and the public health initiatives included in the Health Security Act. Expanded prevention research will ensure the availability of effective preventive measures against existing diseases as well as new and emerging threats to the public health.

Progress in preventing disease will help to offset escalating acute health care costs and the disproportionate impact of disease and disability among women, minorities, and the elderly.

Central to this approach is a restructuring of the personal health care system, enabling it for the first time to emphasize keeping people healthy by promoting health and preventing disease.

The changes in the personal health care system will strengthen and foster the restructuring of the public health system, which we have discussed in previous testimony, making both far more effective in protecting and promoting the health of all Americans and reducing the disparities in the health status among different populations.

I am particularly enthusiastic, Mr. Chairman and Senator Simon, because the President, in developing the proposals, has clearly understood the importance of prevention and has included it in the Health Security Act in four ways: 1) by including a full range of clinical preventive services in the benefits package; 2) by making plans accountable for providing clinical preventive services; 3) by rewarding alliances and plans for keeping their populations healthy; and by expanding prevention research at NIH and providing support to strengthen and expand State and public health programs through the Centers for Disease Control and Prevention.

Our national investment in biomedical, behavioral and social science research yields the knowledge and technology for health promotion and disease prevention as well as for early diagnosis, treatment, rehabilitation and care. This research is translated into practical applications by all the agencies of the U.S. Public Health Service, including NIH, as well as by the medical, nursing and other health professions, by the pharmaceutical industry, the biotechnology industry, and the medical device industries.

The research conducted and supported by NIH provides information needed to assist in adaptation of health plan benefit coverage and the appropriate application of cost-effective methods for prevention and early intervention.

The National Institutes of Health is the premier biomedical research institution in the world and is dedicated to the pursuit of knowledge to improve the health of all Americans, and indeed the people throughout the world. As you both are well aware, the NIH has long used the peer review system to evaluate research proposals in order to fund the highest quality, most meritorious research. The same policies will be followed with respect to the prevention research initiative.

Scientific advances require the continued insight and understanding of the fundamental mechanisms of life, health and disease. Perhaps better than anyone, Dr. Harold Varmus, the new Director of NIH, understands how basic research can and does lead to dramatic and many times unexpected discoveries which can affect the health of a few individuals or perhaps millions of people. And your mention, Senator Simon, of the recent advances in genetic research and the identification of the gene for colon cancer illustrates that point, as does, actually, Dr. Varmus' own research.

Cancer of the colon, of course, is a major problem, and although the genetic factor is responsible for perhaps only 10 percent of the cases, it does begin to lead to a prevention strategy that can flow from this research. And of course, other basic research, we believe will contribute to other preventive solutions with respect to cancer as well as better treatments.

Basic genetic research provides the keys for locating defective genes causing many other genetic disorders in addition to colon cancer. The scientists have already identified and isolated the genes for a number of diseases including Duchenne muscular dystrophy, retinoblastoma, cystic fibrosis, fragile X syndrome, myotonic dystrophy, and Huntington's disease. And although some of these may not be widespread, the devastating effect that they have on individuals merits the kind of research investment that has been made in this area.

Having these genes in hand will allow the researchers to craft the tools necessary to greatly improve control, treatment, and prevention of these disorders. These advances will provide benefits that will touch not only those individuals and their families, but virtually all the rest of us as well.

Prevention research has four ultimate aims: promoting health, preventing the occurrence of disease, preventing the occurrence of clinical illness in individuals who have physiologic or biological evidence of abnormalities, and preventing the progression of clinical disease. I will say a little more about that later.

The initiative spans a wide range of topics and objectives. Research in genetics, molecular and cell biology, immunology, and other fundamental sciences describes the biological basis of disease—what goes awry and why. This knowledge provides a sharp focus for efforts to provide preventive interventions, which can range from lifestyle changes to protecting against damaging biological changes to molecular measures to correct or compensate for acquired or inherited genetic flaws.

While the NIH has long invested in prevention research and has tracked expenditures in this area since 1980, it was felt that an increased investment in NIH research will translate into advances in knowledge that will promote health, prevent disease, and reduce the Nation's expenditures for treatment of preventable illness and injury.

The President's Health Security Act would authorize appropriations of $400 million in fiscal year 95 and a total of $2.9 billion over 6 years for the NIH prevention research expansion. These authorizations are in addition to the current research investment in NIH, including the $2.6 billion NIH is spending on prevention research in 1994. Increases in the NIH prevention appropriations would be subject to the discretionary spending cap.

Our national investment in biomedical and behavioral research, and particularly prevention research, has an important impact on long-term health care and health care costs. In my testimony, I highlight a number of examples, including vaccines, where progress has been really dramatic. In the past recent years, for example, the development of an improved vaccine for hepatitis B and for Hemophilus influenza type b, the latter an important cause of meningitis in children, led to the recommendation that both be included in the universal childhood immunization programs.

Hepatitis B virus causes acute liver disease, sometimes with severe, life-threatening manifestations. And significant savings will be achieved when we get the hepatitis B vaccine widely applied as we are now moving to do in the national immunization program.

Hemophilus influenza type b was a leading cause of mental retardation and deafness in children before the introduction of the vaccine. One in 200 children in the United States developed invasive disease by the age of 5 years. Recent reports indicate that since the introduction of the new conjugate Hib vaccines, the incidence of Hemophilus influenza type b infection has fallen by as much as 90 percent, p eventing an estimated 10,000 to 16,000 cases of Hemophilus influenza type b each year.

Universal immunization has the potential to virtually eliminate Hemophilus influenza type b meningitis in children. The cost savings are considerable. The cost of NIH's research toward development of the Hib vaccines was estimated at $20 million; widespread use of the vaccine can save approximately $400 million a year.

In cardiovascular disease, you are familiar with the progress that we have made and the dramatic reductions in morbidity and mortality as a result of interventions relating to the major risk factors—high blood pressure, blood cholesterol and cigarette smoking.

And I would say that NIH did a really fabulous job in its dissemination of the information based on research on hypertension. As we develop new methods for treatment, those were disseminated by NIH in a very, very effective manner with dramatic results, not only in reducing morbidity and mortality directly from hypertension, but reducing mortality and morbidity from coronary heart disease.

The recently concluded diabetes complications and control trial, a 9-year study, demonstrated conclusively the value of strict control of blood sugar in the prevention of microvascular complications in Type I, or insulin-dependent, diabetic patients. We are now working with NIH, CDC, the Agency for Health Care Policy and Research, the Indian Health Service, the Health Resources and Services Administration, to disseminate this information to practitioners and to public health officials in order that this be promptly applied.

Here is an evidence that there will be dramatic cost savings. Prevention of end-stage rental disease, for example, in diabetic patients eliminates the necessity for kidney transplant and dialysis—savings of millions and millions of dollars, not to mention the improved lives of those individuals.

Senator Harkin, you mentioned Alzheimer's disease and the recent NIH-sponsored research which identified the ApoE gene that is directly related to late-onset Alzheimer's. Further progress in that area, as you indicated, can save untold suffering for individuals and huge amounts of money.

HIV research is another area. I describe in my testimony in some detail the efforts at dissemination of the research findings through various provisions of the plan. The first is the closer cooperation among clinicians and public health practitioners, and the strengthening of public health agencies in order to apply these findings to the populations at large, as well as to individual patients.

The telemedicine initiative of the National Library of Medicine is an area, Senator Harkin, where you have provided us with great leadership and a lot of ideas that in fact are now incorporated in the plan. The Library of Medicine work has also been very important for us in developing the proposals in the plan.

In Iowa, as you know, a group of over 20 hospitals have joined in a network known as the Midwest Rural Telemedicine Consortium. This project seeks to ensure the viability of rural images from CT scans, ultrasound, and MRI; interactive video communications for consultation and education; and administrative information to streamline payment processes and enhance communications capabilities.

We also need more research on how to translate the medical record into the same kind of communications capability. I would say that is the biggest gap right now. But there is a lot of work being done in this area, and we hope we can make some real advances in the near future.

Other areas included in the plan are expansion of health services of research; development of practice guidelines; development of a national quality management program, including the establishment of regional professional foundations to link the research to practitioners.

All this will be included. The President's plan will further promote the diffusion of research and technology by assuring that academic health centers are integrated into the reformed health care system.

Academic Health Centers are where much of clinical research is carried out and first applied. Health plans will be required to contract with a sufficient number of academic health centers to assure that all of their enrollees have access to needed services provided by those institutions.

And finally, in the plan, we include the core grants and the project grants to promote and to deal with public health problems of regional or national significance--all mechanisms to ensure the application of the research findings from NIH.

Let me just close, Mr. Chairman, and stress again the importance of prevention research and this initiative in health care reform, particularly its importance in clinical preventive services, population-based public health programs, quality of care, cost containment, and perhaps most importantly, improving the health of all Americans.

I very much appreciate this opportunity to appear before you and would be pleased to answer any questions that I can.

[The prepared statement of Dr. Lee follows:]

PREPARED STATEMENT OF DR. PHILIP R. LEE

Mr. Chairman and Members of the Committee:

I am pleased to have this opportunity to discuss the Health Security Act (S1757) and
how the National Institutes of Health is integral to the President's plan to improve the
health of all Americans. I am very pleased, Mr. Chairman, that you are one of the
Senate cosponsors on the Health Security Act.

The central role of NIH and the prevention research initiative becomes very clear when
the objectives of reform are viewed from a health perspective, from a quality perspective,
and from a cost containment perspective.

The Health Security Act (S.1757) is unique among the proposals before Congress to
reform the health care system. It emphasizes prevention. It makes health plans
accountable to achieve prevention and public health (population based health)
objectives. It fosters a close working relationship between research, clinical care and
public health.

Prevention research is the foundation for both clinical preventive services *medicine* and the public
health interventions included in the Health Security Act. Expanded prevention research
will ensure the availability of effective preventive measures against existing diseases as
well as new and emerging health threats. Progress in preventing disease will help to
offset escalating acute health care costs and the disproportionate impact of disease and
disability among women, minorities and the elderly.

Central to this approach is a restructuring of the personal health care system, enabling it-
for the first time- to emphasize keeping people healthy by promoting health and
preventing disease. The changes in the personal health care system will strengthen and
foster the restructuring of the public health system, making both far more effective in
protecting and promoting the health of all americans and reducing the disparities in the
health status among different populations and individuals.

Mr. Chairman, I am particularly excited about the Health Security Act because the
President, in developing this proposal, has clearly understood the importance of
prevention and has included it in the Health Security Act in four ways:

(1)   by including a full range of clinical preventive services in the benefits package;

(2)   by making plans accountable for providing clinical preventive services;

(3)   by rewarding alliances and plans for keeping their populations healthy, and

(4)   by expanding prevention research at NIH and providing support to strengthen and
         expand state and local public health programs through the Centers for Disease
         Control and Prevention.

Health Care Reform seeks to provide health security for all Americans by providing universal health insurance coverage with comprehensive benefits including clinical preventive services, containing the escalating costs of health care, improving the quality of care, providing consumer choice, simplifying the system and assuring responsibility. The broader purpose for the Health Security Act, as with all the health programs of the Department of Health and Human Services, is to increase the span of healthy life for all americans and reduce the health disparities among americans. Biomedical, behavioral and social science research, particularly in the area of prevention, is integral to our efforts to lessen the enormous personal, social, and economic toll exacted by disease in all its forms--prematurity and severe childhood illnesses, cancer, heart disease, independence-robbing disorders of the elderly, and unvanquished old and new infectious diseases.

Our national investment in biomedical, behavioral and social science research yields the knowledge and technology for health promotion and disease prevention, as well as for early diagnosis, treatment, rehabilitation and care. This research is translated into practical applications but all of the agencies of the U.S. Public Health Service, including NIH as well as by the medical, nursing and other health professions. The pharmaceutical industry, the biotechnology industry the medical device industry as well as the electronics industry play a large role in the critical translation process.

The research conducted and supported by the NIH provides information needed to assist in adaption of health plan benefit coverage and the appropriate application of cost-effective methods for prevention and early intervention.

NIH Leadership Role in Science and Commitment to Basic Research

The National Institutes of Health is the premier biomedical research institution in the world and is dedicated to the pursuit of knowledge to improve the health of all Americans. As you are well aware, the NIH has long used the peer review system to evaluate research proposals in order to fund the highest quality, most meritorious research.

Scientific advances require the continued insight and understanding of the fundamental mechanisms of life, health and disease. Perhaps better than anyone, Dr. Harold Varmus, the new Director of the NIH, understands how basic research can and does lead to dramatic and many times unexpected discoveries which can effect the health of a few individuals or of millions of people. Dr. Varmus' own work in virology provides convincing evidence of the importance and value of basic biomedical research and I am confident he will be an effective champion of basic research.

The important and unanticipated pay-offs of basic research are illustrated by the announcement last week of the isolation of a gene associated with colon cancer. The function of this gene is relatively well understood as the result of past basic research on bacteria and yeast. The colon cancer gene turns out to be quite similar to genes in bacteria and yeast cells that function as DNA "editors". The gene product acts to ensure that mistakes in DNA replication are corrected. Defects in this editing function therefore result in errors, or "typos", in the genetic material. These errors result in disease.

An estimated 152,000 Americans will be diagnosed with colon and rectal cancer this year and 57,000 will die. While the recently discovered gene for colon cancer is not singularly responsible for all colon cancers, it is estimated to be the cause of about 10 percent of the cases. Clearly, understanding the basis of disease is the first and most critical step to developing measures to cure the defect and prevent disease, and when that is not possible, to screen and monitor individuals with the gene in order to intervene with measures such as a low fat diet and daily aspirin to reduce the likelihood of disease and to detect cancer early and cure the disease at that point. But who would have predicted that understanding bacterial DNA synthesis would be that first step in finding the means to understand and prevent colon cancer?

Basic genetic research provides the keys for locating defective genes causing many genetic diseases in addition to colon cancer. We have already identified and isolated the genes for a large number of diseases including duchenne muscular dystrophy, retinoblastoma, cystic fibrosis, fragile X syndrome, myotonic dystrophy, and Huntington's disease. Having these genes in hand will allow us to craft the tools necessary to greatly improve control, treatment and prevention of disease. These advances will provide benefits that will touch every American family.

Prevention Research and Health Care Reform: Reducing the Burdens and Cost of Disease

As you know, the President has included a Prevention Research Initiative in the Health Security Act (S.1757). More prevention research will generate knowledge that will help to generate such prevention tools as improved methods for early detection of disease and genetic susceptibility to disease; scientifically validated approaches for fostering adoption of dietary and other behavioral practices that protect health; and strategies for reducing or eliminating environmental factors that significantly increase disease risks. While offering returns that can be realized by all Americans, the Initiative gives special consideration to the health concerns of women, minorities, and other populations whose particular health needs have received insufficient attention and study in the past.

Prevention research has four ultimate aims: (1) promoting health: (2) preventing the occurrence of disease; (3) preventing the occurrence of clinical illness in individuals who have physiological or biological evidence of abnormalities; and (4) preventing the progression of clinical disease. The Initiative spans a wide range of topics and objectives. Research in genetics, molecular and cell biology, immunology, and other fundamental sciences describes the biological basis of disease—what goes awry and why. This knowledge provides a sharp focus for efforts to devise preventive interventions, which can range from lifestyle changes to protect against damaging biological changes to molecular measures to correct or compensate for acquired or inherited genetic flaws. The social and behavioral sciences comprise a complementing research area, investigating disease and health in the context of personal choices, social and economic conditions, community and cultural influences, and psychological and environmental factors. We know from social and behavioral sciences research in the past decade, for example, that social class or socio-economic status is a major determinant of health status-particularly how long we live and how healthy we are during our lifetime. Knowledge gained from this research also yields fundamental insights into methods to prevent and control disease. Fundamental research in behavioral sciences is vitally needed to understand both healthy and unhealthy behaviors.

While NIH has long invested in prevention research, and tracked expenditures for prevention research since the 1980s, it was felt that an increased investment in NIH research will translate into advances in knowledge that will promote health, prevent disease and reduce the nation's expenditures for treatment of preventable illness and injury. Expanded prevention research will help ensure the future availability of effective preventive measures against existing disease, as well as new and emerging health threats. Prevention of disease before its onset can be significantly less expensive than treating symptomatic disease.

The initiative will focus on the solutions research can provide to critical preventable health problems in;

> Child and adolescent health
> Reproductive health
> Mental Health
> Substance Abuse
> Infectious diseases,
> Health and Wellness Promotion (including fitness/nutrition)
> Environmental Health
> Chronic and Recurrent Health Conditions
> Elderly Health
> Resource Development

J The President's Health Security Act would authorize appropriations of $400 million in FY 1995 and a total of $2.9 billion over six years for NIH prevention research expansion. These authorizations are in addition to the $2.6 billion NIH is spending on prevention research in FY 1994. Increases in the NIH prevention appropriations would be subject to the discretionary spending cap.

Our national investment in biomedical and behavioral research and particularly prevention research has important impact on the long term health and health costs. I would like to highlight several specific examples of the ways in which biomedical and behavioral research has already impacted on the burden of disease and the cost of health care.

Vaccines

Vaccines provide convincing examples of the successes and cost savings that are achievable through prevention research. It is widely acknowledged, in fact, that immunization represents by far the single most cost-effective procedure in medicine. Universal immunization programs are responsible for much of the increase in life expectancy in the last half-century. In the United States, the use of vaccines virtually eliminated diseases such as diphtheria, tetanus, mumps, and poliomyelitis. In the last decade alone, nine new or improved vaccines have become available. Biomedical research has greatly expanded the possibility for creating new safer and more effective vaccines. In this effort, Government, industry, and universities all play vital roles.

Vaccine development is dependent on advances in basic research, often by discoveries that were unanticipated. In the recent Institute of Medicine report on Childhood Vaccines it was noted;

...Basic research relevant to vaccine development includes such things as the identification and isolation of the protective antigens of a specific pathogen, methods of DNA cloning, the creation of new vector systems, and the development and immunologic evaluation of new adjuvant systems (p 111).

NIH support for vaccine research and development includes basic research as well as clinical trials to assess the safety and efficacy of vaccines. Important recent developments indicate that it may soon be possible to splice as many as 5 to 10 protective antigens into a single virus and bacterium, thus providing protection against many diseases with a single administration. Research involving microcapsules which gradually dissolve after administration offer new prospects for single inoculations of some protective agents which now require 3 or 4 inoculations. Moreover, recent progress in cellular biology, immunology, and biotechnology presents solid opportunities to pursue a new class of vaccines for preventing and treating cancer and other non-infectious chronic diseases.

During the past year, the rapid development of improved vaccines for hepatitis B and for Haemophilus influenza type b (Hib), an important cause of meningitis in children, led to recommendations that both be included in universal childhood immunization programs. NIH funded research played a key role in developing vaccines for these two serious diseases.

Hepatitis B virus causes acute liver disease sometimes with severe, life-threatening manifestations. However, on both an individual basis and an overall economic one, its major impact occurs when an individual does not recover, i.i. becomes a chronic carrier at risk of long-term consequences such as chronic liver disease and liver cancer. Immunization with hepatitis B vaccine is the most effective way to prevent infection and its consequences, and could lead to an estimated annual savings of between $74 and $147 million.

Haemophilus influenza type b (Hib) was a leading cause of mental retardation and deafness in children before the introduction of effective vaccines. One in 200 children in the United States developed invasive disease by the age of five years. Recent reports indicate that since the introduction of the new conjugate Hib vaccines, the incidence of Hib infections in the United States has fallen by as much as 90 percent, preventing an estimated 10,000 to 16,000 cases of Hib disease each year. Universal immunization has the potential to virtually eliminate Hib meningitis in children. The cost savings resulting from the use of the Hib vaccines is considerable. NIH's cost of research towards the development of the Hib vaccines was $20 million; widespread use of the vaccine can save approximately $400 per year.
ㄴmillion

Cardiovascular Disease

The return on investment in prevention research is well demonstrated by the dramatic decline in the death rate for cardiovascular disease. Heart disease mortality has declined 57 percent from its peak in 1963, resulting in more than half a million american lives saved annually. Over the same period, stroke mortality declined 66 percent, so that, in 1992, 260,000 lives were saved. This impressive success story is due both to advances in basic, clinical and population-based research and to innovative programs that transfer scientific results to health professionals and the public. The major modifiable risk factors for cardiovascular disease are high blood pressure, high blood cholesterol and cigarette smoking. Research in all of these areas by NIH has been a major factor in the understanding of these risk factors and the development of effective clinical and public health interventions.

Diabetes

The recently concluded diabetes complications and control trial demonstrated _microvascular_
conclusively the value of strict control of blood sugar in the prevention of complications
in Type I (insulin dependent) diabetes. We are now working with NIH, CDC, AHCPR,
IHS and HRSA to disseminate this information to practitioners and public health
officials _Indian Health Service_

end-stage renal
Alzheimer's and HIV provide examples of the potential reductions in health care costs as
the result of continued investments in biomedical research.

Alzheimer's

Alzheimer's disease affects more than four million Americans and cost the Nation an
estimated $90 billion annually. At present, there is no effective therapy to prevent or
delay the onset of Alzheimer's. However, recently NIH-sponsored research identified a
gene, ApoE, that is directly related to late-onset Alzheimer's. One form of the gene can
predict the likelihood of late-onset Alzheimer's with nearly 91 percent accuracy.
Even a partial victory against this devastating neurological disorder would yield
tremendous personal, social, and economic dividends.

HIV

The cumulative cost of treating persons infected with HIV is forecast to increase by 48
percent over the next three years. The cost for providing medical care for an HIV
infected person from time of infection till death is approximately $120,000. As the basic
biology of the HIV virus is understood, as the pathogenesis of the disease is elucidated,
effective preventive strategies can be developed to control the epidemic and effective
treatments can be developed. In addition, as research advances related to the
opportunistic infections that kill most person with HIV/AIDS, it should be possible to
develop more safe and effective treatments for these diseases.

Diffusion of Research Findings into Clinical Practice

The President's plan promotes the diffusion of research findings into clinical practice and
the public health. It facilitates close cooperation among clinicians and public health
practitioners and it would strengthen the role of public health agencies in protecting and
promoting the health of all Americans.

The Health Security Act provides for the innovative approaches to the dissemination and
application of technology. In addition, the NIH's National Library of Medicine has
assumed a leadership position in encouraging access to data bases for physician in
practice around the country through its Rural Outreach Program. NLM's National

Network of Libraries of Medicine consists of eight regional medical libraries, 135 resource libraries, and 3,600 member institutions. Since 1989, NLM has funded over 139 institutions and groups to introduce "grateful Med to rural health professionals to provide them access to the enormous data resources of the National Library of Medicine.

The telemedicine initiative of the NLM have been greatly expanded in recent years. In Iowa, for example, a group of over 20 hospitals have joined in a network known as the Midwest Rural Telemedicine Consortium. This project seeks to ensure the viability of rural images from CT scans, ultrasound, and MRI; interactive video communications for consultation and education; and administrative information to streamline payment processes and enhance communications capabilities.
outlined.

Telemedicine

The Health Security Act increases funding for health services research at the Agency for Health Care Policy and Research and the Health Care Financing Administration. Health services research plays a critical role in evaluating the application of new clinical and public health interventions in the field to assure that their projected efficacy is realized in all settings and for all populations. Thus, health services research serves as an important bridge between the controlled setting of a clinical research trial to the world of patients seeking care in diverse health care settings. Health services research also provides the information on how to best organize, structure, and deliver cost effective services. Further, health services research makes this information readily available to consumers, health care providers and decision makers at the plan, alliance, state, and national level.

The Health Security Act will enhance the use of clinical research in health care delivery through the development of practice guidelines through the National Quality Management Program. The National Quality Management Council will direct AHCPR to develop, disseminate, and evaluate clinical practice guidelines. These guidelines will be based on the best available research and professional judgment regarding the effectiveness and appropriateness of health care services and procedures. The recent practice guidelines on clinical depression in primary care and on cataracts illustrates both the process and the potential benefit of guidelines. As part of any guideline development, all relevant clinical research, including clinical trials, is reviewed and evaluated to create an updated summary of the state of our knowledge for that condition. These practice guidelines will play an important role in educating practitioners on the appropriate use of the latest clinical management options available to them.

Clinical research findings will also be used in the development of performance indicators for the quality report cards which will measure plan and provider performance and are to be developed by the National Quality Management Program. These indicators will take into account the best available scientific evidence about the impact of care on particular health outcomes.

In addition, the Act provides coverage for routine care costs associated with participation in clinical trials. This expansion of coverage should increase the access to experimental treatments for those who are now uninsured or those without such coverage.

Another provision in the Health Security Act to assure the application and dissemination of research findings is the establishment of Regional Professional Foundations. These Foundations will be established by the National Health Board and will have as part of their charge the dissemination of information about health care quality improvement approaches and research findings. They will also be eligible to apply to AHCPR for ~~funds to support research~~ on health care quality.

The President's plan will further promote the diffusion of research and technology by assuring that Academic Health Centers are integrated into the reformed health care system. Academic Health Centers are where much of clinical research is carried out and first applied. Health plans will be required to contract with a sufficient number of Academic Health Centers to assure that all of their enrollees have access to their specialized services.

Finally, title III, subtitle D, of the Health Security Act includes competitive grants to State health agencies to improve their ability to carry out core public health functions at the state and local level. These core functions include:

- surveillance of communicable and chronic diseases, and investigation of community health problems;
- control of communicable diseases and injuries;
- environmental health (water, food, housing);
- community health education; and
- laboratory services.

These grants also foster greater accountability to the federal government for the definition and reporting of progress in achieving public health objectives.

A second provision in Subtitle D provides grants to public and private non-profit agencies to address preventable priority health problems. Many of these problems do not affect the population of the country uniformly and call for tailored, community based prevention programs. For example, in some areas of the country, diabetes melitis is a major problem; in other areas, priority may be accorded to programs that deal with cigarette smoking; while in still other areas, violence is an issue of great concern.

Mr. Chairman, this concludes my statement today. I would be pleased to answer any questions you might have.

Senator HARKIN. Thank you, Dr. Lee, very much for an excellent statement. We appreciate your being here today.

I want to get right to the heart of the problem right now. You said in your statement that, "The President's Health Security Act would authorize appropriations of $400 million in fiscal year95 and a total of $2.9 billion over 6 years for NIH prevention and research expansion."

You see, I am wearing two hats here. I am on the authorizing committee, so whatever you say about authorizing sounds nice. But I also chair the Appropriations Committee that funds these programs, and I must tell you in all candor, I have all the authorization I need. I do not need any more authorization. I can authorize $400 million next year. If you want $2 billion, I can authorize $2 billion, too—but I do not have the money. I mean, I would have to take it out of everything else because of these budget caps; I could take it out of other institutes at NIH. I could take it out of the Human Genome Project maybe. I could take it out of Heart, Lung, Blood; I could take it out of Cancer and shift it around. I could take it out of Education. I could take it out of Human Services. You get my point, because of these budget caps.

So the authorization, when I hear that the President says he is going to authorize appropriations, it does not mean much unless there is money. Unless the President—and again, my fondness for you and my esteem for you is too much to not let you know that I am speaking through you today, obviously—but unless the President sends a budget up here that has this money in it and specifies where it is coming from, then all of the fine words that you have uttered today will actually be meaningless and will have no impact whatsoever, Dr. Lee, because we will not have the money. We will have authorization, but it will not translate into real funds.

So I guess what I am asking is, is the administration going to include this in the budget they send up in February. You probably cannot answer that question, but I will leave it linger.

Second, is it in addition to the $2.6 billion which we are spending on prevention research now? Is the $400 million on top of NIH's appropriated level for 1994, which is $10.9 billion, or is the $400 million on top of a base of a 4 to 6 percent increase for NIH? Where are we starting from? Can you enlighten me any?

Dr. LEE. Let me just say a couple of things. First, with the authorization for not only the NIH piece, the Agency for Health Care Policy and Research Health Services, but the others, the core public health and the access initiatives, all of those are authorizations. And those were put in as authorizations to have these issues on the table, and because we were not able to resolve all the issues prior to the bill's submission, and not able to work with you and other members of the Congress to identify an assured source of funding, that it was put in in that fashion. But our goal is to identify an assured source of funding for all of the public health initiatives included in the plan, that will be identified and will be included in the Health Security Act by the time Congress enacts it and the President signs it.

In terms of the 1995 budget, as you know, there is active discussion going on with respect to the budget right now. And in terms of the intention of this initiative, it was to be on top of the annual appropriated base. And as you know, in recent years, Congress has increased that at a little bit more than 4 percent per year, and that is the base on which these funds would be added when that source of funding is identified.

So that it would not erode the base, and it would not be part of the base; it would be in addition to the current and the future base increases in NIH appropriations that would come through the normal appropriations process.

Senator HARKIN. Well, let me give you an example. I had to be the bearer of bad news to the President last year when, in a phone call, I had to inform him that he was the first President since the establishment of NIH to send a budget up here that cut funding from last year's level. I think he was rather startled to find that out.

Now, it is true that there were increases in some areas. The Human Genome Project got an increase and a couple of other areas, and that is all well and good, but that was at the expense of other areas that were cut. Well, we finally came through in the appropriations process and were able to even those things out, but I am greatly concerned at what kind of budget will come up here from OMB. Will it be 1994 base? The 1994 base that was sent up here by OMB was not very good. Or will it be the base of what we already appropriated plus a cost of living? I hope so.

Dr. LEE. We are working from the base appropriated by the Congress. That is the base, not what was presented originally in 1994. So we start from the appropriated base. We are in active discussions now with respect to what that level will be, and the decisions have not yet been made by the President.

Senator HARKIN. I understand. Well, again, we have the budget caps, so choices are going to have to be made, and I have said this to Mr. Panetta in the past, that if they want to increase, they are going to have to tell us where they are going to find the money and come up with the money.

The OMB Director, Mr. Panetta, is already proposing a 10 percent cut in outlays for noninvestment programs to make room for increases in the President's investment package. So again, I am wondering where these additional funds can be found within our allocation, which again leads me to the point that Senator Hatfield and I are trying to get at, that we need to find some additional funding outside of the caps. We are going to live with these caps for 5 years, and we are trying to find an additional source of revenue.

Now, it is true that the administration has put in its Health Security Act a 1.5 percent set-aside for training and academic health centers. That comes out to be between $5 and $6 billion a year the way I figure it, but there is nothing in there to increase research.

So again, I just wanted to cover that with you because the $400 million sounds nice. It is for prevention research. It is about 4 percent of the total NIH budget. So if it is just on our base, that is no increase. It has got to be above that.

I think it is inadequate, terribly inadequate, and I am taking advantage of your presence here this morning to send a strong signal to the administration that they are not going to pull the wool over our eyes again. I can tell you that as chairman of the Appropriations Committee, when that budget comes down, if they do not have the funds in there, and they try to just pass it off as some big deal that they are increasing the funds by only authorizing it within the budget caps, I will be the first on the floor of the Senate and whatever audience I can get to pull down this phony cover and to show it for the phoniness that it is.

So again, I fire that warning shot only based upon what happened last year. And again, I am not just pointing it at you, as you understand, Dr. Lee.

Senator Simon.

Senator SIMON. Thank you, Mr. Chairman.

One of the concerns that we have is the arbitrariness of the figures that we come up with. And it is not just at our level; the same thing is true within NIH.

Let me tell you how I got involved in this whole area of research. I was a member of the House, and my son happened to be dating a marvelous young woman by the name of Rachel Mann, who had cystic fibrosis. And through Rachel and her parents, I heard that NIH was cutting back on research on cystic fibrosis, the largest genetic killer of children.

I was sure that it was some mistake and that it was not accurate, and I contacted the head of NIH, and lo and behold, I discovered it was accurate. I was told that a Dr. St. John, who then headed the research in that field at NIH, was retiring, and they had to cut back somewhere, and since he was retiring, that was kind of a natural place to cut back on research.

I mention that simply because it does seem to me that the point of Senator Harkin's proposal, that we have some basic funding there for research, is a desirable thing. If you ask me in theory do I favor earmarked funds, I have to say that in theory, I think they are not a good idea. But I face the practical reality. Just as we have highways funds from gasoline tax and other earmarks, the idea that they have come up with seems to me to be basically sound. Has the administration taken a stand yet on this idea?

Dr. LEE. Not yet, no.

Senator SIMON. Well, I would encourage them to look at this favorably, and maybe this is not the right way to have the funds earmarked, but it seems to me that some stable source of funding is a desirable thing.

Now let me ask a second question in regard to private research. I guess each of us learns through our personal experience. When I was a kid, I got poison oak and poison ivy, and I have always had skin problems. Well, an Illinois citizen whom most people have never heard of—an African American, incidentally—by the name of Dr. Percy Julian developed cortisone and cortisone cream. I have often wondered how many Ku Klux Klan members are putting cortisone creme on themselves without realizing who developed all of this. But this was private research.

I have generally not been too sympathetic to the pharmaceutical companies as I have seen these costs go up. I have voted with David Pryor, our colleague, when he has proposed some limitations. But the pharmaceutical companies say that the administration's proposal is going to cut back on their research abilities. Now, have you analyzed this enough to know if there is legitimacy to what they have to say, or is there not—and this is a question I should know the answer to, but I do not—what percentage of the research that is carried on right now is carried on through nonpublic facilities, non-NIH and universities, and what percentage is in the private sector?

Dr. LEE. To answer that question, we can give you an accurate figure, Senator Simon, because I do not have those proportions in my head, but I know in the last decade private industry has increased their investments in research and development much more rapidly than the public sector, much more rapidly than the NIH funding has been increased. But we will get those figures and the distribution of those dollars.

Senator SIMON. If you could, and we ought to enter that into the record here.

Dr. LEE. On the first question, several things. I have been a student of the drug industry since the 1960's when I chaired the Task Force on Prescription Drugs in the Department of Health, Education and Welfare. We took a broad look—the question then was should drugs be covered under Medicare. We recommended that, and that recommendation indeed was adopted by the Nixon administration, interestingly enough. And with my colleague, Dr. Milton Silverman, we have looked at this industry for many, many, many years, particularly around prescription drug policies.

Two things with the reform. First, with the development of managed care plans, those plans will be negotiating with respect to the companies on the price of their drugs. They will have formularies, there will be negotiated prices. So the companies will have to have fewer detail men, and their marketing costs should be less. There will be more competition with respect to the price of the drugs that they sell. But as they are strong supporters of competition, I cannot see that that will be a deterrent.

With lowered costs for marketing, there should be a greater ability to increase investments by industry in research and development. You cover prescription drugs under Medicare, you cover prescription drugs in the health plans, you expand their market. So there is an expanded market; there is competition on the price side.

The one area I think they have been particularly concerned about has to do with the authority for the Secretary with breakthrough drugs to have an advisory committee that would review the pricing of those drugs, looking at prices in other countries and looking at factors that led them to price a new breakthrough drug.

When you have a breakthrough drug, you do not have price competition as y u would with all the other drugs that are currently on the market, where there are at least generic equivalents, or if there are not generics, there are other drugs that may be used for the same purpose. There are several different drugs that can be used to treat hypertension, for example. So in a sense there is competition on the basis of the quality of the intervention from a physician's standpoint.

But with the breakthrough drug, where there is no alternative, there is not that price competition. That is the area that I think the biotech industries and the pharmaceutical industries have expressed concerns about that particular provision. I think their concerns are—if there is a breakthrough drug, I don't think those concerns should lead them to under-invest in research. They are making very large investments currently. They are very, very important to translating the NIH research into better clinical practice and better prevention. And I think it merits some further discussion with them as to why they believe that would be the case.

I do not believe that a Secretary would ever say that we are not going to put a breakthrough drug on the market. And in fact, the Secretary does not have that authority in this legislation.

So I think those concerns are perhaps overblown, but I do think that there are some very, very good leaders in the pharmaceutical industry, and if they have expressed those concerns to you, I think this merits some further conversation. We need to resolve the questions. We certainly do not want them to diminish their research investments.

Senator SIMON. And it occurs to me that one other way we might deal with that also is some kind of change in our income tax laws so that if they invest "x" percentage in research, then they get certain breaks in their income tax. I do not know. But as we look at research, I think we have to look at this side, too.

Dr. LEE. I totally agree with you that is a very important arena, and because their expenditures have increased very substantially, and of course, they make a major contribution to improving the health of the people and improving care because of that—you look at the research and development on vaccines, for example, where we have had tremendous progress, and a lot of that has been driven by industry.

Thank you, Dr. Lee. Thank you, Mr. Chairman.

Senator HARKIN. Thank you, Senator Simon.

Dr. Lee, I have a couple of other questions. I just want to respond here to my good friend from Illinois on the idea of earmarked funds. I would probably generally agree with you in terms of earmarking funds, but it would seem to me in an area like health, where we are trying to get a control spiralling costs, to make the quality of our lives better, and accomplish all the things that are involved in the Health Security Act, it seems reasonable that of every dollar that a person spends on health care, a certain portion of that ought to go into basic research. How much? Well, as I have already pointed out, it is now less than 2 cents out of a dollar. Any private company will tell you that in order to make the breakthroughs, it has to be much more than that—5 percent, 10 percent. As I said, in defense is up to 15 percent.

Later on, we will hear testimony from Mary Woolley, who is the director of Research America, regarding some interesting polls conducted by Lou Harris that asked people how much they would like to spend on research out of their health care dollar. And if I am not mistaken—she will State it in her testimony—I think it was upwards of almost 25 cents, 30 cents, maybe even higher than that. The vast majority of people would be willing to pay more for basic research.

The problem is there is no vehicle to do that, and that is what we are trying to establish. We need a vehicle to express the public's will, the public's desire to put more money into basic research. The public will support it, but they say we give you a dollar, and it just goes away someplace. If they knew that a certain portion of what they pay was actually going to go into research, I think the support would be overwhelming, and the polls have shown that they would support that.

Senator SIMON. Yes, and I support the idea. Again, it is in theory. If I were teaching a class in political science somewhere, maybe I would be against earmarked funds. But I think the practical reality is that we need them occasionally to achieve what needs to be done. We have done it with the airport money.

Senator HARKIN. Exactly, a certain portion of the ticket you buy is dedicated to supporting the operations of our airports.

Senator SIMON. That is exactly right.

Dr. LEE. On the airports, Senator Simon, someone asked me if I had been in an airport lately that was not remodelled or that was not a new airport. When you think about it, at least I have not, and I have been in a lot of them lately. I do not know about how that is financed, but there is no question that that is an example.

Senator HARKIN. Sure. In my first round of questions, I covered with you the total amount of money that the administration is requesting and whether or not it would be in the budget and how that would be approached. I now want to shift to the targeting of the money itself.

My concern is that the administration is attempting to provide increases only for targeted research. That was the approach taken in the budget that we got in 1994. We did get some increases in women's health, vaccines, AIDS, but what happened then was there was a 2.3 percent cut in all other research at NIH and an historic cut in finding, as I mentioned earlier, for nine institutes.

The approach suggested in the Health Security Act is the same, and I believe it is unwise. Even though I am a supporter of the Health Security Act, as is Senator Simon, I believe that is an unwise approach in this area.

Please explain how the administration intends to ensure an appropriate balance between basic and applied research.

Dr. LEE. I agree with your overall approach on targeting. I do not personally favor targeting. I prefer to let the peer review mechanisms work. In this area, what we would do is to say that this needs to go broadly for prevention. That can be the Genome Project, that can be basic research in human reproduction, it can be research on Alzheimer's. It would include a spectrum of research.

Currently, as you know, about one-quarter of the NIH budget is for prevention research. This would be in those same broad areas from basic to clinical to applied research. We are not talking about taking that money and just using it for applied interventions. But the decisions would be made through the peer review process at NIH. These would be for R-1 proposals. And NIH has provided us with a very large inventory of potential projects on osteoporosis, on child health, on reproductive health, on vaccine development, on HIV, on Alzheimer's. There are a range of areas where there are expansions through this mechanism and through the traditional NIH mechanisms, intramural and extramural.

So you might say it is a very broad targeting, but it is not the kind of targeting that identifies specific diseases as was done last year and says those would be the priority areas. And I think that is something that obviously you all will have to decide. You may say that is not the way you think the money would be spent most effectively, and you would simply untarget the money. That is clearly another alternative.

Senator HARKIN. Again, I would love to have more money in preventive research. I would like to put the whole $400 million toward this end. But, if that means that all the other institutes are held level, then I would be drastically opposed to that. That is why we need a larger sum of money to increase all of the research.

Dr. LEE. Well, the purpose of this was, in my view, only if we were getting the increased base funding through the annual appropriations process. So that you would not be taking money out of one institute or another to fund this initiative.

Senator HARKIN. In my chart on the far right, with that g een line at the bottom, if we just continue on as we have been doing, we will stay right on that green line, and we will not go up. I mean, we have established a level for NIH, and we say that is just where we are going to sit. And we are falling behind. Many of our facilities are in dire need of being upgraded. I hope to get President Clinton to go out and take a look at these. He ought to see them first-hand. They are in terrible shape.

Dr. LEE. As a faculty member at UCSF, I was very familiar with that problem. It is a very serious problem.

Senator HARKIN. And it is not just intramural, but also in the universities. We are working in laboratories that were designed and laid down in the 1940's and 1950's, some of them earlier than that.

We need new equipment. We need new facilities. We need infrastructure, and it is going to cost money. We need it to do the kind of basic research that is necessary. We need to make investments to encourage young people to get into research. How can you encourage a young person to get into research today when the Federal Government is sending the signal that there may not be any money? All you can say is, well, you can work your heart out, you can put in your proposals, and your chances maybe one in five.

Dr. LEE. Yes. Depending on the area, overall it is about 20 percent, but in some areas it is less than that.

Senator HARKIN. So less than one in five of ever getting it approved. And then, if you are approved, you might get it for a couple years, and then you might not. In other words, there is no long-term approach for keeping people in the research area.

I am concerned that in the administration—and not you, Dr. Lee, but in the administration—there is this idea that they are going to target this research, and they are going to put it into prevention research. Fine. I have no problems with that. But if what they mean by that is they are going to keep the basic research at this green line level, then I am going to be opposed to it, and again I will be speaking out against it.

I have something here I am sure you will like. My staff has handed me a quote from Dr. Lewis Thomas, the Nobel Laureate who just passed away last week—not stranger here on the Hill over the last 20 years.

Dr. LEE. A great man.

Senator HARKIN. This is a quote. You will like this, Senator Simon. He said: "It seems to me that the safest and most prudent of bets to lay money on is surprise. There is a very high probability that whatever astonishes us in biology today will turn out to be usable and useful tomorrow. This, I think, is the established record of science itself for the past 200 years, and we ought to have more confidence in the process." That is basic research. And I know I am preaching to the choir here today, but I hope the message gets back to the people at OMB that they just simply cannot play this game with us any longer.

The Health Security Act, we want to see it passed. Both Senator Simon and I are cosponsors of it, and we want to see it move ahead. But I believe the one glaring omission is the lack of a source of funding or a means by which a portion of that health care dollar will be put into basic and fundamental research. It is just not there. And we will do whatever we can to see that it is included.

Dr. LEE. We certainly want to work with you on that to find that identified source, to cover all those initiatives, including the NIH initiative.

Senator HARKIN. I appreciate that.

Do you have anything else, Senator Simon?

Senator SIMON. I have no further questions.

Senator HARKIN. Thank you very much, Dr. Lee.

Dr. LEE. Thank you very, very much, Mr. Chairman.

Senator HARKIN. We have a very distinguished panel of Nobel Laureates here today, but before I call on that panel, I am going to call on a panel of consumers in order to hear the consumer perspective.

We welcome Tom and Dave Robertson from Reinbeck, IA; Joan Samuelson from Santa Rosa, CA; and also Mary Woolley, about whom I just spoke, the president of Research America.

Senator Simon will have to leave very shortly. I am going to ask Ms. Woolley if she could start the panel off by telling us about the poll that she had Lou Harris and Associates conduct. I think that would be interesting to start us off in terms of this consumer panel.

Senator SIMON. And if I could just add, I regret that I am going to have to leave at 11:30, but Dave Robertson, I read your statement, and I appreciate it. And I also want to pay tribute on juvenile diabetes to Ron Santo, whom people may think of as a player for the Chicago Cubs, but whom I think of as a person who had juvenile diabetes and who has been championing the cause of research in this field and has been a very eloquent spokesperson for this cause.

But Dave, I think your statement is a great statement, and I appreciate it.

Thank you, Mr. Chairman.

Senator HARKIN. Thank you very much, Senator Simon.

Ms. Woolley, please tell us about your poll.

STATEMENTS OF MARY WOOLLEY, PRESIDENT AND CEO, RE-
SEARCH AMERICA, ALEXANDRIA, VA; TOM AND DAVID ROB-
ERTSON, REINBECK, IA; AND MARY SAMUELSON, SANTA
ROSA, CA

Ms. WOOLLEY. With pleasure. I am Mary Woolley, president of
Research America, which is a national not-for-profit alliance dedicated to better informing the American public about the value of
medical research.

In partnership with over 250 organizations and institutional
members, Research America is working to assure that medical research has the opportunity to fulfill the promise it holds out to the
citizens of this Nation to deliver the cures, treatments, and preven-
tions that will lead to a better quality of life for all of us today and
for our children tomorrow.

Now, in the course of our statewide public education and outreach programs recently in Maryland and in North Carolina, we
have been struck by the high and steadily growing level of public
support for more medical research. So in November of this year, we
commissioned a national public opinion poll to determine whether
this strong public support for research that we were seeing region-
ally was in fact a national phenomenon.

What we have learned is that adult Americans in communities
of all sizes, from metropolitan Philadelphia to the rural counties of
Iowa, Americans at very socioeconomic level, of every race and of
ever age, strongly support medical research.

Americans want research to be a higher priority in health care
reform. Americans believe that we are not currently allocating a
high enough percentage of the total health care dollar to research.
And Americans are ready to personally pay more to assure that
there will be more medical research.

Research America commissioned Louis Harris and Associates to
ask seven questions about medical research as part of a larger survey that they were conducting on a broad range of current issues
including NAFTA and crime. The survey was conducted by telephone within the United States between November 11 and 15,
1993, among a cross-section of 1,243 adults.

The first finding, which I will show you here, is that the majority
of Americans, 56 percent, say that as we reform the health care
system, the national commitment to medical research should be
higher. While the majority favor a higher commitment to medical
research, 38 percent said the commitment should remain the same,
and only 5 percent said that it should be lower.

In another question, respondents were told that at present, we
are spending about 3 cents of the total health care dollar—and in
fact, it is probably less than that—on medical research, and then
they were asked what percentage they think we ought to be spending. The median response was 10 cents on the dollar, which is over
three times what is currently being spent by Government and private funding sources combined.

We also asked Americans whether they felt that the Federal Government should spend a lot more, a little more, a lot less, or a little
less on several types of scientific research. Ninety-one percent said
that we should spend more on medical research to better diagnose,
prevent and treat disease. Sixty percent in fact said we should

spend a lot more on medical research—and that is more than those saying we should spend a lot more on energy, space and defense research combined.

When asked which one type of scientific research Americans believed was the most valuable, overwhelmingly, people said they favored medical research, with 66 percent naming it as the single most valuable kind of scientific research. Environmental research was next, at 18 percent, followed by energy at 6 percent, defense at 4 percent, and less than one percent for each of space, electronics, computers, and transportation.

It is important to point out that this question about the one type of most valuable research was asked nationally one time before by the Louis Harris Group, 19 months ago in April of 1992. Let me show you the contrast here. The only type of research over those 19 months that garnered a significant increase was medical research, which increased from 49 percent to 66 percent of Americans saying it is the single most valuable kind of scientific research. This 17 percent increase in the level of public support for medical research as our number one national research priority opens a window of opportunity for decisionmakers to significantly increase funding for medical research with the knowledge that the public stands strongly behind such action.

The national opinion poll also explored the question of where is the funding going to come from to assure more medical research. And Senator Harkin, you mentioned that we need a vehicle to express the public's will. We tested some potential vehicles.

We learned that 74 percent of Americans would be willing to spend one dollar more per week—not per year—per week in taxes if they were assured that that money would be spent for additional medical research. We also learned that 75 percent of Americans are willing to spend one dollar more per prescription drug with the assurance that the money would go for medical research. And we learned that 77 percent of Americans are willing to spend one dollar more per week in health insurance premiums if assured that the money would go for medical research—that is 77 percent.

Research American believes that this national public opinion survey presents strong and impressive and growing evidence that the American public understands the value of medical research to the health and well-being of themselves and their family and friends, and that the public looks to elected officials to make medical research a much higher national priority.

On behalf of the members of Research America and all the people represented by our public opinion survey, which is indeed all Americans, I thank you for the opportunity to present this information and would be pleased to answer any questions.

[The information referred to follows:]

Research | America
AN ALLIANCE FOR DISCOVERIES IN HEALTH

MEDICAL RESEARCH AND HEALTH CARE CONCERNS:
A SURVEY OF THE AMERICAN PUBLIC
conducted by Louis Harris & Associates
November 1993

The Harris nationwide poll was conducted by telephone within the United States between November 11th and 15th, among a cross section of 1,254 adults. Figures for age, sex, race, education and region were weighted where necessary to bring them into line with their actual proportions in the population.

Research|America, a national not-for-profit organization dedicated to raising public awareness of and support for medical research, commissioned Louis Harris and Associates to ask seven questions about medical research as part of a larger survey focusing on a broad range of current issues. The margin of error for the survey is approximately 3 percent.

HIGHLIGHTS

1.   *Americans rank medical research as their single highest research priority.*

• When asked which one type of scientific research is most valuable, Americans overwhelmingly favor medical research (66%). Environmental (18%), energy (6%) and defense (4%) finish next. None of the other four types (space, electronics, computers and transportation) is preferred by more than 1 percent.

• The same question was asked nationally in April of 1992. The only type of research to garner a significant increase between April '92 and November '93 is medical research:

Type	April 1992	November 1993
Medical	49%	66%
Environmental	29	18
Energy	10	6
Transportation	3	1
Defense	2	4
Space	2	1
Computer	2	
Electronics	1	

2. *Americans think this nation is not spending enough on medical research.*

• Nine out of ten Americans (91%) believe this nation should spend more on medical research to better diagnose, prevent and treat disease.

• In fact, 60% feel this country should spend *a lot* more on medical research — more than those saying spend *a lot* more on energy, space and defense research combined (35, 10 and 9 percent, respectively).

3. *Not only do Americans want more spent on medical research, but Americans are willing to pay for it.*

If assured the money would be spent for additional medical research:

• 74% are willing to spend $1 more per week in taxes;
• 75% are willing to spend $1 more per prescription drug; and
• 77% are willing to spend $1 more per week in insurance premiums.

4. *The actual amount spent on medical research is well below what the American people believe should be spent.*

• At the moment, about three cents out of each health care dollar spent in the U.S. goes for medical research. The median value suggested by those surveyed: 10 cents per dollar.

5. *As we reform the health care system, the majority of Americans think the commitment to medical research should be higher.*

• When asked about medical research specifically in the context of health care reform, 56% of those surveyed said the national commitment to medical research should be higher while only 5% said it should be lower. Thirty-eight percent said the commitment should remain about the same.

For further information on the survey or other Research!America activities, contact Ray Merenstein at 703/739-2577.

Senator SIMON. Mr. Chairman, I should not interrupt——

Senator HARKIN. No; go ahead.

Senator SIMON [continuing]. But it is interesting as you look at where the public would like to spend the research dollars and where we are spending the research dollars, it is just about the reverse of what we are doing.

Senator HARKIN. That is true.

Ms. WOOLLEY. That is right. I can diagram it for you here. This is the chart that shows the level of public support in blue, at the 91 percent level for spending more on research, and in red, it says let us spend less, in fact. And if you reverse these, you are quite right, Senator, that it is in defense, for example, that we are spending that 15 percent on research. And the public is ready for that to be decreased, according to this finding.

Senator SIMON. Thank you.

Senator HARKIN. Thank you very much, Ms. Woolley. This is the first I have heard of this new poll. I knew you had done one a couple of years ago in North Carolina.

Ms. WOOLLEY. It was actually in May of this year in North Carolina and the previous year in Maryland.

Senator HARKIN. Oh, I see. I remember there was one a year or so ago that was done, and I had seen the results of that, but that was just one State, and this is nationwide.

Ms. WOOLLEY. That is right.

Senator HARKIN. These are very impressive figures. This is the first I had heard of it last night, reading through your testimony. I think there is ample evidence that the support is out there if we take advantage of it.

Senator Simon, did you have any other questions for any of the panel members? I know you have to leave.

Senator SIMON. No, I do not. Thank you. And I apologize also to the scientists who are here. I am taking along the written testimony and I will read it. I really appreciate not only what you are doing in terms of research, but your willingness to stand up and say we have to do better as a Nation. This may be even a greater contribution than what you have done to win that Nobel Prize.

Senator HARKIN. Thank you very much, Senator Simon.

Let us continue with our panel. I will now recognize Tom and Dave Robertson, from Reinbeck, IA, and then we will go to Ms. Samuelson.

Again, your statements will be made a part of the record in their entirety. You can proceed as you so desire, Tom.

Mr. ROBERTSON. Senator Harkin, good morning, and thank you for the opportunity to testify here today.

As you said, I am Tom Robertson from Reinbeck, IA, and with me is my son David.

I appear before you today wearing three hats. First of all, I am here as a former member of the international board of directors of the Juvenile Diabetes Foundation International, a voluntary health organization committed to the simple notion that, through research, we can improve the quality of life for persons living with diabetes and eventually cure this dreadful disease. Over the past 23 years, JDF has raised and awarded over $136 million to diabetes research, more than any other nongovernmental agency in the world.

Second, I appear before you as a concerned citizen about the economic drain of diabetes on our Nation, which is estimated at $91 billion per year.

And third and most importantly, I appear before you as the parent of a son with diabetes. I would like to leave my printed testimony for a minute and also say that I appear before you as a person who, when I was 6 years old, spent 3 months in a polio ward in a bed that was right beside iron lungs. It brought back a flood of emotions when I saw that wheeled in. I was very fortunate; I only suffered paralysis in my left arm, but I certainly have benefited from medical research.

Initially, I was going to come up here and tell you about diabetes and the fears and burdens that David and our family have had to endure for 13 years. But then I thought to myself, who better to tell you about diabetes than Dave himself. So I brought my son along. I am really proud of my son for many, many reasons, but I am most proud of him today because he is willing to sit before you and talk openly about living with diabetes.

My son, David.

Senator HARKIN. Dave, welcome.

Mr. DAVID ROBERTSON. Senator, I was first diagnosed with diabetes 13 years ago on my 7th birthday. I remember celebrating 1 minute and being in the hospital the next. I remember telling my parents that I was sick and that I had diabetes.

I was far too young to understand what diabetes was or what it would mean for the rest of my life, but I knew enough to ask my father: "Does diabetes mean that I am going to die?"

I remember being very scared when my parents began poking my finger with a needle to test my blood sugar levels and injecting me with insulin twice a day, and I was confused when I was told that every morsel of food I ate would have to be strictly monitored. I remember feeling angry and different. Worst of all, I remember learning what the future commonly holds for people with diabetes: blindness, kidney failure, heart disease, stroke, neurological disorders and, God forbid, death at an early age.

Fortunately, I have been free from these complications thus far, but I am acutely aware of what could happen to me in the future.

Speaking to you today about health care reform is especially important to me because I face these terrible complications and because people like me often find it impossible to obtain adequate health care coverage.

For nearly a year, I have been closely, eagerly watching the health care reform debate unfold. In that time, I have had a great deal of discussion on issues relating to coverage, access, and financing. These are clearly very important issues for me and the diabetes community.

But in all of this debate, I have heard barely a whisper about the most effective means of promoting health care quality and reducing health care costs—biomedical research.

Senator Harkin, I thank you and your colleague Senator Hatfield for calling attention to this critical but somewhat overlooked element of health care reform. I urge you to continue your efforts to include a meaningful biomedical research support mechanism in the health care reform legislation ultimately enacted by Congress so that someday soon, I can be cured of this terrible disease.

Mr. ROBERTSON. Senator, my wife and I pray that through medical research, a cure for Dave's diabetes will be found. Thanks in large part to your leadership on the Appropriations Committee, our dream may some day be fulfilled. Because of you and your colleagues' unwavering support of biomedical research, and the National Institutes of Health, near miracles are being achieved every day.

In fact, just last month, two more major diabetes research breakthroughs were announced, one that could eliminate the threat of kidney failure in persons with diabetes; the other which could prevent the onset of diabetes in people who are genetically predisposed to the disease. Each of these breakthroughs is the direct result of Federal appropriations to the National Institutes of Health.

Every research advance brings with it renewed hope for the 14 million Americans who suffer from diabetes and the tens of millions more Americans afflicted with cancer, heart disease, Alzheimer's, and a grab bag full of other dreadful diseases. For this reason alone, I urge you to continue your efforts to include a biomedical research support mechanism in health care reform legislation.

But Senator, there are more tangible benefits that will be realized through an increased commitment to biomedical research. As you clearly understand, biomedical research investments today yield huge health care cost savings tomorrow. In fact, a recent NIH report estimated that for every $1 invested in medical research, $8 is saved in health care costs.

In diabetes research alone, a study initiated by the National Eye Institute led to the development of laser photocoagulation treatment for diabetic retinopathy, a procedure which has been shown to be very effective in reducing the risk of several visual loss from advanced stages of diabetic retinopathy. This study cost the Eye Institute $48 million. The potential annual savings of developing and using this treatment procedure is more than $2 billion.

Senator, we are spending three times as much money providing dialysis services to persons with diabetes than we are devoting to research to eradicate the disease altogether.

Examples such as this one are not in short supply. Despite the billions of dollars in treatment costs that could be saved, our Nation's crown jewel of biomedical research, the National Institutes of Health, desperately wants for adequate resources. For example, the National Institute of Diabetes and Digestive and Kidney Diseases was able to fund only up to the 15th percentile of approved grants last year. When my wife Marion, on behalf of JDF, first visited you a decade ago, this Institute was providing support for almost 40 percent of approved grants.

But increasingly tight budgets is not the only problem confronting the NIH in coming years. Health care reform itself embodies the potential to constrain medical research. An increased emphasis on outcomes research and new cost-cutting pressures on pharmaceutical-based and university-based medical research are likely to further squeeze medical research investment and threaten much of the important progress made in recent years.

Dwindling medical research resources jeopardize more than just our ability to cure the diseases that rob life from our Nation. It also sends a discouraging to young prospective physicians, persuading them to opt for private practice rather than a career in medical research.

Furthermore, diminishing funds threaten the viability of one of the fastest growing components of the U.S. economy, the biotechnology industry. In recent years, the U.S. biotechnology industry has emerged as a competitive economic force internationally. But continued success is dependent upon the continued growth of federally supported biomedical research. Your efforts to invest in biomedical research would provide an indirect investment in the biotechnology industry and a needed boost for the U.S. economy.

Again, I thank you and Senator Hatfield for devising an alternative funding mechanism for biomedical research in light of the withering resources that I have described. As you indicated in your opening statement, such a mechanism could ene te between $5 and $6 billion annually in additional funds for medical research, funds that could go to promising diabetes research at the University of Iowa Hospital, one of this country's premier diabetes research centers.

As your proposal clearly states, however, these moneys must be in addition to, not supplementing, what Congress otherwise appropriates. As such, we support the requirement that these moneys are allocated only if Congress provides a sufficient, predetermined increase to the NIH through the traditional appropriations process.

Mr. Dave Robertson. Senator, JDF and my family are tired of waiting for a cure. The clock is ticking for me and millions of Americans like me. I am delighted that your proposal has gathered steam and acceptance in Congress. This is evident by the inclusion of a similar concept in Senator Chafee's recently introduced Health Equity and Access Reform Today Act.

I hope that supporters of the President's plan will also come to accept this concept and incorporate biomedical research as one of its most important components.

A recurrent theme throughout President Clinton's term has been how investing in our people today will yield big payoffs tomorrow. I can think of no better way to invest in America's health than through increased commitment to medical research.

Senator, I pray that we will not find ourselves looking back over a long line of lives lost and research opportunities foregone because of a dearth of adequate financial support. I hope that Congress will make an investment in America's future through increased support for medical research before it is too late.

Again, I thank you for allowing my father and me the opportunity to speak to this committee today, and for your leadership on this most important issue.

Senator HARKIN. Thank you both very much, Tom and Dave, and thank you for coming a great distance to be here.

Now we will turn to Joan Samuelson, speaking on behalf of research, and I am sure she will tell us the latest in Parkinson's disease research.

Thank you very much for being here, Ms. Samuelson.

Ms. SAMUELSON. Thank you, Senator. It is a pleasure and an honor to be here today.

What I would like to do is submit my statement for the record and then just make my points directly, because I certainly can speak from the heart, as Dave and Tom Robertson just have done.

Senator HARKIN. Please.

Ms. SAMUELSON. As you know, I am afflicted with Parkinson's disease. I was diagnosed 7 years ago, in the first year of my marriage and within the first 10 years of my law practice as a civil litigator in California.

And I must say that I am very pleased that the iron lung is here today, because that maybe gives a glimpse of the terror that comes into the hearts of people afflicted with a disease like Parkinson's, like diabetes, like cancer, like AIDS—like all of those dreadful diseases.

I often embarrass my husband, and I am about to do it again, by mentioning a present he gave me on our first wedding anniversary, which was a framed picture of Mount St. Helen's exploding. That was a joke, but it was also a very good indication of the enormous devastation, disruption, and terror that comes into the hearts of people who are stricken and diagnosed with something like Parkinson's.

I must say the iron lung took me back as I was looking at it, to a moment when I went to visit your former colleague in the House, Congressman Mo Udall, over at the Veterans Hospital. His daughter Ann has been very active with my group, the Parkinson's Action Network, which was formed when we first worked to try to lift the ban on fetal tissue transplant research. Ann has continued as the chair of our group as we have discovered, obviously to our horror, that not only is there no funding for that work now that the ban is lifting, but for none of the other promising developments.

Ann badly wanted me to meet her dad, and I was thrilled with the opportunity. We were driving over in the cab, chatting, and all of a sudden she got quiet. And then she said, "You know, I should have talked to you about this a little bit beforehand. I just realized I am taking you to see your future." She was right.

It was a great honor, and I enjoyed meeting Congressman Udall, but it was also, as she said, a terrifying moment to see him as a prisoner. He was not a prisoner in a machine like that; he was a prisoner in his own body—mute and frozen, unable to communicate with us, and obviously just simply a shadow of the wonderful man that Ann loves so much and that all of us admire and have so enjoyed and respected over the years.

So seeing that machine maybe brings into the hearts of all the people in this room and all Americans a slight flavor for the awful feelings that people who have these sorts of disorders or who live with them as our husbands and wives and parents and children do, and the enormous hope and feeling every day when we wake up, for medical breakthroughs that are going to end the suffering we are living with now and will prevent the suffering that we face in the future.

Parkinson's, as you probably know, is a neurological disorder that occurs when over 80 percent of the brain cells in a certain part of the brain have deteriorated to the point they no longer can produce a neurochemical called dopamine. This leads to symptoms of tremor and stiffness and slowness of movement, eventually increasing to the point where people are unable to move, unable to speak and so on.

There are other people afflicted with Parkinson's in this room who fear, as I do, the day when they reach that point. And that day, if there is not another scientific advance, is not far off. There are examples of other people in my statement who have been afflicted with Parkinson's and who, within the first 10 years of their affliction, no longer could work, are now at the point where they have to hire help to care for them, to turn them over in bed, to help them eat. It is a devastating disorder.

It is one of many, of course, and I feel that part of my role today is not to speak exclusively for the Parkinson's community but for the people who are fighting these diseases from every other quarter—from AIDS, from hepatitis, from diabetes, from Alzheimer's, and so on. There are breakthroughs. Parkinson's is a good example of the role of medical research because of the enormous breakthroughs that are available. It is the thing that gives us such hope and also makes this so very frustrating. In the case of Parkinson's, those breakthroughs are just beyond our arm's reach. I hear neurologists all the time talking about the great breakthroughs that are just beyond our reach in tissue transplants, genetic engineering, nerve regeneration—something that was just considered a fantasy several years ago, the idea that somehow something like a nerve growth factor could be implanted into the brain and bring those cells back to life; that in fact is a reality that can be made part of my life and save my life, as with others, if we have the money.

It is shocking to talk to neurologists not only in the Parkinson's field. I was speaking with one at NIH who is in the Alzheimer's field a couple of weeks ago, and with a bit of envy, he said, "You know, you have the science. The science is there. You just do not have the money."

Another one said, "In Parkinson's, the pieces of the puzzle are on the table; it is just fitting them together."

One thing that I have submitted with my statement is a summary by the National Coalition for Research in Neurological Disorders, which I commend for your study and that of the committee. It is a very good summary of both the costs of neurological disorders and the enormous breakthroughs that are waiting. And for Parkinson's, it quotes the National Advisory Council for the National Institute on Neurological Disorders and Stroke by saying that there are treatments which "would prevent or reverse neurological loss in Parkinson's disease, achievable in this decade, if we have the money." That just echoes the statements by countless neurologists who talk to me about, "Oh, do not worry. We are going to have a cure for you. You do not have to worry—if we have the money." It is that clear.

And as you have said yourself so eloquently, obviously, we do not have the money now. In the case of that institute, the NINDS, they are presently capable of funding 14 percent of the worthy applications that are submitted—14 percent. And as you have described, we had to fight with your leadership to maintain funding in the 1994 appropriations year. We were facing a cut and had to fight hard simply to maintain our funding. And as you said, it does not appear that the health care reform plan addresses the need for medical research at this time.

That is simply unacceptable, and it makes no sense. Not only is it a terrible thing in terms of the human suffering that we have talked about; it is crazy economically, as you know. In the case simply of Parkinson's, there is an estimate that it costs $5.6 billion a year in medical care costs, in disability, in lost productivity. There has been very little study of Parkinson's, and I happen to think that is very low when I look at the cost figures for other neurological disorders which are also reflected in here—all of them in the billions.

The Federal Government is spending $28 million on direct Parkinson's research now—$28 million. Here we have scientists who are saying, "We can get you a cure." That would eliminate $5.6 billion a year in cost. That is how we can finance health care reform. And as you have said, how can we do it without making that investment. It does not begin to use the correct words to say that this is pound-foolish. This is crazy economically.

The other thing that this is doing is creating a very dangerous situation. As you have described, there are disparities in funding, and the disparities in the case of Parkinson's are terrible. AIDS, as one example, is receiving in research over 20 times more per patient in research funding dollars than is Parkinson's. In the case of cancer, it is more than ten times more per patient in research dollars. Just about any disorder is receiving more research funding.

One thing that does is cause our community to think it has got to push to become the next "disease of the month." I was actually pleased to hear the many references to Alzheimer's today, because I greatly respect the work that their community has done to bring to the public eye the horror of Alzheimer's and the need for breakthroughs. And that is, of course, the thing that the Parkinson's community wants to do as well, and we must do it. So there are discussions about getting our own ribbon and our own celebrity spokesperson and our own day and our own march on Washington—somehow getting our very disabled, dysfunctional community together in wheelchairs so that they will somehow get enough cameras that they can come to the public eye.

That is great, to get us into the public eye, but I do not want to spend my time until I am disabled, fighting other sick Americans. And that is what at this point we are being asked to do. You have described the budget caps and so on that you are constrained by, and I so appreciate your leadership in trying to fight against that system, because we must. When we have the will, we have been able to finance things that protect American lives. We did it in World War I and in World War II. We did it with the Manhattan Project, which was intended ultimately to protect American lives. When we simply wanted to go to the moon, which was an amazing achievement, but does not protect American lives, we came up with the money.

We can do it here, and if we do not, we are going to be fighting among sick Americans, one against another, trying to decide which is more important—is it more important to save someone from AIDS? Who is suffering more—is Dave suffering more than I am? Shall we fight each other about whose breakthrough should come first?

The American people, as Mary has so clearly pointed out, would not stand for that, and I give an analogy in my statement of a family sitting in family conference. If Dave and I were brother and sister, would our parents sit in family conference and try to decide which of us would be saved, how they could manage the budget to save one of us because they knew they could not afford the other one, when they were going out to buy a car the next day?

When Americans walk through airports, as Dr. Lee and Senator Simon were talking about earlier, and see improvements and know that that is coming out of the transportation budget, Americans do not think about budget caps; they do not know the nuances of 602(b) and the alphabet soup of the budget process, which I am struggling to learn myself. They know that it is a matter of will and priorities.

We want to help you in your leadership establish those priorities as they should be, because we must.

I thank you.

[The prepared statement of Ms. Samuelson follows:]

PREPARED STATEMENT OF JOAN I. SAMUELSON

I am one of a million Americans with Parkinson's disease. I am testifying today to give voice to my own desperate need for a medical breakthrough, and to that of the Parkinson's community. But I also must speak of the need for an adequate biomedical research budget for all disorders.

I was diagnosed with Parkinson's seven years ago, and a few years ago put aside my law practice when I discovered that medical science was being held back from a Parkinson's breakthrough by the federal government's ban on fetal tissue transplant research. At that point I founded the Parkinson's Action Network, to give our community a voice in that debate. Upon completion of that battle, though, we discovered our work had only begun, because there was no money to fund the research the ban had stopped.

Now we are fighting what most certainly is a life-or-death battle. With adequate funding for promising scientific work, our lives will be saved. Without it, many or all of us will be lost, needlessly.

Parkinson's is a neurological disorder that results from the
degeneration of brain cells that produce a neurochemical called
dopamine, which controls motor function. Symptoms of stiffness,
tremor and slowness of movement first emerge when 80% of those
cells are already dead. The only significant treatment available
is a 30-year-old pharmaceutical discovery known as "L-Dopa." It
does nothing to slow the degeneration, only partly masking the
symptoms, and creating side effects that eventually become as
devastating as the disease. Although the cause remains unknown,
environmental toxins are emerging as a possible suspect, possibly
in combination with a genetic predisposition in some victims.

Medical science tells us it now understands a great deal
about the nature of Parkinson's, and is prepared to produce a
major breakthrough, and possibly a cure, in the next several
years. There are several emerging biotechnical approaches, from
tissue implants to growth factors to genetic engineering, that
hold huge promise. Researchers in each of those fields expect
breakthroughs in this decade.

Even scientists outside the Parkinson's field recognize the
huge potential. As one put it to me, "You have the science,"
indicating that the Parkinson's breakthroughs are there, waiting
for work to be done; that Parkinson's is far easier to beat than
most other disorders Americans presently suffer from.

The Advisory Council to the National Institute on
Neurological Disorders and Stroke (NINDS) confirms that a
realistic research effort would produce treatments that would
"prevent or reverse neurological loss in Parkinson's" by the end
of the decade. They have similar dramatic predictions for stroke
and multiple sclerosis, and expect to at least ameliorate a host
of others, all by the year 2000. I am submitting with this
statement a summary of those promising developments. It is this
potential throughout neurology that caused Congress to proclaim
the 90's the "Decade of the Brain."

But with every such promise there is a caveat: they cannot

produce the breakthrough without funding for the remaining
research. And neurologists also admit that the research is only
inching forward, because it is starved for funding. The primary
source of Parkinson's research, the National Institute for
Neurological Disorders and Stroke, is presently funding only 14%
of worthy applications for grants. I hear stories daily of
research going unfunded, of promising young researchers leaving
the field. And this may not even be the worst of it: the
Administration warns us to brace for a possible cut in 1995.

No one disputes that funding neurological research would
produce great cost savings. Since the fifty million Americans
stricken by brain disorders usually live incapacitated for long
periods, we are very expensive to care for. Parkinson's alone
wastes an estimated $5.6 billion a year in medical care,
disability costs and lost productivity.

From working with the Parkinson's community, I can see this
statistic translated into individual lives. There is your former
colleague in the House of Representatives, Mo Udall, whose career
was cut short by Parkinson's and whose daughter, Anne, works with
us as the Chair of our Network. I think of the couple who have
written me wishing they could die, because of the financially
crippling effect of the expensive Parkinson's medicine that is
steadily stripping them of assets.

I think of Mark Steiner, a 44-year-old San Francisco cab
driver. Diagnosed 13 years ago, Mark has been unable to work for
the last four years, and now requires almost around-the-clock
hired care to help him complete basic functions of eating, moving
about his apartment and caring for himself. Mark is just one
example of the tremendous burden on the social services system
and on the productivity of Mark's immediate family, who must
spend time and money caring for his needs.

There are many others I know -- people trained in computer
science, journalism, accounting -- whose skills and training had
been blunted because the crippling effects of the disorder
require increasingly more assistance to function. In each

instance, even small breakthroughs would translate to substantial savings in cost.

Although I have lost many physical abilities that were tremendously important, I feel lucky to be functioning as well as I am at this stage. But I must recognize that I am steadily approaching the same dependent state. Every simple task, from using a pen to write, to speaking in a clear and distinct voice, is now requiring effort. I see the day coming when my speech is just a soft blur, when walking to this hearing room is not just a project requiring special energy, but an insurmountable obstacle.

For me and these others, the promised timetable for life-saving help is almost entirely controlled by the roadblock of missing funding. If a scientific advance intervenes as researchers tell us it can, we will continue as functioning, taxpaying citizens. But if funding is not improved, we can plan on losing the struggle to walk, to talk, and end up frozen and silenced. These examples are human tragedies, but they also are economic disasters.

In the case of other research areas, such as computers, energy, defense, space, it is popular to discuss the great return on investment that research provides. Like those areas, investing in medical research would improve American scientific stature and competitiveness. That, in turn, would buy economic progress, in jobs in science and medical technology. In addition, there are the two important pluses: reducing human suffering and helping finance health care reform.

Nonetheless, medical research has been subjected to different federal funding rules than many other sectors of the federal budget. Defense, foreign policy, NASA, and many other spending sectors tell the government what they need, and that request frames the debate: they may grumble over the final dollar, but they get the lion's share. Medical science is given a finite sum, unrelated to need, and told to make do.

There is no indication that this approach will change. The Clinton health care reform plan barely mentions the cost-cutting benefits of biomedical research investment, and provides no way to finance it.

As my community comes to realize the stake it has in government funding policy, there is a growing awareness that we need to join the "Disease of the Month" game. Discussions inevitably turn to the need for our own ribbon, our own celebrity spokesperson, our own attempt to organize our disabled community into a wheelchair march up the Mall. The hope is that thereby we can become sufficiently important to access the federal research checkbook. Indeed, we have reason to respect the disease communities that now play this game with great skill: by turning rage and fear into action, they are getting results in special task forces, White House attention, and -- most important -- money.

But with such a tight lid on overall research spending, the government has financed its response to these more vocal, active groups with a "rob Peter to pay Paul" strategy. Funding now is decidedly uneven. Those afflicted with AIDS receive over 20 times more funding per patient for research than do those with Parkinson's. Cancer receives over 10 times more. Almost any disease receives more funding per patient than Parkinson's.

This inequity must change. The slow torture of Parkinson's is just as devastating. Moreover, our needed breakthrough already is on the horizon, and would also produce scientific developments that would benefit a wide array of disorders, neurological and otherwise.

But our fight is not with other ailing Americans. The dollars currently spent to save people dying of AIDS, breast cancer, Alzheimers or any other disorder are a great investment. The problem is a government policy which is forcing America to choose which of us it will save. It is as if a family, when faced with a limited budget and two family illnesses, sat in conference to decide which child's treatment it could afford, while also planning an outing to buy a new car.

Surely the American family would not willfully spend its
national budget that way. It would do as, every day, Americans
on tight budgets must: they grit their teeth, face expensive
temptations and say "we just can't afford that right now."

And, just as surely, there is spending in the federal budget
that pales in importance next to that of saving American lives.
When we fought World Wars I and II, nothing else stood in the way
of an adequate response. When America wanted to build an atomic
weapon, it initiated the Manhattan Project, and did so. When it
wanted to go to the moon, it set a timetable and met it.

The same challenge faces us now. Medical research is the
New Frontier. With lifesaving breakthroughs as close as they
are, any budgetary decision that does not give adequate funding
to medical research is a simultaneous decision to let sick
Americans suffer. There cannot be a higher priority.

Every minute, there are Americans who are losing a race
against time. Like any woman with a new-found lump in her
breast, or any man diagnosed HIV-positive, a person with a new
diagnosis of Parkinson's is fighting against a clock. None of us
have time to spare.

We need our government to make that life-saving choice.
Don't make us fight other sick Americans. Save us both.

Dr. Michael Welsh is a professor of medicine at the Howard Hughes Medical Institute at the University of Iowa College of Medicine.

And Dr. Herbert Pardes is vice president for health sciences and dean of the College of Physicians and Surgeons at Columbia University. Dr. Pardes, of course, was director of the National Institutes of Mental Health in both the Carter and Reagan administrations.

I cannot begin to tell you how proud and honored I am that you would take time from your schedules and travel great distances to be here—all the way from Seattle in one case. I really do appreciate it very much. All of you at this table have achieved a level of prominence that very few Americans ever achieve—very few people in this world ever achieve. To the three of you who have received the Nobel Prize it is something that I could only dream about, and it is something that our young people ought to aspire to.

We have in the past prided ourselves on the number of Nobel Prizes that our researchers have won. I am wondering if we are going to be able to continue that with the level of funding that we have and the lack of incentives to draw young people into making research their life's work.

All of you represent to me the zenith of accomplishment in medical research, and I am just pleased to have you here today.

We will start with Dr. Watson. Dr. Watson has appeared before this committee and my Appropriations Committee many times in the past. We have an ongoing discussion about the Human Genome Project and when it can be finished, and I am going to ask you that question again; I always ask you every time I see you. As I said, Dr. Watson received the Nobel Prize in 1962. He has served on the faculty at Harvard and is director of the Cold Spring Harbor Laboratory. In 1989, he was appointed director of the National Center for Human Genome Research, where he successful launched a worldwide effort to map and sequence the human gene.

Dr. Watson, again, welcome to our committee, and please proceed as you so desire.

STATEMENTS OF JAMES D. WATSON, NOBEL PRIZE RECIPIENT, AND DIRECTOR, COLD SPRING HARBOR LABORATORY, COLD SPRING HARBOR, NY; DR. E. DONNALL THOMAS, NOBEL PRIZE RECIPIENT, MEMBER, FRED HUTCHINSON CANCER RESEARCH CENTER, AND PROFESSOR OF MEDICINE, EMERITUS, UNIVERSITY OF WASHINGTON, SEATTLE, WA; DR. JOSEPH E. MURRAY, NOBEL PRIZE RECIPIENT, AND PROFESSOR OF SURGERY, EMERITUS, HARVARD MEDICAL SCHOOL, BOSTON, MA; DR. MICHAEL J. WELSH, PROFESSOR OF MEDICINE, HOWARD HUGHES MEDICAL INSTITUTE, UNIVERSITY OF IOWA COLLEGE OF MEDICINE, IOWA CITY, IA; AND DR. HERBERT PARDES, VICE PRESIDENT FOR HEALTH SCIENCES AND DEAN, COLLEGE OF PHYSICIANS AND SURGEONS, COLUMBIA UNIVERSITY, NEW YORK, NY

Mr. WATSON. Senator Harkin, I was very pleased to be asked to attend what I think is going to be an historic occasion, what you are doing. Something has got to change.

Just to start with, reacting to what has gone before, listening to these two individuals with Parkinson's and diabetes was very moving because as a member of the scientific community, we really believe now that we can do something, and we want to do it. And seeing people who face future lives which will be clouded by terrible diseases is something we should be aware of.

In light of that, I must say as a lifelong Democrat how disappointed I was in Phil Lee's testimony.

Senator HARKIN. Well, you have told me something I never knew about you.

Mr. WATSON. I know he is speaking in an official way and so on; I know that. But he should have shown a little enthusiasm. He seemed as if he was brain-dead toward a wonderful idea.

There really is a crisis in biomedical research, and it has reached the point where success is not rewarded. Over the past 10 years, medical research has just opened up in a way that none of us could believe as a result of advances in pure science. And the money there—they say 20 percent of the grants are funded—I am dealing with a situation in my own lab where a world class scientist, really world class has a 12 percent priority to work on something related to breast cancer, and they tell me it is not going to be funded. Now, something is wrong, deeply wrong.

So we can go down and see Sam Broder and ask, "What is up, Sam?" and maybe we will get him funded. But 12 percent—that is sick. OK, it is sick.

Senator HARKIN. It is.

Mr. WATSON. And there are really a lot of things we can do.

Senator HARKIN. I like the way you do not mince your words. [Laughter.]

Mr. WATSON. Well, in one case, it got me fired.

Senator HARKIN. That is all right; it did not do you any harm, I will tell you that.

Mr. WATSON. No; it allowed me to speak the truth, which I do today. But we have reached the point where we just cannot go on with these 4 percent increases if we are going to live up to the opportunities which are now available, to do something about diabetes, to do something about Parkinson's, to do something about arthritis—there are a lot of things, and we are just going to get older and sicker, and someone will have to support us. We are going to get older—I want to get older, but I do not want to get sicker too soon.

And we have go to do something about Alzheimer's, and fortunately, because of these genetic breakthroughs, we are beginning to understand what is up; we have not gotten there yet, but it is very exciting, and no one would have predicted how fast this information would be coming in. And with this information, we should start spending the money to follow it up, and we are not going to under the current thing.

So if you do not succeed, the country is in bad shape. And the last thing I will say is that we keep worrying about what is America's future, and it ought to be something better than stopping guns and violence. It ought to be a little better. And I think really having the vision that we can do something to make this a healthier country is the one we should work toward.

Thank you for inviting me.

Senator HARKIN. Dr. Watson, thank you very much. A great statement. It may have been Dr. Pardes in one of our meetings—he can correct me if I am wrong, but I think it was he—who told me that one of the purposes of basic research is so that we can die young as late in life as possible. I kind of liked that.

[The prepared statement of Mr. Watson follows:]

PREPARED STATEMENT OF JAMES D. WATSON

I most welcome the opportunity to speak this morning before the Senate Labor and Human Resources Committee on the need for expanding support for medical research. I do so from the vantage point of my now over 40 year involvement with DNA, the long linear molecule which carries our genetic instructions. Now we realize that each of our chromosomes is a single DNA molecule along which are specified the instructions for several thousands genes, the fundamental units of heredity whose existence was first shown in 1865 by the Austrian monk, Gregor Mendel.

In 1953, I with my English colleague, Francis Crick, proposed that DNA had the form of a Double Helix with the genetic information of genes being specified by the precise sequences of the four nucleotide building blocks along their respective DNA molecules. This original formulation of the structure of DNA has stood the test of time and served as the foundation stone for ever increasingly powerful studies of gene structure and function. Initially, DNA research had little practical significance falling into the category of pure research, pursued for its insights into the fundamental nature of heredity. But starting in 1973, after Stanley Cohen and Herb Boyer devised a powerfully simple way to isolate individual genes, DNA research began increasingly to impact medical research. By today hardly a week passes without leading newspapers reporting some major new advance relating a human disease to defects in our genetic instructions.

By 1986, it was clear that the means would soon be available for scientists to work out the essential chemical features of human DNA giving us precise chromosomal locations and structures for all the human genes. This knowledge would open up the possibility of finding the molecular gene changes in the mutant genes that lead to specific human diseases like Alzheimer's disease or breast cancer. So I with many other leading scientists then proposed the initiation of The Human Genome Project, a 15 year, three billion dollar project to establish the structure and chromosomal locations of the some 50,000 to 100,000 genes, whose coordinated functioning makes possible human development and functioning. This proposal was enthusiastically received by the American Congress, which voted monies in 1988 to the Department of Energy and the National Institutes of Health to initiate this most important human endeavor. I was initially privileged to help bring into existence the National Center for Human Genome Research at the National Institutes of Health, serving as its first director until the spring of 1992. In this capacity, I took pleasure in 1989, 1990, 1991 and 1992 in appearing before Congress explaining how The Human Genome Project, once it got up to speed, would profoundly advance medical research.

Now we are just beginning to see the first fruits of The Human Genome Project. They already have exceeded our most optimistic projections. The ways we think about ALS, Alzheimer's disease, Fragile X induced mental retardation, and colon cancer, for example, have dramatically changed opening up important new ways for their diagnosis and/or therapy. And we can confidently predict that further genetic approaches will radically change how we think about many other important diseases like asthma, migraines, non-insulin dependent diabetes, epilepsy, depression and arthritis. Medicine will become a much more rational endeavor, and the quality of human life will correspondingly improve.

But how much time it takes for these changes to occur will depend upon the rate at which we do biomedical research. Already we have reached a state where NIH grants to first-rate scientists are being in effect rationed. The situation no longer exists where only the second-rate grant applications get turned down. Instead, highly competent medical research no longer can count on being funded after study section review. All too many of our best scientists, particularly those at the start of their careers, have to wait 9 to 24 months before these research projects become funded. This dilemma exists not because the federal monies for science have decreased but because of the great increase in opportunities for future important accomplishments. Because so many important diseases look potentially curable if the relevant pure and applied research gets done, the number of highly original scientists opting for careers in biomedical research is steadily increasing. Yet once they have made that choice, they face the constant threat that their careers will become aborted because of seemingly arbitrary decisions made during the peer review process. I see these dilemmas everywhere, including in my own institution at Cold Spring Harbor Laboratory, where outstanding scientists no longer automatically can count on new grants as rewards for past success.

I am thus very excited about the positive impact upon our country's biomedical research efforts that would result were the Harkin-Hatfield Medical Research Fund to come into existence. The idea of making biomedical research a necessary ingredient in the forthcoming health care reform plan is indeed inspired, for the long term success of the forthcoming legislative effort depends on much better understanding of our various human diseases than is now available. The only way we can effectively take care of an increasingly elderly population is to banish many of the degenerative aging diseases which simultaneously diminish the quality of life while inflicting intolerable financial burdens on our health services. We must thus find the means, for example, to prevent the senility of Alzheimer's, the blindness and kidney failure that come with diabetes, and the constant pain and immobility of those suffering from arthritis.

Such "miracles" will only come from research, and so we should seize the fact that we actually have good ideas to explore and a very well trained cadre of scientists eager to better the human condition. I am, of course, aware that the argument can be made that Congress can never provide enough money to let us soon exhaustively establish the precise functioning of some 100,000 human genes. So even with say double the amount of money now available to NIH, hard choices have to be made. Here I am very reassured by the fact that Harold Varmus has assumed the directorship of NIH. In him, we have a research scientist of the highest qualifications who comes to his office with a deep understanding of the relationship between pure and applied research. Most importantly, he knows the distinction between looking good and doing good. Now that we have so many good leads to follow up, we must be very careful not to spend money merely because the objectives sound good. Even with all the advances of the past decade, there are still diseases whose deadly courses we still see no way to alter. So we must continue to place great emphasis on so-called pure research which aims to understand the essence of life as opposed to understanding the molecular essence of a given disease be it caused by an infective agent or a defective set of vital genes. The real advances we need very often depend upon facts not yet found.

Setting the right balance between pure and applied research will never be straightforward. But I don't think anyone could seriously argue that we have done too much pure research in the past. All too often we have spent vast piles of money on objectives that were beyond the current capabilities of science. Masses of money early in the War on Cancer were spent on 1970's task forces that were to stop breast, colon, and prostate cancer but predictably yielded few real dividends. Fortunately, the monies since then spent on pure cancer research have now created the knowledge that, for example, may now let the currently huge sums allotted for breast cancer to be better spent.

Letting the United States continue to lead the world in the advancement of medicine through research has the added benefit of continuing to provide the ideas and trained personnel needed to retain the preeminent position now held by our major pharmaceutical and biotechnology companies. That American companies so dominate the rising field of Biotechnology reflects not only the healthy state of American venture capital efforts but also the extraordinarily successful deployment of federal monies to support DNA-based research.

But we must never forget that the main wealth that will be created through biomedical research is that which comes from health itself. Imagine, for example, the wealth now consumed by nursing homes instead being passed on to our children in the form of education and housing. When so viewed, it is clear that we must be a more healthy nation. And for that to happen, we have no choice but to place more resources toward biomedical research.

Senator HARKIN. Dr. Don Thomas received the Nobel Prize in Physiology in 1990 for his work on bone marrow transplantation. He is a member of the Fred Hutchinson Cancer Research Center, a professor of medicine emeritus at the University of Washington, and former president of the American Society of Hematology.

Dr. Thomas, again, welcome back to our committee, and thank you for being here.

Dr. THOMAS. Thank you very much, Senator Harkin, for the invitation to be here.

My name is Don Thomas, and I work at the Fred Hutchinson Cancer Research Center in Seattle and am also immediate past president of the American Society of Hematology, which is an organization of some 6,000 physician-scientists who also are on record as strongly supporting your proposal for the Harkin-Hatfield Fund.

I would like to put things in perspective by beginning with a somewhat personal account. My father was a general practitioner in Texas for 50 years, and he died in 1941. I think in many respects he was an ideal family physician. I never knew him to take a vacation. He knew everybody. He was always available, and he was loved by everyone.

But as I look back on his time in medicine, I think his ability to do anything about disease was pitiful. He had two effective drugs. One was morphine, and one was digitalis. The drugs that we now regard as routine—for example, insulin, that we heard about; sulfonamides, the first antibiotics—came along right at the end of his career in medicine.

Now, I graduated from medical school in 1946, and the changes in medicine since that time certainly encompass things that my father never could have visualized. The changes are monumental. In fact, in my own field of marrow transplantation, which was considered a silly idea back in the early 1950's, last year, there were more than 10,000 bone marrow transplants done around the world, with the cure of a large number of young people with otherwise fatal diseases.

The remarkable advances in medical care and medical knowledge coincided with the increased funding for the NIH that occurred beginning at the end of World War II. And I am proud to say that our own Senator Magnusen played an important role in the funding for the NIH.

The discovery of the structure of DNA by Jim Watson and Francis Crick, of course, has ushered in an entirely new era in the life sciences. The door has now been opened to a characterization of the human genome, with profound implications for the understanding, treatment and, most importantly, the prevention of diseases.

I think the Harkin/Hatfield proposal is the most reasonable and perhaps the only way in sight to assure funding and continued funding for research and development. It will also be essential to our biomedical industry in maintaining its world leadership and therefore in creating jobs.

In the long run, an investment in research is critical to our efforts to control the cost of medical care. When we talk about more funding for research, I think one of the first questions should be can we use the money. And of course we can. You have all heard about the low level of funding of research grants, which disturbs us greatly. But in a sense, that is not the important issue in the next year or two. The important issue is that many of our young, brilliant scientists are discouraged about trying to pursue a career in research, because they cannot see the future for them.

We cannot afford to lose these young scientists, because they are the people who will be making the discoveries 10 to 20 years from now that we cannot predict at the present time.

I would like to deviate a little bit to address an additional concern, and that is the support of hospital costs for patients undergoing new forms of therapy. The NIH has had almost no funding for that purpose, and the insurance companies have refused to pay for what they call experimental treatment, which they define, by the way—they define that themselves—as any treatment that is not a part of established practice.

Pity the woman with breast cancer whose insurance company will not pay because her doctor proposes to use a new drug, or a new combination of old drugs.

If we are to translate the remarkable laboratory research advances into clinical practice, we must be able to provide hospital and/or outpatient coverage for those brave patients who are willing to undertake new forms of therapy for the benefit of all.

Let me emphasize that I think this should come through regular patient care funding and should not divert funding from the Harkin/Hatfield Fund, which should be for research.

So in summary, the United States has consistently provided leadership in medical research. It is quite clear that we can expect great progress on the biomedical problems that confront us. Further, we can expect the next 50 years to bring remarkable advances that none of us can now foresee.

The Harkin/Hatfield Fund for Medical Research will help to ensure that the United States continues to play an essential role in the solution of these problems while at the same time providing the best in medical care for all of our citizens.

Thank you for the invitation to be here.

Senator HARKIN. Dr. Thomas, again, thank you, and thanks for coming a great distance. You were talking about getting young scientists and keeping them in. I was looking further at this article that I got, just today, on Dr. Lewis Thomas. He was asked during his tenure as head of the Memorial Sloan Kettering Cancer Center how he chose where to invest limited resources, how he chose which bright, creative minds to support. He replied that often, late in the evening, he prowled the dark halls, listening for telltale exclamations such as, "Damn, that works like that?" or, "What a surprise that is," or for incredulous laughter. "Those are the places I invest resources," he said. I thought that fitting in regard to what you were talking about in getting these young people involved.

[The prepared statement of Dr. Thomas follows:]

PREPARED STATEMENT OF DR. E. DONNALL THOMAS

I am pleased to offer my support for the proposed Harkin/Hatfield Fund for Medical Research. I work at the Fred Hutchinson Cancer Research Center in Seattle and am a former president of the American Society of Hematology, an organization that strongly supports the Harkin/Hatfield Fund.

Let me begin on a personal note. For 50 years until 1941, my father was a general practitioner in Texas, knew everyone, made house calls, was always available, was everyone's dream of a physician. But his ability to provide effective treatment was pitiful. People with pneumonia or a long list of other diseases died or got over it with little real help from the doctor. Many of the drugs that we take for granted today, such as insulin and sulfonamides, came along near the end of his career.

I graduated from medical school in 1946. My 50 years in medicine have seen changes that my father could never have imagined. My own field of marrow transplantation did not exist at the time of his death, but now world-wide more than 10,000 marrow transplants are done each year with resulting cure of a wide variety of previously incurable diseases, including leukemia and genetic diseases of the bone marrow. In Seattle next August we will have a reunion of approximately 1,000 patients who are disease free 5 to 20 years after a marrow graft.

The remarkable advances of the past 50 years have coincided with the increased funding by the National Institutes of Health that began at the end of World War II. In the 1950's, when transplantation seemed to have almost no chance of success, my team was able to get funding which continued over the years. Following the Nobel prize, Secretary Louis Sullivan gave a party at the NIH for Dr. Murray and me. He had tabulated our team's research grant support over the years at $63,000,000. That investment has paid off, not only in the cure of many young people with otherwise fatal disease, but also in setting the stage for manipulation of the marrow stem cells, which will play an important role in the coming application of gene therapy.

The discovery of the structure of DNA by Jim Watson and Francis Crick ushered in a new age in the life sciences. The subsequent developments in molecular biology, including the characterization of restriction enzymes, and the automation and computerization of the technology has made it possible to define the code for many genes, including oncogenes. The door has now been opened to the characterization of the entire human genome, with profound implications for the understanding, treatment and, most importantly, the prevention of disease.

The Harkin/Hatfield proposal is a most reasonable way to assure that an investment in research and development can be a part of our national health program, whatever its final form. Such an investment will benefit all people. Further, it will be essential to our biomedical industry in maintaining its world leadership and in creating jobs. In the long run an investment in research is critical to our efforts to control the cost of medical care.

Can the increased funding be used wisely? Of course it can. We are all aware that a large number of worthy research grants are going unfunded. Many of our brilliant young scientists are discouraged about continuing their research careers because of funding problems. We cannot afford to lose these people because they will be the individuals making the discoveries 10 to 20 years hence.

May I address one additional concern—that of support of hospital costs for patients undergoing new forms of therapy. In recent years, the NIH has been able to provide very little support for patient care costs. On the other hand, most insurance companies have refused to pay for "experimental" treatment which they define as any treatment that is not a part of established practice. Pity the woman with breast cancer whose insurance a company will not pay because her doctor proposes to use a new drug or a new combination of old drugs. If we are to translate the remarkable laboratory research advances into clinical practice, we must be able to provide hospital and/or outpatient coverage to those brave patients who are willing to undertake new forms of therapy for the benefit of all. Provision for these costs should be a part of any new or revised health care plan with appropriate safeguards such as protocols approved by the NIH or the NCI.

In summary, the United States has consistently provided leadership in medical research. It is quite clear that we can expect great progress on the biomedical problems that confront us. Further, we can expect the next 50 years to bring remarkable advances that none of us can now foresee. The Harkin/Hatfield Fund for Medical Research will help to ensure that the United States continues to play an essential role in the solution of these problems while at the same time providing the best in medical care for all of its citizens.

Senator HARKIN. Dr. Joseph Murray is professor of surgery, emeritus at Harvard Medical School. Again, with Dr. Thomas in 1990, he shared the Nobel Prize for his work related to the first kidney transplantation.

Dr. Murray, it is good to see you again, and welcome back to the committee.

Dr. MURRAY. Thank you very much for the opportunity to be here, Senator Harkin.

I am going to give a personal review of how I got into research, because I think it will play the role of basic versus targeted investigation.

As a young surgeon fresh out of medical school in 1943, my first permanent assignment in the Army Medical Corps was to the plastic surgical unit at Valley Forge General Hospital in Pennsylvania, where I served through October 1947. We treated several thousands of battle casualties from the European, African, and Pacific theaters. These included wounds from shrapnel, bullets, mine explosions, frostbite and thermal burns. These occurred anywhere in the body—the head, the body, or the extremities.

Probably the two most difficult problems to treat were explosive injuries to the face, orbits and skull, and extensive "aviator" burns of the face and hands.

One pilot who sustained fourth degree burns of the face and hands in a crash on takeoff while flying the "hump" in Burma required the use of skin grafts taken from a cadaver to save his life. Although we knew that these "foreign" skin grafts would not survive permanently, they could be life saving by controlling fluid loss and infection and thus provide time for nutritional support and final skin grafting from unburned parts of his own body.

This experience influenced and directed my subsequent career. I was curious to know how the body could detect the difference between one's own skin and a piece of skin from some other individual. The accepted dogma was that transplantation between genetically different humans was impossible. In fact, many of my mentors advised me against studying the problem, stating that it was a waste of time and beyond the scope of clinical surgery.

But doctors at Harvard Medical School and the Peter Brent Brigham Hospital where Don Thomas and I both were residents were extensively involved in the study of kidney disease. They had already modified the artificial kidney machine and made renal dialysis possible. Over the next 15 years, our many laboratory and clinical studies were funded initially by private foundations, but subsequently almost completely by the NIH. Without continued NIH support, our program could not have survived, especially in view of the negative attitude of many influential physicians and scientists. In addition, the general public at that time had little or no knowledge of the then revolutionary concept of organ transplantation.

Our group ultimately achieved the first successful kidney transplant in humans between identical twins in 1954; between siblings in 1959; and the first successful kidney graft from a dead person in 1962.

Now, the success of this kidney transplant from a dead person was a result of our close collaboration with Burroughs-Wellcome Company, which produced and supplied the first effective immunosuppressive drug. Our collaborators, Dr. George Hitchings and Dr. Trudy Elion, both received the Nobel Prize in 1988 for "their discovery of important principles of drug treatment."

Our success in breaching the immune barrier could not have been possible without the use of experimental animals—dog, mouse, rat, rabbit, hamster, sheep, horse, as well as the use of many human volunteers. Since our initial reports of successful human transplants in the late fifties and early sixties, doctors around the world now transplant hundreds of thousands of organs—kidneys, livers, heart, bone marrow, heart, heart-lung, intestine and pancreas. These pancreas transplants will help not to cure diabetes, but treat diabetic patients. Simultaneous multiple organ transplants are also done in individuals when indicated.

Originally, organ transplantation was considered "spare parts surgery," the replacement of a worn-out organ with a new one. But the medical benefits and the consequences have turned out to be far more extensive. We now have better understanding of the causes of many diseases. The heart transplant is a perfect prototype for the study of heart disease, the study of diabetes, arthritis, some cancers, pancreatitis—all are either curative or treated by some form of transplantation.

I am going to go to another subject in my personal experience that influenced me—poliomyelitis or infantile paralysis, which we have talked about here. It illustrates the unexpected and unforeseen pathways of research that can lead to the prevention of disease.

In the early 1940's, I was a medical student, and the wards of the Boston Children's Hospital were filled with paralyzed polio patients in iron lungs, wheelchairs, and traction devices. The hospital was filled with them. At that time, one of my immunology instructors, Dr. John Enders, was working on a seemingly esoteric project; he was trying to grow viruses in tissue culture. In the late 1940's, after I returned from the service, I was a surgical resident, and we used to send him bits of tissue from surgical operations, tissues which would otherwise be discarded.

Now, during the polio epidemic of 1952, the hospital was so jammed with patients that I can remember we would go out and examine patients trying to get into the hospital in their automobiles, which lined the streets for several blocks.

Just about this time, late forties, Dr. Enders succeeded in his quest of growing the polio virus in cultures. And in 1954, he, together with Thomas Weller and Fred Robbins, were awarded the Nobel Prizes for "their discovery of the ability of the poliomyelitis viruses to grow in cultures of various types of tissue." That was what they needed. Prior to this time, to get the polio virus, they would have to infect chimpanzees or primates and then grind up the brains from the sacrificed animals to get the polio virus. But Drs. Enders, Robbins and Weller could grow it, and now we had great quantities.

And it was merely a matter of time until the vaccine would be developed. Dr. Jonas Salk came in, I think, about a year or two later, and then Sabin. So this illustrates the cumulative pathway of medical progress. Each researcher builds on the discoveries of the previous one.

So when you start out with the study of, say, treating burned aviators by tissue cultures, you have no idea where it is going to lead. And I think that this idea of the potential conflict between the diabetic patient and the Parkinson's patient, we really want to go back one step further—it is very likely that the person studying Parkinson's will be studying the derivation of the nerve cells and stem cells, and that research may help the other patient with the diabetes. We do not know the end of the road when you start off in basic science.

So those are only two examples, and the third example I am briefly going to mention is cardiac surgery, which now can produce longer lives and better lives for so many persons, and I am sure many Members of Congress are benefiting from cardiac bypass surgery.

It took a long time for the surgeons to perfect the "heart-lung machine." This was in the fifties, and I remember it very well. I worked with many of them; I will not name them all—Gross, Blalock, Lillehei, Gibbon, DeBakey, Harken, Hufnagel, and so on. But they finally achieved success in problems that were previously considered untreatable.

The idea that you could take a little baby's heart, born with multiple congenital anomalies, and at the end of the 3-hour operation, leave the baby with a perfectly normal heart, was unthinkable when Don and I were in medical school.

So research by scientists, whether working exclusively in laboratories or in hospitals, or partially in both—and we need all sorts of basic scientists—clinical, bench, and those that are bridging the role between bench and bed. We can save lives, we can cure disease and improve the quality of living. And of course, as has been pointed out, medical research is cost-effective. Just the Type B, Hib, vaccine, which costs $17 million to produce, saves about $360 million every year. That is just one example.

So finally, today, we as a nation are in a critical period regarding health care. And in our zeal to cut costs and to use our available resources for patient care, we must not be shortsighted. Our Nation's health demands a serious continuing, enlarging investment in research. So the available funds must be to supplement now the available funding.

I thank you as a citizen and as a physician for your zeal in pursuing this issue.

Senator HARKIN. Dr. Murray, thank you very much for your testimony and for being here.

[The prepared statement of Dr. Murray follows:]

PREPARED STATEMENT OF DR. JOSEPH E. MURRAY

As a young surgeon fresh out of medical school in 1943, my first permanent assignment in the Army Medical Corps was to the plastic surgical unit at Valley Forge General Hospital in Pennsylvania, where I served through October 1947. We treated several thousands of battle casualties from the European, African and Pacific Theaters. These included wounds from shrapnel, bullets, mine explosions, frost bite and thermal burns. These occurred anywhere: the head, body, extremities. Probably the two most difficult problems to treat were explosive injuries to the face, orbits and skull, and extensive "aviator" burns of the face and hands.

One pilot who sustained fourth degree burns of the face and hands in a crash on takeoff while flying the "hump" in Burma required the use of skin grafts taken from a cadaver to save his life. Although we knew that these "foreign" skin grafts would not survive permanently, they could be lifesaving by controlling fluid loss and infection, and thus provide time for nutritional support and final skin grafting from unburned parts of his own body.

This experience influenced and directed my subsequent career. I was curious to know how the body could detect the difference between one's own skin and that of every other human on earth, the only exception being identical twins. The accepted dogma was that transplantation between genetically different humans was impossible. In fact, Many of my mentors advised me against studying the problem, claiming it "a waste of time" or "beyond the scope of clinical surgery."

But doctors at Harvard Medical School and the Peter Bent Brigham Hospital in Boston were extensively involved in the study of kidney disease. They had already modified the "artificial kidney" machine and made renal dialysis possible. Over the next 15 years, our many laboratory and clinical studies were funded initially by private foundations and subsequently mainly by the NIH. Without continued NIH support, our program not could have survived, especially in view of the negative attitude of many influential physicians and scientists. In addition, the general public at that time had little or no knowledge of the then revolutionary subject concept of organ transplantation.

Our group ultimately achieved the first successful human kidney transplant between identical twins in 1954, the first successful sibling graft in 1959, and the first successful kidney graft from a cadaver in 1962. The success of this kidney transplant from a dead person was a result of our close collaboration with Burroughs-Wellcome Company, which produced and supplied the first effective immunosuppressive drug Our collaborators, Dr. George Hitchings and Dr. Gertrude Elion, received the Nobel Prize in 1988 "for their discoveries of 'important principles of drug treatment'."

Our success in breaching the immune barrier could not have been possible without the use of experimental animals - i.e. dog, mouse, rat, rabbit, hamster, sheep, horse, as well as the use of human volunteers Since our initial reports in the 1950s and early 1960s, doctors around the world have transplanted hundreds of thousands of organs: kidney, liver, heart, bone-marrow, lung, heart-lung, intestine and pancreas. Simultaneous multiple organ transplants are also performed when necessary.

Originally organ transplantation was considered "spare parts surgery," the replacement of a worn-out organ with a new one. But its medical benefits have turned out to be far more extensive: better understanding of the causes of diabetes, arthritis, some cancers, heart disease, pancreatitis, and enzyme deficiency diseases.

Another medical experience, poliomyelitis (infantile paralysis), illustrates unexpected and unforeseen pathways of research that can lead to the prevention of disease.

In the early 1940s, when I was a medical student, the wards of the Boston's Children's Hospital were filled with paralyzed polio patients in iron lungs, wheel chairs or traction devices. At that time one of my immunology instructors, Dr. John Enders, was working on a seemingly esoteric project, growing viruses on tissue culture. In the late 1940s, when I was a surgical resident, we used to send him bits of tissues from surgical operations, tissues which would otherwise be discarded.

During the polio epidemic of 1952, the hospital was so jammed with patients that those awaiting admission had to be examined in their automobiles which lined the streets for several blocks.

Just about this time, Dr. Enders succeeded in his quest. In 1954, Dr. John Enders and his colleagues, Thomas Weller and Frederick Robbins, were awarded the Nobel Prizes for "their discovery of the ability of the poliomyelitis viruses to grow in cultures of various types of tissue."

The production of a vaccine now became feasible and was produced a few years later, first by Salk and then by Sabin. This sequence illustrates the cumulative pathway of medical progress, each researcher building on the discoveries of a previous worker. Today polio has been virtually eradicated: 21,269 patients with paralytic polio in 1952, none (verified) in 1990.

These are only two examples of the role research has played in prevention and treatment of disease. A third example is cardiac surgery, which predictably can increase both longevity and quality of life. Cardiac operations may require the use of cardiopulmonary bypass, the so-called "heart-lung machine." I recall the dedicated, persistent zeal of the many pioneer cardiac surgeons - Gross, Blalock, Gibbon, Lillehei, Kirkland, DeBakey, Harken, Hufnagel and many others - who finally achieved success in problems previously considered untreatable. All of these cardiac pioneers were supported financially by the NIH.

Research by scientists, whether working exclusively in laboratories or in hospitals or partially in both, can save lives, cure disease and improve the quality of living In addition, medical research is cost effective - e. g., the cost savings with improved Hemophilus Influenzae Type B (Hib) Vaccine for every annual cohort of children vaccinated (over their lifetime), is $359.3 million. In contrast, the cost of the National Institute Allergy and Infectious Disease (NIAID) research on the vaccine was $17.4 million.

Today, we as a nation are in a critical period regarding health care. In our zeal to cut costs and use our available resources for patient care, we must not be shortsighted. Our nation's health demands a continuing serious investment in research. Available funds must be supplemented and increased so that clinical and bench scientists can continue to work and advance our knowledge in the prevention and treatment of human disease.

Senator HARKIN. Next, Dr. Michael Welsh, professor of Medicine at the Howard Hughes Medical Institute at the University of Iowa College of Medicine. He is also director of the Cystic Fibrosis Research Center. Dr. Welsh has made several fundamental contributions to research on cystic fibrosis, and his research has laid the foundation for work on gene therapy.

Dr. Welsh, welcome.

Dr. WELSH. Senator Harkin, thank you very much.

My name is Michael Welsh. I am a physician and a scientist at the University of Iowa College of Medicine. Today, I will briefly tell you about our research, doing so in the context of the discussion on health reform.

I want to emphasize two points—first, security for the people who have incurable diseases, and second, the benefits of basic biomedical research.

Security is a popular catchword now in the health reform dialogue, but what is the greatest threat to a person's security? It is hard to imagine anything more threatening than a disease that deprives the victim of freedom, happiness, or life itself. Today, in too many cases, patients face incurable diseases for which physicians can offer little relief. But they can offer hope—hope based on the fact that medical research has yielded many successes in the past, and you have heard about many of those today.

Medical research provides the only way to give people security, the security of treatments and prevention for incurable diseases. I would like to give you some examples from a disease that I study, cystic fibrosis.

Cystic fibrosis is the number one genetic killer of children. In cystic fibrosis, mucus in the bronchial passages is thick and tenacious, and difficult to clear from the lungs. As a result, patients have repeated infections that destroy the lungs.

A generation ago, the average patient with cystic fibrosis died before entering high school. Today, the average person with cystic fibrosis lives to young adulthood. The dramatic improvement in the length and quality of life is attributable to better methods of diagnosis and better treatments that have been achieved through biomedical research.

But despite this process, cystic fibrosis remains an incurable disease that kills the average patient by the age of 29. It is also an expensive disease. It costs $200,000 to $300,000 per year in the last few years of life. This cost will only be reduced by advances in biomedical research that develop treatments to cure the disease and to prevent its complications.

The goal of my work has been to understand cystic fibrosis and to use that knowledge to figure out how to treat it and possibly to cure it. That work is an incremental process. It has taken many research steps to progress toward that goal, and it will take many more to achieve it. We owe much of our success to the fact that we could build on previous research that has been done by others.

In cystic fibrosis, one specific gene fails to function correctly. That gene was discovered in 1989. In 1990, my laboratory, in collaboration with my colleagues at Genzyme, spliced together the normal gene and inserted it into cystic fibrosis cells in tissue culture. When we put in the normal gene, we corrected the function of those cells.

We thought that discovery was important because it suggested that perhaps we could develop a similar strategy to use in people; that is, perhaps we could develop gene therapy for cystic fibrosis; that is, delivery of the normal gene to people with the disease.

We then went on to try to discover what the gene does and to try and learn why it misfunctions when it is mutated. In late Octobe of this year, we published the first report of our work on gene therapy.

To deliver the normal gene to people, we used a virus called an adenovirus that normally causes the common cold. Parts of the virus that cause disease were removed by genetic engineering. In their place was inserted the normal gene. We were excited to find that when we applied the virus, it delivered the normal gene, and most importantly, corrected the biochemical defect in cystic fibrosis.

But much of our work was dependent upon basic discoveries from scientists who had no idea their work would impact on cystic fibrosis. For example, we used a technique that was first used to study nerve activity in slugs. Who would have guessed that such work would benefit a human disease? We also used gene splicing techniques that were originally developed to manipulate DNA in bacteria. That work gave us the tools to do our studies and is indeed the foundation of the whole biotechnology industry. Again, we profited from basic research that at the time had no apparent relation to a specific disease.

Although our work on gene therapy is not yet ready to be used to treat patients, it does give them hope—hope for the security of a treatment that can cure or prevent this terrible disease. Health care reform should be first and foremost about saving lives and improving the quality of life.

If we are to do that, we have to put in the effort and the investment on the front end, in biomedical research. That investment will also reduce the incredible costs of caring for people like those who have cystic fibrosis. If we do not invest on the front end, we have no hope for cost savings for incurable diseases, and we can extinguish the hope for better health for ourselves and our children.

The National Institutes of Health are a major supporter of biomedical research. They support applied research as well as basic research on problems of fundamental importance to biology. I gave you just a few examples of how such basic research was critical for our work. In turn, I hope that our work on cystic fibrosis and on gene therapy may also be of value in other diseases.

For example, gene therapy is now being tested for treatment of some forms of cancer. There is reason to believe that in the future, gene therapy may be used to treat many other diseases, chronic diseases like rheumatoid arthritis, metabolic diseases like diabetes, dise ses of the coronary artery, and diseases of the brain like Parkinson's.

Senator Harkin, I appreciate your leadership and vision in this area, and I support your and Senator Hatfield's effort to ensure and increase funding for medical research. Any health reform plan that does not support medical research in the end is going to prove shortsighted and ultimately self-defeating. Increased funding for medical research is the best investment we can make in long-term health reform.

Thank you, Senator Harkin.

Senator HARKIN. Dr. Welsh, thank you for your testimony and thank you for being here.

Dr. Herbert Pardes is vice president for health sciences and dean of the College of Physicians and Surgeons at Columbia University. As I mentioned earlier, he was director of the National Institute of Mental Health in both the Carter and Reagan administrations.

Welcome again, Dr. Pardes.

Dr. PARDES. Senator Harkin, thank you very much.

I want to applaud your championship of biomedical research. We need it, and you have just been phenomenal in taking this lead for us throughout the country.

I am right now vice president for health sciences and dean of the College of Physicians at Columbia, and have worked in a number of medical centers and also in the Government, and so have been involved in trying to work for the support and supporting biomedical research in this country.

One of the nice things about the testimony today, Senator Harkin, is that it is almost hearing a wonderful chorus of citizens, families, doctors, Government leaders, scientists—everybody coming together around one unified theme. And many of us in certain ways wear several hats. You might be interested to know that the kind of transplant work that was discussed just a little earlier by Dr. Murray and Dr. Thomas to me was personal in that it saved my son's life about 7 months ago.

I would like to submit my full testimony for the record and briefly comment on some of the highlights.

The effort that you and Senator Hatfield are making in creating an important fund to augment medical research is absolutely critical. Some of the comments you have heard before from other people in scientific settings regarding the topnotch research applications that are not being funded are things that we are experiencing at Columbia as well.

I was just in conversation with somebody who had a score at the 14 percent priority and was told he probably would not be funded. This message is going out to senior scientists and to junior scientists and I think is very ominous for science and biomedical research in general.

I worry about the future of biomedical research and the future of academic medicine. It is my feeling that the future of all health care and all medicine depends upon our support for biomedical research and academic medicine.

Medical research, as you have heard, has produced constant answers for America. We have addressed devastating problems and often have changed the outlook from diseases.

The reference earlier to pediatric cardiac surgery by Dr. Murray—we just talked about this at Columbia and looked at conditions which at one point meant 100 percent mortality and are now providing 100 percent survival.

While we have not won the war on cancer which was started back in the Nixon era, we have found cures for a number of cancers and increased life expectancy in a number of areas.

You pointed out earlier that life expectancy has increased from 34 years of age in 1878 to 75 years today. In fact, deaths from cardiovascular disease have dropped by 45 percent; coronary artery disease by 48 percent; stroke by 60 percent, as articulated in a nice article by Dr. Michael DeBakey, who was also mentioned a little earlier.

The new generation of genetic therapies, imaging devices, and a whole host of new immunological and molecular biological biology research promises our ability to attack a whole host of diseases, and these are happening while at the same time, the proportion of moneys out of the health care dollar going for health research continues to decline—in 1960, 5 percent; currently, probably under 3 percent.

The public, as Mary Woolley said earlier, is totally supportive of biomedical research, and it is important that our Government respond to that citizen call.

You have heard recounted any number of examples of cost savings from research. I might mention one other, and that is that the treatment of manic-depressive disease through the use of lithium has reduced health care expenditures some $6 billion between 1969 and 1984. It has been shown that the amount of money saved just from that one development has been more than all the money ever put into the NIMH for mental health research. I could give you other examples, but I think you have heard them already.

Where have the majority of these discoveries been made—and incidentally, as we have gone through the hearing, people have talked about advances in transplantation, pediatric cardiac surgery; you have heard about current advances in genetics research, regarding Huntington's disease. At Columbia, we have had a number of our scientists involved in advances in the genetics of lymphomas; Huntington's disease, as you heard; spinal muscular atrophy; Wilson's disease—it seems like one discovery after the other is coming, and as Dr. Watson eloquently stated before, we can help. What we need is the support in order to enable us to help.

Many of those discoveries have taken place at academic and biomedical research centers around the country, and these centers must be adequately supported in any health reform bill that eventually emerges through Congress.

The inclusion of biomedical research funding is critical. The funding of research is important to the academic medical center enterprise, and we are concerned about the whole fabric of that enterprise because that is where much of this research gets done.

Arnold Relman eloquently stated that "If we do not invest in biomedical research and academic medicine, the medicine we practice in the 21st century will be the medicine of the 20th century."

There are many laudable parts of the Clinton health plan, but to ensure the vitality of biomedical research and the academic centers where it takes place, we must maintain and enhance this Nation's biomedical research effort, make sure, as Phil Lee said, that all patients have access to the full range of care available at such centers, and rather, bring people to the best of medicine, not homogenize medicine down to its lowest common denominator; ensure that physicians and other health providers have access to the expert consultation services available from such academic centers; allow coordinated relationships between hospitals, physicians, and medical school faculty after changes in antitrust regulations; provide the adequate funding for medical schools so that they may support the full panoply of research necessary to undertake this mission; ensure adequate funding for health professionals so there is a balanced work force of both generalists and specialists; provide adequate funding for the teaching hospitals who, today, provide some 50 percent of the charity in this country; establish the National Biomedical Research Fund proposed by you and Senator Hatfield, and backed by Senator Simon and others; devote a more appropriate and higher proportion of the national budget to the support of research and development essential to improving health, and make certain that these centers where this research is carried out continue to play a critical role in the national quality management of which the Health Security Act speaks.

Again, Senator, thank you for your leadership, and thank you for the opportunity to participate in this excellent hearing.

[The prepared statement of Dr. Pardes follows:]

PREPARED STATEMENT OF DR. HERBERT PARDES

Senator Harkin and distinguished members of the Senate Labor and Human Resources Committee, I am honored to appear before you today to testify on a subject that must be addressed as we move forward in the health care reform environment—the need for continued vigorous support of medical research in any finally-passed health care reform bill. I am Herbert Pardes, M.D., Vice President for Health Sciences and Dean of the College of Physicians and Surgeons at Columbia University. During the course of my own career, I have had the opportunity to work at many fine academic health centers and to provide service to my government as Director of the National Institute of Mental Health in both the Carter and Reagan administrations. In these capacities, I have observed firsthand and participated in supporting some of the most important discoveries in the medical sciences in the last decades. The United States has been the leader in medical research for the world and we must do all we can to make certain that we maintain this important role. Today's innovative and new treatments are tomorrow's common medicine. Health reform must incorporate a "set-aside" for ground-breaking work.

Before I begin my testimony I would like to compliment you, Senator Harkin, and many of your colleagues who have recognized the importance of medical research and have done all you can in the face of grave budget deficits to protect and enhance research budgets. Your contributions in this arena are most appreciated by me and my colleagues. You and Senator Hatfield have made an important additional contribution by introducing a bill that would establish a medical research fund and there appears to be other bipartisan support for medical research in health reform.

My testimony today will focus primarily on the need for such a medical research fund and the costs and benefits of medical research. In addition, I would like to discuss the role of academic medical centers in health care now, potential roles in hearth reform and the important contributions we can make to underserved communities in our areas

A National Medical Research Fund: Importance of Inclusion In Health Reform

There are many laudable goals of President Clinton's hearth proposal and proposals that have been introduced by a wide range of members of Congress. All of us who speak on health reform recognize that the health proportion of the gross national product is 14% today and could escalate to 19% by the year 2000 unless there is some intervention. In addition, we realize that despite the greatness of our system there am problems of access, dissatisfied consumers and frustrated doctors who are increasingly burdened by the administrative problems associated with the multiplicity of insurers their patients have. At the same time that we recognize these problems, many of us in this room, including those testifying today, recognize the importance of biomedical research. Some individuals testifying today have received Nobel prizes in recognition of their work.

Life expectancy has increased from 34 years of age in 1878 to 75.7 years of age in 1992. In an October 1993 article in Science, Dr. Michael DeBakey describes the 70% reduction in live births seen from 1950, when there were 29.7 per 1000 live births, to 1991 when there were 8.9 live births per 1000. DeBakey further notes that deaths from all causes fell 29.2% between 1963 and 1987. During this period, deaths from cardiovascular diseases fell 45.4 %, coronary artery disease fell 48.2 % and stroke fell 60.6%.

Our advances continue to increase at a rapid rate. Genetic therapies hold promise for many areas of clinical applications. The new generation of Imaging devices can pinpoint areas of deviation that make them more susceptible to correction. Precise Delivery of immunological substances and extraordinary advances in transplantation can bring us more and more relief from a variety of devastating illnesses.

These advances have been made in the context of what might be termed a declining proportion of health care expenditures that are dedicated to research. Dr. Donald Harrison of the University of Cincinnati finds that in 1960, 5% of the health care monies were research dollars; by 1990 this had declined to 3.3%. Richardson of Johns Hopkins juxtaposes this 3.3 % to the new and emerging high technology industries that spend 6-12% on research and development.

Scientists are not alone in supporting the need for investments in medical research. According to an April 1992 Louis Harris and Associates survey, 91% of 1,255 adults were in favor of spending more on medical research. 49% of these adults rated medical research as the highest priority when offered a choice of investing in eight major fields of study including environmental research and energy issues. In a December 1992 survey of 900 adults conducted for the Alliance for Aging Research, Belden and Russonello found that 82% felt that more emphasis on medical research should be included In government health reform. This information was provided to the Congress during the last budget cycle by the Ad Hoc Group for Medical Research Funding.

Because we are in a time of tight budgetary constraints, it is important to evaluate what some of the potential cost savings from the fruits of medical research have been. The esteemed Chairman of this full Committee, Senator Edward M. Kennedy, stated in July of 1991 that ". . . the most remarkable achievement of the NIH may be that there has been no net cost to the American people. The health care savings from advances in one area alone—preventive medicine and the development of vaccines—have more than paid for the Nation's 105-year investment in the NIH." There are many examples of costs averted to bolster the Senator's argument. Listed below are some of these examples taken from The Ad Hoc Group for Medical Research's FY 1994 budget proposal and from a document being prepared by the NIH on "Cost Savings Resulting from NIH Research Support, Second Edition, A Periodic Reevaluation of the Cost-Benefits of Biomedical Research." These examples are based on a nonexhaustive list:

Effective prevention of dental disease between 1979 and 1989 through use if fluorides, better dental hygiene and preventive education of individuals resulted in an estimated 39 billion in savings.

Treatment of manic-depressive disorders by using lithium reduced health care costs by 6 billion dollars between 1969 and 1984.

Routine use of angiotensin-converting-enzyme inhibitor drugs for treatment of congestive heart failure has potential, as indicated by NIH-sponsored clinical trials, for preventing 10,000-20,000 deaths each year and about 100,000 hospitalizations, thus saving $1 billion a year in hospital and other costs.

Treatment of advanced stage testicular cancer using combination chemotherapy with cisplatin results in a cure rate of 60-65%. The NIH invested 71.6 million over a 17-year period in this research and estimated that the improved survival rates have reduced premature morality and have an estimated potential of one year savings of $134 million to $178.7 million.

Between 1964 and 1981, NIH invested $31.8 million to formulate a hepatitis B vaccine. The vaccine is estimated to have one year savings of $73.7-$147.6 million. (Statistics based on 1983 incidence rate). Savings accrue from preventing acute and chronic illness and reductions in health care utilization.

The examples above give some measure of the payoffs we see in reduced health expenditures and improved productivity for society. The development of a vaccine for AIDs may one day reduce the scourge of that disease.

These examples and so many others I could point to help to indicate that our country would be remiss if we herald a new dawn of health reform without the important "set-aside" for research. This "set-aside" in the health reform plan ought to be one that is guaranteed. We cannot have this fund substitute for other appropriated funds. It must be an add-on so that we can continue in our grand tradition.

Academic Health Centers

The site of much of American biomedical research is the academic health center that ". . . consists of an allopathic or osteopathic medical school, one or more affiliated teaching hospitals (children's or free-standing cancer hospitals), and one or more health professions schools or programs." DeBakey in his October 22, 1993 Science article indicates that "the medical centers represent a symbiosis of research, education, and practice, where new concepts germinate, are explored, and are then fully tested." Beyond the research that our institutions do, we train and have trained a cadre of outstanding physicians who provide the best medical care in the world. We have trained researchers, clinicians, educators, community leaders and policymakers. The American doctor stands tall in relation to his or her peers in the world.

Beyond research and training, our academic medical centers are centrally involved in providing care where it is needed. In Columbia's situation we are located in one of the most poverty-stricken areas of New York City. Dr. William Richardson, President of Johns Hopkins, indicates that the 287 AAMC teaching hospitals represent the largest such institutions in the country constituting 6% of all hospitals but 26% of gross patient revenues. These centers also absorb 28% of all medical bad debt expense and 50% of all charity care.

In New York City alone, according to Kenneth Raske, President of the Greater New York Hospital Association, many private hospitals that are part of an academic medical center provide $2.5 billion of uncompensated care. The reimbursement mix at Columbia and Presbyterian Hospital is 30% from Medicaid, 35% from Medicare and 10 % self-pay (the rest is from other insurers).

Academic health centers provide top quality care often to individuals with a multiplicity of health problems. In 1990, Drs. Colin McCord and Harold Freeman wrote in the New England Journal of Medicine that a "black male growing up in Harlem has less of a chance of reaching age 65 than a male growing up in the third world country of Bangladesh." Communities such as Harlem are inundated with other problems that complicate health care delivery. Poverty, unemployment, poor and substandard housing, homelessness, poor nutrition, crime, violence and poor education make the provision of health care and the patient compliance with therapeutic regimens exceedingly complex. The health care challenge is further complicated in these underserved communities by the high incidence of AIDS, drug abuse, tuberculosis, child abuse, spouse abuse, and premature births.

Thus, our premiere academic health centers conduct state-of-the art biomedical research, educate the world's finest providers, deliver high quality care to all patients and develop new ways to provide care to complex populations.

Health Reform and the Academic Health Center

As I mentioned most prominently, we at academic health centers are committed to working with this Committee and the Congress to make certain that there is vigorous support for medical research in health reform. There are some other areas that I also want to detail.

Health reform may affect academic health centers in many ways. While one can talk about the academic health center as an employer and all of us as employees, the issue I would like to talk about is the setting of academic health centers, their conduct of scholarly biomedical research and patient care functions and how they may fare in health reform. I would like to particularly look at potential positives and negatives from the sweeping changes.

Overall, I believe that there are many goals in the Clinton reform which are long overdue and most welcome. Prominent among these goals is access to health care for all people in this country.

In addition, the proposal includes a seamless system which protects people so that they are not in jeopardy in the event that they lose their job or move to a different state. The system may decrease administrative complexity. We also hope it will decrease malpractice costs and the diversion of energies and resources to defensive medicine.

All of us should welcome some containment of the cost of health care. I am personally in favor of trying to give comprehensive health care to everybody and I am not reluctant to spend the money it takes to have that happen, but I think it can be done with less threat to the rest of the economic welfare of the country.

The extra functions of an academic center must be supported. In their educational roles, centers are responsible for graduate and undergraduate medical education and nursing education. Additional functions include the transition to education in ambulatory settings, the education of generalists, costs of clinical research, high technology care of patients with complicated disorders, the high burden of indigent care and care to undocumented aliens.

Many of these areas are not the concern of the narrow-based purchaser of health services in the market. Thus, the fact that the Clinton reform plan does pay some attention to the academic health centers is refreshing.

I was part of a group of 15 who met with Mr. Magaziner beginning in April of 1993 and again in September and October of 1993. We have had further conversations with him since. We have also spoken with Mrs. Clinton, and the result of these conversations has been a far greater recognition of academic health centers and their needs in the Clinton plan.

In the health reform plan, we see the following:

1. Special pools of money for graduate medical education and for the needs of academic health centers.

2. An improved definition of an academic health center that recognizes its complex nature.

3. Inclusion of academic health centers in the quality control concerns and evaluation of the health system.

4. Requirements for interaction between the health system and academic health centers so that everyone in this country will have the right and capacity to have access to an academic health center in case of a complicated health problem.

Another important policy shift in the country focuses on the health work force. It has been generally agreed that generalists are needed in the United States—individuals who will serve as gatekeepers and controllers of cost. Some suggest that there are too many physicians in the U.S. and, therefore, resident numbers should be decreased. These policy changes may have varying effects in different parts of the country. For example, some have proposed that the number of residencies be determined by their arithmetic relationship to the number of senior medical students graduating in the United States. Specifically, a figure of 110% has been suggested by some for the number of first-year resident spots that would be available for graduating medical students.

This creates an enormous burden in New York where the number of first-year residency spots constitute 180% of the senior medical spots in New York. These medical residents provide a tremendous amount of the service to the citizens of New York, Residents staff the public city hospitals as well as many of the voluntary hospitals and private hospitals and provide around-the-clock and comprehensive care. Therefore,attempts to regulate resident numbers must also recognize the idiosyncratic nature of issues, populations and costs around the country.

in addition, academic health centers are concerned that clinical revenues could be significantly reduced and in turn impact on many programs in these centers. Dr. Richardson points out that clinical fees constitute approximately 40% of the income at medical schools nationwide. Reductions in payments to physicians could reduce these fees. We also see dangerous inclinations to decrease indirect costs of research. If clinical revenues and true indirect costs are reduced, we are faced with the nonviable options of increasing tuition, expanding fund-raising or seeking increased state support. Students, donors and state budgets are not in a position to respond to additional demands.

A sensible national health reform system that is carefully and sensitively structured would be welcome if it replaces a managed care revolution which moves forward oblivious of the needs of academic health centers. In cities such as Minneapolis and Los Angeles these managed care alternatives have threatened the viability of academic health centers.

Responsibilities of Academic Health Centers

Academic health centers must be actively involved in the health reform debate. I recommend that we do the following:

1. Maintain and enhance the nation's biomedical research effort.

2. Make certain we continue our ability to provide quality care to all patients.

3. Insure that we maintain our roles In research, education, quality care and as models for medicine throughout this country and the world.

4. Work to try to help meet some of the identified problems of the health care system. These include a need for greater attention to general health care, greater attention to delivery in the ambulatory setting, greater attention to the complicating factors of health care, such as poverty, violence, drug abuse, etc.

5. Stress the role of the physician as an advocate for the patient.

6. Focus on specific areas of strength and relinquish the goal of being strong in everything.

7. Make alliances within our own institutions and also outside.

8. Emphasize our work with complicated patients and patients with general health care needs.

9. Establish linkages to the rest of our universities.

10. Reach out into the community to make sure health care is delivered wherever it is needed.

11. Reach out to industry and collaborate on clinical trials and research in order to sustain the overall biomedical research enterprise in this country.

12. Ensure that certain provisions are attended to in any ultimate system. We must make certain adjustments are such that groups of providers who take patients with the most complicated care are not penalized.

13. Examine carefully the question of new monies coming into the system and old monies being taken out.

14. We must articulate the key requirements in order to sustain the academic health centers. These include: a. The right of all patients to access the full range of care available at the academic health center from the routine to the specialized, complex care and new therapies. b. That all physicians and other health providers must have access to expert consultation services available from the academic health center. c. That antitrust regulations be changed to permit coordinated relationships between hospitals, physicians and medical school faculty. d. That medical schools must have adequate funding to support medical education, and the cost of clinical, behavioral and health sciences research, transitional research and technological innovation. e. That other health profession schools must receive adequate funding to support the education of the mix of health professionals required for a balanced health care work force. f. That teaching hospitals must receive adequate funding to support their care of a disproportionate share of illness of high complexity and acuity. This Includes the maintenance of specialized standby facilities and payment for the direct and indirect cost of graduate medical education. g. That a national biomedical research fund, such as that proposed by Senators Harkin and Hatfield be provided to increase funding for critical basic research. h. That a higher portion of the national health budget be devoted to support research and development essential to improving health. i. That academic health centers play a critical role in the proposed national quality management program by the Clinton Administration.

Dr. Arnold Relman stated that if we do not invest in biomedical research and academic medicine, the medicine we practice in the 21st century will be the medicine of the 20th century. It is because our health care capacity and our medical knowledge has moved forward that our longevity has increased, that diseases have been brought under control, that mortality from various diseases has declined, and that Americans can face a longer, more productive and less painful life. Academic health centers have been at the very heart of this enterprise.

Summary

My testimony today has emphasized a number of important points. We must make certain that health reform maintains continued vigorous support for biomedical research. Our investment as a country in biomedical research has reaped many benefits through eventual increased productivity and reduced health utilization.

Academic health centers are the "heart" of the medical research. We must make certain that they survive in a robust fashion to continue to perform their multiple roles.

Senator HARKIN. Dr. Pardes, thank you very much.

I see Dr. Lehrman in the audience now—it was he who told me that about, "die young as late in life as possible." That is what he is shooting for, too, I am sure. I did not mean to embarrass him, but I saw him sitting out there.

I also want to note that Dr. Michael Johns of Johns Hopkins was going to be here today, but was prevented by an emergency, and I will include his statement in the record.

[The prepared statement of Dr. Johns follows:]

PREPARED STATEMENT OF DR. MICHAEL M.E. JOHNS

Mr. Chairman and distinguished members of the committee:
My name is Michael E. Johns. I am a medical doctor, an otolaryngologist/head and neck surgeon by training. I am also vice president for medicine and dean of the medical faculty of the Johns Hopkins University School of Medicine. I appreciate the opportunity to offer your committee some perspective on the role and importance of basic biomedical research to the health of our nation, and to the success of a reformed health care system.

I would like to begin by asking you to imagine having the opportunity to design and create a whole new business entity that could generate 14-15% of our nation's GNP, employ 9% of its working population, an entity that would provide highly desired products and services that improve the life and health of all Americans. And let's say that the plan for this entity was drawn-up, encompassing well in excess of 1400 pages, but said barely a single word about plans to support the research and development that would be necessary to the continuing improvement of the business' products and services and the discovery of new products and services that might better serve the public. Do you think you could sell that plan to investors? Do you think you could sell a plan that looked only at the reorganization of existing services, but not the pioneering of new and better ones for the future?

Well I think most smart investors would perceive a substantial risk there. The risk that the business could not sustain a high level of service and the quality of its products without substantial plans for supporting the research and discovery necessary to meet future needs.

I would contend that the health care system reform plans that have been proposed to date all share this significant defect. At best, research is an afterthought in these plans. At worst it is not even mentioned. And from my perspective as both a potential producer and consumer of these health care products and services, it is a flaw that needs remedying if the American people are to be persuaded to have faith enough to invest their money and their future health in any of the existing plans for health care reform.

One can hardly overstate the extraordinary importance to the continuing health of our nation, of extensive and high quality basic and clinical biomedical research. Sometimes we forget just how far medicine has come in the last several decades. In a statement that reflected the sentiments of many people in the early part of this century, L.J. Henderson remarked that the chances of coming out better after being treated by a physician were about fifty-fifty. Back then this wasn't much of an exaggeration. Those odds increased only slightly for several more decades. In retrospect this is not surprising. For instance, there was no knowledge of bacteria or of viruses. There was no penicillin or antibiotics—no immunizations and little understanding of the etiology of disease or the functioning and response of the body's major organs. Most of what is now the basic core of biomedical science had yet to be discovered or understood.

But about forty years ago this nation decided that health care and biomedical science were of the highest priority. The national institutes of health were established and, as a society, we made an unprecedented commitment to improve the health and welfare of our nation and our world. Significant public funds were earmarked for this effort. Much of these funds were allocated to be awarded on a competitive basis in the form of grants to individual scientists who would submit fully developed research proposals.

The largest portions of these funds were won by biomedical scientists and physicians associated with academic medical centers. It is there that teaching, research and patient care combine to provide the best environment for pioneering work in the biomedical sciences. The extraordinary advances in biomedical science and medicine of the past four decades are a direct result of our unprecedented commitment to improve public health through the peer-reviewed competitive grants process of the NIH. It's clear that the dollars we have invested in basic research have paid-off many-fold.

But if the past one hundred years have been extraordinary, the next one hundred, even the next ten promise even more. We're on the threshold of tremendously exciting discoveries in molecular genetics that will likely revolutionize patient care. At Hopkins, for instance, we're in the midst of exciting developments ranging from switching off colon cancer cells to cloning brain cells. Imagine being able to disable a cancer, or to repair diseased or damaged parts of the brain. These developments are in the laboratory today. Tomorrow, their impact on patient care promises to be remarkable!

A perfect example is the work of Dr. Bert Vogelstein. Bert Vogelstein is a brilliant young scientist at the Hopkins School of Medicine who is using recombinant DNA techniques to reveal the basic processes of cancer. He and his young team of scientists (whose average age, by the way, is only twenty five!) have done several remarkable things. First, several years ago, he and his group showed that mutations in two types of genes in the body will eventually result in the formation of colorectal cancer this form of cancer is the second most common form found in the United States.

Now, there are estimated to be about 200,000 genes in our body. Dr. Vogelstein and his team were able to isolate and identify one gene—called P53—that is associated with colorectal cancer, and with several other types of cancer—including tumors of the breast, lung and brain. They showed that replacing just one mutated P53 with a normal copy of the gene is enough to stop the growth of colon cancer cells.

Next, about six months ago, Vogelstein's group, along with scientists at the University of Helsinki, in Finland, discovered the region of a chromosome that contains the gene for the most common form of colon cancer, which is also the most common known inherited disease. And just last week you may have read or seen in the news that Vogelstein's group has now helped to isolate the gene on that chromosome that is responsible for this most common form of colon cancer; a disease that affects about one out of every 200 people in the western world.

It's hard to overstate what an extraordinary and exciting breakthrough this is. Today, the earliest experimental studies of gene therapy are underway at the NIH. Some day soon, physicians should be able to locate defective genes like those that Vogelstein's group are now discovering, and remove and replace or repair them before they can cause cancer, diabetes, or other conditions.

Now, Vogelstein's work has been done over a relatively short period of time—about five years of intensive laboratory research. This is not simply a fast pace of research. This is a dizzying pace of discovery. Yet it is work that only ten years ago would have been considered science fiction.

Now, there are many other examples of this kind of work that is being done—particularly in research-intensive academic health centers like Hopkins—all across the country. And it is no accident that much of best research occurs at these centers. Over these last forty years, we have invested billions of both public and private dollars, in the research infrastructure—including facilities and brainpower—that are the backbone of our nation's leadership in biomedical science. Yet the costs of this basic research is infinitesimal—totalling maybe 3% of our total health care spending per year—compared to the potential savings in the costs of treating these diseases, in the lost productivity of literally millions of people, and in less tangible costs, like the loss of the basic quality and dignity of life. This has been true throughout this century as we have conquered polio, bacterial infections, and a host of childhood diseases. And as basic science discoveries have been transferred to the bedside so too have we made great strides in treating heart-disease, various forms of cancer, and many other diseases that continue to plague mankind.

This is why I believe that, as we approach the threshold of a significantly reformed health care system, where many Americans will be asked to invest more in their health care, increased support of basic biomedical and behavioral research must become top priority. In private industry, the firms that thrive and become leaders in their fields invest, on average, about 5% of their operating revenues in research. I see no reason why the federal contribution to basic health care research should be any less. The fact that it has been only means that we have missed or have unnecessarily delayed important discoveries and developments that could improve the health of our nation, as well as new technologies and applications that could improve the cost effectiveness of current and future health care delivery.

Basic research is the foundation of the whole enterprise, and our nation's academic health centers are the cornerstones of that foundation. We must commit to increased funding of basic research, and we must commit to supporting the vital missions of our academic health centers that conduct this research while they train the vast majority of our health care workers and provide the world's best medical care. For, it would be a terrible waste if we were to allow the new emphasis on cost-cutting and competition in the delivery of health care to undermine the foundation of our health care system. But this is exactly what could happen if the research-intensive academic health centers are not properly supported, not only in their research mission, but in their combined missions of research, health professional training and patient care. If instead are shunted aside in favor of policies that benefit more cost efficient health care providers, like some community hospitals, clinics, limos and oars whose only mission is patient care and management,then we quickly will find the quality of health care system in decline.

We must recognize that the best guarantee of the success of our health care system is that we train the best physicians, scientists, and other health professionals, and that our nation continue to lead the world in biomedical discovery and the development of new technologies that can improve the care we provide in preventing, treating and curing disease and injury. This cannot be accomplished unless we invest in the research, training, and expert care that are conducted in our nation's academic health centers.

This commitment is to our young people and to the next generation and to the next generation beyond that. It is the same commitment to the foundation of our nation's health security that was made about forty years ago and that has resulted in the development of the world's greatest centers of medical learning, teaching and patient care. It is the commitment that triggered the most extraordinary period of growth in medical knowledge and in our ability to prevent and cure illness and disease, and that has put us at the threshold of an even more promising period when many of mankind's most deadly afflictions might be conquered.

I commend Senators Harkin and Hatfield for their bold and creative proposal to ensure adequate funding for basic biomedical and behavioral research, and for their efforts to ensure that our nation's academic health centers are properly supported in their vital roles at the foundation of our healthcare system.

Senator HARKIN. Dr. Watson, I remember you and I discussing the progress of the Human Genome Project when you headed it, and I kept wondering why we could not do it sooner, and I remember one time our paths crossed in a parking lot, and you said there was some progress made, and that we could do it faster than we thought we could do it before.

What is the latest? How soon—again, if money is not the object—when could we map and sequence the human gene?

Mr. WATSON. Well, we will have a pretty good map in about 2 years. So it is not done yet, but it is certainly within our capability. I think we will have it 10, 12 years from now. I think we will have most of the interesting regions done a little sooner. I think it is on schedule.

Senator HARKIN. I must tell you I was not trying to lead you on. I just remembered that I had been discussing this with Dr. Collins, and thought that with a high level of funding—now, I do not want to ascribe this to him, and maybe it is not him—we might get sequencing done perhaps by the year 2000.

What do you think? Is that possible?

Mr. WATSON. I do not think so. I think we want to get it accurately done. I do not think it is going to set back medical research that much. What we want to be able to do is sequence those regions which possibly have an interesting gene.

Francis Collins told me that 6 months ago, they should have just sequenced that breast cancer region. There were hoping to get it without the sequence.

So I think we have got to build up pretty fast some laboratories which can do one million base pairs in 3 months, because if you are threatened by one of these diseases, why wait?

So the sequencing now can be pushed in a big way. When you asked me that about 4 years, ago, I said, "Wait a little," but now, I will take every cent you can give us.

Senator HARKIN. Well, I still believe that you can get it done faster than what you are saying, but you are the expert in that area, and I am not. I think there are others who say we could do it sooner and do quality work, not leapfrogging things, but actually doing it in the process. But again, it is going to take the massive computers.

Mr. WATSON. It is going to take computers, and we have got to use the information. I should say how pleased I am with Francis Collins, who is my successor. I think he is a marvelous scientist.

Senator HARKIN. I think he is doing a great job out there.

I would like all of you to respond to one thing that was in my opening statement. I mentioned it, and I might have skipped over it a little bit, but there is a feeling among a number of people that I have talked to in this administration that research is fine, but gosh, you do all that research, and it leads to new machines and new technologies, and it just costs us more money. You invent an MRI, and it just costs us more money. You invent a CAT-scan, and it just costs us more money. So that really, a lot of this research is not really doing that much for us, but is just costing us a lot more money in terms of new therapies, new devices, and new procedures.

So again, how would you respond to someone who says something like that? What is the response on that? Does it just lead to new therapies, new procedures, new machines and new equipment that just cost us a bunch of money?

Dr. PARDES. In the mid-fifties, there were 600,000 people in psychiatric hospitals around this country. I think some of them were let out perhaps with some question, but a number of them were let out because there were better treatments, such as lithium, which meant that we did not have to house people in hospitals, at thousands and thousands of dollars, but could really bring their manic-depressive disease under control with the medication. To me, that is pretty straightforward. You save money, you reduce services, and you give people a better life. It did not cost money; it saved money.

Senator HARKIN. Dr. Welsh.

Dr. WELSH. Two other points. I think you could ask them if they would like to forego the advantages that have been brought about by having an MRI or a CAT-scanner. And the second thing is that the iron lung that you brought in here today is really graphic, and it has been used several times today. At the time that was developed, that was an advance, because those people were going to die. It in many cases allowed people to live through a crisis, and then they could go on with their lives. But it was halfway technology.

Now we have technology that prevents the disease. And some of the cost now is in halfway technologies. We are advancing, but research is an incremental process. You do not go from zero to 100 percent usually in one step; it is a series of steps, and sometimes we have halfway technology.

A final point is the use of that technology. Sometimes that is not an issue that we have addressed or that I am expert to address, but it is an additional thing to consider in what the ultimate cost is.

Senator HARKIN. Dr. Watson.

Mr. WATSON. I think we have got to work very hard to reduce the costs of the new techniques, and I was particularly concerned in the genetics area where, if you are going to do genetic screening to see if you are at risk for colon cancer, it should not cost you $1,000. We have got to really work to get the cost down to a reasonable level so everyone can do it. Then, if you have the gene, you have got to somehow get the doctors to be able to look at your colon for less than $1,000 per time.

So I think we simply want someone to be able to look inside your colon, but we want it to be done cheaper. So I think we ought to be inventive enough to get down below $1,000, which your insurance company will say, "Well, you are not really at risk, so why should we pay for this?"

So I think we have got to worry about the costs of these new procedures, and I am sure in the case of the genetic technology, we can reduce the costs.

Senator HARKIN. And the appropriate use of some of this equipment.

Yes, Dr. Thomas.

Dr. THOMAS. Senator, people who say the kind of thing that you have just quoted often do not consider the alternative—how much money is saved by these procedures; how much accurate diagnosis permits accurate treatment, whether it is surgical invasion or not.

I am a case in point. I had back pain that was almost immobilizing me. MRI showed that a very small part of one disc was the part of the problem. That was injected with an enzyme. The total cost was about $1,500. The alternative before MRI became available would have been a major surgical procedure, weeks in bed. I do not know that cost, but it would certainly have been more than $10,000.

These procedures are not only helping patients making accurate diagnoses, but in many instances, they save money. And that has to be factored into such statements.

Senator HARKIN. Yes, very true.

Dr. Murray.

Dr. MURRAY. I think Dr. Welsh had a point, that the alternative is that the patient is going to get the benefit. Jack London, one of my favorite authors, died at age 42 of renal disease. I visited his museum out in Northern California a few years ago, and the doctor's bill—he had diarrhea, and he went into hyperkelia and died of heart irregularity—the bill was $6.46. He died at age 42. Had he had dialysis or a transplant, he might have survived another 40 years, and the loss to society is immeasurable.

So I think those persons' statements are correct, but I do not think it is a criticism; I agree with Dr. Watson that we must keep the costs down, and we must utilize these new advances very carefully. But it is the quality of life which we are trying to save, and I think we would save a lot of money if we did not do any cardiac surgery or if we did no more transplants.

Senator HARKIN. A couple of you mentioned the U.S. leadership role in medical research. Are there any countries which are ahead of us in terms of their commitment to basic research? Do you know if there are other countries making a greater commitment to basic research right now? I am just curious.

Mr. WATSON. No; I think we are still number one, and we should be proud of it. But the opportunities are just opening up so much; you know, there is Alzheimer's, and we should do something about it, and why not the United States? Otherwise, we have got the nursing home bills, which are just going to grow and grow and grow.

Senator HARKIN. True. One last thing. Dr. Lee testified about the importance of prevention. Can any of you comment on your view of the relationship between the research that is conducted at NIH and our Nation's prevention efforts? It is going to be a big part of the health security bill. You are going to hear a lot of talk about prevention next year—keeping people healthy in the first place. But there seems to be a de-linking between prevention and the concept of basic research.

I would just like your thoughts on that relationship and how we can better get that point across.

Dr. PARDES. Well, sometimes I think there is an artificial dichotomy put between the so-called prevention research and basic biomedical research. I think some of the best prevention comes from a solid research program which produces answers and better treatments. And I sometimes find it difficult to draw the line.

I would certainly be concerned that any focus on a different component of research would threaten the base of biomedical research, because I think that has been central. But these things shade into each other. I do not think they are so hard and fast and different. I think that it is reasonable to say, since we are trying to devise a new services system, that we look at services and know more about outcomes and more about epidemiology. But we have to make sure that the foundation of basic biomedical research is supported with whatever additional effort is put on.

Senator HARKIN. Dr. Welsh.

Dr. WELSH. I would like to emphasize that point that things shade into each other. Things do not stay the same in medicine and in genetics. What we think about today as highly experimental may be treatment or prevention tomorrow. I hate to keep coming back to this polio thing, but when that work was done, the work that you described about people just trying to culture viruses in human cells or animal cells, that was a very experimental kind of thing. That was basic research.

Today, we look at the results of all that, and it is just prevention. We do not want to stay where we are. The things that are experimental today will be prevention tomorrow. And there are many other examples—for example, many other vaccines. We have been talking about the treatment of ulcers, so that instead of waiting until someone is in the hospital with a bleeding g.i. ulcer, maybe we can try to prevent some of that, and we are doing that now with the development of few drugs like Tagamet and Zantac. It is full of examples. All one has to do in many cases is look at one's own medical history to realize that what was highly experimental at one time is now prevention.

Senator HARKIN. Well, I appreciate that, and I understand that. It just seems that some of this research we are talking about is going to be targeted. It almost seems like they are talking about some form of applied research. And again, I am not opposed to applied research, but it should not be at the expense of basic research, I think you are just robbing Peter to pay Paul, in that case, and that is what I am afraid they are doing.

Yes, Dr. Murray, and then Dr. Watson.

Dr. MURRAY. Another example of where research in one field can be prevention in another. In the field of transplantation, we try to match a donor and a recipient, and a whole field of tissue typing has evolved internationally, and we are using tissue typing to try to get good donors. But the whole tissue typing field has disclosed a relationship to other diseases, autoimmune diseases—arthritis for example. Arthritis is common in certain tissue types, totally unexpected.

So now you can get the idea that a certain tissue type might be a possible candidate to get arthritis, and you can then try to prevent it from developing, or have that person under more surveillance.

So the nature of research is so fluid that we have just got to realize that it is difficult to predict.

Senator HARKIN. Very true.

Dr. Watson.

Mr. WATSON. I think we are all in favor of prevention, and what Dr. Lee said, that they want to promote prevention, is of course good. But it really just did not deal with the big issue which you are holding these hearings for, which is that the amount spent on pure research is just too small and is leading to a complete crisis. So that is why I was so disappointed in Dr. Lee. I mean, he was sounding good, but I do not think he was doing much good.

Senator HARKIN. Well, we are going to help him do better.

Dr. Pardes.

Dr. PARDES. Just to connect over—and I am sure that Jim would be much better at this than I, but just to introduce the subject— with a fuller knowledge of the human genome and a better understanding of what genes people have within them, you can devise a much more effective prevention program by being able to target the people who are at specific risk for a certain disease by virtue of knowing their genetic makeup. You can help target them with regard to the kinds of behaviors that they should avoid or, on the other hand, they should exercise in order to keep themselves from seeing a full disease realized for which they are at risk.

So that is where a basic research set of developments can lead to a very concrete prevention strategy.

And if I might just make one other comment, while I agree with Jim that the United States is the leader in the world in biomedical research, I would say there are a number of countries that, if we start to slip a little bit, would be happy to take over leadership, and I think that would have profound consequences not only for the health of this country, but the economic health of this country.

Senator HARKIN. Sometimes I do not emphasize enough, and I am going to be emphasizing it more, that if we really want to invest in the future economic growth of this country, a perfect example is the biotechnology industry. Someone mentioned that earlier today. I think it is about a $6 billion a year industry now, and may be up to $50 billion by the end of this century. That is a lot of jobs, a lot of economic activity, and all for a good end. We are not building bombs and missiles, you see; we are building something that is going to help people.

Well, you are all very kind to be here today, and I thank you for your testimony.

This is just the first of what I hope will be a few hearings on research. We need to have a number of hearings on the lack of a commitment to medical research in the health reform bill. It has just simply got to get a higher profile than it has. You are preeminent in your fields; people look to you for leadership, and the positions you take and the statements you make in this area can have a tremendous impact on what happens here in the Congress.

So as this thing proceeds in January, February, March, April, as we go into the spring, I look forward to any opportunity that you might have to inject your thoughts and your advice into this process—and do not just wait on us to call you; you can call us.

With that, thank you very much, and have a happy holiday season. We look forward to working with you next year.

The committee will stand adjourned subject to call of the chair.

[Whereupon, at 12:54 p.m., the committee was adjourned.]

O